Shakespeare
and the Popular Tradition
in the Theater

SHAKESPEARE
and the POPULAR TRADITION
in the THEATER:

*Studies in the Social Dimension
of Dramatic Form and Function*

ROBERT WEIMANN

Edited by Robert Schwartz

THE JOHNS HOPKINS UNIVERSITY PRESS

Baltimore and London

Originally published in German, in a somewhat different version, in 1967,
by Henschelverlag Berlin, entitled *Shakespeare und die
Tradition des Volkstheaters: Soziologie, Dramaturgie, Gestaltung*
(copyright 1967 by Henschelverlag Berlin).

Manufactured in the United States of America

The Johns Hopkins University Press, Baltimore, Maryland 21218
The Johns Hopkins Press Ltd., London

Library of Congress Catalog Number 77-13673
ISBN 0-8018-1985-7

Library of Congress Cataloging in Publication data
will be found on the last printed page of this book.

To
Benno Besson and Manfred Wekwerth,
my friends in the theater
who have come closest to a modern Shakespeare
in the popular tradition

CONTENTS

EDITOR'S PREFACE

Shakespeare und die Tradition des Volkstheaters was first published in Berlin in 1967. Since that time G. K. Hunter has called it "the most important work on Shakespeare to come out of Germany since Clemen's *Shakespeare's Bilder* of 1936" (*Notes and Queries,* June 1970). Dieter Mehl concluded his review of the book in 1969 with the following appeal: "It is, I feel, most desirable that an adequate and perhaps condensed English version of this book be produced as soon as possible, because it would be a great loss to Shakespearean scholarship if lack of communication should prevent its wealth of ideas and suggestions from making their deserved impact" (*Review of English Studies,* 1969).

This revised English language edition of Robert Weimann's study of the social and dramatic dimensions of the popular tradition in the theater and their bearing on our understanding of Shakespeare is designed to answer two compelling needs: the lack of a translation such as Dieter Mehl has described and the necessity to incorporate into such a translation Professor Weimann's most recent scholarship on the subject, as well as some of the results of other significant studies that have appeared since 1967. It has been my primary goal to prepare as expeditiously as possible a clear and compact edition of a book whose publication in English has been delayed at many points after an unsatisfactory preliminary translation was made in Berlin in 1971. The amount of scholarship that has appeared since 1967 on topics germane to this book is surprisingly great; and in close cooperation both author and editor have tried to make reference—whenever possible in the text, but more often in the notes—to at least some of the more important recent works that support, contrast, or expand the original argument.

In addition to Robert Weimann's new introduction, his often extensive general revision of the original text, and my own revision and rewriting of the manuscript, parts of articles that the author has published in English since 1967 have been added to clarify or elaborate the original text: these are included in section 1 of the introduction (first published in "Shakespeare: Theater and Society: Notes Towards a New Synthesis," *Shakespeare Newsletter* [September–November 1974]); in chapter IV, part 4 (first published in "Shakespeare's Wordplay: Popular Origins and Theatrical Functions," *Shakespeare 1971*, ed. Clifford Leech and J. M. R. Margeson [Toronto, 1972], pp. 230–43); in chapter V, parts 1, 2, and 3 (first published in "The Soul of the Age: Towards A Historical Approach to Shakespeare," *Shakespeare in a Changing World*, ed. Arnold Kettle [New York, 1964], pp. 17–42); and in the appendix (first published in "Laughing with the Audience: *The Two Gentlemen of Verona* and the Popular Tradition of Comedy," *Shakespeare Survey* 22 [1969]:35– 42).

Although this edition has been reviewed and finally revised by Robert Weimann, I must accept full responsibility for any lapses of style or clarity or for inaccuracies that may have resulted from my own rewriting and revision of the preliminary and revised translations. I gratefully acknowledge James Richardson for his help in translating the footnotes and Edward I. Berry for reading parts of the manuscript and making helpful suggestions. Both author and editor owe special thanks to Bruce Erlich for his highly perceptive and most helpful comments on matters of terminology and content, and to The Johns Hopkins University Press for its patience and understanding throughout the long and complex process of translation and revision.

ROBERT SCHWARTZ

INTRODUCTION

1

The subtitle of the original German language edition of this book attempted to link its three main concerns: *Soziologie, Dramaturgie, Gestaltung*. But to speak of the links between these three aspects, and even to attempt to work out some of the interrelations between theater, society, and verbal and dramatic art, is, in the language and context of English and American Shakespeare criticism, to invite a host of questions in regard to method and purpose. Based on the conviction that both the purely formal and the image-symbol-myth approaches—like the Romantic character analysis against which these initially rebelled—have failed to convey a sense of the unity and vitality of Shakespeare's work as a social and cultural force in the present world, this book runs counter to a good deal of English and American Shakespeare criticism. Compared with purely literary interpretations, recent interest in Shakespeare as a poet in the theater involves a welcome advance beyond the limitations inherent in exclusively verbal or psychological approaches. Recently revised views of Elizabethan stagecraft, particularly in the works of Richard Hosley, C. Walter Hodges, Richard Southern, Glynne Wickham, Bernard Beckerman, and others, are significant not only in that they should lead, ideally, to better modern productions, but in that they reveal a new awareness of the interaction between plays and audiences, and thus help point up the importance of emphasizing the function of theater in society.

But even though one would not wish to minimize the potential significance of recent critical re-evaluations of the Elizabethan stage, they have as yet produced few clarifications of any theoretical consequence. In particular, they have not produced a viable alternative to the literary and structural modes of analysis, and have not really come to terms with the ways in which the theatrical and the poetic dimensions of Shakespeare's work interact. Although much is now written on the subject, we still do not know, for instance, the extent to which varied forms and qualities of dramatic speech or the changing modes of acting constitute or reflect the social mode of the theater. Thus, while the ahistorical and nontheatrical approaches to Shakespeare criticism have come to be distrusted, a more satisfying approach and a new synthesis have been slow to take their place.

In this respect the older sociologically oriented criticism does not offer an acceptable alternative. It was based, primarily, on the assumption that the theater *reflected* contemporary society and that the social composition and dramatic taste of its audience determined or "explained" the nature of the plays. But such a positivistic approach is too reductive to be useful. It is true that the organization and audience of the Elizabethan theater mirrored a highly transitional social, economic, and ideological balance between the feudal background of the New Monarchy, the nobility and the conservative gentry on the one hand, and the aspiring new gentry, the London bourgeoisie and the *plebs* on the other. But to reduce the theater to a mere "reflection" of its environment seems, even as a generalization, unduly limiting. If, as Marx noted, "art" is "one of the special modes of production,"[1] then surely Shakespeare's theater and his society were interrelated in the sense that the Elizabethan stage, even when it reflected the tensions and compromises of sixteenth-century England, was also a potent force that helped to create the specific character and transitional nature of that society. Thus, the playgoers did not determine the nature of the plays, for although the latter certainly responded to the assumptions and expectations of the spectators, the audience itself was shaped and educated by the quality of what it viewed. Indeed, the sensibilities and receptivity of the audience and the consciousness and artistry of the drama were so mutually influential that a new historical synthesis seems conceivable only through an increased awareness of the dialectics of this interdependence.

It is only when Elizabethan society, theater, and language are seen as interrelated that the structure of Shakespeare's dramatic art emerges as fully functional—that is, as part of a larger, and not only literary, whole. To understand verbal artistry as an element in the total function of the Shakespearean stage, dramatic speech must be considered both as a process between actors and audiences and as a vision of society, as an integral part of the history of the nation that Shakespeare's theater both reflected and helped to create. Hopefully, an increased awareness of the social and theatrical functions of Shakespeare's plays will stimulate more practical criticism and a deeper theoretical grasp of the verbal arts of drama as elements of a total aesthetic and social unity that ultimately goes far beyond language itself.[2]

2

What is needed, then, is a sense of the unity of history and criticism by which both the past significance and the present meaning of Shakespeare's theater can be defined through the structural quality and the social function of his dramatic art, and vice versa. Certainly this is a difficult perspective to develop, but it is necessary, for it is based on two facts about Shakespeare as a historical phenomenon. On the one hand, Shakespeare's theater is irremediably a thing of the past; on the other, his plays have survived the conditions from which they originated and are continually revitalized on the modern stage. For the scholar studying the history or prehistory of the Shakespearean theater it is difficult to ignore these two aspects. The tension between what is past and what lives for us today is obvious; and yet, from the point of view of the function of literary scholarship, it seems impossible to relegate the pastness of Shakespeare's theater to the "pure" historian and its contemporaneousness to the "pure" critic or modern producer.

When, however, we do not attempt to separate pastness from what is alive, history from interpretation, we become more acutely aware of a contradiction between the two that is of some methodological consequence, a contradiction between the history of a work's origins in the past and the story of its effects in the present. This corresponds, on another level, to the tension between the mimetic and the "moral," between the original poetic object of, and intention behind, the work, and the changing responses of the modern audience. If either of these dimensions is ignored, if the critic is concerned only with the question of origins or only with the impact of Shakespearean drama, a dilemma ensues: one is forced to be either uncritically historical or ahistorically critical. Instead, the criticism itself must be a kind of historical activity which, ideally, can be both a product and a "producer" of the history of the effect of Shakespeare's work.

For the literary historian and critic, the problem, then, is not whether to accept both worlds and points of reference, but rather, since each is so inevitable and necessary, how to relate them so as to discover the degree and consequences of their connections. In order to grasp the dialectics of this problem it is helpful to remember that we are not dealing entirely with a case of opposites. On the contrary, it would be a grave mistake to overlook those many points of contact where, for example, Shakespeare's Renaissance values can be considered valid today. This area of identity or interaction, however, is not simply given; it can be enlarged from a contemporary point of view that conceives its own social direction as historical, in the sense that it affirms both the discontinuities and the continuities between the past and the future. Ultimately this relationship involves a social and a methodological position from which both the change and the continuity can be accepted as part of a meaningful movement in history. In our current reception of Renaissance drama, therefore, the area of identity will differ radically between, say, a Marxist interpretation and one based on the premises of Jacques Maritain's or Claude Lévi-Strauss' frames of value. Where the Renaissance heritage is not repudiated, there is bound to be a wide range of living contact in which the "historical" element can be viewed as part of a wider configuration in which the present reproduction of past art is one way to bring about a meaningful future.

Nor is this area of identity, which is, of course, also a human one deriving from man's anthropological status, confined to the Renaissance tradition. We are all—the great dramatists of the past, their contemporary producers and critics, and ours—characters in history; our own points of reference are, like those of our predecessors, the results of history. In this, our present values emerge from the same historical process that is both reflected in and accelerated by Shakespeare's contribution. This is quite obvious in the history of literature, which can only be written with reference to a scheme of values that, among other things, has to be abstracted from its great works, including Shakespeare's dramas. Their greatness has been confirmed by the very contribution they have made in furnishing us with criteria by which to judge—and to judge not only modern plays but also the history of drama as a whole.

The relationship between Shakespeare's vision and the modern interpretation of that vision cannot simply be described as one of conflict or opposition. The difference between Shakespeare's world and ours is obvious enough, but this does not exclude some kind of concurrence. As Arnold Kettle has remarked, "the best way to emphasize the value of Shakespeare in *our* changing world is to see him in *his,* recognizing that the two worlds, though very different, are at the same time a unity."[3] This unity is the basis of all our veneration for Shakespeare; without it the impact of his work would not be possible. At the same time, this unity does not preclude a contradiction that is the basis of all our conflicting interpretations. To oversimplify: the unity creates the need for our interpretations of *Shakespeare;* the contradiction accounts for the need for our *interpretations* of Shakespeare. But actually each is contained in the other, and the interpretation as a whole can only succeed when these two aspects are inseparable: then, perhaps, our research may hope both to revitalize the past and enlarge the present.[4]

3

We will find that the popular tradition, which contributed so much to the past significance of Shakespeare's theater, can provide an important supplement to our understanding of Shakespeare's modern meaning—a much more important factor than a good deal of criticism (or production, for that matter) has allowed. But to discuss the points of contact between the popular tradition before and during Shakespeare's time and the ways in which it can be received today is not an easy task. The degree of concurrence certainly depends on the social functions that a vital, and not merely a technical, renewal of this tradition can be made to serve. If, for instance, the all-important popular actor-audience contact were considered, emphasized but not integrated into a larger conception of dramatic structure and social function, it could easily seem external to the meaning of the play as a whole, little more than a theatrical gimmick. It is the modern director who must ultimately establish the feasibility of regenerating the popular tradition in the theater; the scholar can only provide a methodological framework for the issues involved in dealing with that tradition then *and* now, and a judgment of the extent to which the popular tradition shaped Shakespeare's dramatic art.

While the methodological problem is complex (the "then" cannot simply be grafted onto the "now"; rather, the "now" can be realized to the extent that past structure can be turned into present function), the historical problem is even more formidable. In the first place, the impact of the popular tradition on Shakespeare must not be overestimated, even when it was clearly a part of his drama (and of much more consequence than, say, for Marlowe, Heywood, or even Ben Jonson). Shakespeare's theater was not a folk theater, but a highly complex Renaissance stage. Consequently, by emphasizing the popular tradition in Shakespeare, we refer not to his work as a whole, but to one of the elements that helped to create a new unity in the total shape of his drama. If, in this connection, it is difficult to avoid referring to the popular tradition as a "source," it is the structure and function rather than the influence of the popular tradition that are of consequence in this study. And if neither Shakespeare's drama as a whole nor the entirety of his literary, dramatic, and ideological sources is here illuminated, at least the attempt has been made to express a new sense of the depth and vitality of his relationship to the popular tradition.

One of the burdens that we must bear throughout this study, however, is the fact that many of the sources of the popular tradition are basically unliterary and thus only partially recorded. While the medieval church virtually monopolized book production, hence controlling the preservation of all that was written, and while the contribution of the Renaissance humanists was also a literary one, and also well preserved, the oral and mimetic heritage of the popular culture has sunk beneath the surface of literary history. This is true of the ancient *mimus*, which has been transmitted in meager fragments and through polemical witness, as well as of the folk drama, which survives only in late, corrupt texts. The quasi-dramatic customs of common medieval villagers, the mummings of the towns, the rural Robin Hood plays, and many other sources of popular mimic culture have been lost forever. This explains in part why the popular dramatic tradition was not a very attractive subject to historical philologists who were more concerned with influence than with function, more concerned with source than with structure. But although a historical treatment of the popular theatrical tradition is infinitely complicated by the absence of written texts, the nonliterary nature of folk entertainment was a source of great strength to the popular tradition itself; for the oral tradition insured great flexibility and hence great adaptability in the structure and function of both late forms of ritual and modern modes of representation—a flexibility that allowed for the endless assimilation of new subjects, themes, and modes of verbal and mimetic expression.

To understand the changing pattern and content of this tradition we need only recognize the enormous discontinuity between the ritual origins and elements of folk culture, or even the medieval lay theater, and the Elizabethan stage. Shakespeare himself wrote for a professional Renaissance theater which, as a national institution, attracted an audience from many classes and many social backgrounds. And even if, as Leopold Schmidt notes, the "folk drama in the narrowest sense" was capable of various kinds of development, the limits of its growth were reached when the lay drama, by remaining within the ambit of "internally bound societies," was separated from the development of the nascent professional theater. The tradition of the folk play can be traced through "the mutual permeation of the seasonal and liturgical cycles" back to the formation of "every premedieval and pre-Christian mode of performance," but this does not mean that the traveling Tudor plebeian stage could be described as folk drama in any useful sense of the term.[5]

Obviously what is called for is a distinction that is not implicit in a term like *Volkstheater*; the "theater of the folk" must be seen in relation to the popular tradition, but the two are not identical. The quasi-dramatic culture of the folk is so important because it remained close to those forms of late ritual that the popular stage turned into effective conventions of dramatic speech and action. But since the popular mimic culture is only indirectly and partially preserved, it is never fully possible to trace the popular tradition in its various aspects of growth, adaptability and decay. Still, the little that is left of the older mimic culture suggests a process of change that included important continuities as well as the more apparent discontinuities. Of the continuities we can say that Shakespeare's drama is unthinkable without the popular tradition; but we must add that the popular stagecraft that Shakespeare incorporated into his unique dramatic method was a popular theater already developed to its fullest artistic possibilities.

4

Since the popular theater provides much more than a series of literary sources, the concept of "tradition" that we use in reference to its continuity must be understood in terms of more comprehensive cultural and social activities in history than ever allowed by the accepted conception of tradition (that of the early T. S. Eliot). If tradition is viewed as a cultural force in history—and especially one in the theater—it must necessarily involve an intellectual *and* a practical connection between the achievements of the past and their changing functions in the present— be it Shakespeare's present or ours. For Eliot, tradition was conceived in terms of "the individual talent," never in terms of his audience, and always with regard to an ideal order, never with regard to temporal change and social movement. But as soon as tradition is viewed as a social form of cultural activity, it may well be defined as past culture turned present function. For Shakespeare, the art and experience of playing handed down via the popular stage was part of a meaningful cultural past in the process of its present reawakening, assimilation and change. For him the popular tradition was an ever changing phenomenon in which the imprint of the past and the impact of his present constantly interacted. Shakespeare excelled as a playwright precisely because of his ability to relate the dramatic vitality of a still living past to the drama of contemporary life.

This relationship between originality and tradition resulted in a supreme balance between experimentation, innovation, and revitalization. Wherever else the manifold elements of Shakespeare's greatness are to be found, it is here that one of the most essential springs of his creative power has its source—at a point in the development of culture and literature that fostered a newly complex, but nonetheless balanced, relationship between individual creativity and communal activities and traditions. From this arose the correlation that retained a contradiction between individual expression and communal taste. It is in this sense that in Shakespeare's theater the most original kind of artistry remained compatible with age-old conventions of dramatic speech and action. The new self-consciousness of literary art forms did not eradicate the experience of generations of plebeian actors; rather it facilitated the assimilation and transformation of their experience into the poetic drama of the English Renaissance.

To emphasize the popular tradition at this point is not to detract from the many other, and often more important, traditions from which Shakespeare drew. Comedy alone, as Leo Salingar has recently shown, developed from many sources: Plautus, the drama of the schools, Italian comedy, and medieval stage romances.[6] But of all these, the popular tradition holds a special significance insofar as it was, in contrast to the *literary* culture of humanism (including neoclassical drama), rooted *in the theater*. The vitality and continuing impact of this tradition are not easily explained, but the postritual background of popular entertainment and its close connection with everyday life were important factors that contributed to its long life. It reflected the attitudes of those sections of society engaged in labor and production that were in closest contact with the physical world. For this concrete reality they had a concrete idiom[7] that was reflected in the gestic dimension and the physicality of verbal expression and communication, as well as in the capacity for sensuous action and spectacle that the purely literary drama could never achieve. Wherever the popular tradition was embraced by a national theater and translated into its own creative poetry, the physical and the imaginative united in a wealth of association where language and delivery became one.

Even the masques and quasi-dramatic ceremonies of the court, which themselves began to influence theatrical production, reflected popular modes and conventions. The Queen herself deferred to the tastes of the London *plebs*; the best of the city's drama was always good enough for the court. Apparently the art of the common players had something special to offer not only to the people of London, but to the nation as a whole. But even as the popular theatrical tradition helped to bring about a new unity of word and action, the traditional conventions of speech and gesture themselves changed. As they were absorbed into a larger social context and made to serve new and more comprehensive functions (national, moral, poetic functions), they were so modified and became so much a part of a larger whole that they cannot very well be isolated or considered in any purity.

To separate, therefore, what for Shakespeare was inseparable—the native theater from humanist inspired poetry, Tarlton's heritage from the literary legacy of Terence—is justifiable only for the purposes of analysis: and even then only with the understanding that the popular tradition itself assimilated wholly disparate elements (including classical, courtly, and humanist materials) until it became part of a vastly larger cultural and aesthetic synthesis: the "mingle-mangle" of which John Lyly spoke when he noted that "the whole worlde is become an Hodge-podge."[8]

5

Although the important work of C. L. Barber, Richard Southern, David Bevington, Richard Hosley, and others has remedied somewhat the long-standing deficiency of information relevant to an understanding of the connections between Shakespeare and the popular dramatic tradition, significant omissions persist. Still overshadowing this important dimension of Shakespearean dramaturgy are centuries of subjective criticism which, with its polemical view of the social and theatrical characteristics of Shakespeare's stage, devalued as "vulgar" all popular connections. In the Romantic period, especially, Shakespeare was esteemed not on the grounds of, but rather in spite of, his theatrical achievements. Despite isolated pioneers from Edmund Malone to G. P. Baker and other Victorians, Shakespeare the poet was celebrated at the expense of Shakespeare the dramatist. Early studies of Shakespeare's theatrical heritage conceived under these assumptions (by J. S. Tunison and Janet Spens)[9] did emphasize popular elements, but such studies were unsystematic and entirely ignored the social context of the theater. When the Elizabethan theater came under the close scrutiny of scholars like T. F. Ordish, J. Q. Adams, E. K. Chambers, W. J. Lawrence and others, essential facts about the stage were systematically gathered, but because of their positivistic bias these writers seldom interpreted what they recorded. It was only in the work of L. L. Schücking, E. E. Stoll, and C. J. Sisson, for example, that the reading of the plays themselves began to be affected by the study of theatrical history. In the early work of Schücking, followed up by Sisson and, more recently, by scholars like Alfred Harbage, M. C. Bradbrook and especially S. L. Bethell, some of the social premises of the public stage were so illuminated that the form and function of Shakespearean art could be seen in a new light.

We can only begin to suggest here why these beginnings were pursued so half-heartedly. Obviously, post-1945 Shakespeare studies followed the lead of the thoroughly ahistorical and untheatrical New Criticism. Influential critics like R. S. Crane had already, by the end of the 1930s, systematically turned their backs on literary history. Even Schücking abandoned the sociological focus of his early *Rezeptionsstudie* (1908) and his later *Charakterprobleme* (1919) in favor of a more stylistic approach in *Shakespeare und der Tragödienstil seiner Zeit* (1947). The conflict between historical origin and timeless effect was critically circumscribed rather than resolved. Some careful studies (like L. C. Knights' *Drama and Society in the Age of Jonson* [1937]) did consider the popular tradition, but valued it more for its moral and poetic significance than its theatrical and dramatic consequences. And here too, in the postwar era, the historical approach was much overshadowed by the linguistic "figure in the carpet."

Small wonder, then, that the students and successors of the best known scholars turned away from unfashionable social history and downgraded theatrical history for being "extrinsic." No wonder that only the most penetrating treatments of dramatic art perceived the connection between verbal structure and theatrical function. Where this connection was not pursued, the formal or symbolic interpretation naturally assumed disproportionate importance—the social and aesthetic unity of the popular features of Shakespeare's art remaining virtually undeveloped. Where the conventions of the popular theater have been seriously studied, either their social backgrounds have remained unexamined or they have been biased, as in S. L. Bethell's important book, by an unveiled hostility toward realism, dismissed, in Shakespeare's case, as unfortunate "lapses into naturalism."[10]

The general critical preoccupation with the symbolic inhibited any thorough investigation of the ritualistic sources and mythic analogues of drama. From the ahistorical perspective of New Criticism, the reasonable analogy between myth and art grew into a timeless and boundless identity; the possible pre-historic relationship between Hamlet and Orestes pointed out by Gilbert Murray in 1914 was generalized into the monomythic "fearful symmetry" of *all* literature. Frazer's comparative social anthropology, although already questioned by other anthropologists, was transferred to literature unmodified by empirical ethnography (Bronislaw Malinowski and others) or by postpositivistic religious history (W. F. Otto, Karl Kerényi). The approach of the Cambridge school (Murray, J. E. Harrison, F. M. Cornford) remained essentially restricted to the subjects of classical philology and art, while the only parallel research in the area of later drama, Francis Fergusson's *The Idea of a Theater* (1949), began with the unproved assumption that Elizabethans brought to their theater the same "ritual expectancy" as the audiences of the classical festival performances brought to theirs. This astounding overstatement of the ritual element in Shakespeare—"taking *Hamlet* as a species of ritual drama"!—was a natural outgrowth of the ahistorical orientation of New Criticism. But such an orientation could not and did not provide any useful perspectives on the theatrical functions and the poetic meanings of ritual activity in a secular context.[11]

Of course the very limited survival of popular forms and the amorphous nature of folk culture itself posed serious problems to the literary historian, problems that emerged even in so penetrating an "essay in historical criticism" as Madeleine Doran's *Endeavors of Art*. For while Doran did note the distinction as well as the points of contact between "aesthetic theory and dramatic practice," she did not explain their opposition in terms of the encounter and conflict of the humanistic tradition and the native theater, as we might expect, but rather in terms of the relationship between the humanistic tradition and the medieval epic. While the epic certainly had a profound effect on the native drama, the repeated assertion "that the main roots of Elizabethan drama lie in traditional medieval narrative"[12] rather than in native theatrical conventions betrays a peculiarly formal and untheatrical, albeit common, attitude.

Although the older research of Chambers, C. R. Baskerville, and others into ritual and folk festival customs demonstrated a number of dramatic beginnings, for decades such studies were not applied to a reading of Shakespearean drama. Serious literary historians like Hardin Craig or T. W. Baldwin still strongly favored an approach to Shakespeare through the learned side of Renaissance culture. According to their view, Shakespeare's work owed more to humanist poetics and rhetoric than any previous conception of the "popular bard" or the "natural poet" (in the Romantic sense) had ever allowed. By the time that W. W. Greg and Peter Alexander were looking into the textual-critical subtleties of his plays, Shakespeare, once the native *Urtalent,* the "upstart Crow" as Robert Greene described him, was viewed more and more as the aspiring humanist. No longer imaginable as an inexperienced apprentice or a plebeian "Johannes factotum," Shakespeare increasingly appeared as an artistic power in his own right, as a humanist-educated, ambitious, and, whenever possible, patronized artist. Thus, *Titus Andronicus* was interpreted as an early artistic exercise in the Senecan style, *The Comedy of Errors* as an ambitious emulation of Plautus. This brilliant "apprentice," who mastered Senecan drama and classical comedy on his first attempt, and who emerged as the founder of historical drama, appeared to many to be a "born classicist," an "original poet, educated, confident of himself, already dedicated to poetry; a man passing through the states common to any very great artist, akin to Dante and Milton not only through mature achievement but in the manner in which he began his life-work."[13]

But while the Romantic conception of Shakespeare as the "poet of Nature" is certainly inadequate, the more recent emphasis on his rhetorical and humanist training, although largely justified, in some points lacks balance and perspective. Is it true, for instance, that Shakespeare "intended his works for the same public for which Spenser wrote the *Faerie Queene*?"[14] Shakespeare was, to be sure, a sensitive and deliberate artist who in his own way reflected the highest aspirations of Renaissance humanism. But this does not in any way contradict his positive relationship with the popular theatrical and cultural tradition.

Because most traditional approaches to Shakespeare criticism rely on idealistic methodologies that are preoccupied with a literary or formalist concept of structure or with the history of ideas, we have tended to visualize the poet creating outside of his medium, the theater. Without a complete understanding of the *special* characteristics of the theatrical mode any comparison to a poet like Milton, however interesting it may seem, is a little beside the point. The critic interested in poetics, though he can generally illuminate Shakespeare's conscious artistry, cannot see the "carpet" for the "figures," and therefore usually cannot explain the function of the image within the play as a whole. Such an approach exemplifies in modern terms what Hermann Reich saw as "the bankruptcy of the philological theory as opposed to the great mimic material."[15]

The consequences of this critical myopia have only become clear in the last decade; for as Glynne Wickham has noted, "most modern criticism, with its heavy literary bias, has in fact severed Elizabethan drama from its roots."[16] In 1912, L. L. Schücking wondered "what the vastly numerous smaller and larger theatrical troupes traveling around in the country were accustomed to play." Yet for all the research conducted since then there is still much truth in Schücking's assertion that "we know relatively little about the real drama played by professional players in Shakespeare's youth in spite of the pyramid of scholarly literature which has gradually risen over the remains of Elizabethan drama . . . One can say about English drama in Shakespeare's youth that we know the tributaries much better than we know the mainstream."[17]

Thanks to scholars like David Bevington and others, this is true only on some points—but on some very essential ones. "Despite universal interest in the dramatic literature of Marlowe's and Shakespeare's day," Bevington writes, "scholarship has only belatedly recognized the validity of treating that drama as popular and national, deriving its themes and forms of expression to a considerable extent from its own native tradition."[18] This is valid not only for theatrical history but also for the corresponding dramatic and structural characteristics of Shakespeare's work. Despite the efforts of critics with strong theatrical backgrounds (from Harley Granville-Barker to Bernard Beckerman), the theatrical dimensions of Shakespeare's genius have received less than adequate treatment. The unity of stage and poetic creation embodied in Shakespeare's work has been usefully set forth in terms of artistic syntheses, but dramaturgy and theatrical art have been studied mostly as *technique,* and usually in connection with rhetoric rather than with the historical, contextual, and audience-related realities that bear so strongly on the look and feel of a stageplay at any particular point in time. Certainly there are important relationships between Renaissance rhetoric and contemporary theatrical art, but Shakespeare's drama cannot, finally, be understood as rhetoric or as a self-contained theatrical form. Between the external history of the theater and the internal structure of its dramaturgy there are numerous and multileveled relationships that cannot be isolated from the continuity and change of the total social process.

Shakespeare
and the Popular Tradition
in the Theater

I

THE *MIMUS*

1

Ritual and Mimesis

In its earliest stages ritual is both consecrative and productive, irrational but at the same time organizational; there is a point at which myth encompasses both religion and knowledge, illusion and a sense of reality. In many primitive cults throughout the world the sequence of annual sowing, growth, and harvest was supported by collective emotion and mimetic magic. The biological progression from youth to manhood, considered part of the process of nature and society, was confirmed and crowned by ritual. In such a context, therefore, miming is simultaneously magic and a means of coping with the practical world. Acting things out subjects them to the actor's power (a phenomenon Frazer called "the Law of Similarity"), and so at some level of their development sympathetic magic and the conquest of nature share similar social functions. For magic possesses, as Bronislaw Malinowski points out, "a functional truth or a pragmatic truth since it arises always under conditions where the human organism is disintegrated." Fantasy and "realism" are not incompatible in the ritual context of miming.[1]

There is no need to discuss the rise of primitive acting in order to clarify the ritual context of its origins. The connection between work and rhythm pointed out long ago by Karl Bücher does much to illuminate the origins of the dance and, by inference, certain primitive forms of *mimesis*. This connection has been developed more recently by Oskar Eberle and A. D. Avdeev in their revealing studies of the so-called *Urtheater*. It was their discovery that primitive peoples, most of whom as yet knew nothing of ancestor cults or animism, initially associated miming with their natural means of survival. The water dwellers of Tierra del Fuego, for example, have their canoe play, the Bambuti pygmies

1

their jungle hunting game, the Tasmanians a seal game, and the Kem-mirai of New South Wales a kangaroo game. At this level of culture *mimesis* arises out of a community in which there is little division of labor; the "spectators" take part in the game or join in the acting. The unity of player and audience is complete when each participant shares in the indivisible process of primitive living.

In the more advanced planters' civilizations the identity between player and audience continues primarily in the form of cultic and as-sociative customs, but still sustains its greatest impulse where the original links between mimetic and productive activities are most pronounced. Here, too, the rational function of rhythm—that of making work easier—is augmented by the representation of an illusionary world. But, again, such rhythmic ecstasy in ritual cannot be placed in simple opposi-tion to a sense of reality, since the imaginative inversion of the actual situation—hunger, darkness, cold, or fear, for example—arouses a col-lective energy which in turn is applied to coping with reality.

The correlation between the productive and the consecrative forms of ritual permeates the earliest drama, and is analogous to the primitive functions of mythology: where myth can be understood—in the words of Marx—as an "unconscious artistic processing of nature" by the "popular imagination." In this context, the embryonic functions of miming and the origins of *mimesis* deserve to be considered. In practice, of course, the forms of miming cannot at first be isolated from the uses of magic, especially when they are connected to certain defensive activities—against death and the dead, for instance, as in the belief in demons. But if early *mimesis* can be at all abstracted from its ritual context, certain structures and functions of the primitive imitation of nature may be discerned. For example, a thing, a person, or a gesture is "investigated" and illuminated when it is imitated, when its social *ohm,* or measure, is discovered and exposed. From this point of view, the unity of imitation and representation denoted by the Greek term *mimesis* seems valid for the preliterary stage. The early modern German verb *ahmen* or *ohmen,* which became *nachahmen* (to imitate), implies a measuring and presup-poses a standard not exclusively derived from the object itself. The im-itating subject, or ego, imposes his own standards onto the object and the resultant representation is, as Aristotle was to note later, not merely a passive reproduction of something given, that is, not a simple imitation. It is no accident that the verb corresponding to the Greek word for actor—*hypokrites* (*hypokrinomai*)—means "to interpret," and less often "to answer." The Ionian equivalent of *hypokrites* was *exegetes,* whose charac-teristic meaning is familiar to us today.

More recent research, such as that of Hermann Koller, has clarified the original context of *mimos* and *mimeisthai* and revealed a "close link between mimesis and the dance." Furthermore, it has been observed that *mimos* and all terms derived from it "originally have their home only in the cultic sphere, in the orgiastic cult." If the original meaning of *mimesis* was "expression in dance," then it obviously covered much more than can be included in the term *imitatio*. The elements of expression and evaluation in *mimesis* as opposed to mere *imitatio* can be emphasized without necessarily agreeing with Koller's daring conclusion that *mimos* means "the actor or the mask of Dionysian cultic drama." For if, as G. F. Else argues, the late reception of the word *mimos* into Greek results from its foreign character and the vulgarity of the object it described, an early derivation of the verb *mimeisthai* from *mimos*—the lower Dorian miming—would be quite conceivable. But *mimeisthai* seems to imply a similarity between the object and its mimetic imitation, at least in the sense of a "representational action."[2] From the outset, then, *mimesis* paradoxically included both the element of expression linked with the actor (that is, the subject) in the process of representation, and the element of imitation, which is primarily linked with its object.

It is this paradox that lies at the heart of the tension between the ritual origins and the representational forms of *mimesis*. The structure of this tension changes in history, and the quality of its change reflects the social consciousness behind the movement from irrational myth to rational cognition. It arises from the nature of the object chosen for imitation, but also from the changing means and standards of representation—its more or less rhythmic (dancing) and verbal modes and contents. This change is of the most far reaching consequence in the history of both the ancient and the modern theater, especially in the structure and stagecraft of popular drama. What is important here is that regardless of the gradual movement from myth to realism the tension between the two poles retains its vitality and importance. Significant and fundamental attitudes in the processes of staging and the art of dramatic speech hinge on this contradiction. The tension between the ritual expression of self and the dramatic representation of objects seems especially long-lived in the popular theater where the *actor's* naive self-expression repeatedly finds a place alongside the pure naturalism of his *role*.

This statement of the relation between myth and drama, ritual and *mimesis*, involves sweeping generalizations that must appear unduly oversimplified as long as the structure of the mimetic process is not derived from and studied in the early forms in which it actually existed on the stage. Despite the meager evidence as to its theatrical practices, the ancient *mimus* probably provides the first and least contested example of a popular drama which, unlike the Attic festival theater, developed in direct conjunction with varied strata of society. A genuinely popular theater, the ancient *mimus* received no subsidies and "derived its guiding principles solely from its own immediate experience with the audience." It offered no artistically refined drama, but short, sketchy, naturalistic images of life with motifs and types taken from everyday experience. This, as Arnold Hauser notes, was a theater "which was created not only for the people but also to some extent by the people," although it remains difficult to establish the extent to which professional actors could in fact "remain folk players" solely because they had as yet no connection with the educated elite. Nonetheless, if they were recruited from amongst the populace, they may have shared the general taste and perhaps even "derived their philosophy of life from the common people."[3]

This "unpretentious naturalistic popular theater," even if its social foundations were more complex than such a summary allows, reveals social functions and dramatic forms that are quite relevant to a study of the Elizabethan popular tradition. In ancient Greece the dramatic representation of reality found its characteristic art form not in the stylized festival theater but in the popular *mimus*. It was in this form that drama first "broke away from . . . religion and rose again" in a modern and entirely secular context.[4] Here the principle of *mimesis* was freed, or at any rate was separated from its ritual origins and mythical functions. The popular player, renouncing the buskin, and generally the mask as well, became a "describer of reality," the unmasked imitator and presenter of the actual world around him. Consequently, the process of staging was dominated by a more pervasive sense of realism than that of solemn tragedy; images of everyday life, descriptions of life's pitfalls, realistic portrayals of blood flowing upon the open stage, and the depiction of the crucifixion of characters, were acted out with what must have been a naturalistic effect something like that found in certain mystery plays and to some extent in the Elizabethan theater.

What should be noted about this kind of naturalism, however, is that in the preclassical *mimus* the lifelike and the fantastic existed side by side. It was perfectly possible to combine realism of detail with ritualized conventions in dramatic representations that remained close to the audience. In this way the memory of the cultic, nonillusionary elements in the ancient mimetic dance and song survived. For centuries the erect phallus—ageless symbol of fertility—was carried across the stage, a custom already unthinkable in New Comedy. Judging from fragments that have survived, the *mimus* seems to have been closer to the Old Comedy of Aristophanes than to New Comedy, with its increasingly illusionary effects. And even if, as Arnold Hauser suggests, the classical festival stage is regarded as an "instrument of propaganda," and its dramatists as "state dependents," the relationship between these "state dramatists" and actors and their audiences resembled that of the popular miming theater much more closely than that of the later stage of Menander. This relationship is fundamental to discussion of the changing connections between ritual and mime.

The close tie between magical rite and mimic representation (which survived in phallic fertility symbolism) gradually weakened. To the degree that ritual died out or became fossilized, the imitation of reality became deliberate and effective, thus transforming the function and structure of mimic actions. In ecstatic or magic ritual, the tension between mythical archetype and mimic imitation was suppressed or ignored: the shaman, the poet-priest—as well as the *kōmos*, the community around the cult—did not *represent* the mythic happening for a public; rather, in their possession they *embodied* or incarnated it, and the priest's frenzy was direct evidence of immediate contact with the spirits or of an effective initiation ceremony. As a sense of the gods' power declined, possession became drama and embodiment became representation. Even the ritual community underwent a division of labor, for the specialists in frenzy could no longer simply incarnate their experience, but had to—for a public—re-enact and interpret it. As understanding of nature increased, and the experience of art separated from the life of myth, the "measuring" potential of *mimesis* as *imitation* assumed a new independence. No longer archetypes to be embodied, scenes taken from myth became secular objects of sheer imitation and, finally, objects of parody and comic irreverence. At this point, the heritage of ritual had become the material of dramatic convention.

This rather schematic description (again, deliberately abstracted from the broader connections between social and theatrical history) may serve, provisionally, to separate the "disenchanting" potential of imitation from the "enchanting" power of ritual miming. Even though both existed side-by-side, there developed a curious contradiction involving not only the *mimus* but also Old Comedy and the tragedies of Euripides. The mime, originally the loyal servant and agent of myth, became the derider of the gods. Gestures once sacred became irreverent. Ritual, no longer re-enacted but acted, became conventional, lost its revered status and was placed on the same level as other dramatic representations of life.

The potential for disenchantment implicit in imitation is one of the most sustained elements of parody in the *mimus* (as it remained to a much lesser extent in the medieval mystery cycles); for the dramatic "reassessment of all idealistic mythical values" was even more pronounced in the *mimus* than in the enlightened approach of Euripides. The *mimus*, Reich adds, "brought down from their heights all the ideal figures of myth (the Homeric gods and heroes), made use of them for its own realistic and comic art, and placed them on a familiar footing with all the other miming rabble."[5] It is in this sense that the many accusations of irreverence and coarseness made by the church fathers and ancient writers like Diomedes can be understood. This burlesque element of parody survived with astonishing continuity. Mythological parody persisted within the broad development from the Dorian *mimus*, through the plays of Epicharmos and the Phlyaka, down to the *fabula Atellana*. Its startling *verve railleuse* and blatantly blasphemous nature is probably best illustrated in the pictures painted on Phlyakian vases. Later parody at ceremonial church festivals, and indeed all the anti-Christian miming, as Allardyce Nicoll points out, in no way differs from the earlier burlesques of pagan ceremony. The tradition of parody is, therefore, not restricted to the sensational *mimus* of the later Roman and Byzantine epoch.

What finally emerges is a deeply rooted connection between the more autonomous method of *mimesis* and the burlesque treatment of the cultic. Perhaps it may even be said that there is a tradition that extends from the acting out of baptism and the presence of "church dignitaries, bishops, exorcists, presbyters and deacons on the miming stage"[6] right down to the grotesque appearance of the strange "presbyter" in *Mary Magdalene* (1143–1248), whose irreverent servant must ring the bells, prepare the altar, and recite a sixteen-line "mocking nonsensical service."

The history of parody in the Middle Ages is certainly too broad a topic to be considered under the category of *mimesis*. Its changes through many literary forms and historical periods make generalizations tenuous at best. But one may still reasonably consider the possibility that "thanks to the *mimus*, relics of a tradition of parody were carried over into the Middle Ages."[7] Here it is worth noting that parody and burlesque often flourished in conjunction with pageants and disguises. They survived also in the context of processions and irreverent festivals of the medieval church where myth and ritual, once they were no longer embodied but simply acted, deteriorated into a spirited topsy-turvydom[8] which, in its most varied forms, re-emerged as key elements of dramatic speech, structure, and stagecraft in the popular tradition of drama.

2

The Actor-Audience Relationship

In view of the fragmentary survival of the *mimus*, it would be difficult to support Hermann Reich's claim of an "unparalleled continuity" down to Shakespeare. But even so the *mimus* deserves more attention within the framework of the popular tradition than it has generally received. A comparative history of the popular theater would be as little able to disregard the *mimus* as the Turkish *Karagöz* or the modern *Commedia dell'arte*. It is through a comparative approach to the various forms of popular theater that the changing elements of tradition and innovation can be established and viewed as part of a more basic understanding of the theater as a social institution in history. What is needed is a histori-

cally conceived study of the fundamental elements of popular dramaturgy. This, however, presupposes some attempt at an integration of the perspectives of history and sociology on the one hand, and the study of dramatic speech and structure on the other, as parts of drama in performance. The assumption that the quality and very nature of a performance depend largely upon the relationship established by the actor with his audience supports the critical utility of such an integration. But the relationship between actor and audience is not simply "conditioned by the physical structure of the building that contains them both";[9] rather, it is connected with some of the most basic economic and social forces in history, of which both drama and the theater (as social institution and architectural design) are reflections *and* agents.

These considerations of method are particularly relevant when claims of the continuity of the popular tradition are based not on historical fact, but on some kind of ideal order or preconceived norm. Here it should be stressed that the more the popular theater preserves a nonliterary or amateur character, the more directly it is exposed to the impact of the changing forms and organizations of society. The impact of time and place is most immediate where the actor-audience relationship is flexible, close, and spontaneous. And the flexibility and spontaneity of this relationship are most effective and far reaching in their dramatic consequences where there is no social and architectural division between the worlds of actor and audience, or where such a division can still be easily traversed.

This was the case in the *mimus,* as it was in the old Attic comedy when Aristophanes' actors addressed the audience, or when the actor representing Dionysus asked a priest in the audience for help and hid behind his seat, or when Socrates was represented as a character in the play while he himself sat in the audience.[10] As long as the performance of the play is substantially enriched by the potential social significance involved in the actor-audience relationship, the full meaning of drama may be defined as an image of the impact of this relationship on the performed text. And the more the public is drawn into the world of the play and the more the play is drawn into the real world, the more the essence of the play is brought out *in the course of performance.* The relationship between actor and audience is, therefore, not only a constituent element of dramaturgy, but of dramatic meaning as well.

While Ibsen, Chekhov, and the theater of dramatic illusion can largely, or to a certain extent, be understood from a reading of the text, the purely literary interpretation remains quite unsatisfactory in dealing with the older popular theater. As long as no class divisions separate actor and audience, the spectator remains a potential actor and the actor a potential spectator. Such unity of dramatic production and reception is, of course, never complete, for it contains many contradictions. In the *mimus* and in Old Comedy it must be seen against the background of an ever increasing division of labor; the actor had long since broken away from the native *kōmos* and at least temporarily achieved a specialized function in society. Yet this inevitable division did not simply disrupt the relative unity of actor and audience but rather fostered a series of contradictions which underlie the long and protracted transition from ritual embodiment to dramatic representation. Seen in this light, the tradition of the popular theater can be characterized by the continuity of historical conditions in which social or physical barriers between actor and audience remained undeveloped.

To illustrate some of these conditions it must suffice here to compare the *mimus* theater and Old and New Comedy. From the point of view of the actor-audience relationship, the significant dividing line does not run between Aristophanes and the *mimus* but between Menander on the one hand and both old Attic comedy and the *mimus* on the other. After the defeat of Athens by the Macedonians (322 B.C.), the *theōrikon*—the grant distributed to the poorer citizens of Athens enabling them to pay admission to the theater—was finally discontinued. Consequently, the stage became less accessible to free working citizens, even though they were not forcibly prevented from attending performances. The dramatists themselves were no longer citizens working with an eye to the *polis*, but, like Diphilos and Philemon, even strangers in the places where the plays were performed. As such they no longer thought of themselves as guardians of and sharers in public interests but as paid producers of entertainment. The spirited criticism of the Attic public characteristic of Aristophanes was no longer conceivable in the Menandrian theater. Hence the broadening gulf between actor and audience compromised both the function and structure of Old Comedy, since Aristophanic laughter was a form of self-insight and a means of self-purification which, as Hegel noted, presupposes the identity of the subject and object of comedy. There was a dissipation of the actor's "pleasant sense of subjectivity," as exemplified by Dikaiopolis in the *Acharnians*, who, knowing how to laugh with the audience, laughed at himself more than he was laughed at. Tarlton, Falstaff, and other Shakespearean clowns later recall just such a self-conscious sense of comedy. This Aristophanic laughter was inconceivable without the relative identity of actor and audience, and was bound to die on the lips of Menander's performers. Thus the theatrical conventions of comedy changed together with the change in the actor-audience relationship; Dikaiopolis became Knemon, still a peasant, but a *dyskolos*, a grumbler, a ruffian, a comic old man who, like Molière's misanthrope, did not laugh at himself but was laughed at, ridiculed not as the subject of comedy but only as its object.[11]

These changes in the actor-audience relationship corresponding to far-reaching social transformations penetrated deeply into the structure of comedy and modes of comic characterization. But it was the process of staging that was perhaps most significantly affected. The old Attic scene was not an illusionary locality; essentially, the scene was the theater itself with an audience in it. And the citizen audience, which considered itself involved in what happened on the stage, found a common voice in the chorus, which in many ways itself reflected important aspects of the unity of production and reception—that is, we find a positive and functional relationship between those who performed and those who attended the play. Once this unity was disrupted, the chorus was bound to disappear, as it did from Menander.

In *Dyskolos* or *Epitrepontes* the scene no longer reflected the former indivisibility of play and audience, for its locale was determined not by the audience in the theater but by the fictive setting established within the play. Actors did not perform in the midst of the audience but against a localized scene which the spectators watched but which their presence no longer helped to constitute. This meant that along with the increasing dramatic illusion of verisimilitude, not only did the actor-audience relationship change but also the actor's relationship to the scene. No longer the creator of the scene, the performer needed only to adapt himself to it. Scenic conventions of locality achieved a greater autonomy, and the beginning of a "fourth wall" (which was, of course, not yet impenetrable) was set up between audience and play. The history of comedy after Aristophanes reveals that this process was not initiated by architectonic changes, for an entirely new process of dramatic action emerged in the midst of an essentially unchanged stage structure.

> *Charisios:* ... What are you standing there and listening for?
> *Onesimos:* I?
> I just came out of the door.
> I did not listen. But if you want that
> no one should hear you
> You should not trust the sky with
> your troubles so loudly and freely.[12]

As the scene achieved a more representational quality, the actor began to submit to new conventions (those governing illusion and impersonation) even when he could exploit an awareness of their limitations, as did Onesimos. Charisios' soliloquy, which precedes this dialogue, reflects a convention that nonetheless seems so out of context and dramatically inappropriate that it is easily turned to comic effect. The new illusion of solitude on the stage tended to disregard the presence of the audience, but the illusion of not being overheard still must have seemed so weak that it could be comically dismissed. Even though the technical process of staging was enriched by varied and often quite brilliant devices, the member of the *polis* turned private citizen essentially corresponded to the common actor turned specialist, no longer speaking as representative and on behalf of the spectators but only in the service of what was usually an audience of higher social standing.

As the passage from the *Epitrepontes* indicates, the shift from a nonrepresentational scenery to a new kind of stage illusion is never complete. In Plautus and Terence, as in Menander, the contradiction between unlocalized setting and the more scenic kind of illusion is never absolute, although one or the other usually predominates. Nor should it be forgotten that Plautus, to whom Shakespeare owed so much, wrote for the noisy, unlettered crowd that attended the Roman festivals. In fact he drew inspiration from the *fabula Atellana,* a popular, secular offspring of ritual ceremonies and rural festivals which were acted *ex tempore* and, like the Greek satyr plays and the Elizabethan jig, often appended to a more serious play. The scene was generally rural, with action that focused upon the lower classes. The language was rich in proverbs and filled with popular idiom; choruses and songs as well as a good deal of obscenity were common. Strong elements of parody and conventions of disguise, like those found in the *mimus,* were the legacy of the native Roman theater from which Plautus drew in his creation of robust comic situations and in his depiction of plebeian characters (notably his clever comic slaves).[13] Plautine comedy, once it reached the English public stage, contained submerged elements of another native popular tradition, which, as a matter of course, met with a congenial reception.

Indeed, some structural and verbal conventions display a remarkable continuity wherever a popular theater takes root. These include the mixture of serious and comic elements, frequent use of disguises, and an occasional element of dance. As early as the *mimus* there are recurrent modes of dramatic speech, such as wordplay (in Laberius, for example), the couplets described by Chrysostom and Gregory of Naziantium, and the proverb (of which there is so much literary evidence in Sophron, and especially in Herondas, that Otto Crusius regarded it as a sufficient criterion for defining the *mimus*).[14]

But are there any concepts of moral value or plebeian ideology behind these theatrical and linguistic conventions? Hermann Reich's research suggests that there are, though his findings are based mainly on secondary and literary sources (Sophron and Herondas, and the collected proverbs of Philistion and Publilius). Eduard Norden also refers to these when he writes that "the robust realism of the action was combined with a moralising element, as so often in popular plays." Is it possible, then, to conclude that a "didactic element ... was from the very beginning extremely important in the mimus"? In any case it seems significant that the proverb flourished in the context of specific character types; the merrymaker of the Graeco-Roman world—the μῖμος γελοίων—felt thoroughly at home with the practical wisdom of the common people.

For this reason Reich ventures to suggest that "the mime from the very beginning liked to make use of proverbs in which the common people expressed their wealth of observation and experience." But at present the evidence is too slender for us to assume the existence of a "virtuous moral core ... much of which may have been present throughout the mimus."[15]

3

The Tradition of the Fool

It is the dramatic figure of the mimic fool, or *stupidus*, that preserved some of the peculiar elements and functions of the oldest miming art, for it is in the contradiction and in the unity of fantasy and realism, myth and knowledge, social criticism and utopian prophecy, that the fool's roots are most firmly planted. In spite of numerous transformations, he has never achieved the psychological complexity or ability to develop associated with more modern dramatic characters. Thus he remains, more than any other figure in drama, closest to his early ritual heritage. The descendant of a ritual that has long since lost its original function, the fool is an atavistic agent of the cult, and, through his *mimesis* and parody, its heretic. He is, therefore, both the heir of myth and the child of realism—a contradiction in his genealogy that gives the fool his Janus-like status. But his inexhaustible vitality and unbroken continuity have a good deal to do with the ambivalence of his dramatic functions: he retains the capacity both to enchant and disenchant. He can neutralize myth and ritual through the unmasking and debunking potential of *mimesis,* through his parody, criticism, or cynicism; but he can also generate a ritual dimension through the fantasy and madness of his topsy-turvydom, or through his inversion of values and the transformation of reality into something strange, sad, or comical. Such inversions and transformations in turn recreate a visionary world where Utopia and some echo of primitive society exist side by side.

Although the various forms and modes of dramatic foolery change, the continuity of the type is unmistakable right down to Shakespeare. But any attempt to analyze this figure seems only to result in unhelpful abstractions. It was in the *mimus* that the fool first became an indispensable adjunct of the popular theater, but he has been periodically reborn in the Italian Arlecchino (Harlequin), the English clown or fool, the French Pierrot or Jean Potage, the Spanish Giangurgolo, the Dutch Pickelhäring, and the Viennese Hanswurst, Staberl, and Thaddädl. Through all these transformations the type retains not simply a continuity of attitude but a dramatic consistency that is associated with a particular social,

verbal, and spatial position which in turn reinforces a special relationship between the play world and the real world. Even where the original
unity of theatrical production and audience has disappeared, and
actor-audience contact is minimal, the fool, Arlecchino, Hanswurst, or
Vice remains an atavistic link. In the midst of increasingly illusionary
scenery and localized settings, the fool and his descendants continue to
break through the "fourth wall" (at a time when it already seems almost
impenetrable), and again conjure and renew the old audience contact.
The modern German puppet Kasperle, much like the English Punch,
preserves an echo of the traditional actor-audience relationship when he
asks the director's question, "Are you all there?"

To be sure, none of these types has a "pure" genealogy; Shakespeare's
fool in particular is a rich hybrid in which the court fool, the Vice of the
morality plays, the genius of Dick Tarlton, and individual talents in
Shakespeare's troupe merged with countless other elements of clowning
and popular entertainment. But Shakespeare's fools and clowns are
nonetheless steeped in a tradition that is not primarily one of character
but of social and dramatic functions.[16]

In the *mimus,* the miming fool already appears to have existed in a
number of forms. The bald clown μωρὸς φαλακρός appeared in Roman
times as *sannio* in the motley of Centunculus and made faces when his ears
were boxed. The clumsiness and characteristic greed of this variant contrasts with another version, the μῖμος δεύτερος, the "secondary mime,"
whose comical aping and imitation served, according to Horace, to contrast other characters. The fool, like his descendants, carried a phallus,
or at any rate a club, and wore a hat of rural design—"originally part of
the costume of the Greek or Italian peasant." He usually spoke in prose,
but at times sang; he was also able on some occasions to utter "profound
remarks."[17]

The early dramatic functions of the fool in the *mimus* find a revealing
context in the serious play or theme where he assumes the main role—
that of the martyr, for example, in the anti-Christian dramatic parody.
The best evidence of such a dramatic function is to be found in one of
the rarer tragicomic and "romantic" plays like the Charition fragment of
the papyrus found at Oxyrhynchos. The fragment formed part of a play
that could be called a "scurrilous Iphigenia,"[18] that is, a burlesque version of *Iphigenia in Tauris.* Here the young Greek heroine, Charition,
who probably became the devotee of some goddess in order to escape
the advances of a barbarian king in whose land she is now in danger, is
rescued by her brother, the captain of his ship, a "funny man" and a
friend.

> Scene: *The precincts of a temple.* Charition *is standing with the* Fool. *There is a*
> *noise of shouting without, and the* Friend *dashes in.*

The Friend. Lady Charition! Rejoice! I have escaped!
Charition. Great are the gods!
The Fool.   What gods, fool? The goddess Porde—
Charition. Peace, slave!
The Friend. Wait here for me; I'll go and get the ship
              brought to anchor.
Charition. Go then. For see! here are their women
              come from the hunting.
              [*A crowd of* Barbarian Women *suddenly make their appearance.*]
The Fool.   Ow! What enormous bows they have![19]

Here the fool provides a scurrilous undertone in calling Charition a
fool for praising the gods, a posture that is essentially echoed in Feste's
later banter with Olivia in *Twelfth Night* (I, 5, 52 ff): "Good madonna,
give me leave to prove you a fool." The same comical exchange of roles is
found in both cases despite the differences in occasion and context; the
fool, with his cheeky impunity, turns his mistress' standards upside-
down because he senses that they are foolishly inadequate for the particular situation. However, in inverting his mistress' role, he also playfully challenges her authority as a superior. The fool in the *mimus* does
not believe in a *deus ex machina;* he knows only one "goddess": Porde
(πορδή, the fart)—perhaps an implicit stage direction indicating his in-
testinal response to the threat of the Amazons. The fool's joke is harm-
less enough, but still it retains a kind of subversive function. The capacity
for inversion is, after all, based on a fundamental disrespect for rank and
the hierarchies inherent in the nature of myth. Irreverence becomes the
method, and disrespect the principle of the fool's comic inversion.

It should be stressed that this subversive function has theatrical and
structural correlatives and supports a specific process of staging and a
particular actor-audience relationship. To begin with, the fool's vocabulary provides a striking contrast to that of the god-fearing Charition. But
his scurrilous reply is only the verbal expression of a kind of worldview
that is clearly contrasted to the mythos in the main action. For a moment,
the plot is comically evaluated from the fool's point of view, a perspective
that is not at all implicit in the mythos but which exists totally beyond its
thematic and moral assumptions. This comical, clowning, scurrilous position derives its effect from the tension between the mythical world of
Charition and the actual postritual community of the audience. The
fool's spontaneous remark about the Amazon's "huge bows" is not at all
essential to the action. Rather, it verbalizes the naive (and later the anxious) impression of a person operating outside the heroic ethos and its
dramatic conventions. In this way the fool creates a complementary
perspective that (down to Shakespeare's day) counterpoints the attitudes
of the heroic or romantic characters. His perspective reflects a dramatic
and social position that rejects the assumptions of the mythical or heroic

theme in favor of the common sense attitude of a plebeian or secularized audience. And although not on a conscious level, the fool, as early as the *mimus* fragment, makes use of a self-expressed *ohm*, a plebeian standard whose collision with the mythical is the crux of comedy. The fool's capacity for audience awareness, "anachronism," and social criticism exist primarily by virtue of these contradictions.

Seen in this light, the fantastic, scurrilous, and irreverent fool does not really stand in opposition to the "astonishing realism" that Hermann Reich found in the *mimus*. One need not actually appreciate the banal aspects of the *mimus,* or see in it "the foundation of ancient realistic poesy," in order to detect the struggle between a "refined mythical idealism and a popular burlesque realism."[20] But the disenchanting qualities of this kind of realism cannot be defined exclusively in terms of its opposition to the theater of myth and idealism. Mythical idealism does in fact confront popular realism, but the confrontation is a highly complex one. The mythical substance of the tragedies, as well as that of Old Comedy, reveals an inspiration of poetic truth that would make too rigid or abstract an opposition between the worlds of myth and realism inappropriate. As George Thomson and Jack Lindsay have shown, there is no doubt that it was the *thiasos,* the cult of Dionysus and the Orphic and shamanist traditions, that helped preserve the standards of communal consciousness and social criticism—standards that were not at all opposed to a popular sense of reality.

All this applies to the fool as well as to the comic hero in Old Comedy, and to their assimilation of ritual and realism. "Nonrealistic" and nonrepresentational, he finally becomes an excellent vehicle for the criticism of reality. In the case of Aristophanes' comic characters, such as Dikaiopolis or Trygaios, an ancient, primitive idea of equality is linked to a utopian vision of future peace and plenty. This is not true of the banal, miming merrymaker, but it is partially true of some of the great clowns and fools of world literature. The mature popular theater is unthinkable without the "measure" of truth and knowledge contained in a representation of the world as it is; but it is not at all bound to the artistic principle of imitation. The image of myth and the playful revival of ritual as the "unconscious processing of nature" do not hinder the development of an awareness of the poetic truth of art. It is only when the dramatic representation of objects is no longer reconciled with the self-expression of the subject—the community's longing and despair, hopes and struggles—that the popular theater becomes merely rowdy and *mimesis* becomes naturalism.

II

THE FOLK PLAY
AND SOCIAL CUSTOM

While the *mimus* grew away from primitive tribal culture, the ritual and festival customs of an older agrarian social structure lived on in the folk play, especially in the English Mummers' Play and the Sword Play, and in similar forms of men's ceremonial in Thessaly, Thrace, Rumania, Southern Macedonia, and elsewhere. But as the mimetic element in the *mimus* had lost its magical purpose and meaning, and the dramatic functions of representation and communication came into their own, *mimesis*, in the folk play, became increasingly separated from its ritual origins and context and did not develop in correlation with myth. As a consequence, the elements of action and interpretation never fully came together: "plot" and dialogue in the folk play, in the absence of the development, through *mimesis*, of such universal narrative models as mythos had once offered to drama in ancient Greece, did not receive any mutually stimulating impulse, and the ability of folk drama to fully symbolize human experience remained undeveloped. Nor was the folk play greatly affected by collateral changes in literature. As in the more primitive ceremonials or the ritual dance, it was still the action, not the story or interpretation, which remained central; and whatever links seemed to exist were mostly accidental to both the social function of ritual and the collective uses of the imagination.[1]

Regardless of variations in details and characters, the many versions of the Mummers' Play preserved in various parts of Great Britain contain a number of recurring elements. The basic four-part structure of the play begins with an introduction in which one of the actors addresses the surrounding audience asking for room to play and requesting, sometimes, their attention as well. This is followed by the hero-combat, in which two protagonists (often St. George and the Turkish Knight) appear to boast of their strength and engage in battle; the defeated player is subsequently wounded or killed. A doctor, usually assisted by an impudent young servant, is then summoned to heal the fighter's wounds or to resurrect him from the dead. A number of comic characters appear in the last part of the play, which ends finally with a collection and another address to the audience.

With a few exceptions, like *Grim the Collier of Croydon*, the Mummers' Play left no tangible or direct traces in the Elizabethan theater. Nonetheless, it deserves attention from a comparative historical point of view as a form of dramatic activity, maintained by amateur actors right into the twentieth century, which provides an illuminating contrast to the popular Renaissance theater. Because of its remarkable continuity it indicates the deeply rooted dramatic traditions of the people, as well as the limitations of a nonrepresentational formal kind of popular ceremony, enriched neither by the chivalric or courtly values of feudalism nor by the humanist tradition of the Renaissance. It is true that the Mummers' Play still seems to have interested the landed gentry in the fifteenth century and is mentioned in town records, but in the seventeenth century it was enjoyed only by the "base vulgar"—rural people as yet little affected by the rise of a middle-class literary culture, Puritanism, or the later Enlightenment.[2]

From the point of view of its social function and status, then, the folk play began to degenerate long before the earliest extant records of its existence. Those who perpetuated the form were, in the material forms of their existence and their social consciousness, increasingly vulnerable to, and isolated from, the pressures and movements of society as a whole. Under these conditions it was certainly an exception, not the rule, for rural players to perform *St. George and the Fiery Dragon* along with *Mucedorus* and *Dr. Foster* (Faustus), although a 1741 diary kept by the head of a wandering players' troupe records amongst their plays for that year *Hamlet, Tamburlaine,* and *Jane Shore* as well as *The Mock Doctor*. This late link between rural popular traditions and Renaissance culture indicates that audiences were, nonetheless, prepared to welcome both forms of dramatic entertainment. But the combination had no future; after the yeomen had turned middle class or were expropriated, the rural population was at best capable of preserving an already decadent ceremonial, but not of providing the foundations for the growth of a creative dramatic culture.

Only limited conclusions about the origins of the Mummers' Play can therefore be drawn from the later development of the folk play. If it is assumed (with E. K. Chambers' caution) that the surviving dialogue of the St. George plays should be placed in the sixteenth century, and a literary echo also admitted here and there (of *Mucedorus,* for instance), this would still leave unexplained the evidence that such plays were performed as early as 1348, 1474, and 1511. Its origins must, therefore, be sought at an even earlier date. The same applies to the English Sword Dance, which is likewise documented in the 1490 "dawnce of Sygate." The tradition of the Sword Dance (which Tacitus had already found amongst Germanic tribes) as well as analogous ceremonies in southern Europe justify a search for the ritual origins of the folk play in the fertility rites and the agrarian festivals of prefeudal and pre-Christian village communities. At the same time, the influence of outside forces must be taken into account; for instance, it may well be assumed that "the formal structure of the medieval joust and tournament was taken by the folk and grafted on to the basic Men's Ceremonial."[3]

The folk play reflects a state of dramatic activity that failed fully to interrelate, and to comprehend in one vision, the nonrepresentational embodiment of the rite and the sensuous representation of reality. On the one hand, there is a recurring pattern of late ritual action. Although the gradual separation of performer and "audience" increased the need to interpret cultic action in terms of representational forms, basic elements of a ritual action persisted, albeit in submerged ways: the combat, the cure (with its death and resurrection motifs), the *quête* (with its processional and choral elements), as well as the dancing and the courtship ceremony in the related tradition of the Sword Play. On the other hand, there is an undeveloped element of verbal interpretation, usually varied by local accretions. This verbal drama does involve a certain element of *mimesis* in the form of an impersonation of "St. George," "Oliver Cromwell," or "King George," and it refers, to a certain degree, to the action proper. But a fully representational quality is not achieved when such undeveloped elements of verbal drama are grafted on to the forgotten meaning of a ritual action.

There remains, then, an unresolved contradiction between the elements of ritual embodiment (such as those associated with ancient fertility rites) and the tendency toward a representational mode of impersonation (as associated with the needs and possibilities of amateur acting for seasonal audiences). The *effective* magical purpose of the former and the *affective* communicative function of the latter exist separately, without significantly drawing on the potentialities of a combination of both. The ritual element is not transformed into symbolic action, nor is it gradually secularized and dramatized from within, as in the old Attic theater; rather it withers away, leaving vestigial dramatic and verbal formulae without providing any referential consistency, any continuity in representational form as expressed through fictive images of social action, that is, through plot for the benefit of an audience. Insofar as dramatic representations did gain ground, they did so not in terms of their ritual antecedents—through the already existing medium of some "unconscious artistic processing of nature"—but accidentally, as accretions, from outside.

As a result, the elements of myth and realism did not fully interact; neither the perspective on society nor the transmutations of fantasy developed dramatically. The dramatic interpretations of ritual action did not develop symbolically into a body of mythological images and stories; they remained tied to the seasonal activities of the ritual performer and the decadence of what was once an effective social occasion. Although the amateur actor's own standards, together with his ceremonial activity, were already marked off from the audience, his own social and personal identity, despite his new function as seasonal "entertainer" did not emerge. It was not distinct enough in relation to the social whole to give rise to an imaginative pattern that was, in its links between the art of acting and the activity of living, meaningful as drama.

It is out of these contradictions that the structure of the extant folk play and the direction and meaning of its poorly developed dramatic interpretations of ritual action can best be understood. Once these interpretations are recognized as verbal expressions of, or accretions to, a nonliterary event, one may explore the nature of the relationship between verbal interpretation and nonrepresentational action more meaningfully. This relationship, which is perhaps more profound and pervasive than recent students of the Mummers' Play are inclined to think, can be extremely subtle, but no less valid because we must rely on nineteenth-century versions of the texts as our primary evidence for the folk play tradition. For how, it must be urged, can the *entire* text be a local accretion when its basic elements occur again and again all over the country? Can the text really be "no more than the water breaking, shifting, and receding around the rocklike center of the action"?[4] These questions do not imply that a literary approach to a nonliterary tradition, or even a preoccupation with sources such as E. K. Chambers showed in *The English Folk-Play,* would be at all satisfactory. But to consider the text as mere "shifting" water and the action as "rocklike" and immutable is to misjudge the relationship—itself a changing one—between verbal interpretation and nonrepresentational action. To say that the action is primary and of ritual origin is one thing, but to ignore the way its basic cultic functions have been surrendered *in the course of verbal interpretations* is to close one's eyes to the fact that in the folk play action and interpretation at certain points do affect each other. Such points of contact, even if they do not achieve the artistic form of drama, are very much part of a theatrical tradition—a tradition that cannot be defined in terms of literary drama. There is a point in the folk play where (although never consummated) interpretation becomes *verbal action,* and action—for a brief moment—assumes a symbolic and temporal dimension. At this point, the transitional quality of the links between actors and audience seems arrested. These links, while they still involve spectators as participants in the purposive meaning of the play (the "sympathetic" luck that it is believed to bring), already help to provide the conditions on which the heritage of ritual embodiment achieves the communicative function and interpretative quality of dramatic entertainment.

To stress such transitions and anticipations is not to ignore the truly traditional elements in the action of the play. These provide a matrix of continuity in which submerged echoes of an older social existence might well survive as, for example, in the Ampleforth and Weston-sub-Edge ceremonies, the Revesby Sword Play and the Plough Play of Bassingham.[5] In these and some other plays it seems possible to trace the dim reflections of a more primitive society still fairly homogeneous in its property and class structure. But can we assume that a few elements in these plays reflect not only the older ways of life but also serve a kind of defensive function against the threat of communal dissolution? Some social historians would say yes, and would point out that as late as the fourteenth century peasant communities had immemorial customs dating from "freer days" which helped to maintain their "strength and cohesion."[6]

For this there are, of course, parallels in different epochs, for instance in the continuity of prefeudal heroic attitudes and ideologies which have been shown by Henrik Becker to have served a defensive function against the nascent claims of feudalism. Another significant precedent can be found in the undercurrents of tribal law which are shown by George Thomson to survive in Aeschylus' tragedies. The cults of Orpheus and Dionysus constituted an anti-Apollonic vestige of tribal culture whose prophetic functions were reduced, but not totally suppressed, by the delphic control of the Olympians, and which, as Jack Lindsay has pointed out, lived on in the *hybristika* or Satyr cult. Repeatedly there is a topsy-turvy inversion of normal controls or standards of behavior in a brief festive moment, or a reversal of values "with the dispossessed spirits summoned up to judge the world that has forgotten tribal brotherhood."[7] It is this utopian vision that emerges in a kind of shamanistic context in Old Comedy, especially in *The Birds* with its dramatic image of "a return to tribal democracy in its early forms, to a Golden Age without divisions and exploitations." Here we may recall Nietzsche's insights into the Dionysian tradition which—although largely metaphysical—take account of the lingering primitive forms of agrarian culture, its shamanistic rituals and secret societies and, of course, the powerful cult of Dionysus itself. Such Dionysian undercurrents must have thrived on the practice, or at least the memory, of tribal equality—a "tendency towards popular thinking"—and reflected tribal "efforts towards unity" as promoted in the dissolution of the *principii individuationis* by the cult:

Within the magic of the Dionysian, not only is the union of man with man regained; alienated inimical or subjugated Nature celebrates its reconciliation with man, its prodigal son . . . the slave is now free, all the rigid, inimical strictures which have created misery, tyranny or "rude custom" amongst human beings now collapse. . . . Singing and dancing, man expresses himself as a member of a higher community. . . .[8]

1

Topsy-turvydom in Ceremony and Performance

Whatever echoes of a prefeudal past remained in the folk play, they cannot, of course, be measured by the standards of Attic drama. If there is any "Dionysian" element at all in the men's ceremonial, it is confined to a tradition of inversion that can be traced through two groups of motifs which, for want of better terms, may be called the visions of topsy-turvydom and of Utopia. The element of topsy-turvydom (which we have already encountered in the ancient *mimus*) finds its most explicit expression in the fools and saucy boys of the folk plays. The utopian motif is much less important and less clearly defined. It emerges in brief but repeated references to Cokaygne, a legendary island of "Plenty" in the far west which promised good fellowship and a somewhat ambivalent prospect of equality and freedom. The Cokaygne tradition is almost certainly older than the grotesque two-hundred-line Middle English poem of the early fourteenth century, which nonetheless constitutes its main literary source in England. Echoes of the Land of Cokaygne may be found in various folk plays, often in the most unlikely places, usually complementing the element of topsy-turvydom with a curious kind of verbal inversion or grotesque nonsense speech.[9]

The connection between Utopia and topsy-turvydom is significant. The origins of the topsy-turvy patter may well be sought, as R. J. E. Tiddy has suggested, in formulae of magical invocations whose original function and incantatory nature were gradually forgotten or misunderstood as comic or grotesque. But what seems more directly relevant is the background of medieval traditions of inversion such as the Lord of Misrule or the *festum stultorum*. A consideration of these can perhaps help to clarify related features in the folk play, since the medieval church and village festivals themselves reveal a semidramatic character and so offer the most important evidence for what might be called a Dionysian tradition in the Middle Ages.

What makes these traditions relevant to an understanding of the growth and development of a popular theater is their uncontrolled element of parody as well as some articulation (often disguised) of an "unofficial" or unorthodox vision of the world. There is a remarkable continuity of playfully inverted conceptions of the world which extends from the Roman Saturnalia down to the rural May games, the *episcopus puerorum* and *festum stultorum* of the lower clergy, the *sermon joyeux* and burlesque *sottie* in France, and the urban mummings and masques in England. Whatever the occasion, however varied the forms, and however different the background (ancient, pagan, clerical, or corporative), a grotesque process of inversion achieved through *mimesis* or disguise is again and again the mainspring. This happens when a *rex saturnalitius*, a mock king or Lord of Misrule, a May King, a Boy Bishop (the German *Schul-* or *Apfel-Bischof*), or a clownish priest is chosen to preside over the reveling community, playfully turning the conventional order of things upside down.

As early as the Roman Saturnalia such topsy-turvydom was associated with a utopian dream of the Golden Age. The festive abolition of inequality and the playful exchange of roles between masters and servants defined the "democratic character"[10] of the Saturnalia, which ostensibly served to "preserve the memory of the original state of nature where every man was equal."[11] At the same time there must have been, one would suppose, an element of appeasement in the state sanction of these reminders of a more primitive society, since there was an unquestionable contradiction between the ruling class position of the organizers and the oppressed status of the participants in the festival. Hence, there resulted the kind of ambiguity that was to find its perfect expression in the short-lived liberties of the fool—exercised in full awareness of his impotence. No matter how tame or conventional (and, of course, vastly different) medieval analogies to the more ancient forms of Dionysian and Saturnalian inversion may have been, it was the ambivalent notion of a past state of society recalling some primitive form of equality that remained part of a tradition of ambiguous freedom and release. In the *festum stultorum* or the *episcopus puerorum* the strictly utopian ideal is either absent or submerged in the spontaneous and excessive enjoyment of food (as in the eating of sausage at the altar, or in the Boy Bishop's feast). But the echo of a primitive Christian state of equality remained—a grotesque echo that was all the more effective when it claimed the authority of the Bible: *Deposuit potentes de sede* . . . (Luke 1:52, "He hath put down the mighty from their seats, and exalted them of low degree"). This was the verse from the *Magnificat* which the subdeacons shouted at the top of their lungs before they overthrew church office and travestied divine service in what was fittingly called the *festum subdiaconorum*. As E. K. Chambers noted, "the ruling idea of the feast is the inversion of status, and the performance, inevitably burlesque, by the inferior clergy of functions properly belonging to their betters." These lower clergy were "an ill-educated and ill-paid class," and that they should "perpetuate or absorb folk-customs was also, considering the peasant or small *bourgeois* extraction of such men, quite natural."[12]

A similar inversion of status, although in a considerably milder form, dominated the investiture of the Boy Bishop, who could also be called *episcopus Nicholatensis* since he collected a large tribute and sometimes treated his schoolmates and fellow choirboys to substantial feasts. The feast took place after he had preached from the pulpit and conducted what a royal ban (July 22, 1541) described as "suche other unfittinge and inconvenyent usages" which served "rather to the derision than to any true glory of God."[13]

What is important here is the fact that almost all of these customs had some equivalents in the folk festivals, and that theologians were at least partially justified in regarding them (as they did the popular drama) as the "devilish" heritage of a pagan past.[14] The nature of such mimetic topsy-turvydom and its inversive quality is neatly glossed in Archbishop Grindal's 1576 inquiry as to "whether the minister and churchwardens have suffered any lords of misrule or summer lords or ladies, or any disguised persons, or others, in Christmas or at May-games, or any morris-dancers, or at any other times, to come unreverently into the church or churchyard, and there to dance, or to play unseemly parts, with scoffs, jests, wanton gestures, or ribald talk."[15] Popular customs connected with the beginning of summer were apparently accompanied by the same irreverent behavior as the lower clergy displayed at Christmas; scoffs, jests, wanton gestures, or ribald talk did not stop at the church door. What is so remarkable (and so characteristic) here is the fact that these late medieval modes of inversion were all associated with both "dance" and the playing of "unseemly parts," and that these enchanting and disenchanting patterns of embodiment and *mimesis* almost certainly provided the basic impulse and occasion. It was an occasion, let us note, at which verbal and physical modes of action, "jests" and "gestures," were significantly linked.

Phillip Stubbes gives us what is perhaps the most vivid picture of the ritual background and the pagan character of such release:

then, marche these heathen company towards the Church and Church-yard, their pipers pipeing, their drummers thundring, their stumps dauncing, their bels iyngling, their handkerchiefs swinging about their heds like madmen, their hobbie horses and other monsters skirmishing amongst the route: & in this sorte they go to the Church (I say) & into the Church, (though the Minister be at praier or preaching), dancing & swinging their handkerchiefs ouer their heds in the Church, like deuils incarnate, with such a confuse noise, that no man can hear his own voice. Then, the foolish people they looke, they stare, they laugh, they fleer, & mount vpon fourmes and pewes to see these goodly pageants solemnized in this sort. Then, after this, about the Church they goe againe and again, & so foorth into the church-yard, where they haue commonly their

Sommer-haules, their bowers, arbors, & banqueting houses set vp, wherin they feast, banquet & daunce al that day & (peradventure) all the night too. And thus these terrestriall furies spend the Sabaoth day.[16]

It is interesting to note that once again the church is the object of a processional ceremony that combines festive release, music, dance, inordinate noise, and abundance of food with some ceremonial features— "hobbie horses and other monsters"—in an apparently successful attempt to disrupt the service. As C. L. Barber points out, such a "village saturnalia of the Lord of Misrule's men was in its way a sort of rising; setting up a mock lord and demanding homage for him are playfully rebellious gestures, into which Dionysian feeling can flow."[17] Stubbes tells us very little about the social status of those who "like madmen" and "deuils incarnate" invaded the parish church; but the imagery used ("terrestriall furies") and the connection with the Morris dancers and summer lords pointed out by Archbishop Grindal leave little doubt about the popular roots of this pagan topsy-turvydom.

In view of the formality and "solemnity" with which "all the wildheds of the Parish" elected and crowned their leader, it is reasonable to view their revelry as a late offshoot of those secret ritual communities which, in the case of the Greek *thiasos*, emerged out of the decline of tribal society, and which survived in parts of Germany in the form of the "wild chase" or similar processional customs of disguise and noise-making. There is little doubt today that these were originally connected with fertility rites and vegetation magic, and that, as Stubbes noted, "bels iyngling," "drummers thundring," and all kinds of "confuse noise" played an important role in them. It was precisely the lower forms of pagan mythology—seasonal rites and vegetation magic—that were least affected by conversion to Christianity and toward which the medieval church had shown a great deal of tolerance.[18] There were probably several reasons why in England it was the reformed church that took steps against these heretofore accepted processional ceremonies of inversion, and these must be considered alongside the fact that by the sixteenth century the village community and the traditional pattern of popular culture were either threatened by dissolution or drawn into the inevitable process of differentiation within the traditional plebeian and the rising bourgeois strata of society. As the bourgeoisie and the new landed gentry became more respectable and aspired to positions of power, and as Puritanism raised its head, the traditional ceremonies of the village, long since dissociated from their original functions (and now in the hands of "the wildheds of the Parish"), seemed less and less tolerable.

But although the ceremonies were gradually discontinued, their spirit survived in the gaiety, the "immoderate and disordinate Joye," of the

Elizabethan clown, jig dancer, and "ieaster," who was accustomed, as
Thomas Lodge wrote, "to coine bitter ieasts, or to show antique motions,
or to sing baudie sonnets and ballads," and who indulged in "all the feats
of a Lord of misrule in the countrie."[19] The spirit of misrule, so familiar
to the Elizabethan merrymaker and jester, lived on at least in part in the
jig—a dramatic balladlike dance containing some measure of satire and
burlesque parody. The jig provided "legal parody"; it included the "burlesque of religious forms," and combined an occasional echo of
Cokaygne or a clowning nonsense element with "satire on the ills of
society."[20] This characteristic combination of "the realistic... with an
element of burlesque" is a special feature of the jig, by which means the
folk dance, the ballad, and elements of satire and social criticism were
brought onto the stage. Clowns and jesters like Dick Tarlton delighted in
exploiting "nonsense songs, strings of impossibilities, prophecies, ragman's rolls," as well as "street cries, medleys, parodies, and the like."
Tarlton in particular was a pacesetter in the adaptation and dramatization of a modern, balladesque form of folk art, and, as C. R. Baskerville
points out, "parodies of legal and religious forms ... were probably favorites with Tarlton."[21]

But a good many of these traditions were connected with the figure of
the Vice long before Tarlton's quick rise to fame, and as such were
probably an important source of inspiration to the countless popular
entertainers "in hostels and taverns" who were barely tolerated by the
authorities. Proclamations of 1537, 1543, and 1549 which banned such
"seditious" entertainment, however, reveal that in the midst of general
toleration some action could be, and in fact was, taken against popular
modes of topsy-turvydom. Festivals such as the famous May games in
Suffolk (1557), where "one played husbandry, and said many things
against gentlemen, more than was in the book of the play," had been the
cause of unrest as early as 1517. After that date the celebrations were
enjoyed with diminishing frequency.[22] But the main point is that in all
these cases, as in the Lord of Misrule described by Stubbes and Archbishop Grindal, the processional topsy-turvydom and the attitudes of
festive release were not at all incompatible with some sort of communal
consciousness and some elements of social criticism. In fact, the traditions of popular myth, ritual, and disguise seemed to provide a favorable vehicle for a naively rebellious expression of the common man's
sense of the world and his position in it.

The link between traditional expressions of festive license and modern
class consciousness was of course as slight as it was spontaneous; and
since a distinctively plebeian form of consciousness was itself only in the
process of formation, the subversive dimension of the Lord of Misrule
should not be exaggerated or its importance overrated. These were indeed "playfully rebellious gestures," and little more. Right up to the end

of the sixteenth century and well into the first decade of the seventeenth (that is, before the revolutionary movement gradually undermined the Tudor compromise in the theater) the conditions for the rise of a specifically plebeian ideology simply did not exist. This was so partly because during the dissolution of the feudal order the contradictions between the popular tradition and the culture of the ruling classes were to some extent synthesized with the needs and aspirations of the New Monarchy and were overshadowed by an overwhelming sense of national pride and unity. In a situation like this the social foundations of the traditional forms of culture were extremely complex. The popularity of the Lord of Misrule among the rural *plebs* did not, for example, prevent the court from developing the same custom. Its expression among the common people, however, was already somewhat politically suspect and subject to criticism, especially since at court the custom was considerably toned down and modified as part of the seasonal revels.

The traditions of urban mumming and the Robin Hood Play, which were closely linked with popular ceremonies and processions, were based on equally heterogeneous social foundations. Both were so varied and changeable that they simply cannot be reduced to any single sociological formula—mumming even less than the Robin Hood Plays. While an important variant of mumming appeared in the disguises of aristocratic tournaments, courtly revels, and the later masque, it was the Robin Hood theme that suffered the most severe changes (in pastoral and aristocratic interpretation as well as in its adaptations in Elizabethan drama from Munday to Jonson). Henry VIII himself took part in the yeoman's Robin Hood parade, and the revels organized at Kenilworth Castle in honor of Queen Elizabeth included various kinds of miming. The same is true of the Morris dance, so closely connected with the late ritual element of rural ceremonials; it was popular both amongst the common people and at court in the sixteenth century, and even Castiglione praised it. The popular tradition of dancing, miming, and disguising cannot therefore be isolated or even clearly distinguished against the wider and complex background of its truly national reception.[23]

In mumming or disguising, the popular element can best be isolated where the semidramatic materials of the masquerade produced quite distinct forms of mimic inversion. Masquerading was in itself much more than a mere change of clothing in an age where the separate estates were required to wear strictly differentiated costumes. It is true that, generally speaking, masquerading had many conventional and often respectable aspects. When the Commons of London dressed up as knights, emperors, popes, and cardinals in 1337, for example, and appeared before the future Richard II together with "eight or ten black masques," it is hardly likely that there was any idea of parody involved. But the dice game with the princes that followed, and the dance in honor of the courtiers were, to be sure, a conspicuous *libertas decembris*. What is more, there were political precedents for the subversive elements of mumming; Sir John Oldcastle and the Lollards, for example, were accused of seeking "under the excuse of mumming to overthrow the King and the Holy Church" in a 1414 rebellion. Followers of Richard II threatened Henry IV in the same way in 1400. Under these circumstances disguise offered "convenient anonymity to professional agitators."[24]

But the general social character of the custom was more important than its occasional application in political causes. As Glynne Wickham remarks, "Mumming was the prerogative of those without claim to noble birth." Processions of disguised persons demanded tribute or forced their way into private houses. Once within, the mummers treated the house as "public property"—another *libertas decembris* by which the sanctity of private property was temporarily suspended. It is therefore not surprising that Tudor legislation imposed harsh punishments on masqueraders, especially if they entered the homes of noblemen or other substantial persons. It was the "rowdy, uncontrolled, free-to-all-comers character of the 'mumming' "[25] that recalled the "democratic character" of the more ancient pagan festivals noted by E. K. Chambers. There was, of course, no political ideology underlying the boisterous revelry of the masqueraders; unlike the Roman Saturnalia, these modern conventions of inversion did not retain any justification in myth and there was no direct connection with any of the defensive functions of ritual. At best only a playful kind of resistance to the division of social classes can be found in the variously disguised inversions of rank and authority.

Since the original social function and ancient ritual purpose of these traditions were forgotten or gradually surrendered, they were usually turned into seasonal customs of festive release which served as a source of gaiety and exuberance in a world that had long since ceased to be enchanted. At the same time, some of the more popular conventions of disguise and miming absorbed or adopted new social and imaginative meanings which, even when they were fitted into a postritual context (as in the Robin Hood tradition), achieved a more directly representational and interpretative significance. The ceremonial action associated with such legendary material was apt, in this context, to involve less effective but more affective forms of conscious imitation. The processional leader who impersonated Robin Hood on the village green might still embody a social occasion or re-enact a traditional event, but in so doing he was not simply performing an action, he was imitating one. As the original cultic significance of such customs was abandoned or diluted in playful vestiges like the *quête*, the jingling of bells, or the communal feast, it was these newly interpretative forms of *mimesis* that contained a potential for growth that was native to popular drama, an element that deserves our attention even when it remained, much more than the Elizabethan jig, poorly developed.

Like mumming, the Robin Hood legends took many forms, the most important of which—the popular ballads—are only of incidental interest here. But apart from his place in the ballads, the figure of Robin Hood was incorporated into other forms of popular custom. Many people, Hugh Latimer noted to his chagrin, were more inclined to celebrate Robin Hood's Day than hear a Bishop preach; and, as Nicholas Bownd noted in 1606, most people were more familiar with Robin Hood than with the stories in the Bible, which were "as strange unto them as any news that you can tell them." As he was assimilated into the late ritual ceremonies of maying, Robin Hood could, and sometimes did, become the subject of dramatic action. The legendary story of Robin Hood was thus associated on the one hand with nonrepresentational processions and popular festival customs and on the other with the newly interpretative and explanatory functions of dramatic representation. Just as in the different context of mumming, there was room for the usual "gaderynge" or collection, which was perhaps as important to maying as the *quête* was at the end of the folk play. At the same time, the Mummers' Play absorbed Robin Hood as a semirepresentational hero, as in the Kempsford and Shipton-under-Wychwood plays. Taking the place of the traditional hero in the ceremonial combat, Robin achieved a status similar to that of St. George, and so brought two dramatic traditions together. (Sir John Paston's famous ostler, for example, played all three roles of "Seynt Jorge and Robyn Hood and the Shryff of Nottyngham.") However, since the actual amount of verbal interpretation and, consequently, dramatic representation was strictly limited within the tradition of the folk play, the Robin Hood tradition was usually included in purely processional and nonrepresentational ceremonies. Here his name was often synonymous with the May King ("somer kyng"), who appeared also as mock king or summer Lord of Misrule. In many places the days of maying became simply "Robin Hoodes Daye." A Scottish parliamentary ban of 1555 associates "Robert Hude" with "Lytill Johne, Abbot of vnressoun" and the "Quenis of Maij."[26] Quite obviously, Robin Hood and Marion (the May Queen) were more generally related to some of the most widespread festive inversions of reality.

In order to understand the actual content of these inversions as well as the undeveloped forms of dramatic interpretation in the folk play that were related to it, it seems helpful to consider the social background of the Robin Hood tradition itself. It is perhaps not altogether accidental that the origins of Robin Hood have received totally divergent explanations. Because of the word "yeoman" in the ballads, a number of historians—among them E. L. G. Stone, R. H. Hilton, Maurice Keen, and others—have stressed that Robin Hood almost certainly reflected neither the status of serving man "nor a rich peasant, but simply a peasant of free personal status." But since the lower peasants and serving men shared a good many of the aspirations and assumptions of the free peasant, this did not mean that the ballads were not in fact addressed to, and sung by, men whom the lords and the lawyers would consider servile.

Although historians offer differing opinions as to the nature of Robin Hood's rural background, they remain, as a rule, opposed to an anthropological treatment of the matter. Such an interpretation, as set forth by Margaret Murray or Thomas Wright, can nonetheless be illuminating, even if it cannot convincingly argue, let us say, that the Sheriff of Nottingham is portrayed not as a medieval sheriff but as the spirit of winter. The assumption that Robin Hood is in part a mythical figure need not necessarily contradict the historical approach if it is understood not as a theory of his origin but as an indication of the popular reception of the figure in the context of semiritual processions and seasonal customs.[27]

To oversimplify an extremely complex and changing phenomenon, it might be said that the ballads and the more verbal forms of semidramatic representation and interpretation reflect more of a sociohistorical figure, while the nonverbal and nonrepresentational reception in the context of popular ceremonies and festive customs at least partially redefines the figure (somewhat atavistically) in terms of latent ritual function and semimythological images. Robin Hood could achieve the semiritual status of summer king or Lord of Misrule and at the same time assume the identity of a "social bandit"—the prototype of a "primitive rebel." In either case, a spirit of inversion and social resistance is important, be it in the playfully rebellious "gestures" and actions of ritual processions or in the more representational elements within the folk plays and the emerging social consciousness of the ballads.

Although the Robin Hood tradition reveals how the popular imagination created its own inversions of unjust contemporary standards, it never reflected a revolutionary attitude. Robin Hood, like other social bandits, provided only occasional redress for injustice, and proved that oppression could *sometimes* "be turned upside down." But at such times the triumph of the outlaw becomes the triumph of a higher justice, one that confirms the basic assumption of all the outlaw legends, that "the true relationship between law and justice has somehow, by the wickedness of men, become reversed, and in this topsy-turvy world law has become the facade of oppression and justice can only be found outside it."[28]

These basic motifs found in the ballad tradition, although an appropriate subject for both verbal representation and processional customs, cannot, of course, be projected indiscriminately onto the meager survivals of the Robin Hood Play. It is true that in some cases Robin Hood's presence in seasonal processions may well have been the primary source of his accretion in the folk play. This would support an understanding of the figure according to which Robin Hood, in his role as May King or mock king, may be thought of not as a vegetation god or the personification of fertility, but at best as their minister condemned to die each year. Such a late mythological meaning has obvious connections with the semiritual hero-combat of the rural ceremonial. The connection between village rites and the Mummers' Play was in fact so close that in some folk plays Robin Hood took the place of the older and more established protagonist.

But wherever the elements of verbal representation and interpretation are most imposing, a direct derivation from the ballad offers a more likely channel into the folk play. Even if we consider a French source for Robin Hood as May King and Marion as May Queen which considerably predated the English ballad (Adam de la Halle's *Jeu de Robin et Marion*) two facts remain: (1) the Robin Hood of the summer ceremonial, whatever *his* origin and source, is partly associated with the Robin Hood of the ballads, and (2) it is only by such an association that figures like Little John and Friar Tuck from the same ballad cycle could have penetrated village customs and thence the folk play.[29]

This is significant when we come to consider the increased representational function and interpretative meaning that Robin Hood achieved in the folk play. Here it is the popular figure and his followers from the traditional ballads who are dramatized, while the nonrepresentational element of ritual is abandoned in favor of some more modern dramatic conventions. In two scenes ("Robin Hood and the Friar" and "Robin Hood and the Potter"), which survived in William Copland's *Gest of Robin Hood,* the original link with seasonal ceremonies is clear from the subtitle: *Here beginneth the playe of Robyn Hood, verye proper to be played in Maye Games.*[30] Although a duel climaxes each scene (recalling the combat of the Mummers' Play), the ritual context, if it is present at all, is at best of secondary importance. The hero, plainly "a good yeoman" ("Robin Hood and the Friar," 38), follows the tradition of the thoroughly earthy Robin Hood ballads.

Still, the link with the ritual and the seasonal background remains an important feature in the *staging* of these scenes. For the way in which they are presented involves an awareness of Robin Hood as the potential leader of the May procession addressing a group of ready and willing revelers. The older fragment, for instance, opens with Robin's unmistakable direct address to the surrounding audience: "my merye men all"

(1), he calls them, thus drawing them into the action as potential participants in the play. Friar Tuck does the same thing when he appears to pronounce a blessing on those standing around (24).

Judging from these passages, the audience, while separated from the actors, seems nonetheless to have been close enough to make its presence felt. Since the performers almost certainly had no raised stage, they probably used a circular playing area around which the spectators could arrange themselves. In any case, this must have been the most effective method of clearing sight lines for as large an audience as possible since in this way "the action is set apart from the spectators yet made accessible to all of them. . . ."[31] If this method of staging was in fact used, then the protagonist's first words—"Now stand ye forth, my merye men all"— were not, as J. Q. Adams has suggested, addressed to the actors but to the audience, just as performers who introduced the Mummers' Play and Sword Dance usually called for room and thereby cleared the circle that was used for a stage ("My master sent me here, some room for to provide,/ So therefore gentle dears, stand back on every side," Greatham Sword Dance). The village community, as Phillip Stubbes noted, swarmed into the woods or assembled on the village green, and here performers were, in more than one respect, still *part* of the cheerful crowd that had gathered for the maying ceremonies under the direction of their summer king. These audiences were not passive spectators; they formed part of a communal ceremony in which, almost everywhere in the fifteenth and sixteenth centuries, the nonrepresentational mode of processional ceremonials existed side by side with a newly communicative and partly interpretative form of semidramatic *mimesis*.

2

Folk Fool and Devil

Like Robin Hood, the fool in the May procession also functioned as organizer and presenter of the ceremonial action. In the Mummers' Play and Sword Play (especially in their respective wooing ceremonies), fools or clowns served very similar functions. As processional leaders such characters maintained particularly close contact with the audience, and thus paralleled another group of performers who were retained as a purely choral element in the *quête* (such as Big Head, Father Christmas, Devil Doubt, and the clownish Beelzebub) or as comical assistants in the cure (like the doctor's saucy boy). Like the presenter, these characters stood between the hero-combat or the cure and the festive occasion at which these were performed. Their processional function entailed the opening of the play, a request for room and attention, the summoning of the doctor and the general hubbub of a final song or request for gratuities. These are probably amongst the oldest figures in the play, and their tenacity suggests some more ancient functions which, although now lost, must have been of central importance at some time in the ritual's history.[32] But a faint reflection of these ritual functions remains in the characters' peculiar speech patterns which persist to this day. If their language is regarded as nothing more than some modern or local accretion, then one may reasonably ask why it is so uniform in its non-representational and non-sensical quality. For their speech is characterized by a topsy-turvy patter which is closely connected with the utopian Cokaygne motif. Furthermore, it is these figures who carry the ancient cudgel or clown's club (with its obvious phallic antecedents and links to fertility rites). The point that has to be made, therefore, is that the processional function and ritual significance of these figures correlate in some obscure way with the texture of their verbal expression.

Taken all together, the peculiarities of the clowning figure can hardly derive from Christian sources or be understood as later "comic" accretions. Nor, in view of the relationship between the fool of the May procession, the Mummers' Play, the Morris dance, and the Sword Play, can they be explained in terms of the continuity of the tradition of the ancient fool as seen, for example, in the *mimus*. Similarities certainly exist—the motley, which corresponds to the Roman *centunculus*, the pointed fool's cap (equivalent to the *apex* of the *mimus calvus*), the fool's baldness, of which there is scattered evidence, and finally the cudgel in the *mimus* which resembles the club or staff of the later clown—but these provide no basis for a genetic explanation. Consequently, the origins of the fool in the folk play must be sought in that native tradition of mimetic ritual that is of central importance to all popular dramatic or semi-dramatic activities. It is this background that explains the relationship between the fool's motley and the pagan traditions of vegetation magic, and throws considerable light on some of his most enduring accoutrements, such as the calf's hide which he still wore in the Mummers' Play, the ubiquitous coxcomb or cock's feather, the antlers (which were still associated with the fool as late as Dr. Faustus' conjuring clown), the horns, donkey's ears, and the foxtail still in evidence in the North Country Sword Dance.[33] It would appear that this curious costume can best be explained as the survival of some kind of mimetic magic which, after having lost its ritual function, became alienated from its original purpose and hence misunderstood as a comic attribute.

While an exhaustive study of the origins of the folk fool is impossible here, it is clear that links exist between the early ritual origins of the fool and his social functions in the late Middle Ages. There are numerous Central European ceremonies in which a continuity of processional and associative elements can be established (such as the fools' carnival societies, or the traditional *Perchtenläufe* in continental Europe). There also seems to be a connection between both the choral and topsy-turvying functions of the fool on the one hand and the processional leader of those who performed rites of fertility or were possessed by spirits on the other. For instance, if the ancestor of Arlecchino or Harlequin might be found in *Herlekin* (O.Fr.) or *Her(e)la cynȝ*—a form of Wodan—lord of the host (from Germ. *X^{aria} - Heer*, army), the origin of the fool might be traced back to the possessed ritual leader of magic processions. The pagan *Herlekin* (like the more modern *Erl-könig*) was "connected with the fairies" and was followed by a train of witches and hide-covered creatures; he was branded a "devil" by medieval theologians, and made his early appearance on the stage as a comic devil and prince of the fairies in the *Jeu de la Feuillée* (1262).[34] The links between this figure and his comic descendants in the Italian *Commedia dell'arte* and the ribald French jester are not too difficult to establish when one considers his ritual background, his choral position, and his function as prologue and market crier.

The general development of the English folk fool can be considered in similar terms if he is seen as having relinquished much of his pagan character and surrendered "to the transformation in meaning and values to which Christianity subjected the figures of an inimical cult."[35] Such a view of his origins would account for the folk fool's connection with various hybrid figures like Father Christmas or Beelzebub; the possessed man becomes the clown, the pagan deity becomes the Christian devil. In the folk play Beelzebub may recall features of an old, club-bearing deity;[36] and here, as in the mystery cycles, the devil retains the stigma of a pagan past: the goat's horns, the ass' ears, the cloven hoof, and, as late as the Renaissance, a huge phallus. Such elements of a Dionysian satyr, at times even a spirit of "joyous freedom and unrestrained delight,"[37] live on, however mutilated, in the diabolic attributes of the fool and perhaps even in the foolish attributes of the devil.

The gradual and partial assimilation of pre-Christian myth and ritual did not proceed according to any evolutionary scheme, and stood at least partly in opposition to the doctrinal policy of the medieval Church. As the immense dramatic success of the devil, and later the Vice, shows, the spirits of the past tended to ally themselves with heretical sentiments. Out of this alliance emerged figures possessed of a vitality that was not easily confined by dogma. Although interpretations of the medieval devil and witch cult as some form of plebeian counterreligion seem far-fetched, it would be incorrect to minimize the dimensions of their social background and function. Beelzebub and related heretical figures, according to one historian, "at times even gained ground as a reaction against the more repressive and inhumane forms of Christianity." There is some evidence that Satan was at times reputed to have been the protector of peasants and serfs against feudal oppression.[38]

The connection between elements in pagan and heretic traditions and certain "devilish" and burlesque forms of blasphemy was, of course, more obvious; heresy, sorcery, and anarchy appear "almost interchangeable" to some students of the witch cult. Heresy was "inevitably and inextricably entangled with attempts on the social order, always anarchic, always political."[39] From the point of view of the history of the popular theater, it is important to note that this social tradition (which has survived solely in the documents that record its persecution) definitely favored burlesque mimetic parody of prevailing church ceremonies: the mass travestied in the Black Mass, the sacraments decried, the candles blackened, fasts turned into gluttonous feasts, and asceticism into excess.

3

From Ritual Participation to Seasonal Acting

In the English folk plays, if we are to judge from their largely corrupted and partially bowdlerized texts, neither Beelzebub nor any of the other clowning characters can be seen as comparable agents of heresy. But the element of topsy-turvydom or inversion generally associated with these characters nevertheless deserves attention. It may well be said that the topsy-turvy or nonsense speech which so frequently appears in the Mummers' Play is the "most characteristic of all folk humour."[40] And this form of verbal inversion, while comic in its dramatic associations, is essentially non-sensical and nonrepresentational in its ceremonial context.

The Weston-sub-Edge Mummers' Play, which was recorded in 1864, is opened by John Finney, the doctor's comic assistant, with the traditional call for room. After the conventional hero-combat the doctor is summoned to resurrect the dead fighter. Upon entering, the doctor looks to Finney for assistance:

Doctor.	Hold my hoss, Mr John Finney.
John Finney.	Will he bite?
Doctor.	No.
John Finney.	Will he kick?
Doctor.	No.
John Finney.	Take tow to hold him?
Doctor.	No.
John Finney.	Hold him yourself then.

> *Doctor.*   What's that, you saucy young rascal?
> *John Finney.* Oh, I hold him, sir . . .

After the boy has contradicted his master for the tenth time Beelzebub appears with his club and delivers a nonsensical speech about how he met a bark that dogged him, how he went to a stick and cut the hedge, and so on. John Finney then concludes his scene by turning directly to those standing around and, pretending that they have arrived in Cokaygne, says, "Now my lads we've come to the land of plenty, rost stones, plum puddings, houses thatched with pancakes. . . ."[41]

The play is typical in the way that the Cokaygne motif and the topsy-turvy patter are linked with particular choral figures. At the same time, it reveals a characteristic barrenness in the interaction of verbal comedy and the element of nonrepresentational inversion: what Chambers simply called "the folk at its worst." Similarly, the utopian vision of the Land of Plenty remains undeveloped; it is reduced to the mere appendix of a dream of idle gluttony. To suggest the dramatic potential of this theme it is sufficient to refer to the Cokaygne poem in which the idea of an earthly Paradise involved a good deal of social tension and ambiguous language, as well as some challenging standards of equality. Here were no "Lordinges," for only he who had waded through "swine-is dritte" for seven years and been in filth up to his neck could reach Cokaygne. Only when gentlemen were prepared to suffer this ordeal as a "ful grete penance" could they hope to get there—and then only on the condition that they never return.[42]

In the Mummers' Play the dramatic potential of this rebellious under-tone is very much diluted; all that may perhaps be associated with it is John Finney's cheeky disobedience. But what also remains is some verbal comedy that is not fully integrated into a pattern of dramatic interpreta-tion. At best, as in the Revesby play, the action is comically associated with a topsy-turvy play on words, but its symbolic dimensions are never translated into a fully dramatic meaning. What we have is a fool who counts backwards:

> *Pickle Herring.* . . . You are older than I am.
> *Fool.*   How can that be, boy, when I was born before you?

And when the fool is to be beheaded by his sons, his perspective is once more inverted:

> *Fool.*   . . . I would not lose my son Pickle Herring for fifty
>   pounds.
> *Pickle Herring.* It is your son Pickle Herring that must lose you.
>   It is your head we desire to take off.[43]

What comedy there is results from the inversion of abstractions (such as time) or from a twisting of words and meanings, sometimes amounting only to ribald ambiguity. In the more sophisticated and literary plays this does achieve a vague symbolism which, however, falls short of interpretative drama because it neither absorbs nor comprehends the non-representational ceremony, but falls back instead into non-sensical verbal comedy:

> ... And he that doesn't come before
> He needs must come before.

The clown repeats this refrain twice. The King threatens to cut off his head until, exasperated by the lack of contrast between "before" and "before," he corrects the lines to give them a more ordinary meaning:

> ... And he that doesn't come before
> He needs must come behind.

But the amount of sense that results is, once again, vague, since it is neither accompanied by nor translated into dramatic action. It is futile, therefore, to speculate whether or not the clown's verbal inversions contain some symbolic statement. It would certainly be facile, for example, to read a utopian or primitive Christian message into them; at any rate, there are no indications that, as in Greek tragedy or in some of Shakespeare's fools, the imaginative experience of myth and ritual has become the expression of a conscious poetic image of the world.

The imaginative truths of myth and the social functions of ritual deteriorated, in the folk play, into trivial patterns which, being comically misunderstood, assumed a new and strange kind of significance. Let us take as a representative instance the following clown's *Leitmotiv*:

> In comes I that's never been yit
> With my big head and little wit
> My head's so great my wit's so small
> I can act the fool as well as you all.

> (Clayworth, 246)[44]

This appears nineteen times with very little variation in the thirty-three plays printed by R. J. E. Tiddy. It is repeatedly put into the mouths of the choral or processional figures, including the doctor's assistant. The first line in particular appears so regularly that it can hardly be taken as an "irrelevant" addition or "local accretion" to an independent ritual action. Since the relationship between the underlying function of ritual and the nonrepresentational meaning of its verbal expression is not an interpretative one, we must be careful not to dismiss the non-sensical element in favor of the referential meaning of, say, "little wit" as an assessment of the fool's intellect. It is difficult to decide upon the amount of sense and interpretation achieved when the relationship between "big head" and "little wit" may either be an inversion or a verbal echo of the

ancient fool's headdress or mask, or, for that matter, the "natural" fool's
hydrocephalic condition. In view of the fact that the relationship between ritual action and verbal interpretation remains transitional and
undeveloped, this recurrent formula reflects the unsophisticated function of the fool, who may have emerged from the figure of the fighting
protagonist. This notion, which Tiddy supports on the basis of the
Ampleforth play, is reinforced by the plough play of Bassingham and, of
course, the Revesby sword dance, in which the fool acts as protagonist,
and even as father of the "King."[45]

The ambivalent and varying relationship between the fool's past ritual
function and his non-sensical contemporary meaning can best be studied
in plays where this ambivalence is reflected in modern verbal structures.
As in the Bassingham ceremonial, an original ritual action receives a new
verbal meaning when the older elements are overlaid with more recent
ideas and images of a more representational character. This is what
happens when the fool confronts St. George, the dragon-slayer:

(Enter St. George)

> In comes Saint George,
> The Champeon bold.
> With my blooddy spear
> I have won ten Thousand pounds in Gold.
> I fought the finest Dragon
> And brought him to a slaughter,
> And by that means I gaind
> The King of Egypts Daughter.
> I ash him and smash him as small as Flys,
> Send him to Jamaica to make Minch Pies.
> *(Fool)*
> You hash me and smash me as small as flys,
> Send me to Jamaica to make Minch Pies?

(Fight. Fool falls)

The fool, here the husband of "The old Witch," suffers the same fate
as the slaughtered dragon. His weapons—"Mustard-seed" and a
"crushed toad"—are magical in origin, and although here used in a more
modern and more representational sense they remain, like the traditional club, useless when pitted against Saint George's "blooddy spear."
But since the representational meaning does not finally predominate
over the non-sensical inheritance of ritual action, the fool can emerge as
a chorus after his resurrection and sing the concluding song:

> Come write me down the power above,
> That first created A man to Love.
> I have a Diamond in my eye,
> Where all my Joy and comfort ly.[46]

This varying relationship between ritual function and non-sensical meaning is even more pointed when in Thame, Oxfordshire, St. George follows the dance of the "Morres-men" with:

> These are our tricks,—ho! men, ho!
> These are our sticks,—whack men so!
>> *Strikes the Dragon, who roars, and comes forward.*
>> *The Dragon speaks.*
>
> Stand on head, stand on feet!
> Meat, meat, meat for to eat!
>> *Tries to bite King Alfred.*
>
> I am the Dragon,—here are my jaws!
> I am the Dragon,—here are my claws!
> Meat, meat, meat for to eat!
> Stand on my head, stand on my feet!
>> *Turns a summersault, and stands aside.*
>> *All sing, several times repeated:*
>
> Ho! ho! ho!
> Whack men so!

The Dragon seems to be defeated by the "tricks" and "sticks" of a modern version of the legendary St. George, but it is not clear whether his repetitions of "meat" (or food, cf. O. H. G. *maz*) allude to the man-eater of the older versions. At any rate, the representational meaning of "Meat, meat, meat" is totally ambiguous since it is associated with the nonreferential dancing action that begins with the inversion "Stand on head" and ends with a "summersault." Perhaps the Dragon does retain some mimetic attributes of the legendary monster who shows his teeth and claws, but again, the fact that he is beaten is not a representational action or an interpretation of his defeat. Rather, it serves as a choral introduction to the "Ho! ho! ho!" which recalls the triumphant challenge of the Vice in the morality, or perhaps some more primitive formula.[47] A "Father Christmas" appears at the end, probably as a personification of the festive season, wishes bread, meat, and fire to all those standing around, and then sings:

> Hold, men, hold!
> Put up your sticks;
> End all your tricks;
> Hold, men, hold!

And finally, leading up to the collection, all join in:

> Hold, men, hold!
> We are very cold,
> Inside and outside,
> We are very cold.[48]

Herein lies the final twist, where the non-sensical survivals of a ritual action become symbolic as "sticks" and "tricks" are reinterpreted as a deplorable form of suppression and deceit. The effective means of ritual are turned into the affective metaphors of interpretation. The interpretation is a choral one in which the humanitarian or Christian spirit of the season is moralized into the meaning of the play. Since it is not realized in dramatic action, this choral interpretation seems to be verbally appended rather than metaphorically integrated into the action itself. An interrelationship between ritual action and metaphorical expression is clearly not achieved, even though there are some suggestive links between the inherent potentialities of socially effective ritual and the dramatically affective forms of metaphorical meaning.

One might ask, of course, if, or to what extent, the "tricks" and "sticks" that St. George wields represent a symbolic social action. Certainly, it will not do simply to read the appended choral interpretation backwards into the play and deduce that St. George represents the forces of suppression and deceit. But even when this reading must be recognized as being overly representational, the metaphorical meaning of the chorus generates a subtly symbolic correlation between St. George's "tricks" and "sticks" and the Dragon's "Meat, meat, meat." To judge the relevance of this connection in terms of the nonrepresentational function of the Dragon and his ritual antecedents, the monster must be seen not merely as the legendary adversary of St. George but also in relation to those other "monsters" which, according to Phillip Stubbes, formed part of the train of the Lord of Misrule. There, too, were "hobbie horses" and a "dragon"; and these traditions of dancing and disguised performance might have been more important in defining the ceremonial function of the Dragon than its legendary background.

An inquiry into the origins of such "monsters" will at best yield hypothetical results. Functionally, they were probably quite unlike the vicious unmasked demon of the Christian legend of St. George. Rather, it may be cautiously conjectured that the Dragon formed part of a more primitive tradition according to which he was viewed as a "beneficent creature,"[49] a dispenser of water and food, an original expression of the vital powers of life-giving. And if a correspondence with the Northern Widhug, the guardian of a well, can be established, the context of a fertility ritual does not seem too far-fetched. In this the Dragon's function is not unlike that of some other traditional figures who, like the fool in the Bassingham ceremonial, are threatened with being cut into pieces. The fools, or Jack Finney for that matter, are constantly being beaten. The fool, too, stands on his head and views the world upside down. It is this context rather than the more vicious animal overtones of the St. George legend that most nearly accords with the "Meat, meat, meat" formula.

In the folk play, the ambivalence in the relationship between representational and nonrepresentational elements makes speculation quite difficult. We have to go beyond the men's ceremonial to the professional modern theater to find that the popular theme of the Land of Plenty is no longer ritually embodied but comically impersonated in terms of affected needs and personal experience: it is here that the empty stomach of the clown or servant clown (from Shakespeare and the Spanish theater to Goldoni) inspires the most representational forms of verbal action. Again, the theme's eventual realism does not contradict its fantastical antecedents, not even genetically when one considers the grotesque meal in the *Prima Pastorum* or even Truffaldino's dream of a perfect meal in *Il Servitore.* In the very different forms of modern comedy the utopian ideal of plenty and a playful inversion of order are—in an affective form of topsy-turvydom—finally reunited. But for this, the folk play provides neither a case for origins nor a paradigm of functions. If the seemingly trivial connection between the Cokaygne motif and the fool's topsy-turvy patter points to anything, then it is to the traditional link between the popular latitude for prophecy and clowning, utopianism and inversion. The origins of the art of acting, and a measure of its capacity to enchant and disenchant find a telling historical medium in links such as these.

4

The English Folk Play and Shakespeare

By Shakespeare's time the Mummers' Play already must have been a "sunken" form, no longer capable of genuinely creative development. It is therefore not at all surprising that the Elizabethan drama, which was a fully realized artistic and literate form, received so little inspiration from the folk play. It is true that indirect rather than direct relationships suggest some level of cross-influences between the Mummers' Play and medieval drama, but the matter is more judiciously dealt with as a comparative question and not a genetic one, and as such concerns not sources but the forms in which Shakespeare made use of structural and verbal elements comparable to those of the folk play. The parallels that will be suggested here, therefore, are not submitted as evidence of "influence," but as a contribution to the discussion of the role of the popular tradition in Shakespeare's theater as well as the innovative use that he made of it.

Disregarding medieval drama for the moment, the usefulness of such a comparative method can be demonstrated by juxtaposing different

versions of related motifs. Let us look again at one of the most characteristic forms of topsy-turvydom in the Mummers' Play:

> I met a bark and he dogged at me. I went to the stick and cut a hedge, gave him a
> rallier over the yud jud killed him round stout stiff and bold from Lancashire I
> came, if Doctor hasn't done his part, John Finney wins the game.
>
> (Weston-sub-Edge, 167)

In *King Lear* the image of the barking dog is used in a totally different
context, but as part of another form of inversion:

> *Lear.* What, art mad? A man may see how this world goes with no eyes.
> Look with thine ears. See how yond justice rails upon yond simple
> thief. Hark, in thine ear: change places and, handy-dandy, which is
> the justice, which is the thief? Thou hast seen a farmer's dog bark at
> a beggar?
> . . .
> And the creature run from the cur? There thou mightst behold the
> great image of authority: a dog's obey'd in office.[50]
>
> (IV, 6, 149–58)

Here the "bark" does not "dog," but the ears can see, and the farmer's
dog serves as a striking image of corrupted contemporary justice and
authority. "Change places and, handy-dandy, which is the justice, which
is the thief?" is an explicit inversion that finds an indirect but equally
provocative analogue in the potential meaning of Portia's seemingly
straightforward question, "Which is the merchant here, and which the
Jew?" (*Merchant of Venice* IV, 1, 169). In a comic context, the most completely inverted perception results from the late type of mimetic magic,
enchanting even in its moment of disenchantment, which is "Bottom's
Dream" that "hath no bottom." Thus, after Oberon has ordered the
removal of the ass' head, Bottom propounds his "most rare vision": "The
eye of man hath not heard, the ear of man hath not seen, man's hand is
not able to taste, his tongue to conceive, nor his heart to report, what my
dream was" (*Midsummer Night's Dream* IV, 1, 110–14). The mode of inversion here makes possible a transition, which is effective in a practical
and purely theatrical sense as well as affective dramatically, between the
fairy-tale world of Puck's popular mythology and the newly recovered
ordinary world of the "bellows-mender" and the "tinker"; and its success
could hardly be more emphatic. But it is only in *King Lear,* where the
nonsensical heritage of ritual action is replaced by a new convention of
"reason in madness," that the inverted vision of the world has become a
means of criticizing society and of expressing the profound realism of a
thoroughly dramatic apprehension and understanding of the world.

In *King Lear,* the visionary quality of speech is linked with the conventional notion that "madness" is a dramatic form of social license. At the
same time, the representation of Lear's madness involves new mimetic

standards of psychological realism which supplement more traditional forms of popular inversion and invective. At this level the topsy-turvying vision again raises questions with some utopian significance, but it does so with a different kind of consistency: we no longer have a trivial dream of the Land of Plenty, but rather a dramatic interpretation of the connection between true need (*Lear* II, 4, 269) and a just distribution of goods. As Gloucester says,

So distribution should undo excess
and each man have enough.
(IV, 1, 71-72)

Another example from the same play points to a mode of traditional embodiment by which Shakespeare's fool can relinquish his partially achieved representational function. "In comes I that's never been yit/ With my big head and little wit" was referred to above as the *Leitmotiv* of the processional performer, usually the fool or saucy boy, which recurs most often in the Mummers' Play. To consider it the nonsensical remainder from some forgotten ritual ceremony is to argue that its obscurity cannot be dismissed as low comedy. The antithesis of "big head" and "little wit" should, I have suggested, neither be read symbolically, in the sense of an undeveloped intelligence, nor psychologically, as a deprecatory remark by the clown about his own character. It is safest to say simply that the ritual content has become, in more modern versions, conventional form, a convenient way for the amateur actor to introduce himself. This, more than anything else, might explain its remarkable continuity, but it must not conceal the fact that the phrase "big head" takes on a latent metaphorical meaning as soon as its ritual function is replaced by representational action. Because the replacement is inconsistent and incomplete the formula remains obscure and poetically enigmatic—which is equally characteristic of some of the finest speeches and songs of Shakespeare's fools. Consider, for example,

He that has and a *little* tiny *wit*
With heigh-ho, the wind and the rain—
(*Lear* III, 2, 74-75; cf. *Twelfth Night* V, 1, 375-76)

According to H. H. Furness who reads the "and" as meaning *also, even, and that too,* "and a little tiny wit" should be understood to mean "a little, and that a very little." This, although it is the best interpretation we have, is not very satisfying, if only because of the "tiny" which follows. Reading these lines against the background of the folk fool would be more consistent with the context of the passage as a whole, and might even account for the "He that has" as a distorted echo of the folk fool's negative "In comes I as an't been it." However that may be, these lines are only partially referential in the sense that the Fool could be speaking either of

Lear or of himself. Very much a choral figure, it is Lear's "Poor Fool and knave" (III, 2, 72) who sings this song and follows it with a popular utopian prophecy:

> ... I'll speak a prophecy ere I go.
> When priests are more in word than matter;
> When brewers mar their malt with water;
> When nobles are their tailors' tutors;
> No heretics burn'd, but wenches' suitors;
> When every case in law is right; ...
> Then shall the realm of Albion
> Come to great confusion.
> Then comes the time, who lives to see't,
> That going shall be us'd with feet.
> This prophecy Merlin shall make, for I live before his time.
>
> (III, 2, 80–85, 91–95)

These lines lose none of their significance because they draw on some pseudo-Chaucerian verses, and even suggest a parody of them. The prophecy provides both a vision of Utopia and an inversion of it, and thereby sheds light on one of the tragedy's basic themes: Lear, after he envisions those "Poor naked wretches" and faces poor Tom as "unaccommodated man," tears off his "lendings" and later has his boots removed; barefoot, he takes upon himself the burden of penance and purification. This certainly falls far short of the "ful grete penance" stipulated as a condition for admission to Cokaygne, but the Fool's speech culminates in the prophecy "That going shall be us'd with feet." If this achieves any symbolic meaning over and above its non-sensical content, then the prophecy assumes a choric function which, although firmly rooted in the folk tradition, nevertheless transcends it by providing a metaphorical statement and interpretation of one of the play's major themes. As such it goes beyond the truly non-sensical mode of inversion of the Revesby Fool's song:

> ... And he that doesn't come before
> He needs must come before,

which clearly cannot be read in terms of the dialectic of "true need" and "each man have enough."

The freedom that Lear's fool has to experiment with (and so to go beyond) the folk play tradition emerges once more when, after having associated his own prophecy with Merlin's, he dissociates himself from Merlin's time, making that time a kind of utopian future by defining his own present as a time prior to the age in which Merlin will make the prophecy. Here the theme of Utopia is not merely associated with the inversion motif, it is *expressed* structurally in terms of inversion. The inversion of a vision of inversion is highly experimental and itself amounts almost to a method of reason in madness.

This is a far cry from the naive statement of the same theme—the occasional reversal of time when the folk play fool wonders why the older was born before the younger. In the face of the traditional context which, as we shall see, is amply confirmed by the Vice in the moralities, the inverted form of the Fool's prophecy should be accepted as it stands, and its obscurity viewed as a nonsensical and nonrepresentational heritage from the topsy-turvy patterns of the popular tradition.[51]

To characterize the dramatic qualities of this traditional context is, first and foremost, to perceive the way in which verbal and theatrical performances are interrelated. In taking up the problem of dramaturgy we may recur to Feste's song in *Twelfth Night* ("When that I was and a little tiny boy" V, 1, 375-95). Here *nomen* is *omen*, for Feste himself embodies the spirit of festive comedy: "And we'll strive to please you every day." These are the words of the actor—the same one, probably, who impersonated the Fool in *Lear*—stepping out of his role to address the audience, as did the folk fool, who did not, however, represent any illusion of true life but enacted the spirit of a seasonal ceremonial. The folk fool's refrain, incidentally, often ended in the same way:

I will dance a jig to please you all (Cinderford)
I've come to endeavour to please you all (Kempsford)
I've brought me a fiddler to please you all (Great Wolford)
I've brought my fiddle to please you all (Ilmington)
I'll play you a tune to please you all (Badby)
I'll do my duty to please you all (Waterstock)

These words are generally found at the end of the play; they introduce music or dancing and provide a natural link between the forgotten world of ritual (the hero-combat and cure) and the more processional forms of secular entertainment, which are all integral parts of the seasonal ceremonial as a whole.

Repeatedly it is the figure of the fool who provides this link. No other actor stands so clearly on the threshold between the play and the community occasion. In the continental Sword Dance and Sword Play he stands apart from the play itself and occupies the positions of parodist, organizer, and collector of the *quête*.[52] In the more courtly versions of the Lord of Misrule the fool becomes a kind of Master of Ceremonies. His processional and organizational functions live on in the Vice of the moralities, a role usually performed by the leading actor and "director" of the troupe. These functions are still reflected in the frequent songs and asides of the Shakespearean fools or clowns who, like the Fool in *Lear*, retain, for example, a heightened awareness both of the audience and of their own role, which is perhaps anticipated by the Clayworth fool: "I can act the fool as well as you all." A dramatic situation like this is capable of considerable development, in the course of which both ritual ceremony and dramatic impersonation, together with their non-representational and interpretative levels of speech, become more directly related. In the folk play, both elements (the awareness of audience participation and the consciousness of the reality of the play world) are already present, and it seems only a step from here to the "wise" fool's reversal of roles with the audience, i.e., "you are the real fools, while I am merely playing this role, well aware that it is a role." This supreme form of inversion is not developed in the Clayworth ceremonial, but the Shakespearean dialectic of appearance and reality is naively adumbrated here.[53]

It is this traditional dramaturgy that links all the more processional and choral performers in the folk plays and allows them the unique freedom to move outside the world of the play: John Finney, Beelzebub, the fool, like the clown in the Plough Play and Sword Dance, do not act exclusively within the framework of the combat, cure or wooing scenes (which of course are never really self-contained to begin with). But more importantly their unique potential as processional or communal entertainers is reflected in, and in turn presupposes, particular positions on the stage that are closely linked with specific modes of speech. The Elizabethan clown's jesting, singing, dancing, his punning and proverb-mongering, and, of course, his audience address, have some of their roots here. The fool in Ampleforth, for example, addresses "Ye gentlemen all who in mirth take delight" and "All you pritty lasses, That's sitting roundabout" as he prepares to kiss the latter, thereby transporting his miming into the very midst of the audience. Like Feste in *Twelfth Night*, the "omnipresent fool" of the folk play (as Chambers calls him) embodies the spirit of the season of which the play itself is an expression:

> I always was jovial and always will be,
> Always at one time of the year.[54]

Since neither the place of, nor the occasion for, the play is forgotten, it is natural that the role cannot conceal the performer. The amazing thing, however, is that in the Ampleforth play (as in the Greatham Sword Dance) the tension that results between role and actor is turned into a deliberate dramatic effect. This is how the representational high stature of the King is deflated by a nonrepresentational awareness of the social identity of the actor who, when not playing the King, is no more than a swineherd.

> *King.*   I'm a King and a Conqueror too,
>   And here I do advance!

Clown. I'm the clown of this noble town,
      And I've come to see thee dance.
King.   The clown come to see a King dance!
Clown. A King dance! Ask thee good fellow?
      didn't I see thee tending swine 'tother
      day—stealing swine I meant to say?
King.   Now you've given offence to your Majesty,
      thee must either sing a song, or off goes
      your head.

The Clown easily bridges the gap between illusion and reality, for his position is not derived solely from within the framework of the play but also partly from without, so as to include the perspective of the audience's everyday experience. The contradiction that results from his dual perspective, then, is one of the basic provocations to theatrical self-consciousness, and the fool remains, as in the *mimus,* the character best able to take advantage of the contradiction.

Still at work is the lively heritage of a ritual ceremony, the social occasion, the seasonal procession to which the actual performance is functionally related as part of the communal process of living with which it is affectively (no longer effectively, as in purposive ritual) concerned. Since the ritual element became less important and the purpose of magic was gradually replaced by the function of drama, the relationship between performance, village community, and the social process of living became less comprehensive and more indirect. The seasonal performer, no longer embodying a ritual or festive ceremonial in terms of his own social identity, allows performing to assume the forms of acting, and, as actor, becomes conscious of his role as independent of, or even opposed to, his own identity. The audience, although definitely part of the community occasion and still involved and prepared to participate in the play, at the same time becomes more and more conscious of its function as spectator. It is at this stage that the survivals of ritual embodiment are confronted with the more representational standards of impersonation. The resulting tensions between performer and role mark the potentialities, but also the limits in the interaction between communal awareness and mimetic verisimilitude.

This, of course, anticipates the supreme synthesis of Shakespearean drama and cannot adequately characterize the altogether different and much more poorly developed context of the Ampleforth play. Still, in embryonic form, some of the basic elements of popular dramaturgy are quite clearly there. The performer of the King, who had obviously ceased to embody a ritual action, submits to the more representational standards of *mimesis* and fails to satisfy the independent criteria of verisimilitude. The tension between the semimythical role of the King and the performance of the miming swineherd explodes. The comic effect

presupposes a transitional situation in which the autonomy of the mimetic claims of the performance as dramatic entertainment coexists with
the extradramatic reference to the life of the village or the performer
behind the role. It is the representational standards of *mimesis* that turn
the extradramatic reference into a comic effect, by pitting the referential
status of the role against the social identity of the actor. As in the
Greatham ceremonial, the referential function of *mimesis* involves a new
principle of dialogue as an imitation of unsuccessful communication, so
that the King can misunderstand the Clown's words, or at least not hear
them clearly the first time around:

> 2nd Clown. (to King) Harks thee my canny man, listen what I've got to say,
>   Wasn't that thou stealing swine the other day?
> King.   Stealing what?
> 2nd Clown.   Feeding swine, I meant to say.[55]

The new realism of verbal exchange is integrated into the surviving
framework of ritual action, but the new motive for killing the Clown is so
facetious an addition and so ineffectual an interpretation that the "off
goes your head" cannot be rightly called dramatic action as *mimesis*. The
non-sensical character of the Clown's beheading is underlined by his
grotesque bequest in Greatham and by the significant alternative to beheading (singing a song) in Ampleforth. Here more clearly than anywhere else the ritual performer has become a lay entertainer whose
social identity can be played upon in order to transpose realistic images
into postritual conventions that have lost their original meaning.

Merely to suggest the nature and continuity of this comic form, one
illustration from *As You Like It* will suffice here. In one of his more
acerbic moments, Touchstone comically evaluates pastoral and romantic
conventions as he responds to Rosalind's sympathy for the enamored
Silvius' effusive art of love with images of real rural living: "I remember
the kissing of her batler, and the cow's dugs that her pretty chopt hands
had milk'd," (II, 4, 46 ff.). Here the realistic experience of village life
counterpoints not a ritual action but a pastoral myth. The nature of the
interjection is no longer extradramatic, but even so it reflects a world
that exists largely outside the conventions of the play. The Shakespearean fool no longer alludes to the social identity of the actor, but appeals
to the tension between the illusion of the role and the reality of living.

The larger dramatic context is very different in the two cases, but in
each a contrasting perspective deriving from the world of ordinary
people and their rural labors is brought to bear on the illusions of the
pastoral or ritual conventions. In the case of the folk play, of course, the
image of rural life is not poetically developed. One would have to study
the more literate Revesby play to find in the fool's speech an imaginative

transmutation of actual experience into sensuous images: "And thy face shines like a dripping pan"; "For thy nose stands like a Maypole tree."

Finally, the traditional tensions between the nonrepresentational standards of the performer and the representational mode of the actor can be seen to affect the changing functions of disguise and dancing. In the folk play, figures such as Beelzebub appear in a mask or with a blackened face, and the fool is sometimes clad in a lamb-fell or cowhide, or he may appear with an animal's tail or disguised as a female, just as Beelzebub appears as an old woman.[56] This disguise, which has relinquished its former sympathetic magical function, is preserved in a more symbolic or characterizing context in which, however, it is subjected to changes analogous to those of the verbal forms of topsy-turvydom. After being alienated from or misunderstood in their original context, disguises and masks tend to assume a comic, grotesque, or simply conventional meaning; and only after the performer has surrendered the directly effective standards of ritual can they achieve a more representational and, hence, more interpretative function. In this respect, the Mummers' Play marks the early and undeveloped stage of a process at the end of which the fool's animal fell becomes as conventional a costume as the Elizabethan motley (although the latter is not, of course, derived from the former). But even in Shakespearean drama it is not always quite clear just how representational disguise is, how much of an illusion of actuality it is supposed to invoke.

In the folk play, disguise is almost as important and traditional as the elements of song and dance. And again it is the fool who stands out as singer and dancer, a versatility that is not confined to the English ceremonial but is reflected in the etymology of *Narr*, the German equivalent of "fool," derived from *narro*, which, like the old Indian *nrtú* (dancer), goes back to a common root, *nart* (to dance).[57] Perhaps it is not too conjectural to venture to suggest a primitive background where speech, movement, rhythm, and song originally formed a whole which preceded the isolation of each as a separate art form. Here it must suffice to observe that the singing, dancing, and miming of the fool were all in line with the nonrepresentational heritage of ritual. It should give us pause to think that the song, jig, and clown's dance, which were transposed to the end of the play, retained their importance until Shakespeare's time. The most famous of Elizabethan clowns, Dick Tarlton, excelled in the jig. Kempe, perhaps Shakespeare's greatest comedian, was the most famous dancer of his day; the Morris that he danced all the way from Norwich to London was an event in which elements derived from the tradition of the folk ceremonial achieved a nationwide recognition.

Even though the ritual context of the dance had become quite irrelevant, a residue of mimetic magic survived, clearly recognizable in the leaf pattern and the bells on Kempe's costume. When, finally, Robert Armin reanimated the Tarlton tradition and created the part of the more sophisticated fool, he must have been splendid as the singer of many of Shakespeare's finest songs. As with Kempe, it is tempting to think that this heritage of dance and song was at the center of the changing modes of traditional dramaturgy, which the semichoric functions of the clown and fool both reflected and helped to revitalize. In its own naive and primitive ways, the folk play, albeit in embryonic form, paralleled some of the popular modes and conventions of the Elizabethan stage. Occasionally there was to be heard in the later theater a distant and almost imperceptible echo of some early version of the dialectic of enchantment and disenchantment which the folk play, even where both these forms of *mimesis* were latent, never developed in dramatic verse and action.

III

THE MYSTERY CYCLES

1

Secular Performances and the Popular Tradition in the Middle Ages

The popular element in the secular drama of the Middle Ages poses problems the extent and significance of which can only be conjectured. In contrast to older views, modern research has suggested that a good deal of secular dramatic activity existed in various places at the height of the Middle Ages. Newly found or newly interpreted evidence of *histriones, mimi, joculatores,* and *balatrones* connect the existence of mimes with some impermanent *theatrum* or a *scena* which, as early as the thirteenth century, was a contemporary living form and not merely a scholarly literary echo of the classical past. There are references to dramatized legends of the saints in London at the beginning of the twelfth century, as well as allusions to certain *spectaculis theatralibus* and *ludis scenicis.* This obviously secular *theatrum,* according to Mary H. Marshall, did not have "specific and regularly used theatre buildings" at its disposal; but even so there is a good deal of evidence that various dramatic entertainments were performed in specific localities: public squares or market places, or in "some theatres in the form of a circus." Discoveries of this kind have led scholars permanently to correct theories about the theater in the Middle Ages. Both probability and the new evidence, "even with the most cautious interpretation," seem to favor the assumption of a "continuance of some sort of secular dramatic performance."[1]

The main problem from the point of view of the popular tradition is the continuity of the *mimi,* those secular entertainers who apparently survived the decline of the postclassical *mimus.* In light of the more recent studies by R. S. Loomis, Gustave Cohen, Mary H. Marshall, J. D.

49

A. Ogilvy, Rosemary Woolf, Alan Nelson, and Richard Axton, greater credence should again be given to the older theories and studies of Heinrich Alt, Hermann Reich, Edmond Faral, J. S. Tunison, and Allardyce Nicoll. The frequently accepted notion that Renaissance comedy "can have nothing whatever in common" with the kind of drama practiced by popular players throughout the Middle Ages is probably not the last word to be said on this vexed question. Certainly Hermann Reich's claim that the Graeco-Roman *mimus* had a continuity right up to Shakespeare is extravagant; but the enormous amount of evidence that he compiled should at least be given a very careful second look. Some of his conjectures—about the origin of Jack Juggler in *joculator* (which is etymologically plausible), the surprising continuity of the ass' head motif from the *mimus* down to *A Midsummer Night's Dream,* the traditional antics of the mimes and *joculatores* with dogs as a background for Shakespeare's Launce, and the like—should not, perhaps, be completely disregarded by Shakespeare scholars.[2] What is more, the continuance of some form of public dramatic activity must be considered as a very real possibility if the English mystery plays are to be viewed both in their social functions and in their relationship to the popular *miracula* of saints' lives performed publicly in London, according to William Fitzstephen as early as the second half of the twelfth century. What makes such a consideration difficult is the fact that the evolutionary idea of a gradual secularization of liturgical drama has as a matter of course led scholars to underestimate and, in fact, neglect the secular elements in the early, precycle traditions, and it has severely oversimplified, if not distorted, the complex relationship between the cycles and the popular elements in the early European dramatic tradition. In England, not the least of the difficulties stems from the fact that the full dimensions of secular dramatic entertainment in the Middle Ages can only be grasped indirectly, not through the texts of actual plays. The oldest surviving evidence is that of handwritten fragments dating back to the early fourteenth and late thirteenth centuries, of which the *Dux Moraud* fragment might also derive from a miracle play and the *Interludium de Clerico et Puella* from a French *fabliau.* Information of this kind is too sparse and fragmentary to afford us more than a hypothetical view of the extent and character of popular dramatic activities in England at the time.[3]

It seems likely that the *mimi* in some way influenced the religious drama, but not to the extent that it could be regarded as the fundamental stimulus that Hunningher, for example, thought to find in the dramatizing of the tropes.[4] Actually, the medieval *mimi* could probably best be studied in terms of the *scurrae* and *corauli,* the jugglers and jesters. This is supported by the fact that, at least up to the thirteenth century, the term *histrio* or *mimus* can be equated with *scurra* and *joculator.* There can be little doubt that miming played a considerable, though perhaps varying, role in the art of juggling. Jugglers probably performed and danced in the marketplace or on the platform stage where the mimes acted.[5] Edgar of England already refers, in the tenth century, to mimes who "sing and dance on the market places"; the word for dancing (*saltare*) is here used in a clearly transitive meaning, which suggests that its object must have been some sort of imitation: *haec milites clamant; plebs submurmurant; mimi cantant et saltant in triviis.*[6] The *haec* refers to abuses notorious among monks, which were exposed in a satirical or burlesque manner faithful to the mime's traditional penchant for satire and parody. There were, in fact, many contemporary complaints about the way in which mimes and players held things up to ridicule—*ad illudendum mimis et scenicis.*[7]

There were in all probability links between the traveling mimes and late ritual customs of prefeudal origin. Repeated references to *larvas daemonum,* or demonic masks, support this assumption, especially since, as at the Council of Nantes (890), they were not always attributed to professional players. Some striking evidence for this can be found in the mid-fourteenth century, when the English Bishop Grandisson complained about "a certain obnoxious game" (*quendam ludum noxium*) that was to be performed in 1352 "in the theater of our city" (*in theatro nostrae civitatis*) as a satire of the honorable guild of the *allutarii.* Four years earlier, on July 11, 1348, Grandisson referred to the theater in Exeter as the scene of a highly irreverent performance: a "sect of malign men" calling themselves the "Order of Brothelyngham" had dressed up as monks, elected a crazy fellow as abbot, put him on show in the theater, and parodied his office. They also roamed the streets and squares day after day blowing horns and, under the "colors and integuments of a play" (*sub colore et velamine ludi*) blasphemously demanded a ransom "instead of an offering" (*loco sacrificii quin verius sacrilegii*).[8]

This earliest piece of relatively detailed information about secular dramatic activities in England is remarkable insofar as it points to a kind of *société joyeuse* that was connected with burlesque mimicry. On the one hand there is an indication of a sect practicing disguise (not unlike a semisecret association), and, on the other hand, postritual conventions like noisemaking, processions, and the collection of offerings. Bishop Grandisson had good reason to call these activities heretical and suggest that they were inspired by the devil. Significantly, the blowing of horns is depicted as a characteristic of demons in English medieval church art; and in the *Peterborough Chronicle* of 1127 there is an unmistakable connection between hornblowing and a kind of "wild chase" procession. The roaming of the Exeter sect recalls the noisy games of medieval fools' societies and secret brotherhoods, where offerings were likewise demanded and the "unbearable" noise of "shouting, bellowing and . . . blowing on cow-herds' horns" was common.[9] But in Exeter—and this is what gives the record its unique interest—all this business culminated in the *theatrum,* the same, in all likelihood, in which satirical farce was performed four years later. The noisome and indecorous *ludus* might even have been acted by the same young men who did the hornblowing and set up the mock abbot *in theatro.*

Whatever ceremonies they performed there, the Bishop's account suggests processional forms of disguise and inversion, with elements of a *quête.* Again, *mimesis* became parody and the parody took on an irreverent and topsy-turvying character. The *theatrum,* then, served as the focal point for a mimic sort of topsy-turvydom that remained closely related to the popular traditions linked with seasonal processions and late ritual customs. Even though we do not know how the *ludus* or the role of the mock abbot was actually performed, it is not difficult to compare what went on in Exeter with the scurrilous parody in the ancient *mimus* and the semidramatic mimicry at medieval festivals.

The miming activities of such groups of lay performers were of course not identical with the professional work of the *joculatores* and *mimi.* But if there was any connection at all between the two, the plebeian jugglers and lower *mimi* may have had a bigger share in it than the later *ministralli.* There is recurring evidence that in the Middle Ages the "lower minstrels of the *mimus* tradition," as E. K. Chambers called them, existed side by side with the socially more respectable entertainers and minstrels—the descendants of the Germanic *scōp.* In a very revealing passage in Thomas de Cabham's *Penitential,* three kinds of entertainers are distinguished; one group disguised themselves in "dreadful masks" (*inuendo horribilies larvas*) or "made indecent gestures and leaps; others followed the courts of the great as satirists and mockers; the third, with their music and singing, conducted a less objectionable handiwork."[10] The first of these groups was probably nearest to the tradition of the folk ceremonial, but since there were players who aroused "lust" in taverns even in the third group, the gulf between them could not have been altogether unbridgeable.

Even though students of the medieval and Elizabethan theater have done little to explore the possible extent or quality of contact between the professional medieval entertainer and the traditional culture of the folk, such contacts seem almost certain. A fresh reading of the relevant records and a careful reconsideration of the evidence leads to the conclusion that the rise of the professional actor in the fifteenth century should be studied in connection with the changing social foundations of popular miming. To begin with, the sheer number of professional actors makes it improbable that they were recruited entirely or even mainly from the ranks of the minstrels, whose vocation was on the decline at the time. With the lessening of hospitality at the feudal manor and castle under the duress of a long, drawn-out civil war, the ranks of the *minis-*

tralli had thinned, and the majority of them tried to re-establish their position by joining the musicians' guilds. If they did not merge with the lower vocation of the jugglers in the early Tudor period and join up with what were then the *Fencers Bearewaredes . . . Juglers Pedlers Tynkers Petye Chapmen,*[11] they abandoned their traveling and isolated themselves from the actors' troupes springing up everywhere at the time. The Royal Guild of Minstrels was founded in 1469, apparently in hopes of securing protection against a new kind of competition. The Charter granted them by Edward IV mentions "some ordinary peasants and craftsmen" (*nonnulli rudes Agricolae et Artifices*)[12] who competed with the professional minstrels. Almost a century later, in 1555, the authorities at Beverley recorded the same threat of competition with the order, *expressis verbis,* that no shepherd or husbandman—"no myler shepherd or of other occupation nor husbandman or husbandman servant"—was to be allowed to meddle in the minstrel's vocation.[13]

It seems highly significant that "ordinary peasants" competed with the minstrels since there was almost certainly a connection between the *rudes Agricolae* and those many "freshe starteupp comedanties"[14] of which contemporary accounts so often complained. But if this was so, the whole question of the rise of the "common player" will have to be reopened: were there (and if so, which and how many) points of contact between the traditional culture of the folk and the professional art of the traveling actor? If we accept the view that the actors' troupes, which began to spring up with increased frequency at the end of the fifteenth century, could not have come from the depleted ranks of the minstrels, then we must look elsewhere for their origin. Even a cursory examination of contemporary legislation against vagabondage reveals that "Vacaboundes" and "Common players" were lumped together, and that they were *not* placed on the same level in order to denigrate the profession of the actor. Rather, the association of vagabonds with actors more likely reflects the fact that many vagabonds tried to make their living by acting. Indeed, Giovanni Florio remarked that "as enterlude-plaiers, you shal now see them on the stage, play a King . . . but they are no sooner off the stage, but they are base rascals, vagabond abjects, and porterly hirelings, which is their naturall and originall condition."[15] It was only the Puritan pamphlets that were likely to place actors on the same level as vagabonds with the intention of denigrating the former.

Economic and social history provides an answer to the question of where, at the end of the fifteenth century, these swarms of vagabonds originated. Tudor legislation indicates that the number of propertyless persons increased steadily; there were twelve times as many by the end of the century as there were at the start. Aerial photographs and excavations have located more than a thousand deserted villages and hamlets which were presumably the former homes of the "Vacaboundes."

Modern research, such as Maurice Beresford's study of *The Lost Villages of England,* confirms "the colossal dimensions" of the enclosures of arable land and substantiates Thomas More's complaint about formerly tame sheep having taken to eating humans. However unreliable they may otherwise be, Tudor pamphleteers such as Crowley or Stubbes supplied vivid descriptions and moral condemnation of the expropriation of the rural population which, as Marx was to show in his *Capital,* paved the way for the "primitive accumulation" that helped to make capitalism possible in England. The vagabonds were precisely those people who, as Crowley wrote, were driven to beg although they were able to work: "For there are pore people, welmoste innumerable,/ That are dryuen to begge, and yet to worcke they are able."[16]

When these homeless, propertyless people joined the ranks of the jugglers and players or appeared as "musical rustics," to use W. L. Woodfill's term, they had no other choice but to draw on their former way of life and their own cultural background for a spontaneous source of acting and music-making. For this there is, of course, no evidence, but the sheer weight of probability suggests that certain aspects of the popular tradition were thereby preserved and channeled into professional circles.

The ability of the uprooted "vagabonds" to draw spontaneously on the semidramatic heritage of the people can just as well be assumed as the readiness of contemporary audiences, familiar with folk play and Sword Dance, to appreciate traditional elements in miming and dancing. At the same time, though, the social context and function of these underwent a profound change; and it may be conjectured that under the conditions of an uprooted and commercialized itinerant existence, only the tougher and more adaptable talents were able to make a successful transition to the professional stage. But once this step was taken, something significant happened to the new type of professional play: it did not develop from within a specialized, self-contained group of dramatic entertainers with their closed set of rules and sanctions, but remained closer to a living tradition of popular culture than was possible in any other country in Europe. Under these conditions quite a few points of contact between folk ceremonies and professional dramatic entertainment were possible, from the early morality play *Mankind* to the unique phenomenon of the Elizabethan jig. At least up to the 1570s and 1580s the art of acting and staging, far from being confined to a self-perpetuating group of specialists, reflected the ever changing experience of the nation and drew upon the best talents from widely ranging backgrounds. This circumstance had far-reaching consequences, even at a time when the acting profession had become almost middle-class in its status and offered security and occasionally even respectability to some. The English actors who were celebrated throughout Europe were the heirs of a tradition in

which professional acting was built upon an exceptionally broad foundation of lay actors and constantly fed from this source.

Although it is possible, then, to assert the continuing importance of
the popular element in the secular drama of the Middle Ages, there is
much less ground on which to base a discussion of a popular tradition in
terms of a secular theater. Even though there were theaterlike structures
with scaffolds and platform stages in London, Exeter, and elsewhere at
the height of the Middle Ages, there is not enough evidence of their use
to make an inquiry into methods of staging and the nature of performances really fruitful. The unique processional and dramatic activities
of the "sect" in Exeter and the horribly masked *histriones* of whom
Thomas de Cabham spoke suggest a traditional social and ritual background, but throw no light on the extent and quality of the popular
contribution to the continuance of some sort of secular dramatic performance. When, in the fifteenth and sixteenth centuries, a professional
theater first emerged as a secular and commercial institution, the semidramatic traditions of *rudes Agricolae et Artifices* merged with the ways of
the traveling entertainer, while at the same time their age-old methods
of miming, singing, and dancing combined with the new-found wealth
of ideas and experience of several generations of humanist writers in a
way that held out great promise for the future.

2

The Mystery Plays and Tradition

The rise of the mysteries can fruitfully be related to a number of
traditional ritual, dramatic, festive, and processional activities. Yet when
all the sources and inspirations are viewed together, the dramatic cycles
still appear as a highly original institution, independent, in many important respects, of any one precycle cultural tradition. This is true, first of
all, of the tradition of liturgical performances within the Christian
church. Obviously, this tradition is of the greatest importance, but the
evolutionary conception of the mysteries as having developed through a
gradual or partial secularization of liturgical drama seems highly problematic. (As is well known, neither the actual Resurrection of Christ, the
Harrowing of Hell, nor the guarding of the Sepulcher, if we judge from
the Latin versions of liturgical drama, had any impact on the vernacular
representation of these episodes.) Suffice it to say here that the evolutionary conception no longer accounts for the social, cultural, and linguistic elements that cannot by any means be traced in liturgical plays.
Perhaps Rosemary Woolf, in her recent treatment of the subject, gives
the most balanced assessment when she notes the simultaneous impor-

tance and negligibility of the influence of liturgical drama on the mystery plays.

But if "it is only in trivial instances that the mystery plays draw upon liturgical drama as a direct source,"[17] other traditions do not present a much better case for continuity. For instance, the relationship between the cycles and early vernacular plays like the Anglo-Norman *Adam, La Seinte Resureccion,* and the Beverly *repraesentatio* can hardly be traced in terms of any direct points of contact, even though neither dramatic tradition was directly connected to prescribed church worship. Certainly from the point of view of stagecraft and the representation of action, the early vernacular plays have more in common with the mystery plays and, indeed, the moralities than with the drama arising out of the liturgy. As early as the *Ordo representacionis Ade* we find the basic divisions into *locus* and *platea.* (The Paradise, for example, conceived as a distinct locality, was "to be made in a raised spot, with curtains and cloths of silk hung round it. . . . and divers trees put therein with hanging fruit, so as to give the likeness of a most delicate spot"; the devils and demons, on the other hand, ran, danced, and addressed the audience *per plateas.*)[18] Here the most basic interplay between illusion and embodiment, representation and ritual, appears remarkably early. But these early plays are isolated instances, and unless one attempts to find points of contact through the almost entirely lost tradition of English miracle plays, it seems extremely difficult to consider them as a direct source of the mysteries.

No doubt there is a good deal to be said in favor of the miracle play tradition as an important link, not only between the early Anglo-Norman plays and the cycles but between the early drama and Elizabethan stage romances. Scholars have hardly done justice to this apparently widespread tradition of dramatized saints' legends and romantic plays since C. R. Baskerville and J. M. Manly drew attention to it more than a half a century ago. (There are records of performances, the earliest dated 1097, of plays on such subjects as St. Andrew, St. Eustacius, St. Dionysius, St. Catherine, King Robert of Sicily, and others.)[19] Certainly it is not surprising that the English survivals (the Digby *Mary Magdalene* and, partly, the Croxton *Play of the Sacrament*) provide unmistakable evidence for both the heritage of semiritual speech patter and popular conventions of *platea* and *locus* staging. If we may judge by analogy from some of the plays that have survived in France and the Netherlands, there must have existed some entirely secular romances. Even in the saints' legends and miracles of the Virgin there was, as a recent critic notes, "a large admixture of pre-Christian romance."[20] But although there can be little doubt that this tradition must have helped prepare the way for the early Elizabethan romantic tragicomedies (and even perhaps the romantic plots in Shakespeare's comedies), the relationship between the *miracula* tradition and the Corpus Christi play can only be conjectured. Although most of the evidence is indirect and hypothetical, the Digby *Mary Magdalene* does provide some suggestions as to how elements from the mysteries (biblical history such as the raising of Lazarus by Jesus) and from the moralities (allegorical figures such as the World and the Flesh, Wrath, and Envy) are woven into a swiftly changing series of romantic and miraculous episodes. But *Mary Magdalene* (1480–1520) is a late play, and the elements of synthesis may well reflect a process of decline in the original barriers between the two genres rather than any genetic constellation or any transitional link between miracles and mysteries.

Finally, the relationship between the dramatic cycles and the medieval religious and secular festivals deserves to be reconsidered. Alan Nelson has recently argued "from documentary evidence—much of it previously unknown—that the fifteenth-century English dramatic cycles developed out of fourteenth-century festival processions. A corollary of this argument is that the doctrinal relationship of the Corpus Christi dramatic play to the feast of Corpus Christi is almost entirely incidental."[21] But even though the processional and festive elements in the mystery plays have probably been underrated, it seems doubtful that they provided the most basic impulse and inspiration.

The point that has to be made is not simply that many traditions of precycle origin were involved, but that these must have entered into a conflicting and contradictory relationship with the emerging cycles. As modern scholars like F. M. Salter, A. C. Cawley, Eleanor Prosser, V. A. Kolve, and O. B. Hardison, Jr., have rightly emphasized, there was a pattern of highly diverse influences against which their basic thematic indebtedness to Old and New Testament sources must be viewed. (It is noteworthy, also, that studies of the conditions under which they were staged—at Chester, for example—reveal that the influence of the church on the organization of the cycles could be considerable: the texts of the plays remained under the control of church authorities until about 1530.) To recognize the importance of these sources and to say that the cycles owed more to the Old and New Testament than to any other single narrative source does not, of course, account for their equally important sources of theatrical inspiration and experience. If the cycles do point back to the tradition of liturgical drama (which had, after all, "established certain basic modes of dramatizing the materials of sacred history"),[22] the element of discontinuity in matters theatrical still remains considerable.

Even a hasty glance at the many obvious innovations associated with the cycles reveals that the most powerful forces of change could not possibly have worked from within the tradition of liturgical drama itself. To assume a development from liturgy toward drama and to conceive of it as a shift from *similitudo* to *imitatio*, from the ritual incarnation of the

Christian mass to the mimetic representation of biblical myth in terms of later medieval reality and sensibility, involves more questions than answers. If such a pattern does indicate some very general trends of change, it certainly obscures the basic fact that the movement from ritual to representation does not indicate a progressive development, but rather defines a fundamental contradiction throughout the history of medieval and Renaissance drama. The resolution of this contradiction took place in phases and on various levels with changing emphasis right down to the Shakespearean theater. As a matter of fact, the tensions between ritual performance and representational action which were partially reflected in the folk play were not entirely absent from the mystery plays themselves.[23]

Almost none of the important innovations and elements of discontinuity associated with the mystery plays can be accounted for from within the traditions of either the liturgical drama or the orthodox institutions and controls of the church itself.[24] The large number of lay persons taking part in the performances, the use of the vernacular, the enormous expansion of the plays, as well as their organization and staging by the guilds, involved factors of such great consequence that not only the social function of the cycles but aspects of structure, the scope of their subject matter, the theatrical mode of their presentation, and, finally, matters of social and religious consciousness were affected. In all these, the mystery plays reflected the impact of various changes in society and social consciousness, most conspicuously the increased need for plebeian instruction and entertainment (which was granted by the Church itself) and the growing awareness (which varied from place to place) of the social aspirations and cultural traditions of the rural and artisan populace. The point is, of course, that these factors all tended to move the cycles away from the liturgical tradition; none of them arose, organically or spontaneously, out of the elements in the service itself; most of them developed from impulses that extended far beyond the context of medieval worship. These new social functions and factors did not and could not affect the Christian content of biblical history, but they did succeed in replacing the orthodox liturgical versions with something new.

At its most general level this involved a shift of emphasis in the relationship of nonrepresentational and representational modes of performance. While the function of Christian worship and the element of ritual action remained alive and strong, a new awareness of man's position in the physical world and a new perspective on the social, physical, and causal conditions of his existence increased the scope of mimetic action and symbolic interpretation. Where the temporal quality of objects and the social nature of man were apprehended dramatically, the more descriptive and undramatic paraphrasing of the Old and New

Testament episodes was increasingly abandoned and a new theatrical unity of gesture and language, physical and mental processes, nonverbal and verbal performances, resulted.[25] For wherever the image of man achieved a more autonomous status, the scope for a mimetic and dramatic interpretation of his action increased; and wherever the social quality of communal and individual actions was perceived, their particularity could be viewed symbolically, as part of a dramatization of the temporal world in which the audience was conscious of its own place and function. But while the cognitive and affective potentialities of dramatic representation expanded, the heritage of ritual activity underwent equally significant changes, in the course of which a new popular element of self-expression came to exist side by side with the homiletic content of the liturgical performances. Such self-expression could assume a choric form or it could, as in the First Shepherd's speech of the *Secunda Pastorum,* anticipate the function of prologue or monologue. But there, as in the more important dimension of the comic and grotesque, the representational forms of *mimesis* and the nonrepresentational forms of self-expression existed side by side, and, in the resulting drama, role and actor, the representation of society and the re-enactment of self, became indivisible.

If it can be said that the mystery plays were "humanized by popular influences"[26] these, then, are the lines along which a rationale of such a process might be understood, and the social nature of the popular element more relevantly defined. To view the social context in perspective, it is important to recall the role that the craftsmen's guilds played in the financing, organization, and production of the cycles. With their controls against individual economic enterprise and the rights contained in their bills of incorporation, they had become an integral, though underprivileged, section of the feudal order.[27] Under the advanced agrarian conditions prevailing in England at the time, the guilds' municipal form of organization did not necessarily isolate them from important sections of the rural population. The theatrical endeavors of the guilds might appeal to a mixed audience, "both of burgh and of towne" (*Herod the Great,* 2 and 462). In fact, the wealthier citizens themselves were probably in much closer contact with the common people than their corresponding class in later centuries.

Against this background it is possible to understand that, after the introduction of Corpus Christi Day (1311), and especially after 1377,[28] the cycles became an important social event in medieval towns, a vast communal effort in which almost all citizens participated. The various scenes were so distributed by the corporations that each of the guilds performed one that accorded with the communal division of labor or appealed to its patron. The smiths of Coventry spent more than half of their budget in 1490 to have their scene rolled through the town on magnificent pageants and the play performed in splendid costumes at important central places. The guilds regarded the plays as "a demonstration of their solidarity and prosperity." Countless helpers and all the lay actors were welcome. Unlike the sixteenth-century London bourgeoisie, the town authorities did not think of the theater as a "great wasting both of the time and thrift of many poore people."[29] On the contrary, a system of rewards and fines insured the communal character of the occasion: careless work was criticized, but so was egocentric excess of zeal. A player in York, for example, was fined because he attempted to play more than two parts.[30]

Even if the communal content and function of the cycles helped to introduce and perpetuate elements of a popular tradition, the various scenes and the different cycles still seem too heterogeneous to be reduced to one sociological or ideological formula. The extent to which the contemporary social experience of plebeians and peasants was transmuted into the images and representations of biblical history or found some more direct or anachronistic form of self-expression varied widely. The quality of such transmutation, even as it affected the conception of entire scenes, modes of staging, characterization and speech, must ultimately be assessed for each separate scene.

In terms of their class alignment, the point of view of the cycles was that of the lower and middle free peasants and the urban artisan—that is, "most often that of the yeoman or the small burgher of the towns,"[31] for those classes comprised the major part of the audience and also bore most of the cost. And even though these craftsmen and yeomen possessed some degree of social self-consciousness, it was not uniformly or rigidly defined, and was, in fact, not even truly free from the ideology of the ruling feudal class. But still, to judge from the plays, their point of view must have differed considerably from the official doctrine of the church. Their interpretation of the Gospels involved a different frame of reference—certainly not an irreligious one, but one commensurate with the experience of the common people. Thus, Christ himself was thought of as an elevated example of the common man; the betrayal of Christ was a betrayal to the great of this world, a betrayal of the new laws that he proclaimed and of the idea of the "brotherhede" (York, XLVIII, 250) of all men. "Jesus' chief crime is that he will upset the law"; but the "law" represented by figures like Pilate was "a tool of injustice and oppression."[32] Jesus' words of accusation are not directed against disbelievers or heretics or even enemies of the church, but against oppressors— the rich and hard of heart (XLVIII, 325–49).[33]

For the dramatic expression of this kind of plebeian consciousness, the tradition of native myth and ritual was only of very limited use. But if it could not exert any marked influence on the themes and structures of the mystery plays, there were indirect influences that were of some consequence. Many in the cycle audiences were probably familiar with various forms of secular dramatic or processional activities. No other conclusion is possible in view of the folk play's wide distribution. Without a very large audience already accustomed to semidramatic performances, these plays in which hundreds of people acted and which were watched by thousands of spectators in day-long performances throughout the country would scarcely have been possible. True, several trends within the church must have favored the expansion and reception of the cycles. Efforts at ecclesiastical reform brought about an upsurge of the mendicant orders (and the institution of the Corpus Christi festival which was associated with them) and encouraged lay understanding of the Bible. Like the Corpus Christi festival itself, the performances were processional in many places. But if the church did provide the initial impulse, more than the efforts of the clergy was needed to make the cycles so vast a success.

Although it is extremely difficult to establish the extent to which elements of a pre-Christian tradition were taken over and transformed, there are a number of parallels between the folk ceremonies and the Corpus Christi play that attest to a process of cross-influence. Indeed, several conventions of staging find analogous verbal formulae; among them, the direct address to the audience which often opens the play and sometimes includes a traditional request for room for the actors. One such request precedes the entrance of Octavian in the Chester play: "Make rowme, lordinges, and geve us waie,/ and let octavian come and plaie" (VI, 177–78). The way in which each actor is successively called onto the stage or introduces himself also prompts comparison and suggests similarities in performance. In addition to such elements of staging (which we shall consider at greater length), we may note similar conventions of characterization which cannot have developed independently. For example, it seems significant that the black-headed Beelzebub, a traditional figure in the folk play, has his equivalent in the mysteries. There are also striking parallels between Jack Finney, the folk play doctor's assistant, and Garcio, the cheeky young shepherd in Chester, Colle, the doctor's servant in *The Play of the Sacrament*, or Garcio in *Mactacio Abel*.[34] What is more, these figures share some important conventions of speech and staging which are cultivated further in the morality play and in Elizabethan drama. The most fundamental motif of the folk drama—the death and resurrection of a protagonist—is, of course, paralleled by the Easter tradition of the crucifixion and resurrection of Christ. And even though it would be misleading, to say the least, to argue the matter of "influence" into this parallel, it is obvious that the theme of resurrection itself embodies functions similar to those of the pagan ritual that is reflected in the death and "cure" of the folk protagonist. But even if some "identity of basic patterns" is granted, it still seems difficult, on those grounds, to suppose that medieval folk drama "coalesced with" the Corpus Christi cycles.[35]

The principal impact that the folk ceremonies and other elements of popular culture made on the mystery plays was both indirect and transmuted. On the one hand, the folk tradition helped to prepare for the unprecedented expansion and popularity of a highly organized form of drama in which thousands of illiterate people adopted and adapted traditional modes of secular and semidramatic activities. On the other hand, the heritage of a more ancient native culture was metamorphosed into poetic modes of representation and evaluation of the feudal Christian myth, as, for instance, the grotesque and the burlesque. In either case the popular tradition did not change and grow *in vacuo* or for the sake of its own continuity; it persisted because it helped to sustain, or to modify, or to create anew, those forms of consciousness, imagination, and entertainment which, for many working people, served important functions in the elementary process of living in a socially differentiated society. We must keep this in mind if the immense significance of the burlesque and grotesque, as well as the new element of realism, is to be seen in the perspective of the popular theatrical tradition.

One of the most perceptive historians of the pre-Shakespearean drama, A. P. Rossiter, has pointed out that the element of the grotesque repeatedly produces a curious ambivalence, a "disturbing doubleness of tone and point of view." There is alongside the pathos and agony of Christ an "expression of the devilish as the inversion, reversal or parody of the divine." Such an element of grotesque inversion, the same scholar suggests, derives from "that opposite and antithetic world of the diabolical, in which the shadows of primitive paganism survived";

> where an unholy zest . . . readily turns to a positive zest-for-unholiness in which the Spirit of Negation almost speaks out loud and bold. . . . In all the legacy of Joculator and Jougleur has become one with the spirit of the comic rejoicings of the folk, as a kind of opposite to or negation of their normal religion. A ritual of defamation, sometimes reaching an adumbration of the undermining negatives . . . is the true basis in the English legacy of the clashing comic contrasts of Gothic drama; and this comes down to later times as the most important part of the medieval heritage.[36]

If the grotesque is seen in relation to some forgotten function of ritual in which the disenchanting effect of mimetic inversion serves a secular purpose which is less effective than magic but more interpretative (and hence affective), then it need not be thought of as being independent of, or unrelated to, the growth of the more representational forms of dramatic *mimesis*.[37] Both the grotesque and the realistic (with their disenchanting forms of *mimesis*) are opposed to the symbolic forms of ritual inherited from the Mass and the liturgy; and wherever the continuity of the latter is marked, as in the orthodox scenes of the York plays or the bulk of the Chester cycle, the former are hardly conspicuous. The secular endeavor to appropriate the world through drama is much more than just a manifestation of low style or a result of the "influence" of profane sources or motifs. What is involved, rather, is the complex problem of the rise of a dramatic method—the way in which the worlds of biblical myth and contemporary society are dramatically related to perception and experience in terms of a new, artistic form of social activity. From the point of view of their functions, then, neither the grotesque and the realistic, nor the comic parts can be understood as the "necessary relaxation" or "temporary distraction" that so many critics have judged them to be. To view these elements as "broad fun" or even as "a way of escape from piety,"[38] that is, as a more or less piquant seasoning for an all-too-solemn play, is completely to misunderstand their structural significance and their contribution to the total meaning of the play. And it is precisely the great structural tensions between the serious and comic elements and the interacting levels of main and subplot which will be seen to constitute a tradition that finds its finest expression in the works of Shakespeare.

Therefore, to refer to "realism" in the mystery plays is to be aware of an aesthetic and historical problem beyond the traditional context of the comic or burlesque. The ability of realism dramatically to perceive and comprehend the world cannot be viewed exclusively in terms of representational form. At every stage and on many levels the representational component combined with nonrepresentational techniques of speech and dramaturgy. And wherever a heightened empirical awareness of the actual world and the social, psychological, and temporal relations of man began to inform the dramatists' method, the Christian pattern inherited from the Mass and the liturgy, and even the homiletic and narrative elements in the renderings of the biblical theme were not disrupted, but subjected to a process of change. The immutable world of biblical myth came to be viewed in a temporal as well as a timeless perspective, and both the traditional subject-matter and its contemporary popular treatment were interrelated through various forms of dramatic anachronism. The best-known example is the *Secunda Pastorum*: the shepherds of Bethlehem graze their sheep on the moors of northern England, and the cold wind blows not in southern Palestine but over the fields of Yorkshire and in the skies above Wakefield.

But the image of the temporal world amounts to more than a dramatic representation of life as it is. Far from presenting a self-contained image or imitation of reality, the scene records a new mimetic form of self-expression and self-portrayal, which is inspired by a heightened awareness of class standards and an acute recognition of the common people's need to assert themselves.

Bot we sely husbandys that walkys on the moore,
In fayth we ar nerehandys outt of the doore.
No wonder, as it standys, if we be poore,
For the tylthe of oure landys lyys falow as the floore,
As ye ken.
We ar so hamyd,
Fortaxed and ramyd,
We ar mayde Handtamyd
With thyse gentlery-men.

Thus thay refe vs oure rest, oure Lady theym wary!
These men that ar lord-fest, thay cause the ploghe tary.
That men say is for the best, we fynde it contrary.
Thus ar husbandys opprest, in ponte to myscary
On lyfe;
Thus hold thay vs hunder,
Thus thay bryng vs in blonder;
It were greatte wonder
And euer shuld we thryfe.

(XIII, 10–27)[39]

These English shepherds act out their own fate before the stable of
Bethlehem—the hardships of their existence, the oppression, but also
their determination to resist. They are concerned not only with their
present dilemma but also with its past causes. They assert their own view
of "true need"; the way the "tylthe of oure landys lyys falow" is not, as the
gentlemen and their hangers-on say, "for the best." The shepherds
"fynde it contrary." It is this "contrary" vision that points to oppression
as the true reason for their misery: "No wonder . . . if we be poore." For
them there is no peace, and they pass this curse on to "thyse gentlery-
men": "oure Lady theym wary!" The curse almost amounts to an inversion of the Christmas message; it involves a process of self-expression
and the definition of a social identity which is based neither on the
topsy-turvying forms of late pagan ritual nor on the symbolic mode of
Christian myth but on an artistic perception of the world *as it is*.

3

Laughter and Terror: Herod and Pilate

The new awareness of self and society is not confined to the shepherd
scenes, but can also be found in some traditional biblical contexts. Generally speaking, the Old and New Testament figures that attain the
greatest theatrical vitality are those whose dramatic functions within the
biblical narrative are related either to a mimetic image of the contempo-

rary world or to some grotesque version of myth, or both. Evidently, figures like Herod or Pilate (as well as Cain, Joseph, Noah's wife, and others) who stood, as it were, between biblical history and contemporary reality, were, dramatically, the most flexible. They could draw upon the widest range of temporal, spatial, and verbal points of reference that the medieval stage offered, and they seemed best adapted to interrelating and integrating these three dimensions. Such figures were capable of fully exploiting the dramatic potential of anachronism because they established a broad range of links with, and realized the most affective tensions between, the world and time of biblical myth and the world and time of contemporary England. Furthermore, they enjoyed the most flexible positions on the stage and most varied modes of performance because they moved easily between both the fixed and the unlocalized settings, thereby drawing on the fullest range of theatrical links in space and scene that lay between the more illusionistic scaffold, or *domus*, and the *platea*, or pageant area closer to the audience. They realized, also, the greatest range of physical and verbal attitudes that supported and reflected their various points of reference in time and place. In achieving and interrelating these basic dimensions of the theater, they not only drew on the legacy of popular ceremonies and semidramatic activities but so developed, changed, and refined these traditions that they created many altogether new and original standards of dramaturgy which outlived the decline of the mystery plays, influenced some very important conventions in the moralities, and stimulated the theatrical imagination of Shakespeare and the Elizabethans.

Herod is the most obvious case in point, but not merely because of his Elizabethan popularity. The biblical associations and the highly critical treatment of the figure explain in part Herod's reputation; but the basis of his popularity must be sought not only in the figure as the image of a well known "character," but also in the traditional modes and standards of his portrayal in the popular theater. New Testament and apocryphal sources combined with the postritual tradition of the Lord of Misrule, the *festum stultorum* or similar forms of festive release, and these—together with ideas from the homiletic and liturgical traditions—were incorporated into a new empirical mode of representation and interpretation according to which these figures were viewed as images of the contemporary feudal tyrant. Biblical, homiletic, and ritual elements, together with their narrative, didactic and nonrepresentational equivalents combined in a newly referential and empirical mode of *mimesis*. It is the dramatic figure's capacity to synthesize that accounts for the remarkable transformation of the popular tradition and its no less remarkable continuity.

According to the Bible, Herod is first of all the cruel King of the Jews, described as *iratus* in the Gospel of St. Matthew (II, 16). In liturgical performances he is shown as *furore accensus,* whose excess of wrath is no longer based on canonical precept but corresponds, according to R. E. Parker, to apocryphal and patristic versions.[40] As the legend of Noah's wife shows,[41] the apocryphal tradition was much less orthodox and rather closer to heresy than the canonical writings of the Bible. And as such Herod could well be linked with the *rex stultorum* and other forms of inversion among the lower clergy, since in the play of the *pastores* at Rouen and Autun the *regnum Herodis* was in fact celebrated as a fools' festival and the person who performed the role of Herod was presumably none other than the king of fools himself. In Padua, Herod's boisterous antics were particularly revealing: an inflated balloon (*uesica inflata*) appeared in his train, and he held a staff or wooden spear in his hand (*cum hasta lignea in manu*) which he flung at the chorus in a state of extreme wrath at the beginning of his mock sermon (*et cum maximo furore prohicit eam uersus chorum*). In other places, where the heritage of ancient fertility rituals was not so apparent, the turbulence of the fool's festival or the Lord of Misrule may have had a less marked effect on the presentation of Herod. Still, his grotesque boasting and ranting, which became his proverbial attributes, cannot be derived primarily from the biblical *Herodus iratus*; his association with the spirit of misrule and topsy-turvydom was definitely "popular" and must be considered as part of the genetic background of Herod in the mystery plays.[42]

However, the continuance of a nonrepresentational element of ritual ranting alone cannot explain the theatrical fascination and rich complexity of the figure of Herod. In addition to this late ritual legacy, a newly referential form of *mimesis* was grafted onto the New Testament, apocryphal, and liturgical background: the way he was depicted at Wakefield, York, and Coventry, even more than in the *Ludus Coventriae,* leaves no doubt that he was performed as a contemporary feudal magnate. Such an interpretation was not original to these plays, either. In terms of the "figural" dimension of medieval art, the biblical character must have appeared as some eternal archetype, whose spiritual "reality" might well be reconciled with the shadow of his contemporary existence. Not surprisingly, homiletic versions of Herod had already presented him as "the feudal tyrant of the day."[43] Likewise, there were related figures of a similar aristocratic or tyrannical status, such as Pilate, who were brought to life in much the same way. But the secular image of contemporary society could become so powerful that it was capable of overshadowing the biblical as well as the ritual background of the figure, especially when the characters themselves described their personalities explicitly in terms of medieval feudalism:

> I Tyrant, that may both take and teene
> Castle, tower, and towne . . .

> (Chester, VIII, 163–64)

ffor I am he that may make or mar a man;
My self if I it say as men of cowrte now can;
Supporte a man to day, to-morn agans hym than,
On both parties thus I play...

(Towneley, XX, 19-22)

Here Herod and Pilate seem aware of their representational function; they relate the biblical past to the perspective of "now," which distances the mythical role from the contemporary performer and permits him the deliberately referential and interpretative form of comparison: "as men of cowrte *now* can." Thus, above and beyond his biblical context, Herod was seen as the uncontrolled, violent tyrant, and Pilate as the tyrannical, unjust judge. The anachronism of their English social status was accentuated in their speech: in a number of scenes, at Chester and York, for example, Herod speaks Norman French, the language of the feudal court. But at the point of greatest realism the representational function of speech was turned into a nonrepresentational burlesque appeal to the audience, as when Herod ended his scene with

Bot adew!—to the deuyll!
I can nomore fraunch!

(Towneley, XVI, 512-13)

It is no coincidence that such clowning self-consciousness has its place in the Wakefield Master's *Magnus Herodes,* where the dramatic tension between the representational quality of the biblical and feudal role and the nonrepresentational, burlesque self-expression achieved its most remarkable effect. Perhaps the Wakefield Master's scene does not have the subtlety of Shakespeare's studies of rulers, but it is probably unique in the severity of its portrait of malignant tyranny. "Herode, that lordyng," the introduction says, is "Chefe lord of lordyngys, chefe leder of law." Everyone must obey him "or els be ye lorne." Those around him must indeed be careful:

Downe dyng of youre knees,
All that hym seys;
Dysplesyd he beys,
And byrkyn many bonys.

(XVI, 60-63)

The picture of the tyrant is frightening in its realism, but, again, it is not simply a version of "ritual form in representational terms."[44] The new dramatic method is more complex than this; it would still be an oversimplification to say that this method is "ritual" in its subjectivity and "representational" for its objectivity. Actually both self-expression and *mimesis* coalesce and interact: the resulting dramaturgy sets forth a point of view which is not only that of the frightening feudal object of repre-

sentation, but also that of the victim or subject, the plebeian experience
of contemporary tyranny. What matters is not the person in power but
the impersonation of tyranny, as seen not only through the eyes of the
ruler but also through those of the ruled. Since the dramatic experience
is that of the man who bows down before power but does not recognize
its claim to privilege, Herod's exercise in tyranny is burlesqued, as it is in
York, Coventry, and Chester. In the process of performance the magnate's lust for power has a frightening, but also a comic effect. Once it is
subjected to the *ohm,* or measure, of a popular dramatic sensibility, such
an attitude is judged stupid and uncontrolled. Herod exclaims wrath-
fully:

> My wytt away rafys ...
> My guttys will outt thryng ...
>
> (XVI, 234, 240)

In Chester he is "almost crazy" with rage and, like Shakespeare's
Coriolanus (I, 4, 27), he begins to "sweat" with anger:

> for wrath I am nere wood ...
> all for wrath see how I sweat ...
>
> (VIII, 377, 187)

In the Coventry play of the Shearmen and Taylors:

> I stampe! I stare! I loke all abowtt! ...
> I rent! I rawe! and now run I wode!
>
> (779, 781)

This is not simply comical or farcical: it is a burlesque version of terror
as laughter. Contrary to prevailing scholarly opinion, the center of this
figure's dramatic energy is to be found neither in his comic nor his tragic
dimensions. On the one hand, Herod is no *miles gloriosus,* and his wrath
no farce or "low comedy" (as critics from Hermann Graf to Hardin Craig
have claimed); on the other hand, he cannot be understood as an expression of a "tragic infatuation" or even in terms of "the somber spirit and
tragic essence of the role."[45] Herod is of course both somber and ridiculous, terrifying and grotesque, but the unique force and dramatic effect
of the role are rooted in the tension and interaction of the horrible and
the comic. This effect is not an original achievement of the Wakefield
Master, or of any other medieval dramatist for that matter. It reflects the
dramatic potentialities of a popular theater in which the background of
pagan and Christian ritual and a tradition of nonrepresentational forms
of embodiment and self-expression are linked to, and interact with,
more modern empirical standards of mimetic imitation and interpretation.[46]

In such a transitional context Herod and Pilate are especially apt to achieve a new standard of verbal action according to which a more potent unity of dramatic speech and theatrical movement takes the place of the narrative and descriptive forms in the homiletic tradition. Physical action and emotional excitement, raging violence and angry speech coalesce and interact to such a degree that in a play like *Magnus Herodes* emphasis is placed not on a *description* of the outcome of action but on the *process of doing*, which is itself performed as verbal and physical action. Herod does not narrate: rather, he enacts an experience and he represents a position. The structure of his speech therefore tends to become complex in the sense that it includes perspectives of both identification and dissociation.

In the dramatic representation of Herod, as in Shakespeare's Richard Gloucester, imitative forms and functions are thoroughly compatible with transmuted ritual and with the more traditional elements of non-representational burlesque and audience awareness. The contradiction between the two modes is, as in Shakespeare, essentially creative, and indeed necessary if understood in terms of its functions in the social context of the popular tradition where truth and myth, realism and self-expression constantly mingle. Thus it seems significant that the most intensely realistic versions of Herod achieved the most lively and direct audience contact. At Wakefield and at Coventry the social and theatrical function of this contact was built into the structure of the play itself and into the dramatic meaning of its protagonist. His relationship to the audience is only superficially parallel to the more didactic or homiletic position from which Moses, for example, addressed the audience as "ye folk of israell" (Towneley, VII, 1 ff.) and followed with a recitation of the Ten Commandments. Nor does it correspond to the "communion with sacred history" arising out of Christ's address to the public.[47] Rather, it fulfills different functions that cannot be understood in terms of the liturgical or homiletic conventions of audience participation. One would not wish to minimize the importance of these traditions in the Corpus Christi cycles, but for Herod a really comparable form of audience contact may be found in other tyrannical figures like Augustus Caesar, or Pilate, as well as in Garcio, Cain's clowning servant, and a number of comic demons and devils.

As in the case of Pilate's direct audience address, at least two different dramatic patterns emerge. The self-explanation or self-introduction of the villain who takes the audience into his confidence or calls himself a "Tyrant" (Chester, VIII, 163) is the first:

> I am full of sotelty,
> ffalshed, gyll, and trechery;
> Therfor am I namyd by clergy
> As mali actoris.

(Towneley, XXII, 10–13)

Whether or not this reflects a legacy of nonrepresentational ritual, or a narrative mode of descriptive characterization, or both, this form of self-consciousness by the villains and tyrants is essentially anachronistic; it projects the deliberate reference to the contemporary medieval clergy onto the plane of biblical history. Although possibly didactic, the dramatic consequence of this projection is more complicated than the liturgical communion with, or homiletic address to, the audience. There is more to be considered than the instruction or edification of the audience; a theatrical effect similar to that produced by the unabashed challenge of the devil, or the Vice in the moralities, seems to be present as well. Shakespeare's greatest villains—notably Iago, Richard Gloucester, and Edmund—are often characterized by this mode of direct self-explanation.

Similarly, the horrific-comic or grotesque effect has no liturgical or homiletic precedent either; in many instances it expresses the legacy of the topsy-turvying mode of postritual inversion which, in the folk play, became non-sensical. For Pilate this often occurred at the beginning of a scene—in Wakefield, for example, when he opens with a threatening but also comically boastful speech, comparable to Herod's opening words already quoted.

> Stynt, I say! gyf men place, quia sum dominus dominorum!
> he that agans me says, rapietur lux oculorum;
> Therefor gyf ye me space, ne tendam vim brachiorum,
> And then get ye no grace, contestor Iura polorum,
> Caveatis;
> Rewle I the Iure,
> Maxime pure,
> Towne quoque rure,
> Me paueatis.
>
> (Towneley, XXIV, 10–18)

Pilate calls for silence and room because he is "dominus dominorum." Anyone who speaks against him will feel the strength of his arm, and so on. And the whole rant culminates in a grotesque nonsensical version of a ritual-like noise. Behind this boasting is an irreverent element of mimic parody; the burlesque is as rollicking as it is blasphemous. The terrible threat is both physical and theological—the seeing are to be deprived of sight, the faithful of their blessing. This anachronistic palaver by the "Roman" Pilate is cheerfully heretical. But what is remarkable is that it is addressed to the people of Wakefield, in particular to those who have, in their curiosity, pressed too close for the pageant actors to move. A similar threat to the audience is delivered by Herod who distances his tyrannical role through his comic performance:

Stynt, brodels, youre dyn—yei, euerychon!
I red that ye harkyn to I be gone;
For if I begyn, I breke ilka bone,
And pull fro the skyn the carcas anone— . . .

Peasse, both yong and old, at my bydyng, I red,
For I haue all in wold: in me standys lyfe and dede.
Who that is so bold, I brane hym thrugh the hede!

(XVI, 82–85, 91–93)

He addresses both "yong and old," silencing with his threats the surging, gaping, noisome crowd. The threat is horrifying but also comical; for the seriousness of the actor behind the tyrant's role is as suspect as Bottom the Weaver's flair for the tragic when he suggests that his "chief humour is for a tyrant" (*Midsummer Night's Dream* I, 2, 24).

Perhaps it is impossible to say whether the horrific or the comic effect predominated. If the burlesque performance involved both, as it certainly did, the result must have been strange comedy; a freely associative interaction between the dramatic illusion of biblical or feudal tyranny and the wild self-expressed mimicry of the performer was the probable effect. But whatever enchanting or disenchanting effects prevailed, the forms of non-sensical ritual expression now achieved a new and more functional status as a burlesque foil to, or reversal of, high seriousness.

There is more than one indication of how this burlesque function gained ground. The horrible threats and tyrannical antics may have been intended to quell the noise and excitement first aroused by Herod's exceedingly grotesque appearance. But it is significant that after the usual threats the Herod in York (XXXI, 1–25) had to remind the audience that his words were being spoken in earnest: "It sittis vs in sadnesse to sette all oure sawes." Likewise, Pilate, *after* twenty-two lines of admonition and threats, *still* protests against grinning and screaming: "for þat gome þat gyrnes or gales . . ." (York XXXIII, 23 ff.). It is noteworthy that scolding and threatening tyrants resemble the devils in that the demons also frequently had to call upon audiences to keep quiet. Pilate and Herod are continually moved to call their audiences to order (Towneley XX, 1–5; XXII, 1–4; XXXIII, 1–21; XXIV, 1–9; York XIX, 1–13; XXX, 1–9; XXXII, 1–8; etc.).

Here the dramatic impersonation of biblical and contemporary tyranny mingles with the re-enactment of a postritual form of release and self-assertion. The popular mime's *ohm*, or measure, is enriched by a common stock of social experience existing between the performer and the observer of this highly disrespectful version of the tyrant's role. It seems remarkable that this spirit of self-assertion and the playful rehearsal of the will to survive (or even to resist) feudal oppression find an expression that is not at all didactic or tendentious but entirely theatrical, and, so, great fun. Here the popular tradition, as with the moralities and Shakespeare, excels in the performance of evil: that is, in its theatrical realization, not in its homiletic denunciation. In this sense, horror and laughter are correlated; the enactment of awesome tyranny and frolicsome buffoonery coalesce: "horror is ritualized in sportive forms."[48]

It seems difficult if not impossible to assess the burlesque quality and function of audience participation in a context such as this. The response of the audience probably varied from one performance to another and certainly from one cycle to another. The presentation of Pilate and Herod in Chester, for instance, was not as grotesque as in those plays already cited. In general, though, the horrific-comic characters were the most likely to establish a dramatically effective contact with the audience. The Coventry Herod's nonsense speech and blasphemous boasting may well have led to physical byplay with the spectators. Here Herod declares himself the creator "that made bothe hevin and hell," Prince of Purgatory, "and cheff capten of hell," and a great general and feudal magnate. He is the pillar of chivalry ("manteinar of curtese") who falls into a dreadful rage when it is pointed out that murdering children "Wyll make a rysing in thi noone cuntrey." At this point the stage direction reads, "Here Erode ragis in the pagond and in the strete also" (783–84), that is, in the midst of the surrounding audience.

But as the "King of Kings" (584) mingles with the audience and rages in the open street, he forfeits the reverence and the menace of his station and almost surrenders the representational dimension of his role. At the same time, the audience is drawn into the play and given the role of frightened subjects. In York and Wakefield, for instance, the audience was even supposed to go down on its knees. But the terror that it experiences is a mock fright performed in sport. The intermingling of dramatic illusion and theatrical convention unites the impersonation of the role with the re-enactment of festive release in such a way that the two faces of Herod—the funny and the frightening—become inseparable. The aesthetic effect is close to life and, at the same time, highly complex. The theatrical heritage of ritual release is no longer non-sensical but, in the representational context of drama, fulfills its ancient magical function in the new form of a *burlesque* inversion of the station of the mighty. Terror, playfully experienced, acts as a charm against real terror, or at least reduces some of its more formidable dimensions. The comic version of tyranny has a liberating effect: exaggerated authority becomes laughable. The mighty man appears comic when terrible threats and wrath, once they are subjected to irreverent imitation, are turned into burlesque.

4

Platea *and* Locus: *Flexible Dramaturgy*

The burlesque realism in the social and theatrical functions of Herod does not, of course, correspond to the realism in, say, the nineteenth-century drama. The grotesque imitation of reality complemented the acting out of biblical myth. As in Breughel and Bosch, blasphemy contrasted with piety, heretical parody with Christian pathos, reverence with irony. But how and in what ways is this "disturbing doubleness in tone and point-of-view" related to the popular tradition in the structure and practice of medieval stages and stagecraft?

The actual appearance of the medieval stage and the way it worked is of course subject to a good deal of guesswork and controversy. And recent re-evaluations of David Rogers' "late and garbled," and often "demonstrably false" account of the processional performance of the mysteries have called into question widely held assumptions about medieval staging. The mysteries were not only performed on the big four- or six-wheeled pageant wagons or movable stages, such as those used at Chester and York, but also in stationary acting places—sometimes in the round—where actors spoke from atop scaffold structures or descended to perform at ground level on the "place." The number of these fixed performances has generally been underestimated in the past; recent studies suggest that there were almost as many of these as there were pageants.[49] At Chester, for example, there were more scenes than pageants; and even though two or more guilds could have used one pageant wagon, it has not been conclusively proved that all of the scenes in the cycles were staged on wagons. At any rate, the existence of wagons did not preclude the additional use of scaffolds which, as some evidence from Coventry shows, were probably also mounted on wheels. But again, as little is known about the combination of these scaffolds and wagons as about the structure of the wagons themselves, or, for that matter, about the possibility that groupings of wagons were also used.

Certainly a number of difficulties remain in reconstructing the pageant stage, a structure whose transportation through the narrow streets of a medieval town must have been difficult considering the complexity of some of the more elaborate scenes.[50] New research suggesting that there were movable platform stages in addition to the double-decker pageants makes it easier to visualize the diversity of action in the plays (Mak's leaps and bounds, for instance). But Arnold Williams' belief that "the action was not confined to, but only centered in, the pageant stage" (hence extending the *loca* and restricted acting area of the pageant into the adjacent market or street) is more cautious and, as Glynne

Wickham's hypothetical reconstruction of the platform cart suggests, at least as plausible.[51] This method of staging would be sufficiently flexible for Herod to rage "in the street also," as well as for the appearance of the mounted expositor in Chester and the mounted *magi* of the Towneley plays. The extension of the acting area by a *platea* (in the broadest sense of unlocalized "place") clarifies the scenic arrangement at Wakefield in particular, since it provides a "large and multiple acting area" without necessitating the "circular area or . . . amphitheatre" that Martial Rose and Martin Stevens believe to have been used.[52]

Actually, the difference between the pageant stage and the circular theater may not have been as great as has been assumed. As Richard Hosley has shown, the various kinds of medieval theater used either a "focused" or a "dispersed" mode of production. The famous Coventry stage direction concerning Herod's raging would make equal sense, then, in a round theater, where Herod could easily rage on the scaffold and in the "place" also; "the two theatrical forms are utterly different physically, but the techniques of production are essentially the same."[53] In both, the distinction between a "place" or platform-like acting area (the *platea*), and a scaffold, be it a *domus, sedes,* or throne (the *locus*), is the one factor that is of key importance. Functionally, the *locus* corresponded to the scaffold in the circular theater and to the throne or hut on the pageant stage. In each case fixed, symbolic locations near and on the larger unlocalized acting area tend to define a more particular kind of action.

The combination of *platea* and *locus* is not, of course, confined to the mysteries. It can be found earlier in the stage arrangements of liturgical plays, and it continued later in the moralities (some of which were written for the circular theater). The same principle, in an altered form, had its impact on the interludes acted in Tudor halls. Here too the action was performed in two general areas: the acting area in the middle or at the head of the hall stage (farther away from the audience), and the "place," where the standing plebeian part of the audience sometimes mixed quite closely with the actors (as in *Fulgens and Lucrece*). Originally an outdoor conception in medieval plays, the *platea* thus was adapted to the requirements of indoor staging.[54]

Given the vagueness of the pageant stage arrangement, the circular theater can still provide the clearest illustration of the interplay between *locus* and *platea* that we have. Such a theatrical arrangement was fundamental to the Digby plays, *The Play of the Sacrament, The Creation of Eve,* and also some moralities, like *The Pride of Life* and *The Castle of Perseverance*. Its operation can probably be seen most clearly in the late *Ludus Coventriae,* performed in "N-town" and already acted by wandering players. This mystery provides a wealth of stage directions which facilitate an inductive reconstruction of the play in performance, as well as a number of scenes where the connection between word and action is often unusually close.

At the start of the *Passion Play II,* for example, the following direction is given:

*What tyme þat processyon is enteryd in to þe place and þe herowdys takyn his schaffalde·
and pylat and annas and cayphas here schaffaldys Also þan come þer An exposytour in
doctorys wede þus seyng*

(XXIX, 1)

The "processyon," here probably the entrance of the actors, moves into the *place* surrounded by the audience. After Herod has mounted his *schaffalde,* and Pilate, Ananias, and Caiphas have also mounted theirs (the plural *schaffaldys* is quite clear), an *exposytour,* standing on the *place,* or perhaps striding back and forth on it, addresses himself directly to the audience. He reminds them that the play now beginning is a continuation of the story shown there last year (the *Passion Play I*). Herod then reveals himself (possibly from behind a curtain, in accordance with the direction *here þe herowndys xal shewe hymselfe and speke*) and begins to threaten from his high seat: "Now sees of your talkyng ... Not o word I charge you þat ben here present. ..." The characteristic demand for silence introduces a longer monologue and a shorter dialogue, which are followed by Herod's withdrawal, again into his scaffold pavilion, after he has explained:

Thanne of þese materys serys take hede
Ffor A whyle I wele me rest
Appetyde requyryth me so in dede
And ffesyk tellyth me it is þe best.

(66–69)

These lines correspond to those describing the King's withdrawal in *The Pride of Life:*

Draw þe cord, sire streynth,
Rest I wol now take; ...
Et tunc, clauso tentorio, dicet Regina secrete nuncio

(ed. Brandl, 303 ff.)

A somewhat unmotivated reference to "ffesyk" serves to explain Herod's withdrawal. Thus, a representational (in fact, even a psychological) motive is supplied to justify a nonrepresentational convention: illusion and interpretation first begin to assert themselves in a *locus.* Yet the passage remains a mere verbal gesture that is not integrated into the dramatic process itself, even when it does suggest the more strictly localized character of the fixed or "focused" mode in the handling of the scaffold (as *sedes*). Associated with the scaffold is a rudimentary element of verisimilitude that has not really come to terms with the more episodic and dispersed nature of *platea* production; for in the latter, the play world continues to be frankly treated as a theatrical dimension of the real world.

The tension that Herod's withdrawal creates between the illusion of a representational action and the theatrical convention of a nonrepresentational dramaturgy seems very clumsy and naive. And yet, the unity that contains a contradiction between "realism" and "convention"— which T. S. Eliot considered to be "impure art"[55] in Shakespeare—is remarkable in spite of its awkwardness. (It was to be the interplay between "realism" and "convention" that brought *locus* and *platea* together in the maturing Elizabethan drama.) Herod's "need" to "rest" is itself, for example, a representational indication that his physical presence on the scaffold is to be ignored in the action that follows: for he is not supposed to hear the news that Christ has been taken prisoner, which is brought by the messenger who subsequently enters the "place."

With the messenger's appearance the scene shifts to another scaffold (another symbolic location on the same acting area). But before the news reaches Caiphas and Ananias, and before the prisoner Jesus is brought to their scaffold (97–98), the messenger, fulfilling his *platea* role of narrator, reawakens the audience's awareness of its participatory role as recipient of "Tydyngys, tydyngys":

> *here xal A massanger com in-to þe place rennyng and criyng Tydyngys tydyngys · and so round Abowth þe place · jhesus of nazareth is take . . .*
>
> (69–70)

The messenger's entrance clarifies, to some extent, the overall stage picture: in front of the three scaffolds of Herod, the priests, and Pilate, which were "rownd Abowth þe place," there remained an area surrounded by the audience that was probably circular like that in the plan of *The Castle of Perseverance* or the Cornish *Passio Domini Nostri*. At any rate, there was a large enough distance between the various scaffolds to make it worthwhile for messengers to pace through it. Thus, Caiphas sends a messenger to Pilate summoning him to the "mothalle" at daybreak. Pilate in his turn "syttyth in his skaffald" (214–15), receives the messenger, and sends him back to Caiphas. Caiphas then declares night to be over, descends from his scaffold together with Ananias, and, with the help of his men, *þei ledyn jhesu A-bowt þe place · tyl þei come to þe halle* (244–45). After some discussion Pilate leaves the judgment to Herod. The dramatic process that began at Herod's scaffold returns to it again. As the group approaches Herod's high seat or is already gathered in front of it, the scaffold opens, revealing a new dramatic arrangement:

> *here þei take jhesu and lede hym · in gret hast to þe herowde · And þe herowdys scafald xal vn-close shewyng herowdes in astat all þe jewys knelyng · except Annas and cayphas þei xal stondyn etcetera*
>
> (356–57)

The reconstruction of these scenes in performance not only reveals specific theatrical techniques, but also suggests some basic principles of staging that continued to be meaningful and effective in Shakespeare's theater. At first glance it is difficult to see the connection between the two varying modes of production on the mystery play stage and the form's "disturbing doubleness of tone and point-of-view" involving the interplay of "realism" and "convention." The connection is, however, an important one, and bears not only on the continuing tension between realistic imitation and ritual embodiment, but also on the distinction between the object of imitation and the *ohm* (or measure) of the imitator, that is, the author and actor.

To explore these connections between the technical arrangements and the unformulated intellectual assumptions of the medieval theater is to find that there is no such thing as a unified or homogeneous concept of a "stage." For which is the "stage" in the *Ludus Coventriae*? The scaffold from which Herod speaks? With its probable curtain it comes closest to our modern conception of a raised theatrical stage. It is even called a "stage" at one point: *Here xal annas shewyn hymself in his stage . . . (The Passion Play I,* 40–41). But the high seat of Ananias cannot be the only "stage," since other scaffolds are also used; and as we have seen, each of the other scaffolds is, at some time, completely excluded from the action. It is clear, then, that properly speaking the acting area cannot be exclusively associated with a "stage" as defined in the limited sense of one or more curtained scaffolds.

In addition to these symbolic scaffolds there is an acting area that was called the "place" thirteen times in the *Ludus Coventriae.* This is where the procession of actors makes its appearance, where the messenger moves, and where Jesus is led until "they reach the hall." This "hall," already referred to as the "mothalle" (the court and meeting-place), serves as a scenic unit in midplace, where Christ is brought to judgment and where Pilate, Caiphas, and Ananias meet. This is obviously a focal point of dramatic action, and it corresponds to the "cownsel hous" mentioned in scene thirty-one (635–36) and described in more detail in scene twenty-six:

here þe buschopys with here clerkys and þe Pharaseus mett and þe myd place and þer xal be a lytil oratory with stolys and cusshonys clenly be-seyn lych as it were a cownsel hous . . .
(124–25)

The "hall" is not only an important locality, it is also centrally situated. The stools and cushions to which the direction refers obviously serve to create some impression of verisimilitude, but the phrase "lych as it were a cownsel hous" makes it clear that a real house, which would have interfered with the audience's view, did not stand there. Even without the physical "house," though, this locality would have assumed the function of a central *locus,* which—like some of the scaffolds or frame structures—created a heightened level of mimetic representation and, perhaps, rudimentary elements of the illusion of actuality.

Such a technical relationship between scaffold and "place" allowed, and indeed presupposed, a highly flexible mode of production through which the representation of biblical myth and the expression of self can be seen as integral parts of the "doubleness" and the "strangely comprehensive two-ways facingness" of the late medieval dramatic vision. The dual values of scaffold and "place" do not, of course, provide a causal or mechanical explanation of this doubleness. Neither are the functions of scaffold and "place" always so clearly distinguishable that they can be reduced to a simple formula. Nevertheless, in the *Ludus Coventriae*, as in the related conventions of the pageant wagon, there is an important functional difference between *platea* and *locus*. As a rule, it was the more highly ranked persons who sat on the scaffolds: God the father, the "King" in *The Pride of Life*, Decius (enthroned as in the Fouquet miniature). Significantly, while some high-born members of the audience were also seated on these scaffolds, or at any rate on neighboring scaffolds, the ordinary public stood crowded below in the *champ*. This was the case in *The Castle of Perseverance:* the noble "syrys semly" sat at the sides of the scaffolds while the simple "wytis" were in the "pleyn place," that is, in the middle of the green or field. It was among these simple folk, or in front of them, that soldiers and serfs, the shouting messenger of "N-town," and of course the devil, grimacing "in the most orryble wyse" (465–66), played their parts.

Such functional differences between *platea* and *locus* can perhaps best be discussed in terms of the French theater. In the early Norman Adam play *diabolus* and the demons repeatedly appeared *per plateas* amongst the audience. This arrangement recurs in the later French miracle plays and probably achieves the greatest degree of dramatic consistency in *Saint Didier, Saint Christophe,* and *Saint Bernard de Menthon,* in which a fool repeatedly appears to speak dialect and nonsense, allude to contemporary events, and parody the saint. This fool quite clearly occupies the *platea;* he speaks to the soldiers, servants, and beggars, and to the audience, while the serious or high-born persons in the play seem unaware of his existence despite his lengthy comments on their actions and deportment. Contemporaneous with the audience, the fool here dissociates himself from the world and time of the *locus* as he glosses the symbolic action for the audience: "This must have happened long, long ago," he tells them directly.[56]

Such a clearly defined and far-reaching differentiation between the dramatic conventions of the high- and low-born characters is hardly to be found in the English miracle and mystery plays. The scenic position of the French fool does, however, correspond somewhat to that of the burlesque doctor's servant Colle in *The Play of the Sacrament,* who is expressly directed to come out "into the place" (444-45). The clowning boy Hawkyn in *Mary Magdalene* probably acted close to the audience in a similar way: his grotesque nonsense prayer (1185-1201) ends with an execration, but the *presbyter* and *rex* take no notice of it. In the interlude of the Tudor period it was still customary for the lower characters to move about in a neutral area rubbing shoulders with the plebeian audience: "the comic and disreputable characters (those who call for 'room') . . . speak mainly to by-standers adjoining the 'place'—the least dignified members of the audience."[57]

Such spatial differentiation allowed for complex and sometimes quite rich and suggestive drama. Christ, for instance, moved about the "place" in the *Ludus Coventriae*, quashing spatial and social distinctions, reasserting his common humanity, and giving the *sermo humilis* a new dignity and function.[58] From the point of view of staging, Christ's position corresponded to that of *Humanum Genus*, the central human figure who moved about in the middle of the "place" in *The Castle of Perseverance*, and was led or enticed to the various scaffolds. There it was not the judges and priests who were enthroned, but God, Lucifer, and a host of allegorical figures.[59]

The relationship between *locus* and *platea* was, to be sure, complex and variable; and this rather formal association of figures does not do full justice to that rich variability. But as a rule the English scaffold corresponds to the continental *domus, tentus,* or *sedes* which delimit a more or less fixed and focused scenic unit.[60] On the pageant wagon this might be a shepherd's hut or the stable at Bethlehem; in the mystery plays of Valenciennes these *loca* were set up side-by-side—hall, temple, palace, hell, etc. In Lucerne they were called *tenti,* and in Mons there was a *maisonette.* Scaffolds such as these gradually became the small, temporary, curtained pavilions or porchlike booths that, among other things, answered the need for an "inner stage" or "upper chamber" in the Elizabethan drama.

Unlike these *loca,* which could assume an illusionary character, the *platea* provided an entirely nonrepresentational and unlocalized setting; it was the broad and general acting area in which the communal festivities were conducted. Here the audience could—as in the performance of *The Castle of Perseverance*—share the setting with both the actors and the "stytelerys" who acted as stewards or supervisors. The Latin word *platea* (Gr. πλατεῖα, Ital. *piazza*) originally indicated the open space between houses—a street or a public place at ground level. As Italian usage suggests, the *platea* developed into the ground floor of an auditorium. But, before the separation of actors and audience was taken for granted, the *platea* or "place" corresponded to the "plain" in the Cornish Round or "the green" in Lindsay's *Satire of the Three Estates.*[61]

The changing theatrical functions of this area are extremely important to an understanding of the pre-Shakespearean popular theater. And although Richard Southern originally saw no connection between the *platea* and the Elizabethan platform stage, it may be reasonable to assume that while the main acting area in Shakespeare's theater did not perhaps develop directly out of the *platea* it did take on and expand some of the *platea's* basic functions. The scaffold, once its platform had become the main acting area, was likely to be increasingly dissociated from the earlier representational assumptions of the *loca;* the "place," however, retained the unlocalized quality that remained so important on the later platform stage. In the medieval drama it is the symbolic function of the various *loca* that tended to distance them from the audience. Herod, sitting atop his scaffold, physically objectified his high rank and manner by means of a spatial distance that also facilitated the kind of representational *mimesis* implicit in the drawing of the curtain because of the illusionary need for "rest." Appropriately, this Herod exploited almost none of the comic features normally associated with his audience contact; it is only when the actor, by threatening or raging, upset a sense of distance from within the *platea* or a *platea*-like position that the representational quality of the role disappeared, to be replaced by an anachronistic form of semiritual burlesque and self-expression.

The acting area itself had, of course, no inherent symbolic significance. It was, after all, a public festival ground that assumed a theatrical character only when an actor appeared to create a dramatic role. In transforming the public location into a dramatic setting the actor attempted to divest the *platea* of its public neutrality. But this transformation, if ever really achieved at all, was probably never complete. The surrounding audience, the festive atmosphere, and the temporal and physical realities of "putting on a play" were such immediate considerations that a permanent tension between fictive locality and public place must always be reckoned with.

Dramatic anachronism, so characteristic of the popular tradition, is rooted in this contradiction. Even when the anachronism expresses the general medieval attitude to all past history it is, in the theater, repeatedly emphasized by the audience-actor contact on the *platea*. On the popular Renaissance stage, in which the more direct or naive anachronism had already become secondary to the main or serious plot, it is invariably the figures close to the audience, especially the clowns and fools, who perpetuate the tradition of anachronism. Underlying this continuity are the assumptions of a theater that establishes a flexible relationship between the play world and the real world. One of the most interesting material and practical prerequisites for this relationship is the juxtaposition of the symbolic, representational dimension of the scaffold stage against the actual *platea* in the form of a street, a village green or a marketplace surrounded by spectators. What is involved, though, is not the *confrontation* of the world and time of the play with that of the audience, or any serious *opposition* between representational and non-representational standards of acting, but the most intense *interplay* of both. Such an interplay makes it ultimately impossible to assign to *platea* and *locus* any consistent and exclusive mode of acting. At the same time, this interplay allows (and, indeed, calls for) the mixture of the comic and the serious or the absence of a structural division between monologue and dialogue. In short, both *platea* and *locus* are related to specific locations and types of action and acting, but each is meaningless without the functioning assumptions of the other.

To illustrate the effect of the interplay of the two modes of drama, let us look for a moment at some aspects of anachronism in the *Ludus Coventriae*. Characteristically, anachronism is achieved by conjoining two levels of time or the opposite poles of *mimesis* (its *Subjekt*, or the actor, and its object, or the role). This is so when the religious anachronism in the mystery plays draws on the transcendental heritage of the liturgy as a *repraesentatio Christi*, although this kind of anachronism is hardly capable of further development. In the secular drama the future of anachronism lay in the traditional coexistence of specific dramatic, social, temporal, and sometimes even spatial positions. In the *Ludus Coventriae,* for example, there is a fundamental difference between the *platea* position of the "exposytour" and that of the judges enthroned in their high seats: while the former is envisioned within the context of the theatrical occasion, the judges are more closely associated with the time and theme of the biblical story.

But this example, obviously oversimplified, can only suggest a general principle. In the case of other clearly anachronistic figures, such as Joseph, the spatial position does not have a similar temporal equivalent. When he first appears in the twelfth play, *Joseph's Return*, Joseph must gain access to Mary in the *domus* from the *platea*. The noisy comedy of his appearance from outside ("Who is ther, why cry ʒe so," XII, 3) is quelled but quickly re-animated in a long complaint ("olde cokwold . . .," 55). When Joseph suspects that Mary has deceived him he prepares to leave their hut, i.e., the *locus:*

> Serteynly ʒitt had I levyr
> Ffor sake þe countre ffor evyr
> and nevyr come in here company
> Ffor and men knew þis velany
> In repreff þei wolde me holde
> and ʒett many bettyr than I
> ʒa · hath ben made cokolde
>
> Now alas whedyr xal I gone
> I wot nevyr whedyr nor to what place . . .

(111–19)

Joseph presumably moves into the "place" during this speech, for Mary does not acknowledge his presence in her next speech. She prays to God that He enlighten Joseph; and when her prayer is answered by an angel who descends to Joseph from a scaffold, Joseph is already outside the house. After Joseph has decided to return to his hut ("I walk to my pore place," 168) he thanks "þe god þat syttys on hye" (174) for the angel's explanation. In allowing him finally to enter, Mary ends a theatrical process in which meaning and movement are very closely related. It is a process that is anticipated at the beginning of the play and repeated later when Mary lies in childbed and the anxious Joseph sets out in search of a midwife (XV, 116–76).

While Angelus, Deus, and even Mary maintain an unapproachable position of dignity and aloofness in their *loca,* Joseph acts in quite a different manner. Once again, the nature of his acting is not mechanically determined by his *platea* position, but it does achieve its full significance only in terms of the social and spatial dimensions of the "place." Only here does the anachronism approach the standards and experience of the audience:

> ȝa ȝa all Olde men to me take tent
> and weddyth no wyff in no kynnys wyse
> þat is a ȝonge wench be myn a-sent . . .
>
> (49–51)
>
> Here may all men þis proverbe trow
> Þat many a man doth bete þe bow
> Another man hath þe brydde.
>
> (81–83)

This kind of self-expression is anachronistic in the sense that a contemporary perspective on everyday experience is being enacted. But such a perspective must not be dismissed lightly as comic relief, for it functions as a profoundly well-integrated part of the whole play. In these lines we find a comic challenge to the pathos of biblical myth, one that incorporates a popular experience through content, form, and delivery. Joseph dissociates himself from the world, the time, and the idiom of biblical myth, and in so doing achieves an unlocalized distance from the representational quality of all the *loca.* From this distance he can easily turn to the audience in direct address and appeal to their standards, which are contemporary with the subject (the actor), but not with the biblical object (the story), of *mimesis.* But Joseph's perspective is part of a larger whole, and it is the simultaneity of the contrast between, and the reference to, both worlds that is at the heart of the anachronism. In terms of dramaturgy, this is made possible by the spatial flexibility and the various verbal and dramatic correlatives of physical movement that the popular theater allowed. Against this, a wide spectrum of highly effective tensions and transitions between the world and time of the play and those of the players could be employed, together with corresponding transitions between illusion and convention, representation and self-expression, high seriousness, and low comedy—each drawing physically, socially, and dramatically on the interplay of *platea* and *locus*.

It is not primarily the absence of a historical perspective that is behind this sort of anachronism; rather, a positive principle is at work, according to which the actor may achieve both a specific degree of approach to, and dissociation from, the audience's world in order to move freely between the poles of subjectivity and objectivity, self-expression and representation. In so doing he uses certain conventions of speech and movement that roughly correspond to *locus* and *platea,* conventions by which the audience's world is made part of the play and the play is brought into the world of the audience. Consequently, the *platea* becomes part of the symbolic meaning of the play world, and the *locus* is made to support the dialectic of self-expression and representation. Thus, anachronism points to the contradiction between biblical myth and medieval reality as well as to the connection between subject-matter and interpretation, pathos and burlesque, seriousness and comedy.

Since dramatic meaning, especially meaning generated by anachronism, is so contingent upon the complex relationships established above, it seems extremely misleading to speak of realism and burlesque as just so much "temporary distraction and hence forgetfulness."[62] This is to misunderstand their functional nature completely. To dismiss them as mere "comic relief" is to ignore the way in which they are integrated into the larger theatrical process. With them contemporary reality, especially evident on the neutral *platea,* is projected right onto the scaffold or the pageant wagon to which Herod returns after his raging in the street. The same is true of the shepherds at Wakefield, who first appear in a *platea* position before they make their way to the hut in the pageant. Once the theatrical function of the resulting anachronism is related to the performance as a whole, the recent re-evaluation of the cycles by Eleanor Prosser, O. B. Hardison, Jr., W. M. Manly, and others must itself be reassessed insofar as it involves, among other things, a somewhat questionable attempt to come to terms with the realism and the "broad fun" of the mystery plays. With their literary bias (and their emphasis on orthodoxy) such approaches fail, notably, in the interpretation of "high fraud" and that "strangely comprehensive two-ways facingness" that M. M. Morgan and A. P. Rossiter have observed—phenomena that are difficult to understand fully unless the cycles are viewed as drama in performance. Although any new attempt to read the medieval drama not "as primitive works of art but the final outcome of a slowly developed growth" is only too welcome, a simple reassessment of its *literary* value does not seem to go far enough.[63] It is all very well to argue for the "dramatic artistry" of the plays, but this artistry is definitely one of the theater. An awareness of the theatrical dimensions of this drama can best illuminate those deeper ambiguities which undermine the supposed orthodoxy of some of the plays. Here is a mode of dramatic composition that lives on in Shakespeare's works, right down to "the constant Doubleness of the Shakespearean vision in the Histories" and "the general presence and principles of derisive, debunking, low or critical comedy or farce in the major tragedies."[64]

Already, this argument points beyond issues of production and raises problems of vision and perspective; in particular, it involves the quality of the dramatic and historical correlatives of *locus* and *platea*—a question that will be taken up more fully in the following chapter. Here it must suffice to emphasize the complexity of the social and theatrical functions of *locus* and *platea*. Their effectiveness, which results from the principle of complementarity, is easily underrated: between them, the symbolic forms of *mimesis* and the nonrepresentational modes of self-expression are joined in such a way that the increasing effect of similitude can in no way be opposed to the traditional and the religious elements of ritual. As in the folk play—although here rather in reversed proportion—festival and drama, self-expression and imitation interact; and it is the potency of this interaction on which the dramatic and theatrical vitality of the individual scene is finally based.

Hence the symbolic character of the *locus* and the neutrality of the *platea* are equally compatible with an almost naturalistic verisimilitude. There is "a sort of naive realism so characteristic of the folk play . . . together with an almost incredibly unassuming attitude towards matters of scenic illusion."[65] This accounts for the constant transitions between nonrepresentational and representational modes, between "convention" and "realism" which have been noted. The crucifixion at York, for example, is presented with a Gothic naturalism of detail in which the holes in the wood, the big hammers and long nails, the perforated bones and muscles and the tortured limbs of the crucified body are vividly shown (XXXV, 109–14; et passim). This often-quoted scene is not an exception, either; for in the *Ludus Coventriae*, too, the flesh and muscles seemed to be punctured by the nails, the body stretched with ropes and beaten "tyl he is alle bloody" (XXVI, 445–46; 726–53). There was no difference in this respect, then, between the pageant wagon in York and the place-and-scaffold theater in Lincoln. The medieval theater of France presented the same picture. One has only to look at the frightfully long pincers that threatened to tear the flesh from St. Apollonia's face while she was held down by her hair and stretched out on a rough board and trestle with tight ropes. Against this background, the anecdote described by the Puritan moralist Thomas Beard assumes some deeper significances: "In a certaine place there was acted a tragedie of the death and passion of Christ in show, but in deed of themselves": the actor who played Christ's part "hanging upon the Crosse, was wounded to death by him that should have thrust his sword into a bladder full of Bloud tyed to his side."[66]

As in the *mimus*, "show" and "deed," illusion and reality, can be easily confused. The cross of the actor playing the part of Christ marks a genuine *locus*, but this does not prevent the bloody confusion of role and actor. The bladder filled with animal blood affixed to the body of the crucified man serves to give an impression of verisimilitude, but the element of illusion, even though it applies only to dramatic detail, is confounded with the reality behind the role. On a different level, the shepherds at Wakefield wander over the moors before they reach the stable of Bethlehem. The unlocalized acting area is in Yorkshire, the stable—a *locus*—is more directly associated with biblical Palestine. But again there is a crucial interplay between reality and illusion: the stable stands on and in a public area (whether in front of, or on, the pageant, or in the round of a "place"). The physical presence of the amateur actor counterpoints the illusion of his role, but the illusions of biblical drama in their turn counterpoint the reality of the spectators who know that they have a part to play. This explains why the audience is constantly being addressed and drawn into the action—as servants, as young men and friends of the shepherds, as sinful mankind, as the Devil's accomplices, as people saved through Christ. Thus the more symbolic quality of the *locus* is projected into the *platea* or the street where it incorporates the reality of the audience's world just as the reality and the identity of the medieval festival-goer asserts itself in terms of the play's dramaturgy.

5

Realism and Folklore: Social Function and Dramatic Structure in the Shepherd Scenes

In several respects, important elements of the medieval theater were not far removed from the ritual occasion of the Sunday church service or the seasonal village festival. Still the high point of a communal Christian rite, dramatic performance was, obviously, itself a festival. But this does not mean that the medieval drama incarnated a ritual action, for although the representation of reality and the embodiment of ritual were still closely linked, drama was becoming a secular and purely theatrical activity. Unlike the congregation in the liturgy or the participants in a pagan ceremony, the medieval audience already understood itself to be witnessing a dramatic action that served chiefly not an effective or magical, but an affective and communicative, function. Similarly, while the distinction between performer and audience could be momentarily bridged, it had become too pronounced a separation to be permanently overcome. Ritual was being superseded by representation of an action analogous to what had once been the object of ceremony: instead of incarnation, there appeared similitude; instead of mythic identity, the object of imitation. This new, secular dramatic quality was, of course, to be of great consequence by the time the English popular tradition was received and assimilated by Shakespeare's theater.

Two scenes from the Wakefield Cycle may serve to illustrate this nascent mode of dramatic realism—its social origins and functions and the structure of its theatrical and verbal features. The shepherd scenes, especially the *Secunda Pastorum*,[67] have for a long time been rightly regarded as the finest poetic and dramatic achievements of the Towneley Cycle, and perhaps even "the high-water mark of the medieval drama" as a whole.[68] For this reason alone they occupy a special position in pre-Shakespearean stagecraft. These scenes embody a particularly forward-looking unity of poetic realism and theatrical convention in a mode of dramatic representation that incorporates traditional elements of folklore, utopianism, and corresponding standards of inversion which derive from sources and social attitudes that considerably predate the composition of the Wakefield Cycle. As nowhere else in the medieval drama these traditions are revived and, at the same time, completely transformed in the process of adapting new artistic principles to the popular theater.

In order to reconstruct these scenes in performance it will be useful to follow their spatial and verbal movement closely. The *Secunda Pastorum* opens with the appearance of the First Shepherd, whose introductory lines from the *platea* (close to the audience) reveal his dissatisfaction with the cold weather, the oppression by "gentlery-men" and the arbitrary behavior of the mighty, whose blustering, cruel, and unjust servants no one dares criticize (28–45). The First Shepherd then retires to look after his sheep (46–54) and the Second Shepherd enters to take up and supplement the introductory theme in carefully proportioned parallel to the First Shepherd's complaint (in six strophes, 55–108). His expository speech, again adjusted in imagery and content to a contemporary context (a function of the *platea*), deals primarily with domestic life—with a wife who is "as sharp as thistle, as rough as a briar." Speaking directly to the young men in the audience, he teaches, in proverb form, the folly of a hasty marriage (93).

This narrative speech, which is not so much a monologue as was the Shepherd's self-introduction, is interrupted by the First Shepherd's greeting. A transition from the actor-audience "monologue" to an actor-actor dialogue follows as a dramatic illusion is created in which the content of the initial narrative is re-enacted.

First Shepherd interrupts him:

1. *Pastor.* God looke ouer the raw! Full defly ye stand.
2. *Pastor.* Yee, the dewill in thi maw, so tariand!
          Sagh thou awre of Daw?
1. *Pastor.* Yee, on a ley-land
          Hard I hym blaw.

(109–13)

The First Shepherd, who has been wandering "alone" since the end of his speech in line 54, again comes to the fore with a direct address ("God looke ouer the raw!") in an attempt to rouse the attention and good will of the audience. He then turns to his companion, making the transition to dialogue: "Full defly ye stand."[69] The time that has elapsed during the Second Shepherd's self-introduction furnishes the grounds for a re-proach, by which means the Shepherd's narrative voice (associated with the *platea*, close to the audience) is gracefully transformed into a representational mode: "Yee, the dewill in thi maw, so tariand!" The shift to representation is achieved when the First Shepherd's "wandering" (a nonrepresentational process or attitude bridging the span of time when the Second Shepherd was addressing the audience) is reinterpreted as "tarrying." In this way the *platea* position of the actor is in some measure localized, and, what is more, since the actual process of localization is, as it were, dramatized, it provides a cue for the entrance of Daw, the youngest and poorest shepherd.

Daw repeats and underscores the close interaction of representational and nonrepresentational forms of acting. An opening "monologue" (118–35) again takes up and heightens the theme of the shepherds' hard life, and so further defines a basic theme of the play. The transition to a representational mode is once again effected with remarkable ease: young Daw, making his approach, appears not to recognize the shepherds who are eating their meal. As he nears their camp (a *locus*) from a *platea*-like position, he abandons the time of the real world—the daylight hour of the performance—for the time of the play world, which is identified with the self-contained, farther-removed, position of the shepherds' camp. For those in the camp it is night, and in keeping with the illusion of darkness the actor of Daw pretends to mistake the shepherds for ruffians. Presently, when he "discovers" his mistake, he asks them for food and drink, only to be repulsed by the older shepherds, who berate him for his laziness and tardiness. The enactment of Daw's appearance—an otherwise conventional movement—thus becomes a vehicle of characterization.

The general introduction of the shepherds concludes with a short dialogue (172–89) and a song. The song serves to solidify the relationship between the shepherds who have been introduced separately. But again, the nonrepresentational act of singing achieves a newly representational function, for as we learn in line 182, the song helps to make the night pass quickly. Just as the dialogue grew out of an unlocalized address to the audience, the self-expression contained in the song develops here from a previously established dramatic situation through which the song is psychologically motivated. Again we find the same interplay of dramatic modes that persisted through the moralities down to Shakespeare, and which we will find again in the dialogue of *Hamlet*.[70]

The entrance of Mak, a notorious sheep thief, opens the central dramatic episode in which the two introductory themes—the shepherds' misery and domestic strife—are taken up and dramatized in terms of a highly original comic conflict. Basically, the plot involves a burlesque anticipation and inversion of the birth of Christ in the stable at Bethlehem, which is carefully set up, first, in Mak's self-introduction:

> . . . thi will, Lorde, of me tharnys.
> I am all vneuen; that moves oft my harnes.
> Now wold God I were in heuen, for ther wepe no barnes
> So styll.
>
> (191–94)

Mak's own predicament—"I am all vneuen"—is, from the start, so clearly related to the larger themes that it contributes a serious plausibility to the action that follows: crying children are the result of social, and the cause of domestic, misery. Mak's troubles are not all that ridiculous, for his experience, as the First Shepherd suggests, is essentially that of the others: Mak is a "man that walkys on the moore" and "has not all his wyll" (197–98). This comment echoes the First Shepherd's serious speech about "selys husbandys that walkys on the more" (110), and places Mak nearly on the same level with all those who are "rammed," "fortaxed," and "handtamed." But Mak is unique; his unevenness extends to the strange disguise that he wears, "that Sothren tothe" in which he speaks and his boasts of being the vassal of a "greatt lordyng." This last dissimulation is not clearly motivated; and it remains somewhat doubtful whether, as some scholars suggest, it may be taken as a burlesque image of the infamous lord's servant referred to in the introductory speeches. The wide sleeves of the lackey's costume (189–90; 200) might support the comparison, but they may simply have been a good place to hide stolen goods. But whether Mak's role is that of the "burlesque maintained man"[71] or not, he is, from the start, bent on inversion.

Detected at once, Mak complains of hunger, domestic strife, and a house full of brood. As soon as the shepherds retire for the night, Mak recites a topsy-turvy bedtime prayer ("Manus tuas commendo, Poncio Pilato"), and casts a kind of magic spell over the shepherds that puts them into a deep, snoring sleep, as Mak says to the audience, a sleep that "may ye all hear" (287). This comment reaffirms the burlesque actor's ability to distance himself from the more representational level of the *locus* (the shepherds' camp) and from the illusion associated with the serious theme. While the shepherds snore Mak gets up, steals a sheep and goes off to his hut across the pageant stage, where he is met with his wife's unfriendly words:

> Mak.   ... How, Gyll, art thou in? Gett vs som lyght.
> Vxor eius. Whor makys sich dyn this tyme of the nyght?
> I am sett for to spyn; I hope not I myght
> Ryse a penny to wyn, I shrew them on hight!
> So farys
> A huswyff that has bene
> To be rasyd thus betwene.
> Here may no note be sene
> For sich small charys.
>
> (296–304)

Although the hut clearly represents a *locus*, it remains always in contact with the *platea* (or with an acting area functionally related to the *platea*). The interplay between *platea* and *locus* is here reflected in the transition between two distinct kinds of dramatic speech: the representational, illusionistic dialogue related to the *domus* (the late hour, the supposed darkness and the hut's closed door) and the speech that distances the time and place of this action. Gyll's remarks therefore fall into two general categories: dialogue used to answer Mak's partially understood or deliberately misunderstood entreaties to be let in, and a more general and explanatory solo speech that is addressed to the audience (300–304).

The expression "So farys" introduces the transition from the illusion of dialogue back to a less representational and more general speech. Corresponding to the later Elizabethan "thus" or "such," "So farys" is associated with a theatrical movement that it underlines, while at the same time it signals a change in "voice" without disrupting the smooth flow of verbal and physical action. The words that follow "So farys" are not primarily intended for Mak, the partner in dialogue; they do not express the *role* of Gyll, but reflect instead the self-expressed perspective of an actor who knows his own experience to be like that of the audience. The wonderful realism of this speech arises from a traditional form of stagecraft which so combines *locus* and *platea* conventions that the imitation of the tale and the re-enactment of the plebeian world become indivisible.

Having left off spinning, Gyll lets Mak into the house where they decide to disguise the stolen sheep as their newborn son. Mak returns to the sleeping shepherds and, pretending to awaken with the rest, tells them that he has dreamt that Gyll gave birth to a son early that morning. The two basic themes of the play coalesce in Mak's subsequent lament: "Wo is hym has many barnes,/ And therto lytyll brede" (393-94). Mak then returns, unsuspected, to his hut and lays the disguised sheep in the cradle. Meanwhile, having discovered the theft, the shepherds proceed to Mak's *domus* where Gyll lies groaning in childbed (476 ff.). To clear himself of suspicion, Mak suggests that the hut be searched. Finding no sheep, the shepherds take their leave, but return immediately, having thought to leave some presents for the newborn "day-starne" (577). When the Third Shepherd tries to put sixpence into the cradle and hold the child, the fraud is discovered. Mak and Gyll at first insist that the horned creature is indeed their child over whom a magic spell has been cast (584-619), but finally they relent and plead for mercy. The shepherds decide to deal mildly with this normally serious trespass and only toss Mak in a blanket (625-28).

As the shepherds return to the fields, weary after the punishment, an angel appears (on an "vpward" scaffold) to tell them, in a dream, of the birth of Christ and invite them to pay tribute to the child at his poor stable in Bethlehem. The shepherds approach the stable—very likely the same hut in which Gyll has just enacted the grotesque childbed scene— and find the Christ child. They give to their "day-starne" (727) a handful of cherries, a bird, and a tennis ball (710-36), and are blessed by Mary. The scene ends with a song.

Of the 754 lines in the *Secunda Pastorum* fewer than 120 are based on its biblical source. Any reasonable interpretation of this play must, therefore, reckon fully with the sheer length of the comic secular parts. It is notable that the entire exposition, the central episode which follows, and all the comic and burlesque elements are either derived from folklore or come directly from contemporary experience. Such an astonishing preponderance of secular sources (which, to be sure, is quite the exception in mystery plays) cannot be viewed as a simple contrast to the Christian story of the final part, as, again, just so much comic relief or "broad fun." Between the *mimus* of Wakefield and the myth of Bethlehem there exists a structural relationship that in its own way anticipates some of the most effective correlations of serious and comic themes in Shakespeare's plays. For the Wakefield Master, as for the Elizabethan playwright, the multiple stage was broad enough to allow free movement between high and low, or to shift the dramatic action from Palestine to Yorkshire. The artistic criterion of unity, then, did not rely on the unity of place and time but on the structural interplay between the different modes and parts of the performance. The mythical or legendary past and the temporal present are related to each other through a dramatic method expressive of a theater in which people present their own history while telling the story of the Bible.

Scholars who have studied the folklore background of the Mak episode have found a number of comparable stories in which a sheep or other stolen property is hidden under quite similar conditions. These and other parallels that suggest folklore origins indicate that the basic motif was not original to the Wakefield Master. But, on the other hand, a careful comparison of the extant versions reveals that the Wakefield Master consistently transformed his folklore sources so as to achieve a striking burlesque inversion of the sacred events in the stable at Bethlehem.[72] And so, while many elements in the *Secunda Pastorum* have recognizable popular analogues, actions such as the burlesque announcement of the birth of Mak's "child" through a dream vision, which motivates Mak's departure from the shepherds' camp, are quite unique, as are the coupling of the cradle with the farcical childbed scene, Mak's pleading that his wife "in childbed" be spared, and the shepherds' gift to the monstrous newborn "child."

The burlesque anticipation of the sacred events in Bethlehem is mirrored repeatedly in the shepherd's speech: the Christ child in Bethlehem is called "day-starne," but so is the monstrosity in Gyll's cradle. Such parallels may be said to extend even into Mak's grotesque protestations that magic played a part in the birth of his son. Parallels such as these recall corresponding elements in the *Prima Pastorum,* as well as the burlesque interpretation of the angel's prophecy in the Chester shepherd's play (VII, 369–414) and in the *Ludus Coventriae* (XVI, 78–85). Here, then, is a striking instance of the "zest for unholiness," that irreverent tradition of folk mimicry which from time immemorial had repeatedly turned the sacred into the lowly and confronted a mythic world with the real one. However, it would be superficial to suppose that the blasphemous elements in the Wakefield Master's parody are consciously irreligious. The lyrical intensity of the scene in Bethlehem, like much else in the work, reveals an unquestionably profound Christian attitude. But it would be equally misleading simply to equate the author's basic attitudes with those of the contemporary orthodox church. Characteristically, his dependence on New Testament sources for the language of the play is slight.[73] Keeping in mind always the primary importance of the biblical source and point of view, it seems safe to say, nevertheless, that the Wakefield Master depicts the "low" life of the common people, and that in the presentation of the nature and dynamics of that life we have not only the piety of a sincerely conceived plebeian version of biblical myth, but a dramatic parody of that myth as well. It is still the Christian message that informs the drama, but that message has already become subjected to the *ohm,* or representational measuring, of some popular *mimesis.*

Yet it is not primarily the contemporary theme and not simply the native background that define the new dramatic realism. It is, rather, a new dramatic mode whereby the depiction of events and the development of character are so achieved through action, dialogue, and self-expression that there results a dramatically coherent perspective on the world as it is. As the shepherds wrench Mak's supposedly stiff neck back into place, this new unity of word and action becomes quite evident.

> A! my nek has lygen wrang
> Enoghe.
> Mekill thank!
>
> (380 ff.)

This is precisely the kind of dramatic speech that we find, say, in Lear's befuddled exchange with Gloucester, or in his "Now, now, now, now. Pull off my boots. Harder, harder—so." In each case a remarkable interplay of physical action and verbal expression, a full integration of gesture into the texture and rhythm of dialogue, is achieved. It is no coincidence that this kind of verbal realism, applied here as a vehicle of parody and inversion (in the context of Mak's "spell" and inverted prayer), can also be found to some degree in figures such as Herod, Cain, Garcio, Noah's wife, and the shepherds of the *Prima Pastorum.*

It is this new dramatic unity of language and action that helps neutralize the inherited contradiction between representation and embodiment, between the mimetic and the ritual; and it is the conjoining of these two modes of performance that accompanies and reflects what Erich Auerbach has described as a "dynamic need for self-orientation."[74] What is involved is the dramatic form of a plebeian self-representation in a world that has arrived at an aesthetic awareness of its own historical existence. Extending right into the nature of dramatic production itself, this historical context becomes inseparable from the Christian message. The way plebeian religion and the "need for self-orientation" are linked is not, of course, original to the Wakefield Master. Their linking was anticipated by late medieval Lollard heresies which provided an active breeding-ground for a mode of thought that connected social discontent with religious heresy.[75] One might reasonably ask, then, if any relationship existed between this movement and the social criticism of the Wakefield poet. The reference to Tutivillus as "master-lollar" (XXX, 213) does establish some relationship between the scenes written ca. 1450–60 and the contemporary social and religious movement. Considering the social context of the work as a whole, though, the reference is best considered ambivalent. Opposition to the Lollard view could, as Millicent Carey suggests, just as easily arise out of a more radical instead of a conformist attitude. If Wycliffe's admonitions to unruly laborers and his appeals for "pacience" and "mekenesse" are taken into account, then the First Shepherd's speech cited above (p. 64) might even be understood as a protest against such preaching.[76] Unlike Wycliffe, the poet envisioned the peasants in opposition to the lords and their servants. The treatment of the poor shepherd Daw (XIII, 154-71) does not accord with the ideas of Wycliffe and the older learned Lollards who were more likely to articulate the needs of the poorer gentry and less privileged landowners.[77] The Wakefield poet's perspective on society was more closely in line with the class struggles that culminated in the 1381 Peasants' War, thus covering a middle ground between John Ball's revolutionary preaching and the more reformist idealism of *Piers Plowman*.

Although definitely not anti-Christian, both the Wakefield poet's burlesque and his social criticism do exhibit certain heretical features. Only recently has the "proletarian irreverence and popular scepticism" that underlies early Protestant dissent been more fully studied. As A. G. Dickens has shown, this naive "popular heresy," largely independent of the Lollards' theoretical dispute, usually avoided the martyrdom of outright Protestantism. But there was a deeply rooted "ground-swell of popular dissent," a movement that continued into the Tudor period and found its last and broadest expression in the more radical revolutionary sects in the Civil War.[78] As J. A. F. Thomson has suggested, this form of popular dissent might also attach itself to the vestiges of an age-old pagan culture. For instance, there is evidence of the inversion of the Paternoster, the worship of the sun and moon, the use of pagan spells, and other "popular prejudices" in the context of popular heresy.[79]

It seems noteworthy that the lower clergy (of which the Wakefield poet was probably a member) was in several respects quite close to some parts of this movement. His extensive knowledge of the life of the rural populace, unlike other biographical data, is a proven fact. He may well have been familiar not only with the traditions of the folk, but also with some of the expressions of the popular heresy. Placing a swathed sheep in the Wakefield/Bethlehem cradle recalls, to a certain extent, the attitudes of the later heretic Roger Gargrave, also of Wakefield, who openly declared "that if a calff were uponn the altar I wold rather worship that than the said holy sacrament."[80] Images such as this, like the folklore sources, were, of course, of pre-Lollard origin.

These contemporary links do not reflect significantly on the quality of the Wakefield Master's dramatic inversion of the Nativity. But they can help to place that inversion in a broader social context which, being part of the world of history, points beyond the timeless tradition of folklore. In this larger world of history, the dramatic expression (and correlation) of both a social movement and a culture that remembers old ritual license seems as significant as it certainly was spontaneous. But this correlation was part of a tradition of popular acting that culminated in the sixteenth-century moralities in which, in the context of Christian allegory, a critical sense of reality and a penchant for heresy can be found alongside the fantastic, the grotesque, or the utopian. Once again, the most disenchanting criticism and parody meets and merges with the enchanting, "magical" potential of *mimesis*. Thus while the world of biblical myth is revitalized in the Towneley plays, it is also, and at the same time, correlated with some realistic parody. What is more, the ensuing temporary disenchantment is achieved through the poet's recollection and comic use of another mode of enchantment (the grotesque idea of magic implicit in Mak and Gyll's protestations that the horned animal is their enchanted son, as well as in Mak's earlier pagan spell and his unmotivated disguise).

The drama of popular enchantment finds an altogether different version in the *Prima Pastorum,* where it takes the form of a temporary naive utopia, an imaginary world of summer and abundance. The utopian element in the shepherd scenes would seem, at first, to have no connection whatever with the tradition of dramatic parody; but parody and utopianism both develop from a comparable process of inversion, albeit one that here works in opposite directions: the dramatic parody inverts the mythical world, while utopia inverts the real world. Thus, in the *Prima Pastorum,* Gyb and Horne, like the "foles of gotham" (XII, 180), find themselves engaged in a strange quarrel: Gyb wishes to drive a flock of imaginary sheep ("an illusion of abundance")[81] across the stage while Horne tries to stop him. Like the First Shepherd's "bob of cherys" in the *Secunda Pastorum* or the red cherries also picked out of season in *Ludus Coventriae* (XV, 32–42), the imaginary flock in the *Prima Pastorum* sets the stage for a utopian vision of the good life. Jack Garcio underscores the significance of Gyb and Horne's argument on Christmas eve when he reports that the sheep are grazing knee-deep in grass (189). Like the famous Christmas cherries in the romance of Sir Cleges, these symbols of wintertime fertility represent "tokenyng/ Off mour godnes that is comyng;/ We shall haue mour plenté."[82]

In the *Prima Pastorum* the shepherds sit down to a sparse meal with the question "what is drynk withoute mete?" But then the unexpected happens: a sumptuous meal of calf's foot, pig's trotters, black pudding with liver sauce, roast beef and veal, and boiled and fried meats appears. This peasant's dream of a feast is indiscriminately mixed up with dishes from a nobleman's table: "tart for a lorde," chicken in egg yolk, partridge and chopped calf's liver in grape juice, and other delicacies follow. It is this combination of "high class and low class delicacies" that may give the scene some "humor of incongruity."[83] At the same time, however, this combination allows for a sense of temporary social unity. For here, as in the Cokaygne poem, the utopian conception of plenty entails more than mere gluttony; the idea of brotherly good-fellowship accompanies the feast. The shepherds at once stop grumbling. Slawpase, cursed by the First Shepherd, returns only kind words:

1. Pastor. ... Thou has euer bene curst syn we met togeder.
3. Pastor. Now in fayth, if I durst ye ar euen my broder.

(206–7)

In a similar scene at Chester stress is likewise placed on the way that each shepherd contributes his small part to the common meal (VII, 105–44). In Wakefield, embraces and a song follow; and when Slawpase does not get his share of the toast and calls his fellow shepherds "knafys" and wishes them to the devil, they invert and re-interpret his remark in good-natured wordplay:

3. Pastor. Ye be both knafys.
1. Pastor. Nay, we knaues all; thus thynk me best,
              So, syr, shuld ye call.
2. Pastor. Furth let it rest;
              We will not brall.

(277–80)

This alters Slawpase's mood to the extent that when Gyb decides to pack up the tasty roast Slawpase suggests that the meat be shared with the poor men.

But if the shepherds' feast were realistically presented in an elaborate scene, the dishes must have been visible, even if time might not have allowed their complete consumption on stage. May we not assume, then, that the delicacies named above did not remain on the stage but were passed out amongst the audience? Such an extradramatic action would explain the First Shepherd's otherwise obscure remark, "Geder yp, lo, lo,/ Ye hungre begers, frerys!" (285–86), as well as the Second Shepherd's comment that follows: "It draes nere nyght. Trus, go we to rest" (287). A. C. Cawley's suggestion that imaginary dishes were taken from empty bags (in the similar Chester scene, VII, 105–56) would simply not be very effective theater. In any event, the account books show that a good part of the high cost of these shows was spent for food, drink, and "rejoicing."[84]

If correct, this interpretation confirms an audience contact that was certainly characteristic of the shepherds and which differed considerably from the audience contact of Herod, Pilate, and other biblical figures. The shepherds' songs (found in almost all of the cycles—York XV, 64–65, 85–86; Chester VII, 172–73, 458–59; Coventry 277–78, etc.) offer a marked contrast to the frightening comedy of the tyrants and ragers. The concluding words at York are characteristic of the cheerful mood set by these songs:

And go we hame agayne,
And make mirthe as we gange.

(XV, 130–31)

"Home" is in Yorkshire, and this mirthful departure leads the actors
through the standing crowd. Their stage position while singing is quite
close to the audience; at Coventry they walk across the "place" and
through the crowd as they sing:

> There the scheppardis syngith ageyne and goth
> forthe of the place . . .

(331–32)

Recalling that in the early morality *Mankind* the yeoman audience
(326) is still encouraged to join in an obscene "crystmes songe" (325), it is
not improbable that here, too, in the shepherd scenes, the audience
joined in to the best of its ability. The Second Shepherd of York, at any
rate, puts everything he has into it:

> Ha! Ha! þis was a mery note,
> Be the dede þat I sall dye,
> I haue so crakid my throte,
> Þat my lippis are nere drye.

(XV, 65–68)

But the jolly song ending here in mirth already has a burlesque dramatic
function as an answer to the angel's *gloria in excelsis Deo.* This is also clear
in the *Ludus Coventriae*, where the second shepherd repeats the *"Gloria"*
of the angels as *gle glo glas glum* (XVI, 85), and at Chester, where it is
misunderstood as *glore* and *glere* and followed by a "merry song" (VII,
372, 411, 454).[85]

In addition to the widespread singing of songs and the shepherds'
direct address to the audience, a heightened actor-audience relationship
is underscored by the frequent use of proverbs (XII, 97, 100, 139, 150,
200, 220, 222, etc.). No biblical play contains more proverbs than the
Second Shepherd's pageant;[86] and proverbs are most in evidence where
the popular tradition is most pronounced. In its own limited way the
proverb represents dramatic anachronism *par excellence:* sometimes a
reading of past myth in terms of present experience. It is no accident
that it is frequently couched in direct address to the audience and connected usually with the world of common experience. Appropriately, it
is not the orthodox biblical characters who tend to use proverbial speech,
but Garcio and the shepherds, the demons and devils, and the Vice in
the later moralities.[87]

The grotesque shepherds' feast, like the inversion of the angel's song,
must serve as a paradigm of a drama that merged representational play
with popular festival. Here the function of the theater itself is utopian,
bringing regeneration to the spirit and solidarity to the community. It is
a theater old and new, but consistently original in its incipient awareness
of the spatial, temporal, verbal, and emotional correlatives of dramatic

action. It is a religious theater that developed a new type of secular drama, interrelating the message of Christianity, the representation of society and the self-expression of ordinary people. It achieved this synthesis by providing new modes of correlation between *locus* and *platea*, dramatic role and self-expressive action, mimetic realism and festive convention. In all that, the cycles placed the popular tradition in a wider social context and, by doing so, began to point beyond the tradition.

IV

MORALITIES
AND INTERLUDES

To survey the nature and continuity of the popular tradition in the
moralities and interludes is always to be aware of its changing context
and increasingly complex social foundations. While the mystery plays
were intimately related to the social structure of the medieval town and
guild system and to the relatively static quality of life in pre-Reformation
England, the moralities and interludes began to respond to the needs of
a more dynamic society in which audiences might be assumed to display
more variable attitudes toward, and degrees of familiarity with, popular
cultural traditions. The collective organization of the Corpus Christi
play, which remained close to the spirit and restrictions of the old faith,
interfered—given its severely limited ability to adjust to new religious
and social attitudes—with the thrust of the reformed national Church
and with the nascent spirit of acquisition and individualism. The
morality play, on the other hand, was much more diversified and capable of change. It readily adjusted to economic, social, and political shifts,
and actually thrived on the transition from a lay to a professional theater; at the same time, it easily received the new national, Protestant, and
humanist ideology. But in adjusting to a transformed environment, the
popular tradition in the morality also changed, adapting itself to the new
social milieu with its secular humanism and postfeudal political assumptions. This change, which in the long run helped to perpetuate the
popular tradition until Shakespeare's time, is not, however, sufficiently
linear or indeed coherent to permit its reduction to one schematic formula. Long before the last of the great cycles were discontinued, new
dramatic forms were as varied as the social strata among which the
tradition of the popular theater was, in varying degrees of continuity
and discontinuity, either carried on, changed, or rejected.

A good many of the new elements developed in close contact with the court. The rise of the Tudors was based on a centralization of economic and political power, but one that proceeded at a very considerable remove from the traditional social structure of the medieval country town or the largely immobile peasantry of the feudal era. The growing political and intellectual importance of the propertied bourgeoisie and rising gentry and the role of the English court, as a center from which the new spirit and the activities of the humanists radiated, made the older communal drama appear outmoded. At the same time there were fresh opportunities for actors; the New Monarchy fostered a remarkable upsurge in musical and dramatic entertainment at the courts of the Tudors, their chancellors, and Cardinals. As early as 1490 the choirboys and gentlemen of the Chapel Royal were brought to court to perform plays, and by 1494 at the latest the economical first Tudor monarch had introduced four *lusores regis, alias . . . Les pleyars of the kyngs enterluds* into his household.[1] As the sixteenth century advanced, cultural and theatrical activities at the universities and schools proliferated, a good many of which were learned and strictly humanist. These activities offered almost no direct points of contact with the great medieval theatrical experience of the English people, or with any of the more ancient semidramatic customs of the folk or, for that matter, with the newly uprooted heirs of the popular traditions of miming and juggling, who in their own ways adapted and enhanced the possibilities of the secular medieval traditions of acting and performance.[2]

But the foundations and social assumptions of early Tudor drama were to become even more varied and complex. As a result of the administrative and financial cooperation between the monarchy, the gentry and rich merchants (such as the Greshams), and through the advancement at court of talented members of the middle class (politicians and diplomats like Cromwell and Starkey, artists like Rastell and Heywood), the social boundaries that delimited the class of those enjoying the privilege of education also shifted. What was even more important, as a result of the growing economic power, political influence, and newfound social position of the gentry and bourgeoisie, an increasingly marked process of social and cultural differentiation developed between those groups on the one hand, and the plebeian and peasant masses on the other. This process reached its first climax in the period of the English revolution, although for more than a century before that date it had been almost imperceptibly affecting the background and social assumptions of the popular tradition in the theater. By the time that the leading London bourgeoisie, followed by that of many other larger towns, attempted to suppress stage plays altogether, this differentiation had crystalized into a more or less discernible dichotomy. But well before this time the middle class representatives of humanism were moving away from the social origins of the traditional culture. Its foundations—

among the peasant population and the servingmen and craftsmen—
were either threatened by vast economic and political changes or were
considerably removed from the centers of the new learning. Consequently, these strata had only limited control over the ways in which
the tradition of popular miming was adapted to the needs and opportunities of a changing society.

Yet the popular tradition was the only theatrical heritage that was
really alive and fully adaptable. And as long as the new classicism, the
humanist ideology, and the Puritan consciousness of the middle classes
had not assumed a position of pre-eminence, there was still—for about a
century to come—the possibility of continuity through change. Even
more importantly, a dividing line between the new court culture, the
activities of humanism, the cultural aspirations of the propertied middle
class and gentry, and the traditional culture of the plebeian strata was
still not rigidly drawn. Under the conditions of the Tudor compromise
the emerging class antagonism was not primarily of ideological or cultural consequence, and it was, in any case, countered by the overriding
need for antifeudal or national unity. As long as the New Monarchy
retained its unifying position of pre-eminence and balance in the nation,
the various economic and social contradictions could still be effectively
contained within the Tudor settlement; and the new secular drama
could, even when it responded to audiences that were much more socially varied, move within the mainstream of the popular tradition as the
most central and practical constituent of the new, distinctly national
culture in the theater.

1

Outdoor and Indoor Stages:
Toward a Theater of the Nation

Even the most general survey of the newly diversified dramatic forms
commonly referred to as moralities and interludes would have to distinguish at least three basic types of theatrical entertainment. The first was
characterized by the large communal circular theater, such as that used
for the open-air performance of an early long play like *The Castle of
Perseverance* (1400–1405). Shorter plays, at first barely 1,000 lines, acted
by traveling troupes of four or five players on various occasions in different places for town and country middle-class audiences made up a
second type. These plays (like *Mankind, Hickscorner, Youth*) became
longer and probably more respectable when the troupes grew to seven
or eight actors after about 1500. Such longer new plays included *Like
Will to Like* (1,277 lines), *All For Money* (1,572 lines), *The Tide Tarrieth No*

Man (1,879 lines), and *Common Conditions* (1,904 lines). The third type was the theater in the hall, as used at court and in humanist or academic circles, where the morality or the more openly recreational interlude lent themselves to the treatment of themes sparked by humanism or the Reformation. The writers of these entertainments (Medwall, Skelton, Rastell, Bale), revealing a new sense of individualism, did not remain anonymous as did their predecessors. Their plays—*Nature*, *Fulgens and Lucrece*, *Magnificence*, *The Four Elements*, *King Johan*—broke new ground from both a thematic and a structural point of view, but still maintained contact with important popular conventions, even when these were considerably modified or transformed in the new context of indoor social recreation.

Thanks to the efforts of modern scholars like Richard Southern, T. W. Craik, David Bevington, Richard Hosley, Glynne Wickham, and others, the stagecraft and dramatic assumptions of the moralities, interludes, and later hybrid plays can now be viewed less speculatively than a generation ago. The place-and-scaffold theater of the late medieval tradition (*Ludus Coventriae*, *The Play of the Sacrament*) was not abruptly discontinued, but remained in use for such early moralities as *The Castle of Perseverance* or *The Pride of Life* (1400–1425), and also for *The Satire of the Three Estates* (1540), which was performed before the King at the Scottish court. Even when the large communal circular theater was no longer suitable for the more readily improvised social recreation, some of its basic conventions of acting and audience contact persisted. The *platea*, for instance, remained an important element in the unspecified acting area restricted by "dores" in *Magnificence* and similar plays written presumably for indoor performance. This indoor "place" must have been relatively small, with a mode of production that was more "focused" or "unified" than the traditional "dispersed" or multiple technique that was associated with the various scaffolds in the larger outdoor theater in the round. Once the more focused mode of presentation (which itself had precedents in the popular booth stage or the pageant wagon as a "stage on wheels") gained ground, the stage was set, so to speak, for the increasing importance of an actual indoor stage or a raised platform structure, especially after the mid-sixteenth century. At court and in schools, properties, decorations, and "houses" certainly came to the fore; and, under certain circumstances, their traditional function as *décors simultané* was so modified as to incorporate the more courtly or sophisticated standards "after the maner of Italie" (which Hall noted as early as 1512 in connection with a royal masque) and, especially, the results of neoclassical studies and experiments which led to Sebastiano Serlio's *Architettura* (1551) and the perspective settings of the *Teatro Olimpico* (1580–84) in Vicenza.

But unlike the Italian neoclassical stage, the English indoor theater continued to encourage performance close to the spectators. The addition of a "house" or "mansion" in an academic or courtly production did not upset the basic principles of a stagecraft based on representation through formal symbols. The original "place," retaining its basic character from the open-air acting area, was adjusted to the hall situation, and, although the new theater was utterly different physically, it maintained essentially traditional functions and techniques of production.[3] The smaller indoor space now combined elements of the *platea* with those of a *domus* or mansion. The actors, while still accustomed to enter in the midst of the audience, gained a new and somewhat more symbolic kind of locality: the dramatically important "within." *Platea* and *locus*, then, became more immediately interrelated; the actor's exit and entrance through "dores" or curtains was now more directly related to, and motivated by, the actual content of the dramatic action, such as the dramatic image of leave-taking, returning home, or visiting.

Since the doors, of which there is considerable evidence, were almost certainly identical with the screen doors in a Tudor hall (such as that at Hampton Court Palace), their theatrical use is bound to have brought the actors into almost physical contact with the spectators filling the front side and upper halves of the hall. Again, if the two hall entrances remained uncovered, they must have anticipated the function of the two big doors in the tiring-house facade of the Swan stage. A more detailed comparison of these rear doors reveals many similarities, including the gallery which can be seen both in the Swan drawing and above the screen doors of the Tudor hall. The obvious difference is, of course, that the Elizabethan public theater had a raised stage in the form of a partly roofed-over platform which could not have arisen out of the hall theater but more probably descended from the platform-and-scaffold theater and the stage practices of the inn courtyard.

The indoor interlude theater, then, derives from various sources, the combination of which already—from a sociological point of view— heralded the cultural synthesis of the Shakespearean stage. What remains significant is the fact that a good many of the theatrical traditions that were associated with the older circular theater and the popular stage play of the inn courtyards lived on in the courtly, aristocratic, or upper middle class surroundings of the Tudor hall, not the least of which was a good deal of the old audience contact.

The actors still rubbed shoulders with the plebeian element in the audience, so that in a play like *Youth* the main actor, as E. K. Chambers remarked, "enters for all the world like the St. George of a village mummers' play,"[4] with "A backe, felowes, and gyve me roume" (39). Here as elsewhere in the theater of the hall the actors behaved as if they had to force their way from the doors to the "place." The traditional call for "room" rang out again and again, but not from the lips of all the actors: those who impersonated the virtuous and pious figures never indulged in this kind of audience address. It is significant indeed that the traditional convention of popular audience address remained a trait of the comic or disreputable characters. It was they who broke through the illusion of their role and, in their remarkable capacity for self-expression, involved the least dignified members of the audience in the play world (these actors would "rub shoulders all the time with the inferior members of their audience").[5] But what is astonishing is that such traditional interplay of representational and nonrepresentational modes of drama was not, as E. K. Chambers said about audience contact, restricted to the "more homely interlude"; rather, the popular heritage of self-expression and self-introduction was accepted by the new courtly and scholarly dramatists like Medwall or Skelton, who used the traditional convention before educated upper-class or aristocratic audiences. The resulting tension between the incipient techniques of verisimilitude and an awareness of the festive occasion, and the underlying contradictions between role and actor were effectively stylized in *Fulgens and Lucrece*, where the interplay of illusion and reality was itself turned into dramatic action.

The early Tudor dramatists, in drawing upon important popular conventions, employed them in the service of new secular and social meanings. But it was precisely because they did not ignore the practical experience of the popular theater that the originality of their contribution in its turn promoted the development of a more national theater, one not narrowly limited by the tastes and experience of a privileged audience but one considerably more universal in appeal. As in *Magnificence*, it was the consciousness of a secularized society and the belief in a new nationalism that broke up the pattern of allegorical abstractions: the struggle between good and evil advisers around "a prynce of great myght" replaced the traditional conflict between Virtue and Vice. Here, indeed, was a most advanced sense of political responsibility and a consciousness that allowed for the most generalized and profound expression of "howe the worlde comberyd is." But the author, laureate of both the English universities and, according to Erasmus, *unum Britannicarum literarum lumen ac decus*, did not conceive the play exclusively for the benefit of an academic or courtly audience, but in such a way that it could be performed by a small group of five strolling players anywhere in the country. Thus a play experimenting with a deliberate variety of verse and presumably intended for performance at court was virtually designed for popular touring.[6]

Like the courtier Skelton and Bishop John Bale, the humanist group associated with John Rastell, Thomas More's brother-in-law, also endeavored to draw upon the experience of itinerant players and the tradition of popular stage practice. John Rastell's interlude *The Nature of the Four*

Elements, for example, certainly owes much to the new ideology of humanism: the themes of natural reason and human learning, astronomy, cosmography, and recent geographical discoveries. But all this learned dissemination of knowledge and patriotism was accompanied by the "mirth and sport" of popular entertainment. The humanist and patriot was not ashamed of these concessions but deliberately sought contact with traditions of popular comedy:

> This philosophical work is mixed
> With merry conceits, to give men comfort...[7]

The "mirth and sport" was of course derived from various sources, but amongst them the comic element of the popular morality loomed large. The deliberate attempt to reanimate traditional stage practices went so far, in fact, that Rastell recommended to the professional actor that "ye may leave out much of the sad matter . . . and yet the matter will depend conveniently, and then it will not be past three-quarters of an hour of length."[8]

On the basis of popular stage practice and experience the leading English dramatists of the early sixteenth century, all of them associated with court and church,[9] began to adapt the medieval heritage to the themes of the Reformation, the precepts of humanism, the ideas of nationhood, and the Renaissance concern with dramatic form and propriety, notably in point of genre, artistic symmetry, and decorum. Such beginnings, which were of great consequence, were possible in an age and in a society where the political and social compromise of the New Monarchy necessitated an active cultural synthesis in which the new sense of national independence and identity embraced rather than excluded its popular traditions. But the new dramatists employed by the court and the church (Skelton, Medwall, Heywood, and Bale) could not assimilate the popular conventions without at the same time enhancing their significance. As D. M. Bevington has shown, for example, Skelton and Bale not only drew from the stage practices of the small groups of traveling players but also helped to develop those practices: they improvised upon the principle of distributing more than one role to each actor, and thereby refined the structure of the type of play that the small troupe was capable of performing. This in its turn had a retroactive effect on the popular theater and, after about 1550, noticeably influenced the nature and quality of the traveling troupe's repertoire. Long before the Elizabethan University Wit placed his humanist education and artistic talent in the service of popular dramatic entertainment, there were significant precedents for this synthesis in England. Even a cursory glance at the interaction between popular stagecraft and the humanist contribution to dramatic composition and artistry shows that

Kyd and Marlowe only completed on a higher level what three generations of actors and dramatists had begun.

If an oversimplification of this development (which is as yet difficult to
survey as a whole) can serve for the moment, some three or four cumula-
tive phases can be distinguished in which the tradition of the popular
theater received and reacted to the efforts of humanist dramatists and
(in the resulting transformations) followed new and different lines of
development. A first stage can be seen in the work of the early Tudor
dramatists: in the two pre-Reformation plays by Medwall, in Skelton's
Magnificence (1515), to some extent in *The Nature of the Four Elements*
(1517) by the somewhat younger humanist John Rastell, and, to a much
lesser degree, in the plays of John Heywood (1519–28), the court entertainer and writer of interludes who, with his penchant for French farce,
broke with the morality tradition. At this stage, the varying ways and
degrees in which these dramatists drew upon the experience and practice of the popular theater reveal a somewhat tentative and inconsequen-
tial groping toward a synthesis that could, as in Medwall's *Fulgens and
Lucrece*, achieve true originality but which also retained a good deal of
uncertainty and the need, somewhat deliberately, if not mechanically, to
enliven "the sad matter" with some "merry conceits." In succeeding decades, the work of John Bale and Robert Wever, answering the pressures
of the Reformation, achieved a new level of synthesis. As in *Respublica*
(1553), the dramatist, in an effort effectively to support his cause, quite
deliberately adopted the conventions of popular stagecraft so that he
might appeal to a broader plebeian public. In a third phase,
Psychomachia—the allegorical conflict between the Virtues and the
Vices which the humanists had already reinterpreted as the struggle
between knowledge and ignorance, and which the reformers now saw as
the antagonism between the true and the false doctrine—was superseded by a mythical, neoclassical or pseudohistorical subject. To use A. P.
Rossiter's phrase, this was the work of those "amateur humanists" who,
like John Pikering (*Horestes*), "R. B." (the author of *Appius and Virginia*),
and Thomas Preston (*Cambises*), readily began to cooperate with the
common players. Unlike the drama of the Children of the Chapel Royal
(such as Richard Edwards' *Damon and Pithias*, 1564), the neoclassical
drama of the Inner Temple (*Gorboduc*, 1561), and the work of the Eton
and Westminster Rector Nicholas Udall, these "university half-wits"
were prepared to use some of the cruder but highly theatrical popular
effects, such as elaborating the comic scenes in tumbling verse and using
the rich idioms, pithy metaphors and proverbs of popular speech. Their
plays, which have survived more or less by accident, were written in the
late 1560s and still acted in the years before Marlowe and Kyd began to
write for the permanent London theater. Shakespeare himself was so

familiar with *Cambises*, the best known of these older plays, that he may even have played one of its parts as a young actor.[10]

The remarkable thing about these plays is that, from a thematic and structural point of view, they incorporated and improved upon the innovations of Medwall, Skelton, and Bale, while at the same time testing them against and reintegrating them into the stage practices of the popular theater itself. Thus, their point of departure is not the more literary achievement of the older dramatists, but rather the theatrical reception and modification of those previous innovations at that level of synthesis between literary art and popular stage practice which had in the meantime proved its value in performance for common audiences. In this way, the learned tradition of rhetoric and the humanist concern for form and symmetry were accommodated, however crudely, to the practical requirements of the popular theater with its greater capacity for action, spectacle, and low comedy.

The continuity of this development, and its immense significance for the work of Marlowe and Shakespeare have, in general, been underestimated. From both a sociological and theatrical point of view the Elizabethan synthesis was a gradual process, and one that proceeded in various stages and on varying levels. The "point of junction" of the two traditions (to which P. W. Biesterfeldt perhaps first pointed) brought forth such fruitful results precisely because the long and drawn-out step-by-step process amounted to something more than a mere "*momentary* fusion of the popular and learned traditions."[11] Ever since this fusion became a possibility, the English theater developed toward a more national and universal institution than, say, the French or German contemporary stage could hope to achieve. The English morality and interlude theater, in its changing forms and aspects, anticipated in several important respects the social "hodge-podge" and the cultural "mingle-mangle" that John Lyly noted just before the Elizabethan synthesis achieved its crowning glory.

A brief look at the earliest extant interlude may perhaps best illustrate the way in which the popular tradition, in the process of its adaptation to, and amalgamation with, the new learning, asserted itself in the social context of the Tudor indoor theater of recreation. *Fulgens and Lucrece*, written by Cardinal Morton's chaplain, Henry Medwall, before 1500, is remarkable in that it goes beyond a simple mixture of "merry conceits" and "philosophical work" by exploiting the tension between the two traditions and giving them a structural significance as part of the meaning of the dramatic product itself. In so doing, the play falls back on the popular principle of mimetic inversion, which it uses not farcically, but in terms of an elaborate parody, one that links the manner of the "high fraud" of the shepherds' scenes with important structural tensions between the main plot and the irreverently comic subplot in further anticipation of one of the most basic structural principles of Shakespearean drama. Thus, the correlation of learned and popular elements is turned into a source of dramatic vitality: it informs the dramatic contrast but also defines the relationship between the aristocratic and the plebeian parts of the play such that the social and thematic contrast is juxtaposed to corresponding elements of dramatic performance.

The profound use of tradition seems all the more remarkable since *Fulgens and Lucrece* is distinctly removed from the traditional context of the outdoor communal theater, and the semidramatic folk festivals and entertainments. This interlude was performed in a hall, where it was intended as entertainment at an aristocratic banquet. The subject was of genuinely current interest in early Tudor England. The argument *de vera nobilitate*, that is, the *débat* weighing greater honor and genuine nobility, is answered by Lucrece when, after hearing speeches by both her suitors, she rejects the well-born but unworthy Publius Cornelius and chooses Flaminius, the poorer representative of "low degree" (II, 687),[12] who has, in the past "one or two years," already reached "office and fee" (568) and hence promises to be the founder of a future line of "nobles" (689).

But this ideological apologia for the rise of the bourgeoisie and gentry, which is of course suitably worded so as not to establish "a generall precedent" (432; cf. II, 428–32, 759–67, 884), is made to confront the standards of an entirely different world. The two suitors are given two servants ("A" and "B") who, in their own parallel cross-wooing of Lucrece's clever maid, cultivate dramatic themes and conventions which, as C. R. Baskerville has pointed out, are analogous to elements in the folk play and seasonal festival customs. In fulfilling the double function of "presenter and jester," the servants use phrases that recall the idiom of the Mummers' Plays, make coarse jokes that support the "spirit of misrule," and perhaps point to some late ritual wooing ceremony. (But if this traditional background is to illuminate the play, it must not be overstated by exaggerating the impact of medieval folklore or by equating the servants with the "leaders of seasonal games.")[13]

Wherever Medwall may have found sources for the subplot (and perhaps some echo of the Roman comic tradition of Atellanic popular farce and servants' parody must also be considered),[14] the significance of the subplot is primarily a theatrical one. All through the play "A" and "B" rub shoulders with the humble folk in the hall; in fact, their social identity is dramatically stylized in a brilliant induction. Before the play begins they stand idly about the hall, but since they are "maysterles" (I, 398), and so in search of work, they hire themselves out to the gentlemen suitors in the interlude. The performance begins before they cross the borderline between the real world and the play world, for such a crossing assumes, at the outset, the function of a dramatic effect and indicates the first phase of a significant movement: "spectators" become actors, the masterless servants in the hall become servants acting on the "place." This extradramatic counterpoint is ironically underlined when "B" energetically denies that he is an actor (46 et seq.), so that "A" then fears he will "disturb the play" (363).

The induction reflects a theatrical movement that in more than one way corresponds to the *platea* conventions of the outdoor communal theater or to the acting area of the folk play in which the audience was a constituent element of the performance itself. It also recalls the self-expressive function of Herod's burlesque threats at the beginning of his comic scene. However, Medwall deliberately stylized and refined the extradramatic convention to shift the effect of comic parody into the structure of the play itself, thus anticipating the framed perspective of the play world that was to be used in *The Old Wives' Tale*, *Summer's Last Will and Testament*, *The Taming of a Shrew*, and, most brilliantly, in *The Knight of the Burning Pestle*.[15]

It might be said, then, that in *Fulgens and Lucrece* a world of popular English experience was made to intrude into and confront the illusions of the Roman *locus*, that is, the fiction of the stage world with its noble ideals and ideologies. Realizing that the induction, together with the subplot, constitutes something of an "intrusion" is to point to the immense vitality offered by a countermovement of dramatic parody. But although the technique of popular inversion is sustained, it cannot by itself illuminate the full significance of the play, which is made up of two *interacting* dramatic modes. For while the actors of "A" and "B" continually depart from their roles, address the audience, or refer to its presence, Fulgens, Lucrece, and the gentlemen suitors create a more autonomous world the thematic unity of which is only very seldom interrupted by an extradramatic element (as in I, 354 et seq.; 588 et seq.). This contrast is underscored by the further contrast between the rime royal and the carefully organized formal rhetoric of the more respectable characters on the one hand, and the popular idiom and coarse speech of the servants on the other. Yet the quality of the distinction is not primarily verbal, nor is the structural tension quite identical with that between the induction, or frame, and the "play" that follows. What seems even more important is the contradiction that is achieved between traditional "myrth and game" and the exemplary matter of elevated rhetoric. These two basic poles, each in its different way, comprise "the substaunce of this play." The dramatist is perfectly aware of their problematic relationship when at the end of the play "B," resuming the function of presenter, says:

> That all the substaunce of this play
> was done specially therfor
> Not onely to make folke myrth and game,

> But that suche as be gentilmen of name
> May be somewhat mouyd
> By this example . . .

(II, 888-93)

The distinction is clearly functional, but can it, as a sociological statement, be accepted at face value? The "myrth and game" are presented,
or so it seems, to the "folke"; the "gentilmen of name" are offered the
rhetorical *controversia* about genuine nobility. Now, although the meaning of the term "folke" is not at all, or at least not necessarily, to be
equated with *plebs* (cf. I, 1413), the play does occasionally aim "to con-
tent/ The leste that stondyth here" (II, 43-44)—another, and perhaps a
more valid indication that, from a sociological point of view, the taste of
the Tudor hall audience was not uniform. No matter how complex or
fluid the social basis of the element of "myrth and game" was, the
perspective of comic irreverence and inversion was presented in a dramatic mode that not only owed a good deal to the tradition of the popular theater, but which had absorbed, and now served as the vehicle for, a
view of life and a set of values that were markedly different from those
expressed in the exemplary ideology of the *controversia de vera nobilitate*.
In the last resort it is the much more comprehensive and universal
conflict between these two views of life, one realistic the other idealistic,
one popular the other genteel, that informs the meaning of the play as a
whole.

This basic tension between the serious *débat* and the comic subplot
admits of no facile solution, for it involves not simply the opposition but
also the dramatic relationship between the two poles. With its contrasting
verbal, dramatic, and social modes, this relationship is not mechanical
but functional, and as such anticipates the structure of a play like Shakespeare's *Two Gentlemen of Verona*. It is stressed when the servants "A" and
"B" (somewhat in the manner of Launce, or Touchstone in *As You Like It*)
set up their own version of courtship, which entails not merely some
crude humor but also a rather sobering reflection on some of the more
earthy facts of life and the contemporary state of the relations between
the sexes. The wooing of Joan offers a highly effective complementary
comic vision against which the meaning of the serious theme is inevitably
reassessed. Such a "farcical fantasia on the theme of *de vera nobilitate*"[16]
involves, among other things, a turbulent wrestling match and ends,
finally, with "B's" challenge to "A" on the open field with spear and
shield (I, 1108-1213). This burlesque version of a chivalric duel culminates in a piece of scatology that markedly and significantly contrasts
with the exigencies of feudal courtship.

The virtuous, industrious, abstemious, and patriotic propertied gentleman who invokes the "gifts" of "nature" (II, 659-85) wins the bride's
hand but not the servants' approval. They wonder why Lucrece insists

on accepting this suitor for his virtue and for nothing else. At this point
the plebeian sense of the facts of life and the lofty idealism of the new
standards of marriageable character are utterly at odds:

> *A.* Uertue, what the deuyll is that?
> And I can tell, I shrew my catt,
> To myne vnderstondynge.
> *B.* By my fayth no more can I
> But this she said here opynly,
> All these folke can tell.
> *A.* How say ye gode women, is it your gyse
> To chose all your husbondis that wyse?
> By my trought than I maruaile.
> *B.* Nay this is the fere, so mot I goo,
> That men chise not theyr wyffes so
> In placis where I haue be...

> (II, 842–53)

Skepticism of the idealistic posture and the moral anarchy of mimetic
topsy-turvydom have become inextricably linked here. Still, they reflect
a *platea*-like position from which the everyday experience of ordinary
people can be invoked and pitted against the illusions (both theatrical
and ideological) of the stage world. In more than one respect "A" and
"B" fulfill the same dramatic function as that of the older servant figure
Garcio, and, in some measure, Joseph, as well as that of Shakespeare's
gravediggers and porters. Ordinary experience is made to counterpoint
the moral or social standards of the serious part. The direct appeal to the
"gode women" in the audience, asking whether they would also choose
their husbands according to these standards, contains a veiled challenge
to, if not a direct inversion of, the moral authority of the ruling class.
Regardless of the social identity of the "folke" in the hall, a *platea*-like
form of "myrth and game" and the anachronism (the repeated "nowaday," I, 475, 520, 730) were conducive to the entertainer's reckless freedom of expression. "A's" proverbial remark ("I shrew my catt") is complemented by "B's" empirical standards that have been tested "In placis
where I haue be." Such traditional freedom to express and re-enact one's
own experience as a matter of course extended into the spheres of sex
and social criticism, where again proverbial speech helped to establish a
more effective identification with the "nowaday" world of the audience
("Ye, goth the worlde so nowaday/That a man must say the crow is
white," I, 163–64). The naive self-expression of the base-born servants
rejects the idealism of the serious plot as patently untrue to life, and
motivates the *reductio ad absurdum* of chivalric ideals in the duel over
Joan.

From the point of view of the popular tradition, the dramatic method
and function of the subplot constituted a remarkably effective and

forward-looking way of integrating and incorporating postritual self-expression into the elements of a literate and truly national culture. Here the servants of the early interlude fulfill a provocative function similar to that of the Vice in the morality. In the later hybrid play *King Darius* (printed 1565), for example, the Vice Iniquytie still betrays the same kind of moral skepticism when faced with the ideological embodiment of Virtue.

> *Charytie.* My name (I tell thee) is Charitie,
> Without the which no flesh can Justified bee.
> *Iniquytie.* Yea, truly thou art an holy man,
> As is betweene this and Buckingham;
> I pray thee, tel me what meneth this word charity?
> Because thou doest make it so holy.
> *Charytie.* Peace, man, thou arte vnwyse,
> Neuer a good thought canste thou deuyse;
> For if thou couldest, thus thou woldest not prate.
>
> (Brandl, 64–72)

In his anarchical way the Vice helps to suggest that the meaning of the word "charity," in the real world, is more complex than the moral postulate of the fictive figure so called. Again, the anachronistic allusion to local experience ("Buckingham") casually evokes some empirical standard of judgment which remains impervious to moral abstractions. As Charytie's indignant rejoinder suggests, the Vice combines the expression of his alleged ignorance with some strong irreverence: "Because thou doest make it so holy." This of course does not quash the serious message either in *Fulgens and Lucrece* or in *King Darius*, but it does momentarily question its validity from a perspective outside the prevailing moral and ideological standards. This angle is never clearly defined, for it reflects a naive and spontaneous attitude toward experience that, since it precludes any profound seriousness in its questionings, is not qualified either to refute or supersede the basic Christian or humanist orientation of the play. In terms of its social correlatives, the play is more or less in line with the ideology of the propertied bourgeoisie and rising gentry.

But all this is not to minimize the dramatic force and significance of the naive measure of popular *mimesis* that recalls the topsy-turvying function of the fool in the pre-Christian *mimus* fragment (p. 13). The spontaneous reference to the facts of life in the real world has both a comic and a liberating effect; and whereas in the *mimus* and to some extent in the mystery plays the disenchanting force and the burlesque function of irreverent imitation break through the illusions of myth, they now point up the limits of idealism. The extradramatic awareness of the world of the audience as a constituent element of the performance

itself had, in the past, reflected the half-forgotten communal participation of ritual and its late equivalents in folk festivals and village mayings.
But after the decline of the medieval Christian cycles, the correlation
between ritual and representation gave way. The postritual element of
nonrepresentational self-expression became associated (as long as it persisted in a secular context) with the actor's awareness of his social identity
and function and served as a link between the experience of the real
world and the theatrical and idealistic illusions of the play world. Thus,
the extradramatic appeal to the experience of "ye gode women" or the
anachronistic reference to local "placis" reflects a realism of sentiment
that is not identical with the illusion of verisimilitude and therefore not
at all opposed to the traditional conventions of "myrth and game." On
the contrary, the particular strength of the popular contribution lies in
its unique capacity for reconciling convention and realism in such a way
that both humanist rhetoric and the Renaissance illusion of verisimilitude were eventually assimilated into the native theatrical experience. As *Fulgens and Lucrece* shows, the social and dramatic mode of the
popular tradition served as a component part of a newly comprehensive
form of drama in which high seriousness and low comedy, ideology and
farce, vision and experience became engaged in an extremely complex
relationship out of which the great Elizabethans were to achieve a supreme multiple unity.

2

From Folk Play to Mankind: *Conventions of Speech and Acting*

The achievement of *Fulgens and Lucrece* anticipates the sociologically
and thematically expanded framework within which the English theater
developed at the beginning of the sixteenth century. The interlude
exemplifies an early phase in the synthesis of various dramatic modes in
a theater that was to become a professional national institution. Once the
wider social context of sixteenth-century drama has been taken into
account, such points of contact (as between indoor entertainment,
morality tradition, folk play, and village festival custom) must appear as
characteristic of a wider spectrum of itinerant theatrical activities. Of
course it is a matter of conjecture to decide whether the countless small
traveling troupes may in fact have been close enough to, or even identical with, those uprooted *rudes Agricolae et Artifices* who were denounced
as having illegally encroached upon the established monopoly of the
ministralli. The point that would support such an assumption is that even
when the more successful of these late amateur "professionals" may have

performed in halls from time to time, their relationship to rural audiences must still have been affected by the seasonal traditions that had played so important a part in their own folk background.

Mankind (ca. 1471) is the earliest and perhaps most interesting work of such a troupe. The play reveals a thorough familiarity with the traditional "myrth and game" of country audiences and is in several respects still remarkably distinct from the new indoor entertainment of the great hall or mansion.[17] The early date of this work, and its association with a professional, although still seasonally oriented troupe, make *Mankind* one of the most illuminating of the early morality plays. As many scholars have noted, it is "undoubtedly popular" and has been considered a culmination of the popular elements in the late medieval English theater.[18] Whatever its intrinsic worth as a work of dramatic art (which is indeed controversial), *Mankind* remains one of the most revealing and impressive examples of early professional stagecraft. It is precisely its dramatic achievement that permits us, through a detailed interpretation of the play in performance, to throw new light on the origins and functions of some important conventions of speech and acting that were associated with the native dramatic heritage that Shakespeare finally inherited.

It should be noted from the start, though, that *Mankind* is in many ways a unique play; and so any interpretation of it must avoid generalizations that would not cover the many other moralities which are, in a Christian sense, genuinely orthodox. But *Mankind* does possess some representative features that reflect the new theatrical context of the small itinerant troupe. The play calls for six actors, a relatively large acting area, no special properties, but two kinds of entrances: one through the audience and the other through a covered entrance or scaffold. As the text suggests, the performance was probably associated with a seasonal occasion and the rural audience of a specific district.

The play is opened by Mercy, who addresses "ye souerens that sytt, and ye brothern that stonde ryght wppe" (29).[19] He has hardly finished his pious appeal for "premedytacyon" (44) when he is interrupted by the central Vice figure, Myscheff, who replies with a verse from the Mummers' Play and a topsy-turvy speech. Myscheff introduces himself as a player and jester ("I am cumme hedyr to make yow game," 69), in which function he is supported by his companions New-gyse, Nought, and Now-a-days. They enter in high spirits and call in musicians; the "mynstrellys" (72) appear and play, and the three Vices dance with "mery chere" (77). They reject Mercy's misgivings about "this reuell" (82) with the argument that they do not corrupt anyone this way; on the contrary, "we make them both fresh and gay" (119).

After Mercy has sent these Vices away, Mankynde enters. He is torn between the life of the spirit and a life of sensuality and lust: "For ther is

euer a batell betwyx the soull and the body" (220). However, Mercy's
admonitions finally bear fruit and Mankynde succeeds in resisting the
temptations of the flesh and the whisperings of the Vices, who await
Mercy's departure from a distance and anticipate it with sarcastic remarks addressed to the audience. No sooner is Mankynde alone working
with his spade and remembering Mercy's pious exhortations, than the
Vices begin the work of temptation. Now-a-days and Nought elbow their
way through the spectators, encouraging them all the while to join them
in a jolly song. They appeal to "all the yemandry that ys here" (325), that
is, especially to those standing, not necessarily to the seated "souerens"
(29). An obscene "crystemes song" (325) follows which, according to the
stage direction, all sing together (*cantant omens*). Meanwhile, Mankynde
goes on with his work; but when he is ridiculed by the dissolute
pranksters ("For all this, he may have many a hungry mele," 363), and
when Nought recommends that he dung his fields himself, he becomes
furious and chases the Vices away.

The chief Vice, Myscheff, enters to comfort his three badly beaten
companions:"Ye xall haue a nappyll—tomorrow" (420). But this is only
the beginning of a strange semiritual element in the play. Somewhat in
the manner of the "cure" of the folk play, Myscheff lops off New-gyse's
bruised head and puts it back again—healed. This is taken for a magic
spell—"Yt ys a schreude charme" (430)—but Nought heretically pro-
claims that it was done *"in nomine patri"* (433). At this point, when the
chief Vice is magician, doctor, and fool all in one, the play reaches its
spectacular climax: Myscheff suddenly calls for music; powder explodes;
and New-gyse tells those in the audience not to spare their money if they
want to see the devil Tytivillus in "hys abhomynabull presens" (450–58).
At this climactic point—exactly in the middle of the 907-line play—the
Vice figures mingle with the audience collecting money.

Tytivillus is announced with almost the same words as those used by
the first murderer in *Richard III* (I, 4, 86): "I com, with my leggis vndur
me!" (447). He appears as "a man with a hede that ys of grett om-
nipotense" (454), perhaps with an oversized head-mask, as Brandl
suggests. His self-introductory speech recalls the frightening comedy of
Herod and the heretical kind of hybrid Latin that Pilate used: "ego sum
dominancium dominus" (468; see above p. 70). When, after repeated
questioning, he is convinced of the lesser Vices' poverty, he sends them
off to steal, quoting the names and places of residence of wealthy contemporary landowners in Cambridgeshire and Norfolk who were responsible for administering the law.[20] Tytivillus bestows a blessing on the
thieves with his left hand and, after their departure, hides a board in the
"soil" representing Mankynde's field, in hopes that Mankynde will lose
patience and abandon his work. The devil also hides Mankynde's spade

and corn; he has already won the game when Mankynde goes "in-to thi yerde" (554) to answer the call of nature and free himself of "colic" and "stone." Tytivillus delivers a long speech to the audience as he gloats over his triumph (558-73), but in the tyrant's manner he also tells them to keep quiet:

> ... for me kepe now yowur sylence!
> Not a worde, I charge yow, peyn of xl pens!
> A praty game xall be scheude yow, or ye go hens.
>
> (582-84)

This speech culminates in a proverb ("the Deull is dede");[21] and with a rhymed couplet he finally takes his leave of the audience (598-99).

After having been seduced away from a virtuous life, Mankynde joins in the wild reveling of the Vices. He is accepted into the "cort of Myscheff" (661) with a solemn proclamation and is sworn into a life of immorality, gluttony, robbery, and murder. But in the last part of the play the seduction is followed by conversion. Although at first repulsed and derided, Mercy laments, prays, and appeals to Mankynde repeatedly to forsake his reckless garb and company. When the Vice figures tempt Mankynde to despair and suicide, Mercy intervenes and finally frees him. In the epilogue Mercy imbues Mankynde with trust in the goodness and grace of God, again instructs him, gives him his blessing and speaks a pious final word to the audience.

Although the text does not convey a clear picture of the external arrangements of the acting area (stage directions are few and some are obscure), there is some evidence—running counter to the assumption of a hall performance—that points to a public innyard and the way in which the surrounding locality was made part of the performance. There are, for example, references to an innkeeper ("the goode man of this house," 460) and repeated calls for the tapster (722) and the ostler (725), from whom New-gyse wishes to borrow (and perhaps receives) a football (cf. 726). Mankynde's announcement that he is going "in-to thi yerde" (554) does not necessarily presuppose a hall performance either; it may have been made on a platform stage from which the actors could both descend into the yard or retire through a "dore" (153)—probably into the house.[22] On the other hand, the actors were in a position to enter, at least from time to time, through the audience standing in the "yerde" (cf. 324-25, 457). This is true, at any rate, for the Vices, who sing and joke with the spectators and whose audience contact has a specific function that is inseparable from the occasion and the social function of the play. Performance at Christmas (as J. Q. Adams suggests) or at Shrovetide (as W. K. Smart argues) would explain the many seasonal references—winter threshing, the cold weather, sowing time, etc. (54, 316, 381, 539).

It would also explain the reference to music, dancing, and calls for game and sport as part of a traditional pattern of joyous merrymaking and festive release.

In this context, the points of contact with the folk play and the half-forgotten ritual heritage of men's ceremonies seem particularly significant. As W. K. Smart has suggested,[23] there are some four or five such points in *Mankind*, among them: (1) the mock beheading or "cure" performed by Myscheff (425–40), which almost certainly reflects an age-old ritual of renewal; (2) the collection (448–67), which, as an extradramatic part of the action, in its own way corresponds to the *quête* in the Mummers' Play; (3) Tytivillus' entrance speech (447), which resembles the customary self-introduction of the amateur actor in the folk play; (4) Tytivillus' big head, usually associated with Beelzebub in the folk ceremonies, which may harken back to some more primitive masking, and (5) the traditional warning and request for room ("Make space! and be ware!" 467). Although some of these aspects may very well be original to the immediate theatrical occasion and reflect some basic similarity in the general pattern of dramatic ceremonies rather than any "influence," there can be, on the whole, little doubt about the impact of traditional mimic activities on *Mankind*.[24]

These are most impressively reflected in the Vice's language, which is full of echoes of a peculiar kind of topsy-turvydom. Generally this results from a confrontation between representational and nonrepresentational patterns of speech and acting—a confrontation that involves a good deal of social as well as dramatic and verbal tension. In this context the dramatic function of the Vice Myscheff becomes particularly complex as he moves easily from dialogue to sportive self-expression and back to farcical dialogue. This is how the chief Vice follows up the prologue and Mercy's reference to the Last Judgment, when God will conduct a strict "examynacyon" by which

43   . . . The corn xall be sauyde, the chaffe xall be brente.
                    I be-sech yow hertyly, haue this premedytacyon.

                                                              [*Enter Mischief.*]

45   *Myscheff.* I be-seche yow hertyly, leue yowur calcacyon!
                    Leue yowur chaffe! leue yowur corn! leue yowur dalyacyon!
                    Yowur wytt ys lytyll, yowur hede ys mekyll! ye are
                    full of predycacyon.
                    But, ser, I prey [yow] this questyon to claryfye:—
50   Dryff-draff, mysse-masche,

                    Sume was corn, and sume was chaffe;
                    My dame seyde my name was Raffe;
                    On-schett yowur lokke, and take an halpenye.

	Mercy.	Why come ye hethyr, brother? Ye were not dysyryde.
55	*Myscheff.*	For a wyntur corn-threscher, ser, I haue hyryde;
		Ande ye sayde the corn xulde be sauyde, and the
		chaffe xulde be feryde;
		Ande he prouyth nay, as yt schewth be this werse:
		"Corn seruit bredibus, chaffe horsibus, straw fyrybusque,"
60		Thys ys as moche to say to yowur leude wndyrstondynge,
		As the corn xall serue to brede at the nexte bakynge,
		"Chaff horsybus," *et reliqua,*
		The chaff, to horse xall be goode produce;
		When a man ys for-colde, this straw may be brent.
65		And so forth, *et cetera.*
	Mercy.	A-voyde, goode brother! Ye ben culpable
		To interrupte thus my talkynge delectable.
	Myscheff.	Ser, I haue nother horse nor sadyll;
		Therfor I may not ryde.
70	*Mercy.*	Hye yow forthe on fote, brother, in Godis name!
	Myscheff.	I say, ser, I am cumme hedyr to make yow game;

This opening encounter between Mercy and the Vice introduces the alternatives that will compete for the allegiance of Mankynde. Their confrontation (which is at the center of whatever plot there is in the play) is here reflected in a dramatic language that reveals much about the Vice's use and abuse of words. "I be-sech yow hertyly" to meditate, Mercy says to the audience; "I be-seche yow hertyly" to be silent, Myscheff says to Mercy. Myscheff's aping of Mercy's phrase, which simultaneously changes its thrust from a positive to a negative request, is paralleled by his mode of verbal inversion and parody. Myscheff seizes on the pompous latinism "premedytacyon" and comes up with the unusual "calcacyon" (probably meaning "to draw in," from the Lat. *calcare*—to tread) and the completely fabricated "dalyacyon" (which sounds like dalliance, but is probably no more than a jingle).

To this point any laughter is clearly at Mercy's expense, as it is when Myscheff heretically inverts (and "misunderstands") the biblical proverb about the wheat and the chaff (Matt., 3:12; Luke, 3:17) by means of invective, wordplay, nonsense verse, and dog-Latin (45–47; 48–52; 53–63). Myscheff's first challenge ("Leue yowur chaffe ! leue yowur corn !") is followed by the amazing "Yowur wytt ys lytyll, yowur hede ys mekyll!"—a phrase that echoes the most widespread, and probably the most traditional, verbal formula of the Mummers' Play (see above p. 35), which must have been quite familiar to the audience. Its use, by the leading representative of Vice in so prominent an introductory position defi-

nitely associates Myscheff with more traditional amateur dramatic elements, in particular with Jack Finney and similar comically defiant figures. But Myscheff is no folk play clown; his words are the same, but his
meaning and context are not. If some of his utterances are still largely
nonrepresentational, his language has already assumed the newly referential function of characterization. The "hede," for example, is no
longer literally "mekyll" (large like the mask in the original rite) but
puffed up like an idiot's head—and hollow. However, such a shift in
meaning must not be overemphasized and taken out of its larger context; for the real importance of the traditional phrase lies in its ambivalence, in the unity of its past significance and its present meaning. The
equation of "mekyll" with "hollow" is valid only insofar as it emphasizes
the transformation of the traditional phrase in such a way that the ancient formula can become part of a larger dramatic dialogue which at
least partly aims at the illusion of verbal exchange and conversation. The
meaning of the phrase, therefore, can no longer be read exclusively in
terms of a traditional self-introduction re-enacted in a late ritual context,
but must be seen, rather, as enriched by its new function within the
framework of burlesque dialogue. The same is true of the nonsense
rhyme that follows to heighten the burlesque version of the biblical
metaphor (49–52). Again the Christian vision of the Last Judgment is
effectively countered by a pagan heritage, and Mercy's words are syntac-
tically, semantically, and metrically turned upside down.

Myscheff's jingling of words, grotesque use of rhymes, and alliteration
are further supported by his use of curiously archaic expressions, like
"On-schett yowur lokke" (52). This corresponds to Now-a-days' remark,
"Now opyn yowur sachell with Laten wordis" (128), which in its turn may
recall such Old English expressions as *wordhord onlēac* (*Beowulf*, 259).
Myscheff's extremely alliterative diction is perhaps his most immediately
noticeable verbal feature, and one that is common to the Vices of later
plays (Sedycyon in *King Johan*, Hypocrisy in *Lusty Juventus*, or Haphazard
in *Appius and Virginia*). The link between noncourtly alliterative poetry
and the mystery play has already been pointed out by John Speirs and
other scholars, but the continuity of this tradition down to the language
of the morality Vice has not received its deserved attention. Grotesque
utterances or nonsense speech, which play such an important role in folk
drama, especially in connection with the Cokaygne motif, are equally
prominent, although altered in function, in *Mankind*. But again the traditional significance of non-sensical verbal patterns must not conceal the
more telling fact that such elements have changed in their passage to the
commercial itinerant stage, and with this change point the way to several
important conventions of speech that are found in Shakespeare's plays.

In the folk play, the nonsense patter, which may echo a long since
forgotten ritual utterance, served no representational function. In *Man-*

kind and the popular morality canon, however, the nonrepresentational element of festive release, while it is still operative (especially in the Vice's self-introduction) is already at least partially integrated within the mimetic assumptions of dramatic dialogue. Myscheff's language supports the atmosphere of "mery chere" at the same time that it counterpoints (and blatantly challenges) the serious speeches. It is this almost subversive function of such verbal patterns that, as we shall see, establishes one of the foundations upon which the "antic disposition" in *Hamlet* and the madness and the truth-telling in *King Lear* are based, and from which the hybrid mode of "matter and impertinency mix'd" (IV, 6, 176) draws its traditional impetus. Partially integrated within the representational function of dialogue in *Mankind*, the Vice's "antic" language has made certain adjustments to the mimetic and psychological requisites of coherent conversation. But these are adjustments that the Vice can suddenly and playfully abandon. Thus Myscheff's seemingly straightforward "questyon" following Mercy's reminder of the Last Judgment—"But, ser, I prey [yow] this questyon to claryfye:—/Dryffdraff . . ."—is not really a question at all but an excuse to be impertinent (both in the derived sense of "cheeky" and literally not pertinent to the matter at hand). Here the double meaning of "impertinent" is relevant because it reflects, as it were, the representational and the nonrepresentational dimensions of the Vice. But if the truly *non*pertinent function of the speech is rooted in the tradition of ritual self-expression, the question *qua* question points to what has already become a mixed framework of dialogue into which the grotesque language of inversion has been received. Although the result of this integration is still rather awkward, it does announce the continuing process of literary change by which, in the late sixteenth century, the element of "impertinency" had become an integral and extremely effective convention of dramatic speech in characters such as Shakespeare's Feste, Gloucester, Iago, Hamlet, and Lear.

This realistic aspect (which also includes a social reference) is even more prominent in Myscheff's third attack on Mercy's biblical proverb (54–63). Here the heritage of non-sensical ritual self-expression emerges from behind the imitation of contemporary reality, and the Vice's speech approaches genuine modern dialogue. To Mercy's question about Myscheff's reason for appearing in the vicinity, the latter answers— seemingly quite pertinently—that he has come to be hired "For a wyntur corn-threscher" (54). But this leads to another mode of inversion, for the Vice proceeds to accept the biblical metaphor literally, on its level of (in I. A. Richards' term) "vehicle." In "the corn xall serue to brede. . . ," the religious image and its allegorical suggestions are reduced to the simple terms of peasant life in which chaff is "goode produce" for horses and straw may be burned "when a man ys for-colde." The reduction of a

moral metaphor to rural concreteness obliterates its theological overtones and didactic function, for the symbolism and the sacred teaching
of the Church are irreverently confronted by a new, naively empirical
experience of the world. The result is therefore comic, as the grotesque
mixture of Latin inflections and English wordplay transforms both the
realism of the dialogue and the conventions of dramatic conversation
into the language of foolishness or play ("Corn seruit bredibus, chaffe
horsibus, straw fyrybusqye," 58–63).

Myscheff's own interpretation of this dog-Latin is hardly addressed to
Mercy, his partner in dialogue. Again the Vice, as with the nonsense
verse (49–52), abandons the illusion of dramatic conversation by appeal-
ing directly to the "leude wndyrstondynge" (58) of the spectators. This
shift from marginal dialogue to direct audience address is effected with
remarkable ease. The Vice has no problem whatever either in carrying
on a genuine conversation, or, whenever necessary, in freeing himself
from the dramatic and psychological discipline of dialogue.

3

From Nonsense to Dialogue: "Matter and Impertinency Mix'd"

The heritage of non-sensical self-expression, already so diversely integrated into *Mankind*, thrived not only in the popular itinerant theater
(from *Hickscorner* to *Cambises*) but was adapted in Medwall's *Nature*, Rastell's *The Four Elements*, Bale's *King Johan*, the children's court production
of *Appius and Virginia*, as well as *Lusty Juventus*, *The Trial of Treasure*, *The
Tide Tarrieth No Man*, and a number of other humanist plays. In addition
to these, many other moralities may be cited that contain "impertinency"
without a satirical or burlesque function or a dramatic effect that "depends upon [the] irrelevancy of the combined ideas."[25]

Self-introduction that stands apart from the dramatic action proper
can be found in its simplest form in an early popular play like *Hickscorner*
(ca.1500–1520). The Vice Hickscorner, appearing in the guise of a seaman (like Myscheff as "threscher"), introduces himself directly to the
audience by means of an extensive itinerary:

> Syr, I have ben in many a countre;
> As, in Fraunce, Irlonde, and in Spayne,
> Portyngale, Sevyll, also in Almayne, . . .
> I have ben in Gene and in Cowe,
> Also in the londe of Rumbelowe,
> Thre myle out of hell;
> At Rodes, Constantyne, and in Babylonde,
> In Cornewale, and in Northumberlonde,

Where men sethe russhes in gruell;
Ye, syr, in Caldey, Tartare, and Inde,
And in the Londe of Women, that fewe men dothe fynde:
In all these countres have I be.

(Manly ed., 309-25)

The travel theme, which recalls the well-traveled doctor of the folk play, does function to preface the Vice's peculiar character. But again, within this representational function, there remains the traditional echo of an imaginary land which, like the Island of Cokaygne in the Mummers' Play, suggests a submerged utopian element and some measure of topsy-turvydom (the rushes "sethed" in "gruell") that tends to frustrate any representational kind of characterization. This fundamental tension, which continually complicates the inclusion of the traditional antic theme within representational drama, is even more pronounced in *The Nature of the Four Elements*, where the Vice Ignorance sings a song about Robin Hood that closely resembles the nonrepresentational nonsense of the folk play.

Robin Hood in Barnsdale stood,
And leant him till a maple thistle;
Then came our lady and sweet Saint Andrew.
Sleepest thou, wakest thou, Geffrey Coke?
A hundred winter the water was deep,
I can not tell you how broad.
He took a goose neck in his hand,
And over the water he went.
He start up to a thistle top,
And cut him down a hollen club.
He stroke the wren between the horns,
That fire sprang out of the pig's tail.
Jack boy, is thy bow i-broke?
Or hath any man done the wriguldy wrag?
He plucked muscles out of a willow,
And put them into his satchel! . . .

(Dod., I, 49)[26]

The astonishing presence of such an antic song in a humanist interlude reveals a set of contrary artistic and aesthetic values that are far from reconciled. On the one hand the song seems to be a fairly reasonable concession to popular taste and the popularity of the folk play's tradition of topsy-turvydom. On the other, the context in which the song appears provides an implicit deprecatory criticism of character; for the nonsense song is put into the mouth of the "rude beast Ignorance" and taken as an example of his folly (I, 50). Nonrepresentational mirth or a functional mode of characterization? The antic song is both, or rather something in between both.

In a late play like *The Trial of Treasure* (1567), Inclination's self-introduction is still far from smoothly integrated into dramatic dialogue, but his ludicrous speech is neither as irrelevant or grotesque as others were in the first part of the century.

[*Enter Inclination, the Vice.*]

> *Inclination.* I can remember since Noe's ship
> Was made, and builded on Salisbury Plain;
> The same year the weathercock of Paul's caught the pip.
> So that Bow-bell was like much woe to sustain.
> I can remember, I am so old,
> Since Paradise gates were watched by night;
> And when that Vulcanus was made a cuckold,
> Among the great gods I appeared in sight.
> Nay, for all you smiling, I tell you true.
> No, No, ye will not know me now;
> The mighty on the earth I do subdue.
> Tush, if you will give me leave, I'll tell ye how; ...

(Dod., III, 267)

The narrative structure of the Vice's speech here approaches the dramatic form of monologue. Inclination remembers, for example, the troubled building of Noah's Ark on Salisbury Plain, a detail that underscores his ancient and checkered career. But the anachronism ("the weathercock of Paul's") and direct address to the audience turn these mythic allusions into a comic consciousness of the present. The age and power of the Vice lend themselves to the uses of topsy-turvydom, and yet the self-expressive function of this language is no longer solely nonrepresentational or grotesque. For the heritage of antic ritual expression has been incorporated within the allegorical form of dramatic action—an integration assisted by certain qualities of the English morality tradition itself. Unlike the seamless allegorical web of Dante, these dramatic structures remain generally open and fragmentary, but they, too, are characterized by what Walter Benjamin, in his discussion of allegory, called *das Primat des Dinghaften vor dem Personalen*—the dominance of things over sentiment, of the reified over the personal. As a result, the normally ambiguous, polysemous quality of this drama becomes heightened, and leads the grotesque effect to a new and even more open-ended level of meaning; multiplicity of meaning being, of course, the foundation of allegory.[27] Although the ageless Vice's determination to subdue "The mighty on the earth" now serves the functions both of individual characterization and allegorical personification, it does neither consistently. In fact, he may simply be scurrilously inverting the *Magnificat*. But regardless of such inherently contradictory modes of dramatic presentation, there is in the passage a quality that is finally and supremely echoed in a modern Iniquity—in Goethe's Mephistopheles who, equally ancient, "bids defiance to the Naught,/The clumsy lumber of the Aught":

> I am a part of the Part which in the beginning was all,
> A part of the darkness which gave birth to light,
> To that haughty light which is struggling to usurp
> The ancient rank and realm of its mother Night,
> And yet has no success, try as it will,
> Being bound and clamped by bodies still.
>
> > (trans. Louise Macneice)

While he does not, of course, achieve this depth of symbolic expression, Inclination does generate a meaning that transcends the convention of allegorical personification:

> Forsooth, I am called Natural Inclination,
> Which bred in old Adam's fostred bones;
> So that I am proper to his generation,
> I will not away with casting of stones!
> I make the stoutest to bow and bend:
> Again, when I lust, I make men stand upright;
> From the lowest to the highest I do ascend,
> Drawing them to things of natural might.
>
> > (III, 268)

Here the late ritual nonsensical patter, by virtue of its newly representational function, has developed a more flexible social and metaphorical frame of reference whereby the omnipotent Natural Inclination rises from "the lowest to the highest" and can, if he wishes, "make men stand upright" (the *double entendre* being obvious).

In breaking with some important conventions of medieval allegory, this speech paves the way for a more complex relationship between dramatic action and verbal expression. The increasingly representational mode is, in this sense, not limited to the depiction of character alone, since it may be said to influence the larger dramatic structure of the play. Hence, Ambidexter's self-introduction in *King Cambises*:

> *Enter the Vice [Ambidexter], with an old capcase on his head, an olde paile about his hips for harnes, a scummer and a potlid by his side, and a rake on his shoulder.*

> *Ambidexter.* Stand away! stand away! for the passion of God!
> Harnessed I am, prepared to the field!
> I would have bene content at home to have bod,
> But I am sent forth with my speare and shield.
> I am appointed to fight against a snaile,
> And Wilken Wren the ancient shal beare.
> I dout not but against him to prevaile,—
> To be a man my deeds shall declare!

If I overcome him, then a butter-flie takes his part.
His weapon must be a blew-specked hen;
But you shall see me overthrow him with a fart.
So, without conquest, he shal go home againe.
If I overcome him, I must fight with a flie;
And a blacke-pudding the flies weapon must be.
At the first blow on the ground he shall lie;
I wil be sure to thrust him through the mouth to the knee!
To conquest these fellowes the man I wil play.
Ha, ha, ha! now ye wil make me to smile.
To see if I can all men beguile.
Ha! my name? My name would ye so faine know? . . .
                                                              (Adams ed., 126-46)

The effect here is comic and burlesque, but clearly the once autonomous
element of nonsense speech is more thoroughly and more skillfully integrated into the play as a whole. The curious fanfare that accompanies
the armored Ambidexter's entrance (perhaps from the audience who
must make room—"Stand away! stand away!") may contain an echo of
the *miles gloriosus*, and so recall direct audience address. (Ambidexter's
black pudding and blue-spotted hen may bear some remote connection
to the Land of Cokaygne and the folklore dream of plenty; but from a
functional point of view such nonrepresentational elements remain of
secondary dramatic importance.) The self-contained quality of this introduction is superseded by a new kind of thematic consistency since
Ambidexter's grotesque speech is functionally related to the serious
theme in Cambises' opening lines from the throne. The King will wage
war against the Egyptians,

Them to subdue as captives mine,—this is my hearts intent;
So shall I win honors delight, and praise of me shall go.

                                                              (18-19)

Ambidexter's clowning references to "spear and shield," "weapon" and
"conquest," are, therefore, a burlesque ethos drawn against the background of the major heroic action. And as such, his speech recalls the
kind of complementary perspective which, in *Fulgens and Lucrece*, is set
against the glory of the knights' duel and anticipates Falstaff's famous
alternatives to honor and death on the field (*1 Henry IV* V, 1, 127-40; 3,
29-38). But this comparison can only underline the particular limitations
of the structural uses of the tradition of nonsense in *Cambises*. Ambidexter relies on a fairly common folklore background,[28] one that emerges,
for example, throughout *A Midsummer Night's Dream* and in Mercutio's
Queen Mab speech in *Romeo and Juliet* (I, 4, 54-94).
    As long as the antic element is directly associated with and limited to
the account of a journey (as in *Hickscorner*), the presentation of a song

(*The Four Elements*), or the traditional self-introduction (*The Trial of Treasure, King Cambises*), its dramatic functions, not to mention more specific psychological or thematic dimensions (as, for example, feigned or pathological "madness"), are not fully developed. At the same time, its contribution to the metaphorical quality of dramatic speech is likewise limited, even though it does prefigure a new complexity of verbal texture. The Vice Haphazard in *Appius and Virginia*, for example, makes his entrance with a traditional self-introduction which, despite an increasingly mimetic form, retains important elements of a more ancient self-expression. The popular tradition, even when it was assimilated by a children's company that performed at court, persisted in a changing context and expanding social frame of reference.

> *Haphazard.* ... Yea, but what am I? a scholar, or a schoolmaster, or else
> A lawyer, a student, or else a country clown: [some youth.
> A broom-man, a basket-maker, or a baker of pies,
> A flesh or a fishmonger, or a sower of lies?
> A louse or a louser, a leek or a lark,
> A dreamer, a drumble, a fire or a spark?
> A caitiff, a cutthroat, a creeper in corners,
> A hairbrain, a hangman, or a grafter of horners?
> By the gods, I know not how best to devise,
> My name or my property well to disguise.
> A merchant, a May-pole, a man or a mackerel,
> A crab or a crevis, a crane or a cockerel?
> Most of all these my nature doth enjoy;
> Sometime I advance them, sometime I destroy...
> As big as a beggar, as fat as a fool,
> As true as a tinker, as rich as an owl:
> With hey-trick, how troll, trey-trip and trey-trace,
> Troll-hazard with a vengeance, I beshrew his knave's face;
> For tro and troll-hazard keep such a range,
> That poor Haphazard was never so strange:
> But yet, Haphazard, be of good cheer,
> Go play and repast thee, man, be merry to-yere.
>
> (Dod., IV, 118)

Here the Vice no longer introduces himself simply as winter "threscher" or seaman; he has become as multidimensional a character as, say, Hamlet, although on a different level. Hamlet, likewise a scholar and student, calls himself a "rogue and peasant slave," a "dull and muddy-mettled rascall," and compares himself to "John-a-Dreams" (II, 2, 543, 561), a popular figure "usually associated by editors with John a Droynes, a country bumpkin."[29] Such verbal parallels, while certainly striking, are probably quite accidental; they prove no "influence," but do indicate that the new symbolic or thematic complexity was associated with a social, theatrical, structural, and verbal synthesis of which the popular traditional Vice was the most universal and vital vehicle. Here, then, was a popular convention of character that could be developed outside the confines of any single social class or estate. Since it was such a thoroughly theatrical creation and was readily adaptable to the *miles gloriosus* and other types, it achieved a greater range of synthesis and continuity than most other popular, humanist, or neoclassical conventions of characterization.

It is mainly from this point of view that the comparison with Hamlet seems justified. But although Hamlet's speech indicates an even greater flexibility of language, character, action, and staging, Hamlet himself ultimately assumes the image of a more poetically unified individuality. And this is precisely what is lacking in Haphazard; for the inexhaustible catalogue of his imaginary identities precludes the unity instrumental to any poetic definition of character—one derived not from the extent but rather the relatedness of detail. Still, the variety of elements in Haphazard's speech opens up a promising complexity of social points of reference and begins, at least, to define the background (involving the breaking up of the barriers between the medieval estates) against which the growing "range" in the interplay of action and verbal characterization took shape. (Haphazard, before he finally recommends "good cheer . . . Go play and . . . be merry to-yere," self-consciously calls attention to his more widely referential position in the play world where he must "keep such a range./That poor Haphazard was never so strange.")

At this point there seems to be no clash or opposition between the new breadth of social reference, together with its related range of dramatic action, and the popular tradition of impertinent speech and antic behavior. In spite of the greater variety of referential contexts, some of the most important popular verbal and theatrical conventions were retained by the Elizabethan Vice. Popular types of alliteration, such as "trey-trip and trey-trace," recall a background of verbal topsy-turvydom closely linked with direct address to the audience, although the subversive festival spirit of *Mankind* is no longer operative. But the playful inversion of reality in a brief festive moment can give way to a deliberate subversion of the once ruling ideology: the saturnalian release moves into history, and the reckless defiance of ritual can be turned into the *mimesis* of Lollard politics.[30]

But if the wider range of social reference and the traditional modes of acting did, when put together, seem "strange," such synthesis was best achieved by making the Vice's function more self-contained. Thus, slowly but inevitably, the extradramatic was filtered out; whatever antic expression or pure jingling alliteration remained was fitted to the dialogue. But in assuming a more representational quality, the convention of antic speech gradually developed its latent capacity to generate a bold kind of popular imagery, one rather unlike the figures derived from the neoclassical rhetorical tradition. Consider, for example, Haphazard's comments on Appius' design to rape Virginia:

> For Conscience was careless and sailing by seas,
> Was drowned in a basket and had a disease,
> Sore moved for pity, when he would grant none,
> For being hard-hearted was turned to a stone:
> And sailing by Sandwich he sank for his sin.
> Then care not for conscience the worth of a pin
> And judgment judge[d] Justice to have a reward
> For judging still justly, but all now is marr'd;
> For gifts they are given where judgment is none.
> Thus judgment and justice a wrong way hath gone.

(IV,129)

Here nonsensical inversion becomes a component of metaphor as soon as the nonrepresentational statement is related to theme and character. And even though the result is not particularly impressive from an artistic point of view, the general outline of a new dimension of dramatic metaphor seems unmistakable. "Conscience was careless and sailing by seas,/Was drowned in a basket . . ." already reveals the suggestive interplay of allegorical meaning and metaphorical freedom which, in its reliance upon a symbolic mode of reasoning ("For being hard-hearted was turned to a stone"), transcends the traditional blend of sense and nonsense. And although the highly alliterative line that follows seems to be something of a relapse into true non-sense, its newly symbolic dimension inspires the allegorical whole of the passage with the sensuousness and the dynamic movement that became such an integral part of Shakespeare's imagery. (But even before that this language was adopted by Elizabethan clowns: one of the greatest of them all, William Kempe, used the same image in a related context of social criticism: "Farewell Bowe, haue ouer the Bridge, where I heard say, honest Conscience was once drowned.")[31]

Haphazard's relatively urbane speech differs noticeably from the more earthy language of *Mankind*, but its continuity in the Vice tradition is unquestionable. Although verbal refinements have accrued, the Vice's traditional modes of address and his critical perspective remain more or less intact as he sums up and distances the theme of "judgment and justice" introduced by the final "Thus." Here the actor can still distance the world of the play, as well as his own role, through a perceptive critical poise which links the illusions of the theater with the reality of society.

This clarifies, in part, the context in which the "mad" Lear inverts "justice" and "thief" (IV, 6, 154), and in which Hamlet's antic sarcasm is most effective. As in the case of Myscheff, Inclination and Haphazard, sense and nonsense, bold criticism and "mad" impertinence, are not mutually exclusive. On the contrary, only when Lear, Edgar, and Hamlet assume their strange "range" of madness do their visions of injustice achieve their most penetrating vitality. It appears, then, that there is an important connection to be drawn between the postritual tradition of madness and the ravings of Prince, King, and outcast son which drive home a profoundly serious criticism of society. In view of this it is something of an oversimplification to follow too closely the customary derivation of the convention of madness—its dramatic functions and metaphorical energies—from classical tragedy (via Kyd), such as Seneca's *Hercules furens*.[32]

Hamlet's "antic disposition" is, no doubt, the most complex case of combined madness and impertinency, and as such an extraordinarily good example to consider in discussing the background, structure, and functions of dramatic madness. To begin with, an element of madness can be found in the oldest parts of the Hamlet legend. Amlethus, the hero in Saxo Grammaticus who has parallels in the Icelandic saga of Ambeles and a fragment in the Prose Edda, has his roots in Germanic folklore and myth. The theme of feigned madness goes back very far, and the hero's disorderly dress and unkempt appearance, his offensive, obscene, and obscure speech, his "unfathomable cunning" and mingling of "craft" and "candour" can already be found in the *Historiae Danicae*. If these sources are based on some folklore tradition (as seems likely), there is something to be said for a more or less direct analogy between Hamlet's regicide and the ritual killing of a king, and the belief that the entire legend of Hamlet's regicide essentially paraphrases a basic ritual situation, of which a comparable derivation, based on myth, may be found in another killer of kings, Orestes, who is also mad, unkempt, fond of obscure utterance and not fond of women.[33]

But it is one thing to be aware of myth and ritual in the legend of Hamlet and quite another to read Shakespeare's play, especially the element of madness, primarily in terms of its obscure folklore sources. Although interesting, such highly speculative interpretation, as suggested by Gilbert Murray, certainly loses touch with the drama at hand when Gertrude is compared to the pre-historic Earth Mother Rhea, or when Shakespeare's *Hamlet* is read by Francis Fergusson as "a species of ritual drama."[34] Even though Hamlet's "antic disposition" is indeed related to the "foolish and grotesque madness" extending through the *Historiae Danicae* and the *Histoires Tragiques*, its dramatic function and delivery can hardly have been derived from these narrative sources. Besides, Shakespeare's Hamlet does not save time, allay doubts, and protect himself by feigning madness; if anything, his antic pose arouses suspicion. Shakespeare's assimilation of the antic theme, in spite of its relative inappropriateness to his hero's immediate psychological needs or indeed the necessities of plot, suggests that the theatrical tradition of madness must have carried considerable weight. Hamlet, of course, is no Vice figure, even though his "flashes of cynical irony" and his sardonic verbal "delight in unmasking,"[35] which he himself calls "knavish speech" (IV, 2, 22), go back to the morality tradition which often fostered a "mad sort" of discourse:

> Haphazard. ... And Hap was hired to hackney in hempstrid:
> In hazard he was of riding on beamstrid.
> Then, crow crop on tree-top, hoist up the sail,
> Then groaned their necks by the weight of their tail:
> Then did Carnifex put these three together,
> Paid them their passport for clust'ring thither.
> Appius. Why, how now, Haphazard, of what dost thou speak?
> Methinks in mad sort thy talk thou dost break.
>
> (IV, 147 f.)

Juxtaposed to this "mad sort" the originality of Hamlet's "knavish speech" is easily appreciated. But still, Haphazard's lines here (more so than his image of conscience "drowned in a basket") indicate at least some mediation between "mad" release and the broader social and dramatic contexts of a diversified and highly sensuous imagery. Again, the autonomous expression of nonsense, as soon as it is related to the larger context of the whole play, becomes suggestive and metaphorical. This bold kind of popular metaphor (for example, "hoist up the sail," for hanging), although still relatively undeveloped, sportive, and heavily alliterative, nonetheless correlates the idea with the "vehicle" of the image and so inspires both with a new dramatic significance: the associations of hemp prophesy death by hanging. As in Haphazard's previous speech, this "mad" kind of metaphor develops essentially through a broad range of implied correlations between the actual world and the nascent unity of the images (as distinguished from the conceptual allegory) of the play world. Shakespeare refined this "mad sort" which, in a play as multileveled as Hamlet, materializes as an almost deliberate dramatic mode: "Though this be madness, yet there is method in't" (II, 2, 203). The supreme synthesis was achieved on the level of representational "matter" and postritual "impertinency": "O matter and impertinency mix'd! Reason in madness!" (King Lear IV, 6, 175).

The ingredients and proportions of this "mixture" changed as it was received by Elizabethan dramatists, but it was a part of stage business long before an "English Seneca read by Candle light" gave it a new rhetorical and psychological dimension. Abandoning the late ritual self-expressive autonomy and self-introductory function of "mad" speech, Shakespeare and Kyd found the device consistent not only with their sources but with contemporary psychology, such as Timothy Bright's 1586 Treatise of Melancholy. They reconciled the native antic tradition with the classical theme of madness by treating it as an assumed or pathological dimension of character.

But while this treatment of madness turned away from the festive residue of late ritual sport and game, an element of traditional impertinence remained, even when it ran counter to the mimetic requisites of modern dramatic dialogue. Polonius gives testimony to the strength and undiminished vitality of this component when he considers Hamlet's distracted speech:

How pregnant sometimes his replies are! a happiness that often madness hits on, which reason and sanity could not so prosperously be delivered of.

(II, 2, 208-11)

"Pregnant" (here closer to the OFr. *preignant* than the Latin *praegnans*) calls attention to the capacity of bold metaphor and irreverent wordplay expansively to discover and correlate.

In general the transitions from "matter" to "impertinency" grow out of, and in turn stimulate, a flexible mode of staging in which the heritage of *platea* extensions into the audience bear a significant relation to the representational *loca* of the play world. Hamlet, for example, is partly given a *platea* position, of which he is repeatedly able to dispose with varying degrees of consistency. From his very first punning words ("A little more than kin and less than kind." I, 2, 65), Hamlet is set at a distance from the court society—a distance underscored visually by his black suit of mourning, already abandoned by the rest. These first words—alliterative, proverbial, spoken in aside—begin to mediate between the etiquette and show of courtly decorum and a consciousness of nonaristocratic standards shared with the Elizabethan public audience. Rural and plebeian experience, images drawn from the most common aspects of everyday life, play an exceptionally large part in the tone and substance of Hamlet's speech. His famous cryptic observation, "I am but mad north-north-west; when the wind is southerly I know a hawk from a handsaw" (II, 2, 375 ff.) draws not only from the aristocratic background of falconry ("I know a hawk from a heron"—i.e., a hernshaw), but also from the background of the common worker ("I know a mortar board from a handsaw"—i.e., "hawk" as a plasterer's tool). Of the one hundred and forty proverbs that M. P. Tilley has found in the play no less than seventy-one are spoken by the Prince.[36] And Hamlet, like the old morality Vice, also sets the pace for wordplay by using more puns than any other Shakespearean character—about ninety, according to M. M. Mahood.[37]

Although these characteristics reflect only one side of Hamlet's social, verbal, and intellectual perspective, they have an immense vitality, not only as a body of complementary social standards and conventions, but as matters of speech and delivery that would almost always call for a downstage position or some form of audience awareness. Admittedly, this physical and intellectual proximity to the audience varies greatly from scene to scene; but a general flexibility of stagecraft, one that constantly recalls the *platea* tradition of the Vice, is unmistakable in those scenes where Hamlet's "antic disposition" and his "madness" loom large. He is not only an aggressive critic, but a "chorus" (III, 2, 238), a "jig-maker" (III, 2, 120), and a source of remarkable obscenity (III, 2, et passim). It is significant that his irreverent popular perspective is focused primarily on the more corrupt, senile, or eccentric members of court. It is somewhat in the manner of Myscheff (see p. 116) that Hamlet parodies the foppish Osric's "golden words" by exaggerating his pompous latinisms.

Hamlet's extradramatic closeness to the audience (through his stage position and the nature of his language) becomes especially effective when coupled with the dominant mode of representational *mimesis*. The play is acted, therefore, on a level of dialogue as well as of narration. Rather than conflict, though, these two dramatic perspectives merge to form a true "scene individable, or poem unlimited." Consider the following characteristic bit of impertinency:

> *Rosencrantz.* Good my lord, what is your cause of distemper?
> You do surely bar the door upon your own liberty,
> if you deny your griefs to your friend.
> *Hamlet.* Sir, I lack advancement.
> *Rosencrantz.* How can that be, when you have the voice of the
> King himself for your succession in Denmark?
> *Hamlet.* Ay, sir, but 'While the grass grows'—the proverb
> is something musty.
>
> (III, 2, 328–35)

Here Hamlet's impertinent reply functions ironically to goad Rosencrantz's curiosity. But to this new effect is added the more traditional nonpertinency of anachronism: Hamlet's allusion to the complaint common among Elizabethan university graduates reflecting the lack of opportunity for advancement[38] serves to extend the play world into the real world, and so intensifies both the tensions between role and actor and the potential meanings of the dramatic action. Here is no simple extradramatic effect, but a perfectly sustained progression of dramatic irony. Hamlet recklessly teases his false friend by both provoking his suspicions and exposing his purposes. Hamlet's second response, a contemporary proverb ("Whylst grass doth growe, oft sterves the seely steede," Whetstone, 1578), not only maintains the provocative challenge, but suggests a race between revenge and perfidy illustrated by the grass growing under Hamlet's feet.

But unlike the irrelevant or provocative impertinency of the Vice, Hamlet's reply is heard and even understood by those who move on the level of the purely representational *loca*. Partners in dialogue, Hamlet and Rosencrantz are both part of one dramatic action, even though they operate on different levels (those of *platea* and *locus*). Thus, they bring a new representational crux to the fore; namely, the problem of communication while arguing at cross purposes, which finally expands to a new sense of the drama of human relationships. Since Hamlet's impertinency is so nearly integrated into the form of dialogue, Guildenstern naturally attempts to bring it more closely in line with conventional conversation:

> *Guildenstern.* Good my lord, put your discourse into some frame,
>   and start not so wildly from my affair.
>
> (III, 2, 299 ff.)

Hamlet's "discourse," however, transcends the "frame" of reference marked by a *locus* position, and so the fact that his impertinency has been fitted to the form of dialogue leads ultimately to a communicative paradox, an abstract pun on the concept of formal communication where the convention of "dialogue" has separate and conflicting meanings and potentialities. When the burden is too great, Hamlet simply washes his hands of the whole matter—itself another form of impertinency:

> *King.*   How fares our cousin Hamlet?
> *Hamlet.* Excellent, i'faith; of the chameleon's dish. I eat the
>   air, promise-cramm'd; you cannot feed capons so.
> *King.*   I have nothing with this answer, Hamlet; these words
>   are not mine.
> *Hamlet.* No, nor mine now.
>
> (III, 2, 90–95)

Mistaking the word, like playing on it, has its nonrepresentational side as sport or game; but Hamlet's reinterpretation of Claudius' question is fully functional in providing a quibbling paraphrase of the action. Claudius explicitly dissociates himself from Hamlet's answer, which alludes to thwarted ambition and calls forth the image of young fowl fatted for the slaughter (answering the reinterpreted question "How eats our cousin Hamlet?"). But if Claudius dissociates himself from their failure in communication, Hamlet mimics Claudius in doing precisely the same thing, thus revealing that he can distance himself from the *platea* position and the antic mode as easily as from the self-contained illusion of the scene. This flexibility in the levels from which Hamlet speaks reflects the multiplicity of social and theatrical perspectives as well as the twofold function of *mimesis* ("enchantment" and "disenchantment"), which we have seen to be so fundamental a part of traditional popular drama. To ignore this and to explain the antic side of Hamlet's language, without recourse to these perspectives,[39] can be seriously misleading.

Again, consider Hamlet's shifting position within the scene:

Hamlet.   [*To Polonius*] My lord, you play'd once i' th' univer-
            sity, you say?
Polonius. That did I, my lord, and was accounted a good actor.
Hamlet.   What did you enact?
Polonius. I did enact Julius Caesar; I was kill'd i' th' Capitol;
            Brutus kill'd me.
Hamlet.   It was a brute part of him to kill so capital a calf
            there. Be the players ready?

                                                          (III, 2, 95-104)

Hamlet's question precedes the appearance of the actors and so is clearly
pertinent to the matter at hand. But although his first two questions are
accurate imitations of conventional conversation, his final comment,
with its heavy-handed wordplay on "brute" and "capital," is not intended
to continue the illusion of dialogue. To begin with, Hamlet no longer
addresses Polonius: he does not say "It was a brute part of him to kill
you." Instead, Hamlet points at Polonius from a position that was more
common to the popular commentator and parodist. This draws Hamlet
completely out of character, for it is the actor, not the role, who
momentarily comes to the fore, inverting not merely the illusion implicit
in impersonation, but the complacent ramblings of an important representative of the court society. If the quibble appears a bit labored and
unprovoked, it is so only by the standards of *mimesis* and not by those of
traditional irreverent parody. Even so, *mimesis* and sport are not always
completely reconciled in the service of a larger dramatic function or
effect; dramatic meaning was at times replaced by the sheer vitality of
verbal games, a tendency that Dr. Johnson found to be Shakespeare's
greatest fault.

4

"Sporte" and Mimesis *in the Structure of Wordplay*

It is against the background and continuity of the popular tradition,
especially, though not exclusively, in the moralities and interludes, that
Shakespeare's verbal art and stagecraft can be seen as interacting elements and as parts of the larger social institution that was the
Elizabethan theater. It is true, every new study of Shakespeare's
wordplay will be deeply indebted to the work of editors, such as John
Dover Wilson, to linguists, such as Helge Kökeritz, and to such perceptive studies of the subject as M. M. Mahood's *Shakespeare's Wordplay,* in
which Shakespeare's puns are viewed in their structural context and

meaning.[40] Also there is the interesting connection between Shakespeare's wordplay and the tradition of Renaissance rhetoric; and certainly the critical habit of close reading and verbal exegesis has considerably increased our awareness of the presence and import of Shakespeare's puns and their connections to that rhetorical tradition.

Still, to conceive of Shakespeare's plays as some kind of symbolic or dramatic poetry, or to relate their dramatic speech exclusively to the practice and theory of Renaissance rhetoric, has imposed limitations upon an understanding of the origins and dramatic functions as well as the total meaning of Shakespeare's wordplay. If the forms and figures of his language must be seen as the work of "a competent rhetorician" who, as T. W. Baldwin says, had grasped right from the beginning all "the fundamentals of the current rhetorical system,"[41] this does not mean that Shakespeare's use of the arts of dramatic speech can all be traced to, or understood as part of, his reception of Renaissance rhetoric and logic. Surely the claim once made by Sister Miriam Joseph now appears excessive and in several respects questionable: "Rightly to appreciate Shakespeare's puns, one should regard them as examples of four highly esteemed figures of Renaissance rhetoric."[42] Unfortunately, this approach to Shakespeare's wordplay, like the approach to his plays as symbols or poems, is based on, and has brought with it, a certain methodological perspective in the light of which the intimate links, in fact the interactions, between Shakespeare's stagecraft and his verbal art, have largely been left unexplored. But the more we understand Shakespeare's work as that of a poet in the theater, the more comprehensively the forms and figures of his language, including wordplay, can be seen, not merely as part of some poetic or symbolic structure, but functionally, in the context of the theater in which verbal art and social action have become indivisible.

To advocate a more comprehensive approach to wordplay in the drama is not to belittle Shakespeare's artistic originality, or to question the immense importance of his rhetorical training, or to minimize its impact on his dramatic language. But it may be one way of drawing attention to the significance and the complexity of popular traditions of speech and acting in Shakespeare's medieval heritage. Even though Shakespeare's debt to the diction of common life has quite often been observed,[43] it seems characteristic of the direction of Shakespearean studies over the past thirty years that we do not have even an exploratory study of the native popular sources of Shakespeare's wordplay. To say this is to argue not for an uncritical type of source study, but for an approach to origins as an element of structure—structure not in the formalist sense of an autonomous aesthetic or linguistic whole, but as a moment in the social mode and theatrical function of dramatic speech.

In the morality, wordplay exists primarily by virtue of the contrasting dramatic modes which distinguish the verbal expression of postritual sport (nonsense, impertinency, etc.) from the representational standards of true dialogue. Such wordplay cannot, of course, compare with the elaborate and subtly conceived wit of Lyly or the infinite variety and ingenuity of Shakespeare's quibbles—forms enriched by artistic self-consciousness, rhetorical training, and the larger social, cultural, and educative context of a rapidly changing English language.[44] Nevertheless, wordplay in the popular morality—even though a good deal of it is jingling, rhythmic, alliterative *Sprachspiel*—does have a meaning and dramatic function that is, in its way, superior to anything found in the sixteenth-century Senecan tradition or the humanist drama of the schools. Its meaning is closely connected with the Vice's penchant for physical and intellectual inversion and is inseparable from the heritage of a largely communal kind of theater in which dramatic speech and audience address, dialogue and aside, role and actor, constantly interact. Such wordplay crystallizes and, in a way, perpetuates the transition from ritual to representational drama in a process of verbal action: it reproduces the movement (and it retains the contradiction) between nonsense and dialogue, between the non-sensical heritage of ritual and the representational form and dramatic illusion of verbal communication.

But it is important to note that the movement or process of verbal action is not a progressive one from ritual *to* representation; for the dialectic of popular dramatic wordplay is such that representational and nonrepresentational elements, sense and nonsense, engage in some kind of an interrelationship: representational meaning is created through playful *metaphor*, and nonsense is the result of semantic or phonetic *imitation*. Such unity of metaphorical play and nonsensical imitation underlies the Vice's quibbling speech as long as this achieves meaning through inversion and inversion through apparent meaning. Usually this involves the confusion of two or more semantic or aural units. The confusion, however, is a contradiction, and reveals a broader context in which one element (often the more abstract) is undermined by a more concrete concept.[45] In metaphor both levels of the relationship come together in a momentary unity of association and expression, which involves both evaluation and *mimesis;* but in wordplay these remain separate. Consequently, the meaning of wordplay, like that of the riddle, must be guessed: its effect presupposes an awareness of the incongruity between the two apparent meanings. Its affective function can be quite complex: unlike metaphor, there is no union in a new and encompassing level of perception. Since the playful or riddling side of wordplay is inherently confusing, it is particularly well suited to the Vice's "Dionysian" self-expression and obscene foolery. The retention of these nonrepresentational survivals within the nascent framework of illusion and dialogue gives wordplay its curious dramatic function in the morality.

Several examples which illustrate that function can be found as early as *Mankind*. Myscheff, as noted above (p. 119), follows Mercy's introductory exhortations with a literal inversion of the didactic metaphor concerning the "corn" and the "chaffe," as the chaff from threshing is confused with the chaff at the Last Judgment—the symbolic generalization reduced to a concrete picture. This banter at the expense of the biblical meaning not only includes jingling alliteration ("Dryff-draff, myssemasche") but also semantic play ("Raffe"—the name Ralph; raff—rifraff). This play on word, sound, and image is characteristic of the Vice, and crops up again and again in other corruptions of the sense and sound of liturgical and biblical expressions. The repeated play with new words like "dalyacyon," in the most widespread of all folk play formulae—

> Leue yowur chaffe! leue yowur corn! leue yowur dalyacyon!
> Yowur wytt ys lytyll, yowur hede ys mekyll, ye are full of predycacyon
>
> (46–47)

is tame compared to the daring play upon the phrase "pardon be lymett" (indicating limited absolution—"pardon by limit"—but turned into "pardon bely mett" in line 138, a "belly-measured pardon"). The Vice New-gyse's transformation of the Dominican Order into "the demonycall frayre" (148) is just as bold, and may even add a touch of Lollard historical reality.

In the context of dialogue, such nonsense becomes sarcastic, critical, blasphemous buffoonery, no longer merely playful jargon. But a primitive link with the purely non-sensical remains, in Myscheff's dog-Latin, for instance, which appears to follow the form of dialogue but in fact remains outside the mimetic and psychological illusion of conversation. It is important to recognize in these early types of wordplay a social and dramatic mode that anticipates the same function of verbal inversion that in some of Shakespeare's quibbles can serve, according to Mahood, as "an outlet for scepticism about authority," by undermining the "social prestige" of words such as "blood," "state," "great," "high," and "grace."[46] This particular function of wordplay generally occurs in a specific dramatic context—a context that is seldom precipitated by dramatic action or psychological need. Such wordplay is most often gratuitous: proof of the actor's spirit or quick intellect, for instance. It is used by the Vice and his comic or rascally descendants who comment cynically, obscenely, obtusely on the didactic or serious themes of the play. As is the case with Myscheff, wordplay often supports the speaker's proximity to the audience and its cheerful, festive or self-expressive mood. It encourages the audience to think along.

The structure of verbal inversion, in much of the morality, is in at least one respect quite traditional: an object, an individual, an attitude, a manner of speaking, an image is "disenchanted" as it is playfully exposed to some aural or semantic *mimesis*. But the semantic or aural cue is seized upon only that it may be willfully twisted in the process of impertinent imitation. This twisting, however, constitutes a verbal element of dramatic action and as such points beyond those forgotten functions of ritual which, in the folk play, had resulted in a completely detached kind of non-sense: "I met a bark and he dogged at me," for example (see above p. 40). Even when such late ritual speech patterns are taken up by the morality Vice, their meaning, in the context of the Vice's speech, is no longer completely detached from a larger dramatic context. Such speech patterns, in the morality, began to enter into a dynamic relationship with dialogue and the larger meaning of the play, and as such are integrated into the causal, psychological, and formal requisites of dramatic communication and the representation of social action.

This, of course, greatly oversimplifies matters. But if this points to some basic pattern of development, even in its broadest sense, it would explain why wordplay, albeit primitive in form, occurs so early amongst wandering players, long before the influence of Renaissance rhetoric can be traced, and why it is connected, in the mystery plays, with figures mainly pagan and ritual in origin. This connection, which deserves to be considered a little more closely, points to an important element in the background of the morality Vice. Merely to suggest the profound implications of such links with pagan ritual and popular custom, we may recall the relationship between wordplay and the riddle, as well as A. W. Schlegel's derivation of wordplay from some of the functions of *mimesis*: if language can at all hope to recover "the lost similarity between word and thing"[47] then wordplay whose object, or "thing," is language can indeed be said to fulfill this function in a playful manner. By creating simultaneous levels of both incongruity and congruity, wordplay resembles the traditional riddle in function if not in structure. Interestingly enough, the riddle in the popular tradition can achieve an almost utopian dimension, as in the riddle of the featherless bird which, having fallen from the sky, was found by shepherds who "cooked it without fire" and "ate it without mouths." Critics and historians have repeatedly pointed out the "close connection between the riddle and the older magic formula" of "ancient magic saws."[48] And even though this observation cannot be mechanically transferred to the riddling element in wordplay, it is interesting to recall that the "witches' incantations, the obscene sexual and blasphemous ambiguity" which can be traced in the ritual and pagan background of some riddles[49] are not so far removed from the heretical, obscene, impertinent speech of the Vice.

Riddle and wordplay, as Robert Petsch has pointed out, are connected not only in origin but also in function, since both must be cogitated and interpreted. In this respect they are, as Heywood noted in his 1607 *Apology for Actors*, educative; they presuppose and precipitate social interaction. Richard Tarlton, the greatest folk actor of the pre-Shakespearean theater, was a master of the jest that turned on a riddle or wordplay.[50] And there is a direct line to Shakespeare through Tarlton's pupil Robert Armin. Keeping in mind Armin's *Nest of Ninnies,* there is some link between this kind of popular jesting and the verbal comedy that he was to perform (as in the characters of Feste, Touchstone, and Lear's Fool). A good deal of this was anticipated by William Kempe's older, more rural clowning: "the mimicry ... the delight in paradox, the singing, the nonsense rhymes, the pleasure in good living."[51] Both Kempe and Armin had their roots in the clowning tradition of the English theater, the theater from which Shakespeare drew so often when he combined riddle and wordplay and placed them mainly in the mouths of plebeian characters. Such utterances can be highly pertinent to the play's serious message: the riddling, punning, obscene Porter in *Macbeth* turns a critical eye to the world around him, reminiscent of the equivocation that has preceded and anticipating the disorder that is to come. The cobbler's brilliantly conceived riddling wordplay in *Julius Caesar* (I, 1, 10–30), where tension and excitement first build and then slacken, approximates the larger historical theme of fickle allegiances.

But even when stressing the plebeian context of the links between wordplay and riddle, it should be noted that it is impossible to approach wordplay, or the riddle, solely in terms of their popular functions. Wordplay, in Shakespeare's day, was not the exclusive domain of any one segment of society or any particular occasion—as was the case with several other popular traditions and customs. For instance, merchants, burgomasters, gentlemen, and knights, as well as "honest Country fellows" enjoyed William Kempe's nine-day Morris dance; he dedicated his *Nine Daies Wonder* to a lady in waiting, but on the way he also danced a good mile with a village maid in russet coat, "brown as a berry" and "with short, fat legs." In much the same way, the clown's wordplay was appreciated by people from various walks of life, from plain folk to scholar.[52] Thus, it was the cultural "mingle-mangle" that proved a fertile breeding ground for both the popular and humanist sources of wordplay and related verbal comedy (Lyly, as far as his dramatic work is concerned, cultivated the pun, particularly in the servant scenes—as in the language of his Licio, Petulus, and Manes—even when his decorative euphuistic prose had almost nothing in common with wordplay).[53]

If it is at all possible, then, to isolate and to study the prehumanist forms and nonrhetorical functions of wordplay, the uses of verbal inversion in the medieval drama, particularly in the mysteries, deserve special attention. Here it is the language of the Garcio type that is perhaps most illuminating. Garcio (also called Pikeharnes) definitely has much in common with the cheeky servant of the Mummers' Plays,[54] and also with Rubin, the doctor's servant in the German *Salbenkrämerspiel.* He is a poorly paid underling, always hungry, always impudent; he appears as Slawpase in the *Prima Pastorum* and as Daw in the *Secunda,* and is related to Froward in *Coliphizacio,* Garcio of Chester, Brewbarret of York, Colle in *The Play of the Sacrament,* and the boy Hawkyn in *Mary Magdalene.* In the *Prima Pastorum* this type heralds the relief from winter affliction; in Chester he grumblingly asks for his wage (VII, 229-32). This type's persistently ribald banter with his master in Chester recalls Garcio's rollicking back talk as Caym's servant in *Mactacio Abel.* It is here that Garcio (by recalling the speech of Jack Finney and anticipating that of the Vice) provides a significant link between the medieval traditions of the folk and the popular culture of the Renaissance.[55]

Very much at home on the *platea* and always close to the audience, Garcio opens *Mactacio Abel* with direct address reminiscent of Jack Finney in the Mummers' Play: "All hayll, all hayll . . . For here come I, a mery lad!" (1-2). At once he reveals himself to be an unruly boy, for he begins by cursing, in aside, his master, who is toiling at the plow. The interchange that follows, as Caym hands over the reins to Garcio, clearly recalls Jack Finney's disinclination to hold the "doctor's" horse (see above p. 33). Garcio rebels to the point where he counters his master's blow with "equal weight and measure" (51). His final curse to the "old and yong" in the audience, like the Vice's curses in the morality, takes the form of a blessing: "The same blissyng, withouten end,/ All sam then shall ye haue,/ That God of heuen my master has giffen" (444-46).

Both the old folklore and new class consciousness merge within and enrich the parody and the wordplay in this entirely unbiblical mode of clowning. As in the case of Mak or Herod, cultic tradition and contemporary realism are not at odds, but rather combine to form an original speech pattern quite unlike the descriptive narrative of medieval prose and the sermon. Anachronism links the biblical murder with fifteenth-century England, for Caym seeks the pardon customary for certain contemporary crimes. Before proclaiming his master's innocence, Garcio is instructed in gaining the people's attention:

> *Caym.* ... Bot thou must be my good boy,
>   and cry 'oyes, oyes, oy!'
> *Garcio.* Browes, browes to thi boy!
>
> (415-17)

The *Sprachspiel* here is not homonymic ("browes" for "stew"); even the homophony is limited to the internal and end rhyme. The verbal twist is, however, very playful, and symptomatic of the boy's impudence as well as his heritage of topsy-turvy folk patter. Similar jingling wordplay is put in the mouth of Rubin, the doctor's impudent and obscene servant in the German drama. "Misunderstanding" the Marys' complaint—"heu, quantus est dolor!"—Rubin interprets it in purely material terms: "What hay,

what hay, what hay,/ what say you about hay?"[56] In both cases the
wordplay derives from an inversion of what has directly preceded. And
like Rubin, who elsewhere demands his wage and a *guten faisten praten*[57]
(good roast meat), Jack Finney and Garcio are both essentially requesting food; the twisting of words as quoted above is consistently reduced to
a plea for enough food. The *Sprachspiel* with "browes" is no coincidence,
for this motif crops up again and again.

> *Caym.*   I commaund you in the kyngys nayme,
> *Garcio.*   And in my masteres, fals Cayme,
> *Caym.*   That no man at thame fynd fawt ne blame,
> *Garcio.*   Yey, cold rost is at my masteres hame.
> *Caym.*   Nowther with hym nor with his knafe,
> *Garcio.*   What! I hope my master rafe.
> *Caym.*   For thay ar trew full manyfold.
> *Garcio.*   My master suppys no coyle bot cold.
> *Caym.*   The kyng wrytys you vntill.
> *Garcio.*   Yit ete I neuer half my fill.
> *Caym.*   The kyng will that thay be safe.
> *Garcio.*   Yey, a draght of drynke fayne wold I hayfe.
> *Caym.*   At thare awne will let tham wafe.
> *Garcio.*   My stomak is redy to receyfe . . .

> (419–32)

While Caym reads his proclamation in an attempt to acquit himself of
the curse of fratricide, Garcio chatters about roast meat, soup, and his
empty stomach. He twists and adds rhymes to his master's self-
proclaimed pardon, interrupting him a dozen times. Like Jack Finney
with his Cokaygne-oriented chatter, Garcio uses the call for food as a
crux for inversion, fitting it all the while into the "dialogue" as a rhyming
game, as a nonsensical form of reply. Although these sarcastic interjections cannot properly be called wordplay, a truly impertinent verbal
incongruity follows from Garcio's nonsensical rhymes on his master's
serious words.

This irreverent rhyming game arises out of a dramatic situation quite
similar to that which informs Myscheff's wordplay and clowning. Like
Myscheff, Garcio stands between his partner in dialogue and the audience; and Caym can hear no more of his servant's interjections than
Mercy can hear the Vice's wordplay. In much the same way that Richard
III, Iago, Thersites, and Apemantus and others tended to remain closer
to the audience than to their partners in dialogue, Garcio and the Vice
figures so twist and corrupt didactic or plainly serious language that
their distance from the main action has almost reached the point of
aside. But the term "aside" is misleading here, since it refers to a point of
view developed in a later, more illusionistic theater, one that no longer
had a platform or *platea*-like stage to foster the dissociative effect of

speech conducted on two or more different levels. These levels account in part for the curious tension between the illusion of dialogue and the sense that wordplay generates of being closer to the audience, a tension that remained down to the banquet scene in *Timon of Athens.*

As similar to the rebellious Jack Finney as Garcio in *Mactacio Abel* are Colle, the "lechys man" in *The Play of the Sacrament,* and Hawkyn, the boy in *Mary Magdalene.*[58] But as servant to the cultic presbyter, Hawkyn represents a style of topsy-turvydom that comes even closer to Myscheff's rebellious blasphemy. The fact that the presbyter appears as a pagan priest hardly detracts from the blasphemy, for all of the accoutrements of the Christian priest remain: the sermon, the parish, the bells that Hawkyn must ring, and the altar that he must prepare, all in "grett solemnyte" (1147). The boy, of course, completely misunderstands his instructions when he is called on to perform his duties: "whatt, master, woldyst þou have þi lemman to þi beddes syde?" (1149). A very impious exchange follows the priest's objection to, and attempt to correct, Hawkyn's mistake, an exchange filled with lewd talk of affairs with women, a comment on the priest's devilish paunch, and a gross obscenity that ends in a good beating for the boy (1153–77).

But all this is merely a prelude to the actual topsy-turvy wordplay, a nonsensical prayer that parodies the Latin liturgy after the manner of Myscheff—a flood of rank, obscene, and grotesque alliteration, nonsensical latinisms, and twisted conventional usage.

> . . . skartum sialporum, fartum cardiculorum,
> slavndri strovmppum, corbolcorum,
> snyguer snagoer werwolfforum,
> standgardum lamba beffettorum,
> strowtum stardy strangolcorum,
> rygor dagor flapporum,
> castratum ratyrybaldorum,
> Howndes and hogges, In hegges and helles,
> snakes and toddes mott be yower belles;
> ragnell and roffyn, and other, In þe wavys,
> gravntt yow grace to dye on þe galows.
>
> (1191–1201)

"Begynne þe offyse of þis day" prompts the presbyter; but the boy has hardly begun to sing his song when the presbyter interrupts:

> Hold yp! þe dyvll mote þe a-fray,
> for all ow3t of rule þou dost me bryng!
>
> (1228 f.)

This, indeed, is precisely what the Hawkyn type and the Vice figures are repeatedly called upon to do. By putting meaning, sound, and song "ow3t of rule" they put their master or the representative of Virtue

"owʒt" as well. The presbyter's exhibition of some grotesque relics—
"mahowndes own nekke bon . . . Mahowndys own yee-lyd" (1233 ff.)—
completes the parody with obvious references to contemporary abuses
repeatedly seized upon and criticized by the Lollards.

Like Hawkyn, Colle confronts his master and manipulates words to
similar effect. Following the traditional Jack Finney and Rubin, Colle is a
doctor's servant and crier who ridicules his master's quackery, his shabby
suit, his ability to make the well man ill and send the sick man to his grave
(*The Play of the Sacrament*, 489–92, 531–39). His topsy-turvy announcement recalls similar nonsensical inversion by Rubin in the Innsbruck
Easter Play:

> die blinden macht er sprechen,
> die stummen macht er eszen,
> her quam czu erztige also vil
> also eyn esel czu seyten spil.[59]

Colle's doctor does not "lead the blind to speak" and "the deaf . . . to eat,"
nor can he see with his ears (like mad Lear, IV, 6, 151), but he can see as
well by day as by night and with the vision of the blind man.

> He seeth as wele at noone as at nyght,
> And sumtyme by a candelleyt
> Can gyff a judgyment aryght
> As he that hathe noo eyn.

> (457–60)[60]

Colle's statement sounds very much like Garcio's rhymed introduction
of Caym or the burlesque proclamation in *Mankind* (659 ff.), but shows
even more striking similarities to the Vice's parody in *All for Money*
(printed in 1578) in which the stage direction itself describes the topsy-
turvy banter that follows: *"Here the vyce shal turne the proclamation to some
contrarie sence at euery time all for money hath read it, and here foloweth the
proclamation...."*[61] The connection between this direction and the an-
nouncements made by the young Finney, Rubin, Garcio, and Colle is
supported by the Vice's question prior to his improvised "contrarie
sence": "Shall I in my mannes voyce or in my boyes voyce it declare?"
(1007).

Colle, although not specifically directed to improvise, is directed to
speak toward "the place"; and so he begins, appropriately, fully conscious of the audience around him: "Aha! here ys a fayer felawshyppe!"
(445). Colle's speech probably contains only one genuine wordplay,[62] but
a number of playful expressions that seem to reiterate his master's words
while actually scurrilously and ironically inverting their meaning confirm the boy's ready wit (516, for example).[63] Like the Vice of the
morality plays, Garcio, Hawkyn, and Colle combine the sportive effect of

traditional license and inversion with a new impulse toward satirical *mimesis*. The result is rarely profound in the sense of any structural significance for the play as a whole, but rather critical, heretical, or obscene impertinence, often disguised as "misunderstanding," spoken usually from a position especially close to the audience.

By the time that the Christian allegory of evil is coupled with, or even grafted on, the traditional context of sportive inversion, there is a continuity as well as some discontinuity in the peculiar forms and formulae of the language of wordplay. The persistence as well as the change in function cannot, of course, be separated from the social foundations of some underlying cultural need which, it seems, was best met by the continued proximity of clowning and realism. But the ritual heritage as adapted by the culture of the popular mimes is eventually confronted and, of course, profoundly affected by an early modern consciousness of history and individuality involving the "self-determination," and that "free consciousness of human aims, involvements and fates"[64] from which, according to Hegel, drama first emerged. And although there are obvious and enormous differences in artistry (we really cannot compare the quality of the language in the mystery, or in the morality, for that matter, with that of Shakespeare) it was the art of the itinerant actors that achieved and perpetuated the most effective and fruitful links with the social and verbal conventions of the Garcio type—conventions centering on the Vice, the Janus-faced descendant of both ritual and realism.

To discuss the Vice's contribution to the developing art of wordplay, a few examples must serve to illustrate the expanding functions of the pun in the earlier sixteenth century. For instance, let us consider his language in *King Johan,* where the Vice Sedycyon interrupts Johan and Ynglond in their dignified dialogue:

> Sedycyon. What, yow ij alone? I wyll tell tales, by Jesus!
> And saye that I se yow fall here to bycherye.
> K. Johan. Avoyd, lewde person, for thy wordes are ungodlye.
> Sedycyon. I crye you mercy, sur, pray yow be not angrye;
> Be me fayth and trowth, I came hyther to be merye.
> K. Johan. Thou canst with thy myrth in no wysse
> dyscontent me,
> So that thow powder yt with wysdome and honeste.
> Sedycyon. I am no spycer, by the messe! ye may beleve me.
> K. Johan. I speke of no spyce, but of cyvyle honeste.
> Sedycyon. Ye spake of powder, by the Holy Trynyte!
> K. Johan. Not as thow takyst yt, of a grosse capasyte,
> But as Seynt Pawle meanyth unto the Collossyans
> playne:

"So seasyne yowr speche, that yt be withowt
disdayne."

(43–55)[65]

The Vice interrupts the serious characters with sheer impertinence, an
interruption that is almost as unprovoked as the cheeky impudence of
the boy servants just discussed or the gratuitous remarks of the Vice in
Mankind. And yet, here is already more of an illusion of a dramatic
situation, of a misunderstanding, than in Myscheff's provocative "impertinency": the semiritual quality of the actor's self-expression has been
more firmly integrated into the art of dialogue. Still, the basic social
mode and metaphorical process of punning are the same: here, as in
Mankind, an abstract or moralizing concept of grace or propriety is reduced to its metaphorical vehicle, which is taken from the world of
physical objects. The Vice ignores the abstract concept, or "tenor," and
jumps to perceive the ordinary, everyday referent of the image, which is
chaff and corn for Myscheff and "spyce" for Sedycyon, a procedure that
is paralleled later in Shakespeare when Speed prefers the physical *vehicle*
of his "master's ship" to the more abstract *concept* of "mastership." This is
pure verbal comedy, even when the object of such good-humored inversion is rank and authority. But as soon as "nobility and tranquillity,
burgomasters and great oneyers" (*1 Henry IV* II, 1, 73–77) are involved,
the quibble can perform a truly subversive function; for these worthies,
says one of Falstaff's company, "pray continually to their saint, the
Commonwealth; or, rather, not pray to her, but prey on her; for they
ride up and down on her, and make her their boots." The pious word
"pray" is, just as "powder" in its hortatory meaning, reduced to a more
realistic frame of reference. For Sedycyon (as for Launce) it is another
instance of common misunderstanding in which the down-to-earth referent obscures the symbolic or abstract content. It certainly is not fortuitous when, ultimately, the inversion is one of ideology, and popular
impertinence and humanist criticism merge in an attack on the
rationalized sanctions of the newly formed nation. (As Thomas More
had said: "when I consider and way in my mind all these commen
wealthes, which now a dayes any where do florish, so God helpe me, I
can perceave nothing but a certain conspiracy of riche men procuringe
theire owne commodities under the name and title of the commen
wealth.")

Sedycyon's ostensible design—"I came hyther to be merye"—closely
parallels Myscheff's admission that "I am cumme heder to make yow
game." And although the more rigorous moral negativity of Sedycyon
makes him less the practical joker than Myscheff, his ironic and irreverent parody and his self-introduction remain, for all intents and purposes, quite traditional.

> *Go owt Nobylyte and Clargy.*
> *Here Sedycyon cummyth in.*

Sedycyon.   Haue in onys a-geyne, in spyght of all my enymyes!
              For they cannot dryve me from all mennys
              companyes;
              And, thowgh yt were so that all men wold forsake me,
              Yet dowght I yt not but sume good women wold take me.
              I loke for felowys that here shuld make sum
              sporte:
              I mervell yt is so longe ere they hether resorte.
              By the messe, I wene the knaves are in the bryers,
              Or ells they are fallen into sum order of fryers!
              Naye, shall I gesse ryght? they are gon into the stues;
              I holde ye my necke, anon we shall here newes.
                       [*He hears Dyssymulacyon*] *seyng the Leteny.*
              Lyst, for Gods passyon! I trow her cummeth sum hoggherd
              Callying for his pygges. Such a noyse I neuer herd!
                       Here cum Dyssymulacyon syngyng of the letany.
Dyssymulacyon. (syng) *Sancte Dominice, ora pro nobis!*
Sedycyon.   (syng) Sancte pyld monache, I be-shrow *vobis!*
Dyssymulacyon. (syng) *Sancte Francisse, ora pro nobis!*
Sedycyon.   Here ye not? Cocks sowle, what meaneth
              this ypocrite knaue?

                                                              (626–41)

Audience contact continues to play a significant part in the dynamics of Sedycyon's character and actions. His physical position here can truly be described as "aside," especially after Kynge Johan's exhortation, which amounts to a stage direction: "I saye, hold yowr peace, and stand asyde lyke a knave!" (112). From this position Sedycyon grotesquely travesties the litany (639), for Dyssymulacyon either does not hear him or ignores him, so that Sedycyon must call attention to himself with the abrupt, "Here ye not?"

But not only the word of the church can thus be mistaken; the words and standards of the ruling class can equally be reduced, as when, in *All for Money,* the Vice Sinne is asked about the "degree" from which he is descended:

Money.   May I be so bolde to knowe of what kindred,
         Or else from what stocke you are proceeded.
Sinne.   The last stockes I was in was euen at Bamburie,
         The be worme eaten which shewes them ancient to be:
         If they were mine because they be so olde,
         I would burne them in winter to keepe me from the colde.
Money.   I meant of what degree you were descended.

                                                           (937–43)[66]

Just as the chaff has, beyond its metaphorical reference to the Day of Judgment, its use in feeding horses, so can the worm-eaten wood of Sinne's "stockes," when burned, keep him from the cold.

In *King Darius*, Charytie speaks of the treasure of brotherly love, but the Vice Iniquytie reinterprets it as the love of money.

> *Charytie.* ... For the Prophets requyre of vs no more,
> But that a faruent loue wee keepe in stoore.
> *Iniquytie.* That I shall, I wyll kepe it faste.
> *Charytie.* What wilt thou kepe, tell me in haste?
> For I thynke thou art a deceytfull person.
> *Iniquytie.* You bad, I shuld kepe my money, least it were gone,
> And I made my pursle so close and so hard,
> That it will not be lost .iii. halfpence...
>
> (84-91)[67]

The Vice, it seems, is impervious to the moral concepts of both aristocratic and Christian living, and grotesquely persists in challenging accepted moral standards. A popular figure in *Fulgens and Lucrece*, for example, asks, "Uertue, what the deuyll is that?" (II, 842), while Lust, in *The Trial of Treasure*, again confounding idea and ideology, asks, "I pray thee, tel me what meneth this word Charity?" (Dod., III, 68). This, then, is the thematic dimension of wordplay as a dramatic form of inversion and "misunderstanding," where two levels of perception confront each other—the one abstract, the other concrete, one idealistic, the other naive and materialistic.

The same context accounts not only for the expression of disrespect and irreverence, but also for the element of obscenity. To say this is to argue that it would be misleading to consider obscenity in pre-Shakespearean wordplay to be exclusively what Mahood has called "a safe outlet for repressed impulses."[68] For such wordplay seems at least in part a relic of a preascetic and pre-Puritan culture; and as such it survives in *Mankind* (338), in the obscene pun on "hole" and "holy" in *King Johan*, and in Wager's *Life and Repentance of Mary Magdalene* (ca. 1550), where the "prick of conscience" has, for the Vice Infidelity, its full phallic implications. Shakespeare's own obscene wordplay is likewise very much in this tradition. Ambidexter's lewd reinterpretation of the clown Snuff's remark that "in eche corner I will grope" as "What and ye run in the corner of some prittie maide?" in *King Cambises* (174-76), nicely glosses the use of "corner" in *Othello* (III, 3, 276).

Likewise, the play on sound, rhyme, and alliteration in the various forms of the nonsemantic pun has a continuity from *Mankind* and the works of Bale down to the drama of the sixties and seventies, even to semiclassical plays like *Appius and Virginia*: from Colle's "rebyll-rable" in *The Play of the Sacrament* (520) and Myscheff's "dryff-draffe, myssemasche" in *Mankind,* to Sedycyon's "dyble-dable . . . byble-bable" (160–61), Hypocrisy's "smick smack . . . tick-tack" in *Lusty Juventus* (Dod., II, 85), and even Haphazard's "tugging . . . lugging . . . pugging" in *Appius and Virginia* (Dod., IV, 120).

Again, the jingling language of the Vice may well recall Lollard heresies. After Ynglond's pious wish "to governe this realme in peace" and King Johan's subsequent call for "plentyus increase," Sedycyon replies much in the way that Gadshill reacts to the language of "burgomasters and great oneyers" and all those who "pray continually to their saint, the Commonwealth":

> Sedycyon. Of bablyng-matters, I trow, yt is tyme to cease.
> K. Johan. Why dost thow call them bablyng-maters? Tell me.
> Sedycyon. For they are not worth the shakyng of a per-tre
> Whan the peres are gone; they are but dyble-dable.
> I marvell ye can abyd such byble-bable.
>
> (156–60)

The proverbial mode of impertinence, together with anticlerical obscenity (162–67), amounts to an astonishing inversion of orthodoxies old and new. In the immediately preceding dialogue between Ynglond and King Johan, the divine sanctions of both monarchy and the state are heavily emphasized: the word "God" alone recurs half-a-dozen times, the Bible is quoted in Latin, and St. John's "most blyssed gospell" (118) is directly cited. If, in this context, the jingling Vice derides all this "byble-bable," he must have been close to that Lollard (and those sympathizing in the audience) who held "that it was no better for a layman to say the Lord's Prayer in Latin than it was for him to say 'Bibull babull.'"[69] Such popular heretics usually were (as was the Vice Sedycyon) men "of symple dyscrescyon" (161). They were the type of men of whom Colet complained when, in 1512, he declared that "We are nowe a dayse greued of heretykes, men mad with marueylous folysshness."[70] Again, the Vice's impertinent jingling must have been close to such "marueylous folysshness," and his "mad fancies" (*King Darius,* 60) were readily acknowledged as late as in *The Conflict of Conscience* where he presented himself "like a madman" (Dod., VI, 56). There must have been a connection, which is difficult to trace now, between the "mad sort" that Haphazard boasts of and the heresy of which contemporaries were so conscious when they charged the player of plays with "extolling Pagan Idol-gods" and "propagating Atheisme and Idolatry."[71] But it is precisely this context in which the popular wordplay, especially the jingle, thrived together with other submerged late ritual echoes of the punning, rhyming, singing, and dancing Vice.[72]

But although Shakespeare retained the critical perspective on "nobility and tranquillity," the "mad sort" of *Sprachspiel* was virtually surrendered in favor of more highly functional and integrated forms of wordplay. In keeping with its adaptation to the Renaissance art of dramatic dialogue, wordplay came to be more and more important beyond its impertinent dimension, especially in the definition of theme and character. But even when wordplay had assumed a host of functions—comic and tragic—it still remained, for Shakespeare, the Vice's hallmark, inextricably linked with this peculiar character. Since the jingling play on sound was not quite as easily integrated into dialogue as the more semantic, homonymic wordplay, the importance of *Sprachspiel* diminished in the language of his drama.[73] As the autonomy of sport and game declined and a more realistic imitation of conversation developed, there was a concurrent, though not consistent, interest in the causal, spatial, and psychological side of dialogue—action and reaction, statement and counterstatement, question and answer tended to attain a more representational status. The provocative figure of "folysshness," no longer quite as free to argue at cross-purposes with his victim as he was in *Mankind,* became subordinate to a more exacting representational mode of scene and language.

Still, the tradition of popular wordplay continued to reflect the most basic contradiction of the pre-Shakespearean theater itself: the tension between the nonrepresentational uses of the *platea* or platform close to the audience and the increasingly self-contained illusion of reality in the dramatic portrayal of action and character. Enriched by classical and rhetorical elements, the integration of wordplay into scene and action proceeded unevenly. But we can, nonetheless, detect a basic pattern: the actor provoked by the wordplay no longer simply ignored it, but acknowledged it and tried to clear it up as if it were a misunderstanding. This attempted clarification naturally led nowhere, since the "misunderstanding" was not a mistake in the first place but a deliberate talking at cross-purposes. The question posed in response to the "misunderstanding" can, however, be telling, both of character and psychology, and offers an easy and effective means of drawing the hitherto isolated wordplay into dialogue.

A rather interesting compromise between the emerging self-contained unity of dialogue and scene on the one hand, and the Vice's nonrepresentational position on the other, resulted in no less effective verbal and theatrical play:

> *Lust.*   My lady is amorous, and full of favour.
> *Inclination.* (*aside*) I may say to you she hath an
>   ill-favoured savour.
> *Lust.*   What sayest thou?
> *Inclination.* I say she is loving and of gentle behaviour.
>
> (Dod., III, 292)

The Vice's interjection, fully understood by the audience but not by his partner in dialogue, is at least partially reconciled to the dramatic illusion of a self-contained scene in that it is technically spoken in aside. But the technique achieved its full potential—scenic, spatial, psychological, causal—when Shakespeare recreated the Vice in a new context:

> Gloucester. [Aside] So wise so young, they say, do never live long.
> Prince.   What say you, uncle?
> Gloucester. I say, without characters, fame lives long.
>   [Aside] Thus, like the formal vice, Iniquity,
>   I moralize two meanings in one word.
>   (Richard III III, 1, 79–83)

Clearly, then, Gloucester's use of the aside and proverb was not "a new stratagem in dialogue,"[74] as the most thorough commentary on *Richard III* suggests, but a traditional element in the sixteenth-century popular theater.

Such a synthesis of an awareness of the audience with a sense of a self-contained imitation of dialogue combined to open up a variety of forms of speech and staging that were accessible neither through Seneca and neoclassical tragedy nor even through Plautus. Once Shakespeare's receptivity to the "language of the people" (W. Franz), the "ordinary word" (D. S. Bland), the "diction of common life" (F. P. Wilson) is considered more seriously in its dramatic context and consequences, there can be no doubt that he, too, was (as Gabriel Harvey said of Nashe) receptive to "Tarlton's precedent" and other popular forms of language and dramaturgy.

Although the Roman servant type, the tradition of the court fool, the humanist *Praise of Folly,* and other factors contributed to the makeup of the fool as he descended to, and was recreated by, Shakespeare,[75] the connection between wordplay and the Vice remained an important and a direct source of inspiration, especially when traditional popular conventions of sport and foolery were correlated to the Renaissance standards of dramatic dialogue. Here, let us recall that Launce's reduction of his "mastership" is followed up by Speed's telling remark: "Well, your old vice still: mistake the word" (*The Two Gentlemen of Verona* III, 1, 276–79). Like Feste, Launce is a "corrupter of words" (*Twelfth Night* III, 1, 34). But there is a growing self-consciousness in the new context of the old modes of verbal inversion: "every fool," as Lorenzo says, "can play upon the word" (*The Merchant of Venice* III, 5, 38).

The point that finally has to be made is not simply that Shakespeare adopted the wordplay in the Vice tradition but rather that he so adapted and developed its theatrical and poetic context that he used it in many more functions—comic and tragic—than the traditional kind of "impertinency" ever allowed. This must be stressed even when—as we have seen—Shakespeare himself quite deliberately and repeatedly associated the art of mistaking the word with the Vice tradition. But when Shakespeare, as it were, quoted the "formal vice," he did not simply incorporate the quotation but stylized it with a new kind of effectiveness characteristic of the general mode of his reception of the popular tradition. For Gloucester's reference to the "formal vice, Iniquity" is—like Speed's—itself in the form of a pun, and it is a vicious and highly sophisticated kind of "contrarie sence" in which Gloucester uses the verb "moralize." The sense of the verb is sarcastically inverted, but this inversion works on two levels and has a twofold function: first, it achieves a sarcastic irony that is entirely in line with the new task of the mimetic creation of character as based on the illusion of a certain psychological coherence. But second, behind the new psychology of this role there is still a residuum of the actor's awareness of his own social function and identity, so that the actor—in the quibbling use of the verb "moralize"—does not simply use a pun but seems to acknowledge its source by referring to the origins, in the morality tradition, of such a technique of confounding two meanings in one word. "Moralize," in this sense, is a metaphorical statement about the literary history of the verbal figure that the actor uses with a remarkable consciousness of its theatrical origins and functions.

Richard Gloucester is, in his own way, a "corrupter of words," and the vicious tradition of moralizing two meanings in one word is very much alive in Shakespearean comedy as it is in tragedy, where the convention of madness provides an effective frame in which the device of impertinent "contrarie sence" (to use once again the stage direction from *All for Money*) still fulfills important dramatic functions. When, for example, Prince Hamlet corrupts the verb "fare" by using it—in the manner of the Vice—in the material sense of eating, not in its general or abstract meaning (of "how do you do"), he does indeed, as Guildenstern reproachfully observes, transcend the "frame" of dramatic discourse. But to "start . . . so wildly" from the affair of the dialogue corrupts more than words: it corrupts, as it were, the dramatic illusion of conversation. The result is not merely of a verbal nature: it affects the actor's relation to both the scene and the audience. For Hamlet at such moments releases himself from his own role of the Prince of Denmark: with the help of popular proverb and aside he momentarily dissociates himself from the illusion of the world of the court and revives a late ritual capacity for reckless sport and social criticism.

Hamlet, however, is no Vice, and his genetic relations with the mischievous figures in the morality are much more tenuous than in the case of Richard III or even Shakespeare's clowns. The Vice was, even for Richard, a "formal vice"; for Feste, too, he was something to be quoted and recalled: "I'll be with you again/In a trice,/Like to the old Vice,/Your need to sustain" (IV, 2, 118-21), as he was for Speed: "Your old vice still" (III, 1, 279). These qualifications are, in Shakespeare, perhaps the most illuminating: the Vice was the *old* Vice, but *still* he could be used or referred to; and the words "old" and "still" indicate the dialectic of innovation and tradition by which Shakespeare's wordplay actually thrived upon the diminishing tensions of *mimesis* and ritual, matter and impertinency. It did so because the traditional pun itself continued to serve as a highly significant medium of interaction between the mimetic form of dialogue and the communal expression of festive release, between role and actor, drama and audience—an interaction that was still central to the basic process of the popular Elizabethan theater.

5

Vice against Virtue: The Comic Double-plot

If wordplay can serve as the most telling verbal paradigm of the changing popular modes of dramatic inversion, then the Vice's "contrarie sence" must be seen both as qualified and generalized when it assumes structural as well as verbal functions. After all, the Vice is the only thoroughly farcical character among many other figures in the allegorical scheme. Primarily an instigator, he stands for himself alone; it is his opposition to, and provocation of, Virtue that precipitates the broader dramatic conflicts in which the allegorical representatives of mankind initially find themselves. Only an awareness of the full context of this conflict can help clarify the nature of the Vice's social and dramatic functions and indicate his structural significance in the development of what was, along with the mystery play, the most important dramatic genre before Shakespeare.

Once again, *Mankind* can be taken as a revealing example, especially since the social positions that Virtue and Vice occupy are so easily discernible. Myscheff appears first in the role of peasant and "wyntur corn-threscher" (54). His language is derived from a characteristically rural experience and plebeian background. Like the later language of Thersites and Lear's Fool, Myscheff's vocabulary is further distinguished by its vivid contrast to that of the serious or official characters that confront him. In the first five lines of his introductory speech alone Mercy uses no fewer than nine abstract and generally clumsy latinisms (lauatorye, condycions, rectyfye, humility, reuerence, remocyon, gloryfye, partycypable, retribucyon, 12–16). Myscheff's language, and that of the other Vices, is markedly different in this respect; they talk of winter, cold weather, horses, saddles, and straw.

> *Mercy.*   A-voyde, goode brother! Ye ben culpable
>   To interrupte thus my talkynge delectable.
> *Myscheff.* Ser, I haue nother horse nor sadyll;
>   Therefor I may not ryde.
> *Mercy.*   Hye yow forthe on fote, brother, in Godis name!
> *Myscheff.* I say, ser, I am cumme hedyr to make yow game;
>
> (64–69)

While Mercy complains about the interruption of his "delectable" admonitions, Myscheff speaks the language of the contemporary land laborer. And when Mercy later encounters New-gyse and Now-a-days to
pursue the "communycacyon" of his "denomynacyon" (122), he is met
with the impudent yet accurate exclamation, "Ey! Ey! yowur body ys full
of Englysch Laten!" (124). Now-a-days compounds the deflating effect
by asking Mercy to describe, in his scholarly and clerical language, an act
of scatological dexterity:

> *Now-a-days.* I prey yow hertyly, worschyppfull clerke—
>   I haue etun a dysch full of curdis,
>   Ande I haue schetun yowur mowth full of turdis.
>   Now opyn yowur sachell with Laten wordis,
>   Ande sey me this in clerycall manere!
>
> (125–29)

In addition to the striking disparity of decorum in the vocabulary of
Virtue and Vice there is a corresponding difference in the meter of their
speech. Such contrasts between both the content and the form of vicious
and virtuous speech reflect the fundamental antagonisms implicit in the
juxtaposition of different patterns of social action. Mercy, whose
"clerycall manere" is only an extension of the clerk's Latin education,
conforms to a social stratum relatively close to, if not congruent with, the
ruling authorities of church and state. Placed on the plebeian stage this
figure could easily become the butt of burlesque *mimesis* and caricature;
and it is not unlikely that the playwright "deliberately made fun of
Mercy" in his attempt to please the tavern audience.[76] On the other
hand, however lewd and reprehensible the Vice's antics may have been,
they were always expressed in a thoroughly understandable language,
an Anglo-Saxon speech that was familiar in a way that the unctuous
prattling of a latinized cleric could never hope to be.

The dramatic potential of the Vice's language and social position was
complemented by the frequency and facility with which he addressed the
spectators. The Vice sang songs with the audience, walked amongst
them rattling his collection box, chatted with the innkeeper and occasionally sported with those around him. The unique relationship between the Vice's jolly Christmas or Shrovetide spirit and the audience's
festive mood was reflected in a *platea*-like position that the Vice assumed

on the stage. This dramatic difference between Vice and Virtue is crystalized when Now-a-days, expressing his boredom with Mercy's "doctryne," clearly chooses the Vice's penchant for freewheeling diversion:

> Men haue lytyll deynte of yowur pley,
> Be-cause ye make no sporte.
>
> (260-61)

The Vice criticizes from the audience's point of view. He sees in Mercy not the allegorical representative of Virtue but the actor ("yowur *pley*") performing a dull role; his is the standard of values associated with the *platea* as against the quite different claims of a *locus*-oriented Virtue. Thus the relationship between Vice actor and audience does not operate at the level of moral fiction or dramatic illusion, but exists rather on the very boards of the stage; for the Vice stands, as champion of "sporte" and game, between the fiction of the moral action and the audience's festive expectations.

To recapitulate the social and theatrical background of the Vice is to point to his showmanship as one of his most spectacular structural functions in the play as a whole. But this function, even when as well developed as in *Mankind,* is an ambivalent affair; nor is it the Vice's only function. For despite his special relationship with the audience, the Vice remains a grotesque character who is both entertaining and repulsive, gay yet evil. The faint residuum of a more primitive pagan culture is revived as the touch of hell and damnation, and as such it remains indelibly branded on him (and usually much more strongly than is the case in *Mankind*). And yet—and this is the Vice's paradox—his "vicious" action retained its fascination, a vital dramatic quality that seemed to survive all moral teachings and ideologies. It is a fascination at once free of the fears and horrors of hell and also allied with them, a vitality that becomes both ugly and attractive because it has been branded as evil.

Seen in this light, the Dionysian laughter of the Vice has a truly disturbing undertone which almost explains the hostile polemics that were soon to be unleashed against the frivolous antics of actors, such as Stubbes' indignation at "those Mockers and Flowters" with their "blasphemie intollerable," which included the mixing of "scurilitie with diuinitie."[77] Stubbes' remarks are revealing; they help to define a popular tradition of itinerant players by confirming that mimetic inversion was an element of structure and by almost suggesting a formulation of the basic structural contradiction of their plays: "scurilitie" *contra* "diuinitie"—the amoral and immoral outlook of the Vice versus theological morality.

However, the Vice's centrality to this conflict is actually not as clear-cut as it would first appear. He is himself a divided figure: the division is part of his own ambivalence. On the one hand he provides a clowning re-enactment of semiritual sport and showmanship, but on the other he carries within himself an element of homiletic condemnation. Insofar as the Vice is an allegorical manifestation of sin, this conflict cuts right through his motley being, drawing sustenance from quite orthodox sources: the Psychomachia, traditions of allegory like the Seven Deadly Sins, and contemporary sermons. These sources have great resonance and an undoubtedly important effect on the Vice, which at times can be stronger than the popular heritage of late ritual expression emphasized in the present context. Usually, the Janus-faced character of the Vice is most evident where the plebeian background of the drama can be most certainly assumed: in the anonymous plays of the wandering troupes, those "doble dealing ambodexters" (Stubbes) whose repertoire had little chance of ever being printed and, hence, preserved. Myscheff may well have been typical in many ways of the Vice in these works. He advocates sensual release and moral irreverence, but at the same time he morally disclaims them. In the end the Vice is, like Goethe's Mephisto, free only to negate. Although bringer of "game" (69), "sporte" (78), "mery chere" (81), and "reuell" (82), the Vice is no pure and simple image of a Dionysian rebelliousness, or even of man "both fresh and gay," but rather the grotesque embodiment of anarchy, farce, and corruption.

Even so, the moral disapproval of sin can be less convincing than wantonness itself. The sensuous portrayal of moral backsliding challenges the didactic message and asserts itself in the Vice's basic contradiction between farce and allegory, between the comedy and the tragedy that medieval drama so skillfully made inseparable. The farce itself can embrace the spirit of negation in the form of satire. But the Vice's satiric aggression is not unselective: church, monastery, priest, lawyer, the rich in general come under attack, while "laborers, peasants, the poor, the unfortunate, are never made the object of his satire and mockery."[78] If there is any single social trait or attitude that is consistently made the target of vicious satire it is *covetyse*. In his social criticism this antiacquisitive position is always present from the early *The Castle of Perseverance* to late moralities like *All for Money, Enough is as good as a Feast*, or *The Tide Tarrieth No Man*, and it remains a dominating concern.[79] But, again, the Vice's function is that of an *ambidexter*: he is both object of and spokesman for the attack on *covetyse*. Being an object of satire he can best satirize himself, and hold up his own attitudes for scorn and laughter. He has the unique freedom to represent and to reprehend, to build up and to annihilate, his own standards. Laughter and terror, merriment and satire go together on a *platea*-like stage where actors, and especially the main actor, had a capacity for both creating and distancing the values and illusions of the play.[80]

This dual quality is the source of considerable dramatic vitality. The Vice, in coping with the inherent tensions between terror and laughter, completely offset the structural balance of the original homiletic allegory of the Psychomachia. Just as the singing Nichol Newfangle in *Like Will to Like* climbs jokingly onto the devil's back, many of his fraternity face the gallows with a sardonic joke. As he rides off to hell, Nichol takes his leave: "till I come againe" (Dod., III, 357). This kind of terrible exuberance lived on while, increasingly after 1500, the traditional morality structures of Vices and Virtues changed and the allegory of *humanum genus* retreated into the background. With the symmetry and the homiletic allegory of the Psychomachia thus upset, the original homiletic victory of Virtue over Vice and the grouping around the symbolic human figure were neglected or forgotten. The Vice, of course, had not become the victor, but he did become the most important agent within the framework of these structural changes. For one thing, he came to dominate the stage: Inclination, the Vice in *The Trial of Treasure*, occupies the stage for three-quarters of the acting time (1,561 of 2,081 lines); Perverse Doctrine of *New Custom* remains on stage for nine-tenths of the play (966 of 1,076 lines); the Vice Courage in *The Tide Tarrieth No Man* is there for three-quarters (1,459 of 1,879 lines) and Nichol Newfangle is on stage for five-sixths of the performance (1,077 of 1,277 lines). Although this high proportion decreases in the hybrid moralities of the late sixties and seventies to make room for the nonallegorical main character, the Vice still remained structurally central.[81]

As the morality declined, allegorical figures on the whole assumed roles less and less important to the total dramatic effect. But the Vice continued to make an impact on dramatic structure right up to *King Cambises* and *Horestes*, that is, up to the rise of Tarlton. There are probably many practical reasons why the Vice persisted in this way. The fact that his long part, which could not be doubled, was taken by the main actor may have contributed to his stability. That the actor of this role also spoke the prologue and epilogue—presented and dismissed the troupe—must also have been conducive to his prominence. These practical considerations must not be underestimated; still, they cannot in and of themselves explain why the Vice's impact on language, staging, and structure survived the decline of his traditional allegorical counterparts. But it would certainly be reductive to explain the Vice's longevity in terms of the alleged similarity between his style of speech, and the direct speech and exhortation used by the parish priest. Interpreting the Vice on the basis of a "homiletic principle," understanding the "relationship between stage and audience" as a "homiletic" one, and overemphasizing the "primary and enveloping homiletic dimension that links him directly to the audience" falls far short of explaining his double function and his continued structural importance. Considering the Vice's audience contact as "homiletic intimacy" and "homiletic duty," his vitality the result of "homiletic jest," "homiletic zeal," and even "homiletic showmanship" can be as misleading as seriously interpreting Ambidexter as "a homiletic comment on Sisamnes." From the point of view of structural development, the vital element in the continuity of the morality form went against the grain of the homiletic and didactic heritage; hence, it does not seem plausible that the Vice's audience contact survived, as Bernard Spivack suggests, as a "homiletic function."[82] Such an interpretation, generally accepted by D. M. Bevington, F. M. Salter, and the majority of the students of the morality tradition, seems quite out of touch with the most basic facts of the contemporary theater itself.

The suggestion that "the mirth of the moralities ... consistently pursued a homiletic purpose" is as misleading as the related idea that the Vice's "popularity and the mirth his antics provided" can be explained as "relief from solemnity."[83] This explanation seems as inadequate in fathoming the structural depth and the implications of the Vice's ambivalent functions as the comparable notion that the comedy and the realism in the Wakefield shepherd scenes served simply as "broad fun" and an "escape from piety." This does justice neither to the tension built into the Vice's grotesque double-dealing with allegory and farce, nor to his astounding adaptability within the changing structure of the morality.

If, therefore, the varying structural functions of the Vice are taken into account, at least three aspects must be examined more closely: the Vice as protagonist and opponent to the figures of Virtue; the Vice as intriguer and manipulator of the representatives of humanity; and the Vice as producer, manager, and commentator. These divisions are, of course, somewhat arbitrary and mechanical, but an examination of each can hopefully illuminate their mutual points of contact.

The comic Vice as the only serious opponent of Virtue is clearly the role most directly pertinent to the allegorical contest of souls. In this confrontation with his virtuous counterpart, the structural framework of the Vice's aggressiveness is predetermined. His function, as Politic Persuasion puts it in *Patient and Meek Grissill*, is deceptively simple: "To vex and harme those wightes, whose liues most vertuous are" (935). And although he is generally brought to account by the triumph of Virtue and Order in the end, he remains a powerful symbol of negation and unending rebellion.

> Well, yet I will rebel, yea, and rebel again,
> And though a thousand times you shouldest me restrain.
> *Lead him out.*

> > (Dod., III, 299)

Such powers of negation are not restricted to passive confrontations with the figures of Virtue or Order; for the Vice has his own positive energy to act as manipulator and intriguer. Since this latter function provides an inexhaustible stimulus for dramatic action, the Vice exercises an inordinate amount of control over the course of the plot. And the more clearly he emerges as an independent instigator of actions and reactions, the less he remains part of a balanced contest of allegorical figures.

The Vice, already removed a step from the Psychomachia as a result of his manipulation of it, achieves an even greater distance from the allegorical convention through his role as *conférencier* and chorus. In so standing between the text of the play and its theatrical realization, the Vice mediates between fiction and reality, the drama and the social occasion. Although his predetermined opposition to the virtuous figures does subject the Vice to a more or less prescribed range of attitudes and actions, his developing capacity for original intrigue and his theatrical buoyancy made him an incessant plotter. This accounted for what were frequently unconnected episodes, a mixture of allegorical scheming and pure farce held together with the loose coherence of something like the old picaresque novel. The result was a principle of free structural composition in which this episodic sequence was, in Hegel's sense of the word, so "suspended" that it achieved a vastly superior kind of unity. But only because the growth of structure had long since emancipated itself from the rigor of the homiletic antithesis was the comical-farcical subplot in a position to be fully and freely correlated to a serious secular theme.

If these suggestions as to the Vice's functions in the structural growth of the morality and hybrid plays are—despite the obvious oversimplifications—even remotely accurate, it would appear that the Vice's structural importance follows generally his increasing distance from the Psychomachia. Given this inverse proportion, the Vice's increasing and continued prominence can hardly be explained in terms of his allegorical function or as a consequence of the lingering impact of the pulpit or of allegory alone. How, then, did the Vice achieve and retain, for almost a century, such a profound structural impact? At this point, his sociological background and the late ritual festival traditions of the figure by themselves no longer offer satisfactory answers, for the symbiosis of allegory and farce already presupposes these. It would be more to the point to ask how and why the element of comical farce came to play such a major role in the structure of morality drama.

Here we must recognize that the comic language and character of the Vice belonged, for the most part, to the nonallegorical part of his heritage. Since comedy at first had little intrinsic relation to the struggle between good and evil powers for the soul of man, the comic effect came "primarily from the comic figure, but not from the story or action."[84] As soon as the allegorical representation of sin combined with elements of clowning and the self-expressed *ohm* of popular *mimesis*, the grotesque figure of farce emerged. This combination facilitated the assimilation of the traditional fool's or saucy boy's *game* and showmanship to a generalized *idea* of evil and negation. Richard Tarlton, who—as he did with the jig—reconciled folk culture with the professional stage, had consummated this development, and was remembered for it:

> Now Tarlton's dead, the Consort lackes a vice:
> For knave and foole thou maist beare pricke and price.[85]

The strange combination of clowning release and self-confessed knavery roughly defines the general pattern of allegorical farce. Transforming itself from within the morality, the concurrence of allegory and farce grew in importance, just as the Vice, who provided the omnipresent incarnation of this dramatic synthesis, pointed to the central structural principal of the allegorical-farcical drama.

In the Renaissance, the underlying duality asserted itself in many ways, as "countervoice" (Wolfgang Clemen) or "two-eyedness" (A. P. Rossiter), all in the tradition of "high fraud" (M. M. Morgan). From the Wakefield shepherd scenes and *The Play of the Sacrament* to *Fulgens and Lucrece, King Cambises,* and *Locrine,* down to *The Famous Victories* and *Doctor Faustus,* the incorporation of comic plebeian elements produced a characteristic two-level structure in which the descendants of the Vice gradually became the nonallegorical center of the comic subplot. In its varying relation to the main plot, the subplot might consist of only one or two intermediate scenes or some irreverent farce complementary to the serious action. In this way, age-old traditions of disenchanting *mimesis* filtered into the plays preceding the great works of Renaissance drama. The emerging unity of the main and sublevels of meaning and dramaturgy was closely associated with the traditional unity of the serious and the comic. This association, which was in the nature of an interaction, may well be viewed as the continued attempt, in the sixteenth century, "to expand the framework of the main action limited by the subject matter so as to provide a more comprehensive image, a generally valid image of the world, not conceived exclusively against the background of the central [serious] problem actually dealt with."[86]

This broader picture of the world is derived (as in *King Cambises* or *Locrine*) from the additional perspective of a comic and sometimes burlesque action, which in the final analysis complements or even inverts the serious (heroic or courtly) substance of the main plot. In implementing this, the native popular tradition of topsy-turvydom reasserts itself as a *structural* principle. Over and above its verbal dimension it becomes a deliberate poetic principle of composition, an overriding perspective that informs both dramatic speech and dramatic action.

In Shakespeare, this perspective is especially closely associated with the heritage of the Vice which affects not only (as Bernard Spivack seems to think) the tragedies, but also, and perhaps even more so, some of the comedies and histories. But at the same time, this traditional perspective is no longer exclusively connected to the descendants of the Vice. Wherever the modern representative of evil (Gloucester, Iago, Edmund) tends to dominate the serious part itself, other figures, such as Brakenbury or the Scrivener in *Richard III*, or Poor Tom and the Fool in *King Lear*, are brought in to enunciate a complementary vision of the main theme. Their dramatic function is not a farcical one, but involves that special relationship with the audience which results from a *platea*-like position and allows the statement of generalized truth in a choric mode. Theirs, indeed, are "countervoices"—voices from outside the representative ideologies—ushering in a contrapuntal theme, some countervision which, even in a comic context, cannot be easily dismissed in its thematic implications for the main plot. Thus, for all their immense difference, their dramatic function is similar to that of Shakespeare's porters and gravediggers or, for that matter, of Launce or Falstaff: they all help to embody some counterperspective of self-expressed interest and truth, a naive and joyous, or bitter, sense of freedom from the burden of the ruling ideologies and concepts of honor, love, ambition, and revenge. In this sense, the ritual sources of popular disenchantment and the Vice's irreverence, in helping to characterize the clowns and porters, suffer a sea-change. The power of negation is turned against the representatives of the *vicious world* itself: the negation of negation dialectically gives them a positive structural function.

But usually this function is restricted to a single scene or a series of comic variations and extrapolations of the main course of serious events. It is only when, as in *Richard III, Hamlet, Othello*, and, partly, *King Lear*, the dramatic heirs of the Vice usurp and direct the main plot that their changing structural significance becomes infinitely expanded. Their extradramatic awareness becomes submerged and is adapted to the needs of a more highly self-contained dramatic action. Richard Gloucester, for instance, is presented as the image of a royal person in history, but at the same time he remains the punning, self-expressive ambidexter directing, in continuous contact with the audience, his own murderous rise to the throne. So the structural impact of the Vice tradition is felt inside the main plot and even as a grotesque stimulus to the main character as well. But the more consistently the vicious capacity for negation is integrated into the framework of a royal plot (centering on the throne, the *locus* of supreme ambition) the less Gloucester can—as chorus or commentator—remain outside the autonomous realm of a self-enclosed action. Consequently, the traditional energy of self-expressive topsy-turvydom is rechanneled into the needs of the growing illusion of a powerful new form of *mimesis*. Thus, his self-introduction—on the neutral platform stage directly facing the audience—remains intact but assumes the additional and combined functions of prologue and exposition. Actually, the exposition (I, 1, 1–13), with a characteristic quibble on "this sun of York," *precedes* the regular self-introduction ("But I—that am not shap'd for sportive tricks," 14–31) only to be taken up again by what Wolfgang Clemen has called a *"Planungsmonolog,"*[87] which sets out the plan for things to come and things to do (32–40). Even more important, the traditional convention of vicious self-expression is retained in order to assume a newly mimetic and characterizing function: Gloucester's self-introductory isolation from the courtly world of the play is used psychologically, for it is made to explain and to anticipate the individualism of his climactic "I love myself" (V, 3, 187). But the most astonishing fusion of tradition and innovation is, perhaps, contained in the irony of his protests that he is not "shap'd for sportive tricks." On the level of representational action this is certainly true enough; but Gloucester's own deformity has a residuum of that ancient nonrepresentational quality characteristic of Punch's hunchback. The dramatic paradox is that Gloucester, *because* he is made to assert the psychological realism of an "unfashionable" Duke of York, can (out of and beyond the mimetic requirements of a *locus*-oriented royal personage) still assert the ritual heritage of an amoral inversion—even from within the world and the values that he both shares and destroys.

Thus, the Vice's heir, in ironically abdicating his traditional responsibility to provide "sportive tricks," reassumes it on a tragic scale. By becoming part of the dramatic representation of society, the Vice's descendant turns both *provocateur* and victim, not merely of his own doings and undoings, but of those social relationships of which the dramatic action is a poetically heightened image. The ancient freedom of topsy-turvydom has, finally, become the modern passion of self-destruction. But this, most important of all, marks the point of departure for modern tragedy as distinguished from that of classical Greece. It is not the *Schicksalsdrama,* not the inscrutable workings of the gods, that finally tips the scales of life and death but the *Charakterdrama* of an individual passion and a self-willed personality "determined to prove a villain" (I, 1, 30). *Richard III,* of course, only points the way, but the pattern seems clear. It was not the humanist tradition of neoclassical tragedy that alone, or even primarily, was powerful enough to bring forth the basic structural design of the modern tragedy. Rather, as in *Doctor Faustus,* tragedy develops from an aesthetic context that neoclassical canons of style would find lowly. The first great artistic portrait of a nascently tragic figure as central to the drama develops from a character—the Vice—deeply rooted in the popular tradition and now turned to a distinctively modern representation of reality.

V

THE ELIZABETHAN DRAMA

1

Toward the Culture of a Nation

When the Elizabethan theater flowered in the 1580s, England was in the midst of an economic expansion and national awakening.[1] The medieval structures of life, which still predominated in other European countries, with their rural agricultural systems based on payment in kind and their unwieldy guild organization in the towns, had been greatly weakened or even superseded in England. The growth of a market—first for goods, then for land and labor, and finally for money—as well as the development of an extensive cloth industry serving overseas export markets, the great influx of American gold and silver, and the sharp rise in prices dating from the midcentury all proved powerful dissolvents of the traditional economy. As productivity accelerated, so did building, shipping, and trade. The decline of feudal social organization and medieval habits of life ushered in a new era of prosperity for England—an age fundamentally of an economic revolution which nonetheless, despite the profound disruptions, was also an era of social compromise that achieved a temporary political stability and a cultural synthesis of old and new. Here was the basis of a modern national consciousness and of a newly found creative cultural potential that enriched and transformed the sixteenth-century theater.

The rise of what was at the time a small nation did not come unannounced, however. As early as the fourteenth century a monetary economy had to a considerable extent replaced the direct exchange of goods, and feudal villeinage had in many places given way to payments in tender. But the collapse of the feudal organization of the rural economy was a process greatly accelerated by many other circumstances. Disastrous plagues produced an acute labor shortage, so that farm laborers were often able to escape the patriarchal control of their landlords. The enclosures, which became increasingly common after 1470, also helped to weaken the old system in many parts of the country. English landowners, particularly in the south and east, turned their backs on the local market economy and began to produce wool for Flemish, and, soon after, for home manufacture.

The number of people dislocated by the conversion of arable land into pasture was further increased by the dispersal of feudal retainers under Henry VII and the extensive sale of church lands during the Reformation. Without work and without masters, those released by an outmoded economic structure sought new protection or sold their labor to the manufacturers and landowners who operated the new system. Stiff laws insured that the majority of those expropriated adapted to the new economy, especially as paid workers.[2] Those who could not adapt were persecuted and punished as outlaws, vagabonds, or jugglers.

The uneven development of capitalism in the various parts of England was accompanied by what modern historians have noted as the gradual dissolution of the medieval estates in favor of a greater "mobility of social classes" (A. L. Rowse), and even a "babylonian confusion of classes" (J. B. Black),[3] especially true in the earlier part of the century and still evident by the end at Court, in London, and in parts of the eastern and southern countryside where the majority of the population still lived. The Elizabethan chronicler William Harrison provided a vivid description of the changes under way in rural England when he noted that "the ground of the parish is gotten vp into a few mens hands, yea sometimes into the tenure of (one) two or three, whereby the rest are compelled, either to be hired seruants vnto the other, or else to beg their bread in miserie from doore to doore."[4] These changes profoundly affected the ancient cultural traditions and customs which the shared land of the medieval village had immemorially fostered. Once the land was enclosed and made an object of speculation, traditions associated with it were, when not completely destroyed, severely threatened.

But economic conditions were not the only factors working to transform the old, collective elements in the feudal village culture. The new Puritan morality, with its sexual repression, thundered against the "Dionysian" freedoms characteristic of popular custom. Contemporary pamphleteers, like Phillip Stubbes, were quick to adopt the new moral and ascetic viewpoint:

Against May, Whitsonday, or other time, all the yung men and maides, olde men and wiues, run gadding ouer night to the woods, groues, hils, & mountains, where they spend all the night in plesant pastimes; & in the morning they return, bringing, with them birch & branches of trees, to deck their assemblies withall. and no meruaile, for there is a great Lord present amongst them, as superintendent and Lord ouer their pastimes and sportes, namely, Sathan, prince of hel.

But the cheifest iewel they bring from thence is their May-pole, which they bring home with great veneration, as thus. They haue twentie or fortie yoke of Oxen, euery Oxe hauing a sweet nose-gay of flouers placed on the tip of his hornes; and these Oxen drawe home this May-pole (this stinking Ydol, rather) which is couered all ouer with floures and hearbs, bound round about with strings from the top to the bottome, and sometime painted with variable colours, with two or three hundred men, women and children, following it with great deuotion... And then fall they to daunce about it, like as the heathen people did at the dedication of the Idols, wherof this is a perfect pattern, or rather the thing it self. I haue heard it credibly reported (and that *viua voce*) by men of great grauitie and reputation, that of fortie, threescore, or a hundred maides going to the wood ouer night, there haue scaresly the third part of them returned home againe vndefiled. These be the frutes which these cursed pastimes bring foorth.[5]

Stubbes' description illustrates both the continuity of traditional culture and the threat posed to it. The rural May festival was obviously still enthusiastically and devotedly celebrated within the village community, and its exuberant and sensual overtones indicate the strength of surviving pagan traditions. But puritanical anathema, which equated the elected leader of the festivities, the May King, with Satan (as it later did with the popular actor), proceeded hand-in-hand with a new individualistic ideology. Why should the whole town, the whole parish, the whole village and land have the same festival day and celebrate such revels? "But why at one determinant day more than at another (except busines vrged it)?" This was the pamphleteer's new social and ethical outlook, a perspective that challenged the communal elements in the traditional culture because it rejected its underlying assumptions. The Protestant individualism that abandoned inherited and collective religious authority (Pope, bishop, and confessional) manifested itself in the social sphere as an ethic of private choice as opposed to the traditions of an entire community ("yung men and maides, olde men and wiues"). For Stubbes, it is the individual who chooses to enjoy the festival, the wine, and the love, but at the risk of losing business, sobriety, and chastity. The associations between sensuality and sin are clear: "plesant pastimes" become "cursed pastimes," and involvement is condemnable, for "sweet nose-gay" here turns abruptly into "stinking Ydol."

But rural custom was not the only part of English life revolutionized by economic and ideological development. Too long organized around guild systems of diminishing practicality, the towns changed as the old apprentice-journeyman order became outmoded. (The 1563 Statute of Artificers was a compromise measure characteristic of this transitional period.) Even in the fourteenth century, the simple craftsman formed what Lujo Brentano called a "separate estate of workers," which became, according to W. J. Ashley, "a labour class" excluded from commerce on an open market that was dominated by wealthy and established traders.[6]

At the same time, merchant capital was no longer accumulating in the hands of a few privileged masters, as was the case in the Middle Ages, but instead remained in circulation and thereby spurred new production. Since, therefore, neither money for investment and wages, nor labor without personal means of support, were then scarce in England, all that was needed for the rise of "manufacture" (the first specifically capitalist mode of production) was a bringing together of large numbers of wage laborers to work at various enterprises. This new economic organization developed with great rapidity, especially whenever the guild system had become less strict or had never been completely effective.

Consequently, what W. H. B. Court called a "rapid development of manufacture," or even an early "industrial revolution" (J. U. Nef) took place in the second half of the sixteenth century. Coal mining alone developed so rapidly that deliveries to London increased more than threefold between 1580 and 1591 (1580: 11,000 tons; 1591–92: 35,000 tons). Shipments of coal from Newcastle grew from 33,000 tons in 1563–64 to 163,000 tons in 1597–98. On the eve of the Civil War, England was mining three times as much coal as the rest of Europe put together. Iron production likewise increased, and processing was vastly improved. The number of furnaces, estimated at about twenty-five in 1550, had, according to H. R. Schubert, tripled by the end of the century.[7] Similar observations can be made about the increased production of glass, tin, and copper, and improvements in methods of transport. The full extent of the growth in production, building, and repairs in Shakespeare's day has only recently come to light in W. G. Hoskins' study of contemporary records and in recent research into local history.

This construction boom may even have been more important than the concurrent increase of cloth production. It stimulated the home market and absorbed the import of capital that resulted from voyages of discovery, expanding mercantile ventures, and pirating. Newly formed trading companies were able to pay their shareholders record dividends from profits of 4,700 percent, as in the case of Drake's voyage around the world.[8]

These drastic social changes were bound to affect the relationship between traditional communal life and popular culture on the one hand, and the changing experience of contemporary life on the other. Even in the northern and western provinces, where traditional habits were at first little affected, the cultural impact of the Renaissance must have been felt. *Tamburlaine* and English history plays were performed by troupes of wandering players in small towns all over the country, and these were probably at least as popular as the biblical drama. In spite of H. C. Gardiner's and F. M. Salter's accurate conclusion that outside interference by the state, church, and Privy Council accelerated the decline of the pre-Protestant cycles, E. K. Chambers' point that the mystery play was itself "an institution which had almost outlived its day" by the early sixteenth century remains valid. However often the cycles were still performed in the midsixteenth century, as a theatrical tradition they were connected with a socioeconomic system that was undeniably on the wane. Historians have shown that many craftsmen's guilds were declining not only in London but also in provincial towns like York, Coventry, and Chester. In these and other places the guilds had lost so much authority that they could no longer rely on the loyalty of their members.[9] Salter illustrates this with what was undoubtedly an extreme case: in 1575 Andrew Tailer preferred to go to prison rather than pay his contribution to the play. And Salter adds that others certainly grumbled at the cost of the festivals as well.[10] New ethics of work and community life underlay this attitude, and contemporaries were well aware of them. Of course there was still a sense of the corporate functionality of the guilds; but while the old social order was by no means completely supplanted by new conditions, the guild spirit sustained little of its original strength and appeal.

In political life, as in the economy, the old and the new confronted each other. The hegemony of the barons was past, and their bankruptcy was military and political as well as economic. After the Wars of the Roses their ranks were thinned, their castles and strongholds had become too vulnerable, their housekeeping too expensive, and their retainers unlawful; after the last feudal rising, the Northern Rebellion of 1569, their decline was an irrevocable trend. But while the feudal aristocracy was no longer in a position to rule the country at large, those sections that a hundred years later succeeded in winning the Civil War were as yet too immature to achieve political supremacy. The bourgeoisie, together with the "improving" gentry and the lower middle classes that ultimately shared (or aspired to share) their modes of living, were not yet politically emancipated. They were more concerned about the settlement of the succession, the threat of foreign invasion, the maintenance of civil order, and their more immediate economic interests, than with challenging state power by advancing their own (as distinct from the national) policies and ideologies. Like the merchants, the moneyed landlords who owned most of the abbey lands, enclosed the commons, and introduced capitalist practices into agriculture, did not for a moment think of challenging the prerogative of the Tudor monarchs under whose peaceful rule they had obtained vast estates and had thrived so unprecedentedly. Policy-making was as yet the undisputed privilege of the crown.

It was the crown and the court, then, that became the focal point of the nation's political, religious, and cultural life. The immense prestige of the monarchy, the homage paid to it by men such as Ascham, Spenser,

Hooker, and Bacon, cannot be dismissed as empty eulogium; for the Tudors—as Shakespeare viewed them in *Richard III*—had overthrown the warring factions of the nobility and thus made possible that "smooth-fac'd peace,/ With smiling plenty and fair prosperous days" (V, 5, 33-34) of which the Elizabethans were so gratefully conscious. Although themselves of the nobility, the Tudors were prepared (and indeed they had no other choice) to compromise with those forces which had opposed the disastrous rule of the barons and which still were suspicious of the rebelliousness of the over-mighty subject. By providing favorable conditions for trade and shipping the Tudor monarchs developed their customs revenues; by promoting a stable and more centralized administration, they reorganized their fiscal system and controlled their own landed revenues much more effectively; at the same time, they advanced the economic development of the country by welding together hitherto local communities of exchange into a larger national whole. In doing all this, the Tudors, without breaking with the more conservative aristocracy, promoted the interests of the newer gentry and the middle classes which, especially in the economically advanced south and east, were moving closer together. In Tudor England those who upheld the independence of the nation supported the sovereignty of the crown; its authority was accepted not only against the claims of the Roman church but also in the face of domestic unrest and foreign invasion.

The New Monarchy, even before the secession from Rome, found active supporters in the newly promoted aristocracy from which, in Elizabeth's time, the great courtiers and administrators were to be recruited. These were the Dudleys, Russells, Seymours, Sidneys, Herberts, Cecils, and, of course, Ralegh and Walsingham. In contrast to the more conservative Norfolk, Sussex, Oxford—the remnants of the older nobility and the unenterprising country gentry—such men were firmly committed to the expansion of commerce and industry. They stood behind the maritime expeditions of the "sea dogs" and often advocated a more aggressively protestant foreign policy. At home men such as Leicester, Sidney, Herbert, and Russell patronized or shared in the pursuit of humanist knowledge and letters.[11]

Even before their patronage became most effective, many of the earlier humanists, who were mostly descended from burgess families, had been preferred by the monarchy. Despite his barbarous treatment of More and Fisher, it might be said of Henry VIII that "throughout his reign he regarded the relation between humanism and affairs of state as indispensable."[12] But as the monarchy, aided by the new aristocracy, encouraged a learned vindication of its new policies and the use of a more polished Latin in diplomatic intercourse, the humanists themselves were commissioned with practical tasks. With men such as Thomas

Elyot, Edward Fox, Thomas Starkey, and Richard Morison, humanism and patriotism became fused; to them learning was no longer a private form of virtuosity but a means of public service. Of burgess descent, supported by the monarchy, in close contact with the new aristocracy, the new pedagogues were permitted to introduce their political and educational ideas into the many new or reorganized schools. The humanists, here as elsewhere, endeavored to implement a policy which, while it served the absolutism of the Tudors, helped to consolidate the autonomy of the nation. And it was Elyot and his followers who had sown the seeds that came to fruition in many of the grammar schools throughout the country in which the young generation, among them Shakespeare of Stratford, received their introduction to the classics and to a view of human nature that was, in essential points, no longer medieval.

At the same time, the New Monarchy, directly as well as indirectly, helped to bring about and consolidate social and political modes of organization in which the newly adaptable forms of popular culture could be amalgamated more richly on a national and, as it were, a universal scale. They could do so by shifting the hard and fast lines that had divided the feudal estates with their hitherto rigid hierarchical divisions. Thus, it may well be said—as Marx said about the absolute monarchies in western Europe—that the New Monarchy presented itself as "a civilizing center, as the initiator of social unity," in fact, as some kind of "laboratory, in which the various elements of society were so mixed and worked, as to allow the towns to change the local independence and sovereignty of the Middle Ages for the general rule of the middle classes, and the common sway of civil society."[13] It is important to emphasize here that in the period we are concerned with the middle classes (although steadily advancing) were as yet in no position to repudiate the Tudor compromise, and that the monarchy, whose rise to power was based on a transitional balance of socioeconomic forces, endeavored to maintain the equilibrium politically.

It was this endeavor (and it accounts for both the success and the ultimate contradictions of the Tudor position) that determined most of their legislation, ecclesiastical as well as economic. The Elizabethan church settlement was in itself the epitome of that "laboratory" in which "the various elements were so mixed and worked" as to contain all the parties within the platform of a national alliance. Elizabeth's one distinctive doctrine was the doctrine of royal supremacy; once this was accepted—and there was no reluctance to do so, since "royal" was as yet synonymous with "national"—the queen did not bother to press for ideological definitions or really strict conformity. On a different plane, economic legislation such as the Statute of Artificers or the Usury Act (1571) was Janus-faced, designed to serve both trade and stability: the monarchy was willing to consider the bourgeoisie as a junior partner, but determined to prevent any rapid growth of those new men who, like Peter Wentworth, had a way of becoming too independent too quickly.

And yet, as the balance of power gradually changed, it became more and more difficult to contain the Puritans and to conceal the cracks in the Tudor alliance. Elizabeth, as late as 1601, still could fall back on compromise measures and the crown's long-standing prestige, which neither her subtle evasiveness nor her many studied ambiguities were quite able to undermine. As James Harrington sarcastically remarked, she succeeded in "converting her reign through the perpetuall Love-tricks that passed between her and her people into a kind of Romanze."[14] Part of this "Romanze" may, in the words of a later historian, have consisted in "bribing her people with prosperity." But when the old queen died, prosperity—now that it was taken for granted—was no longer good enough at its traditional level; and what proved more important, there were indications that its growth was to be less secure than before. At the same time, the compromise in religion and the foundation for an all-inclusive national church had become increasingly tenuous, until James I discovered (in 1604, at the Hampton Court conference) that "Presbytery agreeth as well with monarchy as God and the devil." Now Hooker, in the seventh book of his great *Laws*, might well deplore "those extreme conflicts of the one part with the other, which continuing and increasing" were reminiscent of "those words of the Prophet Jeremiah, 'thy breach is great like the sea, who can heal thee?'" English absolutism ceased to be an absolutism by consent, and out of the national alliance emerged the gradual (although by no means straightforward) formation of two increasingly antagonistic class positions.

Facing these far reaching divisions (there were significant, if almost imperceptible, changes from at least 1588), how was the humanist scholar or poet to react? Was he still, like Gabriel Harvey, to consider the court as "the only mart of praeferment and honour?" Or could he honestly, as Stephen Gosson did, throw in his lot with the Puritans? As early as 1586 the death of Sidney, followed by that of Leicester, was a blow to poets and all those who might have continued to reconcile humanism with the principles of militant Protestantism; in affecting the national position of both movements, it was an event scarcely less significant than the execution of Essex (1601) to whom, in the 1590s, the leadership of Leicester's court party and the popular support of the citizenry had passed. But while the new aristocracy was losing valuable territory at Whitehall, the court—at least since the appointment of Archbishop Whitgift to the Privy Council—was drawing nearer to an Episcopalian church increasingly determined to oppose and suppress Puritan innovations. As the court grew, under James, to be part of a corrupt administration (in which preferment and a public career had for a long time become rare to underprivileged scholars), the more advanced sections of the bourgeoisie showed an increasing hostility to the arts and a growing impatience with the philological traditions of Christian humanism.

Thus, the foundations of the national compromise—so essential to Gascoigne, Sidney, or Spenser—were crumbling away, and neither side proved really acceptable to the humanist imagination. Classically trained poets, even before the end of the century, turned to satire, and their writing reflected an attitude toward experience more sardonic, somber, and savage than that of the earlier decade. The melancholy malcontent became a symbol of the disillusioned academic, and the Italianate courtier—his affected imitator, the fashionable "gull"—was held up to ridicule, while the covetous Puritan was attacked with equal scorn.

But in the theater, the growing antagonism between the realigned classes did not, at this stage, endanger the dramatic images and poetic transmutations of submerged conflicts and tensions. As long as important links remained between the traditional background of the popular culture and the new sense of nationalism embraced by both the middle classes and the aristocracy, the theater supported widely divergent viewpoints. More than any other social institution, the theater still resembled a "laboratory in which the various elements of society were . . . mixed and worked" on. Just as in education, religion, philosophy, social ethics, and other moral attitudes, the old confronted, and often held its own against, the new.[15] Older conceptions of honor were confronted by the new pride of possession, hatred of usury by the fervor for gold, the idea of service by the idea of profit, deeply rooted community consciousness by passionate individualism. Feudal family pride mingled with the bourgeois sense of family, pomp with thrift, frivolity with chastity, pessimism with optimism. In the late sixteenth and early seventeenth centuries these heterogeneous ideas and attitudes jostled each other, and the resulting wealth and depth of conflict was reflected, more than anywhere else, in the Renaissance theater, where the popular tradition was free to develop relatively independent of, and yet in close touch with, the conflicting standards and attitudes of the dominant classes.

2

"Scene individable": Toward a Sociology of the Elizabethan Stage

The capacity of popular Renaissance drama to accommodate and synthesize differing cultural and ideological perspectives was the result of specific sociological conditions upon which the Elizabethan theater, its audiences and their tastes, were based. But although the playhouses themselves and the staging of plays in them have frequently been studied, their sociological foundations have received considerably less attention. It is true that facts about the social context of the founding of the first public theaters are few, but those that we have are fortunately reliable. They include, among others, the contract for the construction of the Fortune theater, Henslowe's diary, and the records of the law suits concerning the site rented for the Theatre. These documents not only tell us something about what the first theaters looked like, they also reveal some facts about the social status of their founders. The Theatre, the first permanent public playhouse, was built by James Burbage in 1576; the Curtain followed shortly after, and a few years later the Rose (1587), the Swan (1595), and the famous Globe (1599), which was built with materials from the dismantled Theatre.

None of these, of course, was a spontaneous product of popular culture. Burbage was originally a carpenter, his brother-in-law and partner, John Brayne, was a prosperous shopkeeper; Philip Henslowe was a busy merchant and speculator, and Francis Langley, who built the Swan, was a goldsmith. Their theaters were private commercial enterprises, erected only after projected profits had been carefully calculated. It is especially clear from the history of the Theatre that business and not communal spirit urged these particular theatrical ventures. Alleyn, the Theatre's owner, and Burbage and Brayne fought bitterly for the profits to be made in their playhouse.[16]

But in spite of the postfeudal, postpatriarchal business ethics that made these theaters commercially viable, they were still dependent on large plebeian audiences—people who remained attached to the old miming and festival traditions and still removed from the new Puritan ethos. This is clear even from the sites on which the first theaters were built. It was no accident that they were built in Halliwell, to the north and outside the city walls (on the grounds of a former priory), and on the southeast edge of Finsbury Fields, on the big playing fields where Londoners went on Sundays to practice archery and engage in other time-honored amusements. Here they were outside the jurisdiction of the city authorities (controlled by the London bourgeoisie), but perfectly congruent with local traditions. Halliwell—"holy well"—was, like Clerkenwell and other local shrines, associated with legendary powers of healing, and probably still a meeting place for festivals—such as the May festival—in Shakespeare's day.[17]

Bankside, on the south bank, where the later Rose, Swan, and Globe theaters were built, was also closely connected with the sports and pastimes of old London. Well before the theaters were built people congregated there to watch bear-baiting, bull fights, wrestling, and fencing, as well as juggling and other displays. In fact, there is some evidence that elements of the May games and Morris and Sword dances lived on in the

* Giles Allen owned the land. Burbage and Brayne fought over profits. Alleyn did quarrel with B., but was in the troupe occupying the Theatre.

growing city; and it is only in light of these still living traditions that the remarkable popularity of Tarlton and Kempe can be understood. If there was any place in London where the older popular miming culture, the lay drama, and the Robin Hood plays were vividly remembered it was in Finsbury Fields and Bankside. It was the common people who met there, who engaged in the pleasure and the games, and who brought with them an appreciation for traditional arts of acting. Like those who watched the mystery plays, the simple London public was well able to bring a surprising amount of intelligence and understanding to the theater. At any rate, they were prepared to spend their pennies to maintain several large playhouses in what was, by modern standards, still a small city. Thus, while growing capitalism and its related asceticism had *not yet* become a way of life for the masses, the new economy and corresponding social changes had *already* created conditions whereby a permanent public theater independent of the controlling influence of clergy and conservative guilds, could develop.

This illuminates not only the rise, but also the remarkable range of the new theatrical culture. London was a city of only about 160,000 inhabitants in 1600, but it supported more than half-a-dozen theaters, each with a varied program, in the years when *Hamlet, King Lear,* and *Volpone* were first performed. According to Alfred Harbage, during the 1605 theater season (when attendance was at its highest) nearly 21,000 Londoners probably went to the theater every week. This means that about thirteen percent of the population of London regularly went outside of the city to attend plays.[18] At the same time, or soon after, bourgeois or Puritan opposition to the theater intensified. The theater, it was said, spread the plague, kept apprentices from their work, and, according to Puritan pamphleteers and numerous complaints by the city fathers to the Privy Council, constituted a pagan glorification of the devil, a form of idolatry. Although exaggerated, such complaints had some truth. Audiences, Phillip Stubbes wrote, "are alwaies eating, & neuer satisfied: euer seeing, & neuer contented; continualie hearing, & neuer wearied; they are greedie of wickednes, and wil let no time, nor spare for anie weather (so great is their deuotion to make their pilgrimage) to offer their penie to the Deuil." And it is that same word—devotion—perhaps suggesting more homage than a play warrants, that Stubbes used in his attack on the May festival (above p. 163). There may well have been more than moral prejudice behind the equation of "playes and bawdy enterluds" with "hethenrie, paganrie, scurrilitie, and deuilrie it self," for such performances may indeed have harkened back to the late ritual heritage of those "doble dealing ambodexters" to whom the Puritans so deeply objected.[19]

The fact that the Elizabethan theater was in constant and bitter conflict with both nascent Puritanism and the leading London bourgeoisie shows very clearly that despite its popularity, its social position was precarious. Yet puritanical attacks and municipal interference, at least until the second decade of the seventeenth century, were limited in their effects, especially in light of the protection that the theater received from court patronage. Such patronage was perfectly in keeping with the New Monarchy's interest in culture and the arts. It was officially justified by the argument that actors needed professional experience in order to provide suitable entertainments and diversions for the Queen during the Christmas season.[20] So long as the bourgeoisie as well as the middle classes and the crown were allies in an "absolutism by consent," or even "a middle class despotism," so long as the great compromise was practicable, patronage represented not only royal protection, but cultural distinction as well.

The Queen not only protected actors, she also saw their performances, for, as some complained, the common players "present before her maiestie such plaies as haue ben before commonly played in open stages before all the basest assemblies in London and Middlesex...."[21] Such points of contact between court art and plebeian drama were indeed remarkable. It was not unknown for the Queen to decline a play prepared for her in favor of a "company of base and common fellows." Often success on the common stages meant success at court, where performances by troupes popular in the city were frequent. Costumes used for court performances were lent to the actors, who wore them as they played "in the cytye or contre."[22] The popular Renaissance theater enjoyed a truly royal reception, and as a national institution was, to be sure, "a theatre of the people and of the court."[23]

Nor was the cultural function of the New Monarchy simply an external one. As early as Bale's *King Johan* it is "Imperial Majestie" that overthrows the enemy "Sedycyon" so as to make room for the triumph of "Cyvyle Order": this is a major motif taken up and varied from the humanist *Gorboduc* to the popular chronicles and history plays. Under the transitional conditions of Elizabeth's reign the crown would assume the role of arbiter pretending to what Hooker regarded as "the soundest... and most indifferent rule." It kept in check not only the feudal reaction of the Northern earls but also (in Crowley's words) those new "men that would be alone on the earth, ... that would eate up menne, women and chyldren."[24] It protected the stage against the chronic indignation of the city authorities and helped both the playwrights and their audiences in preventing the Puritans from "preaching awey theyr pastime."[25] Most important of all, the crown stood for and upheld the conditions to which the theater owed so much. By deliberately promoting mercantile capital and blurring the lines of gentry and aristocracy, old and new, the Tudors helped to bring about that "mingle-mangle" which the theater in its organization and audience, the drama in its

genres, structures, and speech conventions, reflected. This "gallimaufrey" was clearly perceived in the 1580s by John Lyly, a humanist in close
contact with the court:

At our exercises, Souldiers call for Tragedies, their obiect is bloud: Courtiers for
Commedies, their subiect is love: Countriemen for Pastoralles, Shepheards are
their Saintes. Trafficke and trauell hath wouen the nature of all Nations into
ours, and made this land like Arras, full of deuise ... Time hath confounded our
mindes, our mindes the matter; but all commeth to this passe, that what heretofore hath been serued in seuerall dishes for a feaste, is now minced in a charger for
a Gallimaufrey. If wee present a mingle-mangle, our fault is to be excused,
because the whole worlde is become an Hodge-podge.[26]

Unlike Sidney's assault on "mongrell Tragicomedie," this statement is
already confidently apologetic, but its classically trained author is still too
bewildered to realize that the contradictions (which he points out) are
about to yield a new and superior kind of unity. For Shakespeare it is the
awareness of both the possibilities of, and the contradictions contained
in, the social and theatrical "mingle-mangle" that can be shown to inform
the range and richness of his dramatic language and structure. But Lyly
stood at the very threshold of the new "gallimaufrey": it opened up a
synthesis to be achieved by the great Elizabethan laboratory—so remarkably effective both in society and in the theater. Against the "hodge-
podge" of a transitional age, the medieval estates of the realm were no
less mixed and transformed than the various dramatic genres: the craft
cycle tradition, the drama of the schools, the interlude of the hall, the
masque and courtly revels were now no longer "serued in seuerall dishes."
Instead they were so "minced" that in the country's metropolis the result
was a drama neither farcical nor learned nor courtly. It was a drama
unlike any of the continental burgess or classical or pastoral genres, but
one whose bewildering medley of kinds could indeed be defined as
"tragedy, comedy, history, pastoral, pastoral-comical, historical-pastoral,
tragical-historical, tragical-comical-historical-pastoral, scene individable,
or poem unlimited." It was in truth a theater "individable" with a poetry
"unlimited" in its social and aesthetic appeal; for it embraced many of
the popular, humanist and some of the courtly elements, together with
their theatrical equivalents such as rhetoric, allegory, singing, dancing,
clowning, dumb-shows, disguisings, and corresponding modes of
speech, presentation and acting. But by fusing these elements in the light
of a unifying and exalting experience of nationhood, the Elizabethan
theater brought forth something new which *nevertheless* appealed to all
sections of its audience ("from potboy to prince," as a great authority on
the subject writes). "This three years," says Hamlet (V, 1, 136 ff.), "I have
took note of it: the age is grown so picked that the toe of the peasant
comes so near the heel of the courtier, he galls his kibe." It is an observa-

tion that might have been made by a spectator in Shakespeare's theater. Its audience was made up of every rank and class of society; its greatest literature so written that (as a contemporary observed) "it should please all, like Prince *Hamlet*."[27] Through underlying tensions and in the face of imminent divisions Shakespeare's theater achieved a "unity of taste."[28] It was a multiple unity based on contradictions, and as such allowed the dramatist a flexible frame of reference that was more complex and more vital to the experience of living and feeling within the social organism than the achievement of any other theater before or since.

The integration, in the theater, of heterogeneous elements is a historical process, and as such it affects the history of the stage as a social institution; but it also—and more deeply—affects the quality of the plays themselves, their themes, forms, and structures. If it is a truism to say that Shakespeare's subject-matter is as rich in potentialities of experience as the world in which he lived, it perfectly corresponds to his own ideas of how the art of the theater was related to the contemporary world. Hamlet's words about "the purpose of playing" (III, 2, 21) illuminate a relationship, which, in an earlier scene (II, 2, 535–36), is summed up by a reference to the players as "the abstracts and brief chronicles of the time." The point that is worth making is of course not that Shakespeare's drama—in line with the Aristotelian concept of *mimesis*—reflected the issues of his time (in this he was not at all unique); but that he, more than any of his contemporaries, succeeded in the discovery of how the issues of his time, its "form and pressure," could most significantly be turned into material for great art. It was a discovery that involved the capacity for so absorbing and molding the varied themes and modes of drama that its latent tensions might be released into dramatic poetry.

As an illustration we might select one of those plays in which Shakespeare most freely transforms reality into poetry. In *A Midsummer Night's Dream* the "form and pressure" of his age—far from being at all consistently reflected in plot or character—is transmuted into that larger imaginative vision which comprehends, and is expressed by, the sum total of the characters' dramatic interrelations and statements about the world. Its basic levels are well-known: the courtly world of Theseus and Hippolyta is brought into contact with the amorous intrigues of "Athenian" upper-class society, which contact, in turn, is related to the playmaking of the craftsmen, as well as the fairy creatures who, like Oberon, Titania, and Puck, are a fantastic "mingle-mangle" blending classical and Germanic mythology with native folklore. It is through the intimate interplay of delicately woven threads (one silken, one homespun, one sheer gossamer, as the Victorians might have said) that the varied attitudes and moods are made to merge in one complex perspective which defines the unique quality of the play. When the muddy boots of the mechanicals thump through the airy wood of the fairies the result is much more than a series of colorful contrasts: their imaginative interrelation is such that the varied attitudes and statements illuminate one another, and the play as a whole achieves a poetic substance infinitely larger than the sum of its parts. Thus the craftsmen's robust sense of reality at once heightens and limits the airy phantasia of the fairies, while in turn their graceful intrigues form a dramatic commentary on the thick-witted earthiness of late medieval amateur acting and guild life.

It is the dramatic integration of varied social values and cultural elements that, as Shakespeare progresses from his early work, makes the structure of the plays so balanced and the poetic perspective of experience so satisfying. In *Twelfth Night*, although it does not blend courtly romance with popular custom and the fairy world, the exquisite poise of the play's vision is, despite the romantic exuberance, maintained through the comic interplay of material nonexistent in Shakespeare's Italian source: Malvolio's "yellow-legged" stalking (with its Puritan undertones) and Sir Toby Belch's merry banquets (somewhat in the old style of feudal hospitality) flank the central plot of romantic love and comic disguise, but are so closely integrated that they can no longer be described as a mere subplot. By illuminating one another, these varied attitudes again heighten and help to define the play's comic vision as expressing a complex poetic impression of life. At its center, in the country house of Olivia, it is Feste the fool rather than Olivia or even Viola who is closest to it. As in other plays of this period, the fool's part becomes so important because his attitude (and, for that matter, the cultural traditions behind this figure) epitomize the theatrical "gallimaufrey" on which Shakespeare, in contrast to Beaumont, Fletcher, and their followers, could still draw so successfully.

It is the pregnant interplay of varied social and theatrical elements that is so characteristic of Shakespeare's plays. The richness and complexity of its dramatic effects, however, must not be dismissed as a happy exploitation of colorful subject-matter or a skillful arrangement of contrast and relief. Nor is the customary (and somewhat impressionistic) reference to Shakespeare's "breadth" or "width of outlook," his "objectivity" or "impartiality" likely to be much more helpful. These, indeed, have for a long time been his proverbial epithets, but they can hardly claim to focus the essential qualities of the plays themselves. To say, at this stage, that the richness of their dramatic content draws on the contradictions and tensions in the larger social "laboratory," may be yet another hint at their historical background but, as criticism, is likewise unsatisfying. None of these gives us a meaningful suggestion of what constitutes the living quality and the moral nature of Shakespeare's art.

It is perhaps an oversimplification to say that in the Elizabethan drama the astonishing range of values and attitudes is dramatically usable because it achieves an imaginative dimension as large and as lively as the social organism itself. To make this dimension an imaginative possibility, it is clearly not sufficient to have, say, various social concepts of "honor," "merit," or "virtue" existing side-by-side (as by and large was the case in many European countries at the time). For in Shakespeare's England the varied moral attitudes toward experience did not merely coexist: their relative strengths were so balanced and hence so "minced" that popular dramatists were capable of evaluating experience from a singularly fortunate position. As we see from *Henry IV*, the concept of "honor" could still be dramatically defined in terms of Hotspur's attitudes, but it was no longer possible to view it solely as "bright honour," exclusively from the angle of feudal chivalry. Falstaff's complementary commentary on the same subject reveals an alternative of considerable vitality. But while important standards of the older class-morality could already be questioned, the social attitudes of the new era of capitalism (among them, individualism, acquisitiveness, etc.) were not yet their *necessary* alternative; in neither social morality nor dramatic conventions were they yet accepted as a matter of course.

It was from this singularly fortunate position that the dramatist proceeded to realize the dramatic and imaginative possibilities that the conflicting standards of his age allowed. As in *Twelfth Night*, Shakespeare could now express moral evaluations in terms of structural organization: for the dramatist, through Malvolio and Sir Toby, comically rejects both the Puritan disapproval of, as well as the cavalier indulgence in, sensuous pleasure. Instead, something healthier than either asceticism or hedonism is envisioned from a position whose strength and moral poise are altogether admirable. Here, as in the great tragedies, this involved a relative independence of either social alternative as long as it was possible to fall back on a living tradition of popular attitudes to experience. These were in many ways related, but not subservient, to ruling-class concepts of morality. Consequently, there was a margin of imaginative evaluation that embraced, but was not quite identical with, the ruling social standards. Thus, the playwright could dramatically juxtapose *and evaluate* the ideals or attitudes of *both* service and individualism, honor and property, family pride and family feeling, lasciviousness and chastity, sophistication and simplicity, cynicism and naivety. These attitudes were usable in dramatic composition precisely because the resulting tensions were not slurred over but transformed into tragic conflict or comic incongruity. (On a different plane, they informed important conventions of speech and disguising: Falstaff imitating the king, Orlando a shepherd, Edgar a Bedlam beggar, King Henry a soldier—these and similar extensions of character were part of a dramatic convention, but the effectiveness of the convention was due to the proximity of the actual attitudes, not to the loss of their social identities.)

The vast range of conflicting values and standards within the

Elizabethan situation retained its imaginative pregnancy just as long as the dramatist was in a position honestly to face and incorporate their tensions within his poetic vision of society. He could do this only as long as he possessed, as a touchstone to test any experience or concept, a standpoint involving more freedom, or "license," and imagination than the particular social attitude or moral concept in question. Shakespeare's superiority over his material was of course based on his incomparably deep feeling for reality and humanity; but it was so secure and remained essentially unshaken because he could still fall back on the techniques and the standards of a popular culture in a national theater which gave his vision—amidst the temporary "mingle-mangle" of social values—the strength to achieve contradictions within new areas of universality, conflicts within new levels of unity. This was a position only partly of genial detachment, amused tolerance, and dispassionate irony. For apart from the negative virtue of avoiding a facile identification with any of the emerging class concepts, this vision possessed (through its freedom and skepticism) the positive capacity for bringing to bear varied perspectives on the actions and morals of men, thus creating the experience rather than the ideologies of heroism, love, and tyranny. The universalizing pattern in Shakespeare and the "myriad-mindedness" of his art were never outside history, but they lived beyond the historical conditions that made them possible. The basis of Shakespeare's "negative capability" is itself sociohistorical, and it is unthinkable without the freedom, the detachment, and the imagination made available to him by the popular tradition in the theater.

3

Humanism on the Popular Stage: From "Mother Wits" to Doctor Faustus

During the years when the young Shakespeare was growing up in rural Stratford an end was reached and a new start was made in the status and function of the popular tradition in the theater. In 1580 sixteen-year-old Shakespeare was still able to see performances of the mystery cycles in Coventry, a few miles away from Stratford. But after that the cycles were gone; the communal spirit of these plays conformed as little to the Protestant ideology of the national church and the Privy Council as to the new mercantile spirit and secularized culture of the English Renaissance. In London and in other developed parts of the country little of the medieval "organic community" survived (if indeed such a thing ever existed). As the pamphleteer Robert Crowley said of London:

... this is a Citye in name, but, in dede,
It is a packe of people that seke after meede; ...
But for the wealth of the commons not one taketh pain.
An Hell with out order,
I may it well call,
Where every man is for him selfe,
And no manne for all.[29]

And William Harrison, in the second edition of his *Description of England,*
went out of his way to insert the warning that "everie function and
severall vocation striveth with other, which of them should have all the
water of commoditie run into hir owne cesterne."[30] Such contemporary
reactions (and there were many) are scarcely reconcilable with an unbroken continuity of communal festive attitudes toward the theater, even
though it must be granted that the statements of Elizabethan pamphleteers cannot always be taken at face value. The point that has to be
made is not, of course, that acquisitive and competitive attitudes had
already displaced the communal spirit but that the latter—existing side
by side with the new—became increasingly vulnerable to the pressure of
the former, that the continuity of traditional standards was being slowly
but gradually undermined until, sometime in the first decade of the
seventeenth century, the effects were acutely felt in the declining attendance at the public theaters. It was at this time that those who held that
theatergoing was a "great wasting both of the time and thrift of many
poore people"[31] first began to triumph. In this way, the paradox of the
popular tradition in the Elizabethan theater clearly emerged: the tradition began to make its greatest impact and revealed its greatest capacity
to synthesize disparate standards, conventions, and ideologies at a time
when its communal functions were growing steadily weaker. The
Elizabethan popular tradition no longer rested on the corporate foundation of the medieval community, and yet it remained a potent cultural
and theatrical medium.

On the continent, in the French *confrères de la passion* and the German
Gilden, the social background remained traditional; but one reason why
we should not be unduly nostalgic about the decline of the medieval
community is that where it remained intact it did not produce great
drama, but the *Fastnachtspiel,* while in Paris (through the theatrical
monopoly, since 1548, of the French *confrères*) it stubbornly resisted the
inspiration of humanist letters. In England this was not so, and the
popular tradition in the drama, once it was no longer controlled by
conservative guilds, became free—before it seriously decayed—to enter
into fruitful combination with whatever elements of a more broadly
national culture offered themselves. Among these humanism was
foremost: it had developed in closest touch with the growth of a national
(as distinct from a provincial or corporate) outlook, whether in political
theory, education, translation, or drama.

The contribution of the humanist drama, its models in Seneca, Terence, and Plautus, the French imitations by Garnier and Jodelle, its classical examples as seen in *Gorboduc* and the later tragedies by Fulke Greville and Sir William Alexander, need not detain us here. What is less of a commonplace is the changing moral nature and the deeper dramatic significance of the humanist contribution, as it reached, and was transformed by, the popular stage. The familiar interpretation (which reached the textbooks long ago) stresses the ways in which—beginning with Kyd—Senecan elements, such as the revenge theme, the declamatory uses of rhetoric, the stricter adherence to the unities, the prominence of the monologue and so on, in comedy, the *miles gloriosus,* the parasite and servant types, parallelism in construction, etc., constitute the humanist contribution to the Elizabethan drama.

However, these elements (whose importance is not in question) do not adequately define the moral vision and the dramatic potency of what humanism—as an approach to art and method rather than as doctrine or philology—gave to the theater. If we approach it at its greatest level, as seen in *Doctor Faustus* or *Hamlet,* the inadequacy of the customary approach becomes evident: the humanist element in either of the plays (insofar as it is possible to abstract it) can no longer be reduced to its Senecan sources or understood in terms of the older synthesis of Christian faith and classical reason. Once humanism had entered the popular theater and modified the rigid neoclassical poetics, it achieved a new social dimension and a new freedom of imagination through which its artistic potentialities were tremendously enriched. Although it remained deeply indebted to the study of the classics and to traditional concepts, such as the hierarchical analogies and "the great chain of being," it was now able to question their meaning and validity through imaginative conflicts with more practical and revolutionary principles. In *Tamburlaine* and *Doctor Faustus* these involved a new confidence in man's capacity for self-determining action, a new awareness of "nature's treasury" and the freedom of man to be "on earth as *Ioue* is in the skie,/ Lord and commaunder of these Elements." It is out of the new consciousness of the "aspiring mind" that the "fearful pride" of Tamburlaine results,

> ... whose faculties can comprehend
> The wondrous Architecture of the world:
> And measure euery wandring plannets course,
> Still climing after knowledge infinite,
> And alwaies moouing ...[32]

This spirit (if it can be summed up in a quotation) achieves so great an importance in the drama precisely because it is *not* a doctrinal statement but part of an imaginative perspective from which a great poet illuminates human experience. It produces the grand rhetoric of Marlowe's "mighty line" and, through this, the towering stature of his heroes. Less

directly it informs the enhanced capacities for tragic action in Shakespeare and Webster, where human destiny is no longer subject to some
inscrutable fate—determined by arbitrary gods or the wheel of
fortune—but ultimately conditioned by the deeds, though not the will, of
men.

Once the humanist contribution to the drama is seen in its wider moral
and imaginative implications, it can more significantly be related to the
popular tradition. The interplay of popular taste and humanist endeavor has indeed often been observed; it has been pointed out that
classical models, Senecan or Terencean, enriched the popular drama
while the popular tradition, in its turn, saved the drama from academic
stiffness. Hence resulted "the union of classical artistry and refinement
with Romantic life and vigour, of the classic sense of form and simplicity
with the Romantic love of colour and luxuriance, of the classic care for
words and style with the Romantic insistence on action...."[33] This is all
very well as far as it goes, but scarcely suggests the strength and meaning
of the ties between the popular and the humanist traditions. In explor-
ing their relations, one might be tempted to ask why and how in the
1580s a number of young university-trained poets first were prepared to
popularize their rhetoric in public places of entertainment traditionally
associated with fencing, bear-baiting, clownage, and the jigging veins of
rhyming mother wits. From this, many further questions arise that do
not admit of a simple answer. Is the young poets' readiness to be attributed merely to the desperate position of penniless intellectuals in want of
either preferment or patronage? Or did they willingly assume the roles
of public moralist and dramatic commentator? And if so, were they
flattered by popular fame or attracted by the remarkable freedom of
expression that the theater allowed them? To ask these questions is to
realize that the poetic achievement of the University Wits cannot be
explained in terms of their private intentions. Biographical evidence,
even if it were exhaustively sifted, will hardly illuminate the distinctive
quality of their work, which involves the seeming paradox that, as leaven
to art, humanism in the drama was greatest when closest to the people.

In order to illuminate the problem we may refer to Marlowe's greatest
play which is so profoundly indebted to a popular source *par excellence*—
the *Volksbuch*. Or we may ask: why is Nashe's satire and prose most
effective when most intimately in contact with popular speech and jest
book traditions? Again, why is Shakespeare's greatest single representative of humanism so created as to be not only in favor with the multitude,
but in intimate touch with popular speech—as appears in the very imagery of *Hamlet*? (It would be possible to ask similar questions about the
work of Boccaccio, Rabelais, and Cervantes.) Since the Renaissance
allowed for an astonishing proximity of popular tradition and humanist
innovation, some kind of common ground might be expected to exist
between them.

Here we may recall that humanist criticism of society—never more scathing than in More's *Utopia*—finds a good many parallels in popular literature from *Piers Plowman* to the mystery and morality plays, where a similar tradition of critical attitudes toward landlords and "thyse gentlery men" can be traced. But if some ultimate concord between the humanist and popular points of view seemed at all possible, this must have been particularly so in the 1590s when patriotic sentiment and national unity still served as unifying factors among humanist-trained playwrights and popular audiences. When, at the turn of the century and shortly after, divisions among the ruling classes gradually upset the much-praised harmony of city, court, and country, important sections of the theatergoing population were likely to remain unimpressed by either the case for Puritanism or that for the prerogative of an increasingly conservative (not to say corrupt) court. For a few precious years, the "public" (as distinct from the increasingly important "private") playhouses not only defied the emerging social divisions but actually seemed to thrive on the richness of their contradictions. Consequently, the humanist-trained popular dramatist continued to find in the theater the support that allowed him a measure of independence of the rival ideologies. Outside the theater his position as author was, by and large, one between the declining patronage of the aristocracy and the as yet immature opportunities of a money-market for books. This, too, involved contradictions which fostered a relative blurring of class alignments and a certain kind of double-edged social criticism which a popular audience might be expected to encourage rather than resent.

As an illustration, the Janus-faced point of view in Nashe's picaresque *Jack Wilton* and the blurred commitments of his pamphlets are perhaps most characteristic. For Nashe, like most of the humanist-trained popular writers, was fearless in his attacks on Puritans and newly-rich landlords: "There is none hath any wealth which he getteth not from another," he could write—without, however, making concessions to "the ruinous wals of Venus court" and corresponding standards of aristocratic literature and ideology (as in *Jack Wilton* the ironic rejection of chivalry in the description of the Florence tournament reveals). Nashe could *in one sentence* attack the hypocrisy of the trading Puritan and the dishonesty of the warring knight. Thus he defines "our common calamitie, that the cloake of zeale shoulde be unto an hypocrite in steed of a coate of Maile"—an extraordinary statement which, summing up the twofold perspective of popular humanist criticism, indicates the way its emphasis was gradually shifting.[34]

It was the University Wits—Greene, Peele, and Marlowe—who paved the way even before Shakespeare had made his impact on the London stage. They had rebelled against the clerical or middle-class careers for which they had been trained, and found in literature only a precarious subsistence. At this point it was the existing London theater that offered

them their meager livelihood; in their state of uncertain independence
popular entertainment may well have been free enough and profitable
enough to outweigh the stigma attached to writing for such an "unliterary" institution. Greene, Peele, Nashe, Kyd, and Marlowe were certainly
familiar with the mainstream of the popular theatrical tradition of which
so little has come down to us today. And Marlowe, in his famous Prologue to *Tamburlaine,* noted the link with nonliterary folk art as represented by the likes of Dick Tarlton:

> From iygging vaines of riming mother wits,
> And such conceits as clownage keepes in pay,
> Weele lead you to . . .
>
> (1-3)

With this Marlowe signaled one of the boldest experiments in world
literature. And he was well aware of the popular foundation upon which
he built the new verbal and dramatic structures reflected in his "tragicke
glasse." Some of his contemporaries, like Greene, merely adopted the
old popular forms; and so Gabriel Harvey spoke scornfully of Greene's
"Greenesse" and "piperly extemporizing and Tarltonizing."[35] But Marlowe did not just adapt the old to the new. Writing for a stage on which
jigging, clowning, and extemporizing thrived, Marlowe changed and
broadened the horizons of his own humanist education. The results of
his humanist training, the neoclassical theories, and the principles that
he had learned at Cambridge, were applied to new and vastly different
functions when they came into contact with the practical perspectives
and the sensuous spectacle associated with the popular tradition:
academic standards of logic and poetics are nowhere so clearly replaced
by the criteria of a more practical kind of experience as in *Doctor Faustus*:

> *Bene disserere est finis logices,*
> Is to dispute well, Logickes chiefest end. . . ?
>
> (35-36)

The academic abstract is abandoned, not in favor of the mundane, but in
favor of an aspiring concreteness, a wildly ambitious worldliness:

> Wouldst thou make man to liue eternally?
> Or being dead, raise them to life againe?
> Then this profession were to be esteemd.
>
> (52-54)

Through the imagery of magic and the bald hedonism of the story, we
catch a glimpse of a new humanism oriented toward a more secular
definition of the potential applications of knowledge. The popular theater and the jigging veins of extemporizing mother wits confronted the
humanist endeavors in the arts with the need for a new directness and

sensuousness of expression, for a grasp of practical reality, and an awareness of the physical dimensions of the written and spoken word. The result was an unprecedented synthesis of old and new, of spiritual and practical, of speech and spectacle. The popular story of *Doctor Faustus*, for instance, was presented with the aid of several allegorical conventions found in the moralities: the appearance of the Seven Deadly Sins, of the good and bad angels, the homiletic figure of the old man, and the grouping of the actions around a "universal" personality. Mephistophilis corresponds in some ways to both the Vice and the devil of the mysteries, and like them he serves to link serious and comic scenes. Yet these elements of the native tradition were not simply revived by Marlowe. The good and bad angels, for example, transcend the moralizing schema of the purely allegorical debate and become dramatic metaphors of the moral conflict raging in Faustus' breast.

In all of this Mephistophilis is instigator and tempter, bringing the conflict to a head. Like the traditional Vice, Mephistophilis hates women, has traveled widely, and is a master of ambivalence. But unlike the Vice, Mephistophilis sustains little of the traditional aggressive audience contact. Even at his most symbolic (as in Haphazard or Inclination) the old Vice never achieved the sheer poetic power and depth that we find in Mephistophilis. In *Faustus* the element of burlesque farce is relegated to the subplot, where, in burlesquing the serious pursuit of the necromantic arts, Faustus' ambitious thirst for knowledge is paralleled to Robin's physical thirst for "white wine, red wine, claret wine, Sacke, Muskadine, Malmesey and Whippincrust" (820–21). Similarly, Faustus' hunger for power, honor, and omnipotence is juxtaposed to the clown's physical appetite: "and so hungry, that I know he would give his soule to the Divel for a shoulder of mutton" (360). We have seen this method of burlesque and this hunger before: in the *Secunda Pastorum,* where the Lamb of God is turned into a stolen sheep; in *Mankind,* where the chaff at the Last Judgment is turned into fodder for horses; and in *King Johan,* where Sedycyon turned the metaphorical "spices" for which he was admonished into seasonings for food.

But to these elements of its popular heritage *Doctor Faustus* added language influenced by Seneca (especially in Faustus' long monologues), and the humanist challenge of scholastic philosophy and theology. Faustus, like Tamburlaine, seeks the unattainable, but his elusive quest is no longer a medieval alchemist's fantastic search for gold; rather it is a desire—not fully realized in its implications—to:

> ... make a bridge through the moouing ayre,
> To passe the *Ocean* with a band of men,
> Ile ioyne the hils that binde the *Affricke* shore,
> And make that land continent to *Spaine* ...

(341–44)

The tremendous pride betrayed in this design is as much a part of the Renaissance hero as is his longing for Helen's incomparable beauty. The desire to control the continents and the forces of nature, like the worship of Helen's beauty, goes far beyond the legend of Faustus or its English translation.[36] The charlatan has become a predecessor of the new science, his vulgar curiosity turned to thirst for knowledge, his naked lust to *eros* drunk with beauty. The magician's arts become, finally, the over-reaching of a restless spirit storming the heavens: "And burned is *Apolloes* Laurel bough" (1479).

Given all these humanist modifications of the traditional representative of humanity, Faustus cannot be viewed simply as a modern Everyman (although he remains deeply indebted to the morality figure's Psychomachia).[37] To begin with, Faustus is no longer an allegorical picture of the human dilemma but the portrayer of his *own* destiny. Unlike Mankynde, Faustus is not a passive victim, a didactic figure exposed to this or that temptation. Temptation arises within the hero's own breast, regardless of the encouragement or discouragement of the good and bad angels.

> I, these are those that *Faustus* most desires.
> O what a world of profit and delight,
> Of power, of honor, of omnipotence
> Is promised to the studious Artizan?
> All things that mooue betweene the quiet poles
> Shalbe at my commaund, Emperours and Kings
> Are but obeyed in their seuerall prouinces:
> Nor can they raise the winde, or rend the cloudes:
> But his dominion that exceedes in this,
> Stretcheth as farre as doth the minde of man.
>
>   (80–89)

Faustus' aspirations are not inspired by the whisperings of a Vice; they are desires born of a superadded consciousness aimed at "the end of euery Art" (32). However sinful he may be, Faustus craves "a greater subiect" (39); and this longing puts him far beyond the homiletic frame of reference. The challenge and inversion are not effected from the outside; they well up from within. Mephistophilis does remain the devilish tempter, but at the same time he is the hero's intimate ally, the poetic projection and dramatic vehicle of Faustus' own desires.

In shifting the spirit of inversion to within the hero himself, Marlowe created a new kind of character, one who is not only the object but also the *Subjekt* of the dramatic conflict, not only the victim but also the *provocateur* of a cosmic antagonism. This dramatic conflation of corrupter and corrupted cannot be understood solely from a Christian homiletic perspective or solely in terms of a popular theatrical background, but only through an appreciation of the remarkable interaction of both points of view as assimilated within a modern and more practical kind of humanism. What was new in the secular humanism of the Renaissance did not achieve its full artistic potential until it came into contact with what was old on the popular platform stage. Along with the new hedonism and individualism something of a utopian vision survived, but this was no longer a clowning dream of plenty. The popular myth of Cokaygne was a thing of the past, and Marlowe, apparently unaware of More's vision of the ideal society, took up the theme of the Golden Age as a contemporary secular dream of satisfaction that contained all the misery and glory of Renaissance individualism which, two centuries later, Goethe was to challenge at the end of the second part of his *Faust*.

4

Country Jig and City Clowning: The Triumph of Dick Tarlton

The vitality and broadly based social appeal of the popular tradition were inseparable from the transitional social structure of the late English Renaissance. By the time that Dryden, Rymer, and even Pope were criticizing and editing Shakespeare, the literati had very clearly dissociated themselves from the plebeian element in his art: from the language of a "wheelwright" and a "ragman" (Dryden on *Hamlet* II, 2, 489 ff.), the older tradition of plays acted by "Carpenters, Coblers and illiterate fellows" (Rymer, *A Short View*), and in general from "the common old stories or vulgar traditions of that kind of people" (Pope).[38] This change in attitude toward popular culture was certainly not fortuitous; even before the Commonwealth interregnum the balance of social forces on which the Elizabethan settlement was based was beginning to change, and with it the conditions that supported a widespread reception of the popular tradition.

The vitality of plebeian cultural forms in the sixteenth century was based largely on the relative social and cultural unity of bourgeois, peasant, and plebeian strata which, at that time, had not been radically affected or differentiated by the ideology of Puritanism. In matters of social custom and dramatic taste there was as yet no clear division between the rural *plebs* and the London middle classes. This meant that there was little difference between the middle class and the plebeian reception of the Morris dance, the jig, clowning, and the like. The middle strata of craftsmen and the more wealthy dealers and retailers enjoyed these entertainments just as did the lower strata, the laborers, carriers, servants.[39] One would not have found in the Elizabethan pit the "great contrast between the bourgeois and the peasant-plebeian opposition" which, according to Friedrich Engels, was reflected in the course and outcome of the peasant wars that divided Germany. In the theater the ideological and cultural differences between the middle class sections of the gallery audience and the groundlings "who presse to the forefront of the scaffolds,"[40] were minimal.

As a result of this relative homogeneity, urban and rural versions of popular culture did not necessarily conflict. The links between country and city plebeian cultural forms were bound to dissolve sooner or later, but in the decade in which the drama reached its greatest heights these links remained quite intact. Outside of the theater they had enriched jest books, pamphlets and popular religious literature. And while the London groundling may no longer have possessed what Engels termed "a significant grain of healthy peasant nature," his tastes and attitudes were still influenced by the traditional values of a largely agrarian culture.[41]

The unparalleled success of Richard Tarlton, the greatest popular actor of the early Shakespearean era, was based on this rural and urban cultural unity. Tarlton, who rose to fame in the 1570s, was the first plebeian artist to achieve national recognition in England. According to Thomas Fuller, Tarlton was minding his father's pigs when he was discovered by a servant of the Earl of Leicester.[42] But Robert Wilson claimed—probably with ulterior motive—that he had been a London water-carrier's boy. Whatever his plebeian origin, Tarlton's russet costume and countrified manner, as well as his sharp and ready wit, made him the favorite of laborer, city burgher, nobleman, and Queen alike. Tarlton was canonized on inn signs, renowned at court (he was to become the most famous actor of the Queen's Men, founded in 1583), and well known to the new nobility. His legendary jests appeared in three sections, which underscore the broad social base of his appeal: *Tarlton's Jests, Drawn into three parts: His Court Witty Jests; His Sound City Jests; His Country pretty Jests* (1611).

This remarkable unity of court, city, and country jesting paved the way for the Elizabethan clown and was of considerable consequence to Shakespeare's dramatic method. The drumbeating, jigging Tarlton, always in touch with his audience, achieved and sustained this unity: a national (as opposed to a corporate or regional) institution, he already enjoyed a certain detachment from the plebeian and rural forms of culture from which he had sprung. This allowed him to adapt traditional forms to the needs of a popular Renaissance theater. Thus, he transformed the rural jig into a balladesque performance that combined dance and song. The drums that had once accompanied the ritual Morris dancers beat time to a secular English lyric. In this way Tarlton made use of what Gabriel Harvey called the "newfounde phrases of the taverne," and together with his pupils, the great Shakespearean actors Kempe and Armin, and the famous Robert Wilson, created the modern clown and fool of Renaissance drama combining elements of the morality Vice and the outmoded court fool.

The old Vice was a negative figure, though, and Tarlton's major innovations were the dissociation of the role from the heritage of its purely didactic and allegorical meanings, and the development of a clowning self-awareness that went far beyond the Vice's earlier homiletic self-consciousness. Tarlton completely secularized the Vice, thus completing a change of character and function already anticipated in *Mankind*.[43] At the same time he brought the jig to the Elizabethan stage, a form described by C. R. Baskerville as a "professional offshoot of the folk art of song and dance."[44] Although it was not assimilated into the drama proper, the jig did survive on the Elizabethan stage as a dance performed at the conclusion of a play. The jig employed a balladesque action, usually juxtaposed realism and burlesque, and contained elements of semiutopian nonsense as well as attacks on contemporary social abuses.[45] From a basically plebeian point of view (albeit one that accommodated national as apart from corporate ideology), the jig parodied Catholicism, Puritanism, and legal and religious ceremonies. Such "parodies of legal and religious forms," according to Baskerville, were "favorites with Tarlton."[46] Thus, age-old conventions of disenchanting and irreverent parody, which we first encountered in the ancient *mimus,* were received and integrated within the public theater of the Renaissance; for Tarlton's capacity for burlesque action was not restricted to his performance of the jig, but extended also into his role as clown.

Few of the parts that Tarlton created are known to us today, but one which has survived is that of the clown Dericke in *The Famous Victories of Henry V,* the first extant chronicle play. Here, Tarlton's clowning anticipates basic elements of the Shakespearean synthesis, since the clowning action is so skillfully related to the larger meaning of the play. In the well-known Chief Justice scene, for example, Prince Henry boxes his judge's ears because the judge has refused to release one of his cohorts. The judge, although he accepts the blow ("Well, my Lord, I am content to take it at your hands," Adams ed., 496), has the Prince led off to Fleet Prison—"to teach you what prerogatiues meane," (510). This scene is immediately parodied by Dericke (played by Tarlton) and John Cobler:

> *Dericke.* Faith, Iohn, Ile tel thee what: thou shalt be my Lord
> Chiefe Iustice, and thou shalt sit in the chaire; and Ile
> be the yong Prince, and hit thee a boxe on the eare;
> and then thou salt say, "To teach you what prerogatiues meane, I
> commit you to the Fleete."
>
> *Iohn.* Come on; Ile be your iudge! But thou shalt not hit me hard?
> *Dericke.* No, no.
>
> *(John Cobler takes his place in the Judge's seat.)*
>
> *Iohn.* What hath he done?

Dericke. Marry, he hath robd Dericke.
Iohn.   Why, then, I cannot let him go.
Dericke. I must needs haue my man.
Iohn.   You shall not haue him!
Dericke. Shall I not haue my man? Say "no", and you dare!
            How say you? Shall I not haue my man?
Iohn.   No, marry, shall you not!
Dericke. Shall I not, Iohn?
Iohn.   No, Dericke.
Dericke. Why, then, take you that [*boxing his ears*] till
            more come! Sownes, shall I not haue him?
Iohn.   Well, I am content to take this at your hand. But,
            I pray you, who am I?
Dericke. Who art thou? Sownds, doost not know thy self?
Iohn.   No.
Dericke. Now away, simple fellow. Why, man, thou art Iohn
            the Cobler.
Iohn.   No, I am my Lord Chiefe Iustice of England.
Dericke. Oh, Iohn; masse! thou saist true, thou art indeed.
Iohn.   Why, then, to teach you what prerogatiues mean,
            I commit you to the Fleete.

                                                        (534–71)

In this parody the delicate subject of princely prerogative is played out once more, but this time from a complementary and thoroughly plebeian point of view. Here the ambidextrous nature of "authority" is emphasized (a theme that Lear in his madness will take up again): the double vision of "what prerogatiues meane" is implicit in John Cobler's observation that they "should have bene hangde" (532) had they done what the Prince did. As the offense is playfully re-enacted, the plebeian awareness of the ambiguity of "prerogatives" is linked to an awareness of the two valid answers to the question "who am I?" Since the question has been asked by both the judge (500) and John Cobler (565), both the mimetic representation of the aristocratic role and the playful re-enactment of the actor's plebeian self interact within a larger artistic unity. Dericke mimes the role of the Prince, but as Prince he refers to Dericke (who was robbed earlier in the play), that is, to himself. The comic development of an identity that is personal as well as social is complete when another inversion of roles is achieved, and both John and Dericke lapse back into their true clowning selves. But what is remarkable is that this redefinition of self ("doost not know thy self?") stops short of an extradramatic self-introduction of the actors. Rather, it is perfectly well-integrated into the representational action of the play in the sense that it is the emotion and excitement of representing the roles of judge and prince that make John and Dericke momentarily forget their theatrical identities. At this point John Cobler no longer sees a re-enacted prince, but Dericke, the actor. Tarlton-Dericke takes the cue (winking to the audience, one may suppose) but only in order to teach the "simple fellow" to "know thy self": "thou art John the Cobler." By inverting John's role Tarlton helps him to recover it, but again, only to return after this scene to call John a fool for letting his ears be boxed.

Shakespeare probably used this scene as a model for the very similar parody in *1 Henry IV* (II, 4), where Falstaff plays the role of the king and later that of Hal. In both of these roles the actor Falstaff talks about the character Falstaff; the first role is suspended in the second. In such a case, even when the dramatic illusion is not completely broken, the interplay between art and reality becomes both the object and the method of the drama. Like Falstaff, Dericke is the actor who is both the laughable object and the laughing *Subjekt* of his own comic role, constantly double-dealing with illusion and reality: the parodied Prince is always in part Dericke, but Dericke is also always the famous jester Tarlton. Like the football-playing Vice in *Mankind* who passes among the audience to collect money, Tarlton has only one foot in the illusion of the play to begin with. In providing game and sport as part of his role as actor Tarlton stands halfway between the festive tradition of the extra-dramatic Vice and the more representational quality of Falstaff's game and sport.

It is interesting that the popular dimension of Tarlton's role in the *Famous Victories* emphasized the double-dealing function of the clown, and that it did so by inverting an already inverted role. One day, according to a contemporary anecdote, Tarlton went still further by playing the parts of both the clown *and* the judge:

At the Bull at Bishops-gate was a play of Henry the fift, wherein the judge was to take a box on the eare; and because he was absent that should take the blow, Tarlton himselfe, ever forward to please, tooke upon him to play the same judge, besides his owne part of the clowne: and Knel then playing Henry the fift, hit Tarlton a sound boxe indeed, which, made the people laugh the more because it was he, but anon the judge goes in, and immediately Tarlton in his clownes cloathes comes out, and askes the actors what newes: O saith one hadst thou been here, thou shouldest have seene Prince Henry hit the judge a terrible box on the eare: What, man, said Tarlton, strike a judge? It is true, yfaith, said the other. No other like, said Tarlton, and it could not be but terrible to the judge, when the report so terrifies me, that me thinkes the blow remaines still on my cheeke, that it burnes againe. The people laught at this mightily: and to this day I have heard it commended for rare; but no marvell, for he had many of these....[47]

Obviously the audience was fully aware of the tensions between illusion and reality, and was quite capable of distinguishing between the famous actor and his double part: it was clear that the blow received in the role of judge also struck the actor Tarlton. The point of the joke, enjoyed and praised by so many, depended on Tarlton's ability simultaneously to *represent* the judge and to *express* his clowning self, and involved a recognition on the part of the audience of Tarlton's role playing as well as his extradramatic identity. The fictive fright at the thought that a judge has been struck ("the report so terrifies me") and the actual pain of having received that very blow interact in the unified perception of the character as Dericke-Tarlton: both the character's fright and the actor's change of role (Tarlton as judge and now Dericke) explain the red cheek. Tensions such as these are the very stuff of popular comedy. As in the Mummers' Play and *Mankind*, the traditions of the postritual festival and the representation of reality are not mutually exclusive; rather, they heighten the dramatic effect by presupposing a fairly complex conception of *mimesis*. What the comedians behind the roles of Dericke and Falstaff perform is an enactment of their clowning selves through the *mimesis* of *mimesis*. The nature of reality is explored by the imitation of imitation.

Underlying this conception of *mimesis* is what S. L. Bethell called a "principle of multi-consciousness,"[48] a complementary perspective such as we have seen time and again in the *mimus*, the secular plot of the *Secunda Pastorum*, the servant scenes in *Fulgens and Lucrece*, in fact, wherever the Vice burlesques the main action—even in a late hybrid play like *King Cambises*. A similar double vision was present in some servant scenes of the Roman drama that were indebted to Atellanic folk farce. The viability of this "multi-conscious" mode did not rest, ultimately, on a metaphysical principle; rather its vitality depended on the continuity of a style of acting that bridged the gap between play and audience, a stage position such as that occupied by the Garcio or Vice types, or the Elizabethan clown. (This type, when it followed the traditions of festive misrule or the popular fool, tended to combine with the figure of the intriguing servant, as in *Appius and Virginia*, *Horestes*, *Cambises*, for example, and in the 1580s—that is, before Tarlton's death in 1588—it can be said that "the figures of the Vice and the clown merged with each other.")[49]

The function of such "two-eyedness" (to use A. P. Rossiter's term) is connected especially to the social, spatial, and verbal modes by which specific traditions of comic characterization persisted, as well as to important elements of dramatic structure, such as the Elizabethan double plot. These conventions of staging, characterization, and structure cannot be dissociated from our understanding and appreciation of the relationship between the dramatist's own vision and the meaning of his plays. Consequently, critics like Rossiter have done well to emphasize "the constant Doubleness of the Shakespearean vision"; they have read the subplot of *1 Henry IV* as "a critical commentary" on the heroic ideal and the official interpretation of historical events.[50] The same inverting and irreverent complementary perspective has been traced in the tragedies in the form of "derisive, debunking, low or critical comedy or farce."[51]

Even though the continuity of a burlesque double plot cannot be traced directly to Tarlton and his innovations in the Vice and clowning tradition, his work must be recognized as a major link between the popular tradition and the more artistically developed Elizabethan drama, especially since it was his pupils who played the roles of Falstaff, Launce, and Touchstone. The most outstanding of Tarlton's disciples was Will Kempe, who was known to his contemporaries as "Jestmonger and Viceregentgenerall to the Ghost of Dick Tarlton." If, as Dover Wilson suggests, Kempe acted the part of Falstaff,[52] he must have done so in much the same way that Tarlton had played Dericke in the Chief Justice scene of the *Famous Victories*. In this respect, as J. A. Bryant has pointed out, Falstaff was "an immortalized Tarlton."[53]

It is important to recognize, though, that Tarlton's clown, however much Shakespeare owed to him, was not identical to the Shakespearean clown or fool. Tarlton's fame was based on his extemporal wit, his gift for improvisation, which, although it provoked hearty laughter, was nonetheless out of place in the more self-contained artistic unity of the Renaissance play. In his speech to the players, Hamlet himself confirms the drastic change in the clown's role within Elizabethan drama: "And let those that play your clowns speak no more than is set down for them . . ." (III, 2, 37 ff.). Small wonder, then, that in *Macbeth*—as far as we can tell from what is probably an abbreviated folio text—the amount of traditional clowning has considerably decreased and become more episodic in contrast to the length and centrality of Falstaff's role in *Henry IV*. Such a decrease, considering the vitality and long life of the Vice on the popular stage, was symptomatic of the decline of the most important traditional figure in the popular theater. In this Shakespeare followed contemporary taste, which had, under increasing aristocratic influence, lost interest in clowns and fools.

Still, compared to his contemporaries—Beaumont and Fletcher, Jonson, Chapman, and Joseph Hall—Shakespeare adhered quite tenaciously to popular traditions that were already being denounced freely. Even when the popular tradition was well-received in the Elizabethan theater, that is, long before the admirers of Beaumont and Fletcher dissociated themselves from the pantaloon wit of the wandering players, Joseph Hall was already attacking the "base clown":

A goodly hotch-potch: when vile Russetings
Are match't with monarchs, and with mighty kings.
A goodly grace to sober Tragick Muse,
When each base clown, his clumsie fist doth bruise,
And show his teeth in double rotten row
For laughter at his selfe-resembled show.[54]

At this time the attack on the Tarlton tradition was bound to be an attack on Shakespeare as well. Of course, Shakespeare's clowns, and especially his fools, were firmly integrated into the action as a whole: the clown appearing as Proteus' servant Launce, the fool as Olivia's court fool Feste. The actors of these parts—Kempe and Armin—no longer re-enacted their clowning selves, but represented, at least in part, fully developed dramatic *roles*. In this sense Shakespeare broke away from Tarlton's "selfe-resembled show," although he continued to mingle "vile Russetings" with the finer robes of "monarchs" and aristocrats. When it came to the practical considerations of speech and stage action, Shakespeare used and developed popular traditions within his larger artistic synthesis. The porter in *Macbeth* and the gravediggers in *Hamlet* represent this dramatically integrated mode of clowning at its most mature. Even when the conventions of clowning occasionally remained strangely unintegrated (as in *Othello* III, 1; III, 4), Shakespeare—in striking contrast to his late contemporaries—never quite forsook the heritage of Tarlton. As late as *The Winter's Tale* and *The Tempest,* Shakespeare preferred "a goodly hotch-potch" in which "vile Russetings" stood side by side "with monarchs, and with mighty kings."

5

Popular Myth and Dramatic Poetry: Robin and Puck

While certain aspects of the older Vice and newer clowning traditions were being adapted and modified by Renaissance dramatists, entirely separate popular traditions began to make their mark on the drama as well. Notable among these was the native English lower mythology, to which Shakespeare, for example, owed some of his most fantastic creations: Puck, Ariel, Queen Mab, and the other witches, fairies and hobgoblins that inhabit plays as diverse in form and content as *A Midsummer Night's Dream, The Merry Wives of Windsor,* and *Macbeth.* Figures like these were not a part of the older popular theater; the mysteries were built mainly upon biblical sources, and allegorical homily and the Vice's farce in the moralities did not readily lend themselves to the fairytale and un-Christian world of lower myth. But as drama broke away from its allegorical models and classical mythology assumed a new importance in modern poetry, this dimension of popular culture, still very much a part of the daily lives of countless Elizabethans, was assimilated and put to new uses in the theater.[55]

Unlike the gods of the pagan past, the creatures of the lower mythology, because they were everyday house, forest, and meadow sprites, made a much smoother transition into a postmythical culture, thereby retaining much of their imaginative vitality. Growing skepticism, and new insights and discoveries in what Bacon, in the Second Book (I, 5; VII, 1) of *The Advancement of Learning,* called "Historia Mechanica" and "natural philosophy," did not stand in their way. On the contrary, the fact that the seriousness of the belief in such airy creatures was more and more widely undermined made their playfully imaginative treatment in the public theater possible. At that time, the language of native myth must have especially attracted those writers and playwrights who found in them some "unconscious artistic processing of nature" whereby the realities of "nature and the forms of society itself"[56] might be conceived in widely known popular images and stories.

It was in this highly transitional situation, when the new natural philosophy and corresponding attitudes in the reformed church had unsettled the previous social functions of these superstitions without quite extinguishing their traditional fascination, that the fantastic products of the popular imagination were able to make the transition from an oral tradition to a fully literary and dramatic one. Under these conditions the general revival of interest in classical mythology—primarily a result of translations starting about 1553—made it easier for popular pamphleteers and dramatists to raise folklore from the threat of extinction and the stigma of possible heresy to national popularity in what has since been judged "our great period of fairy literature."[57]

Unlike the fays of the chivalric epic and romance, Robin Goodfellow—the prototypical hobgoblin—was not associated with heroic deeds done in distant places, but with the lives and labors of the common man in familiar local settings. Like other fairies and kobolds, and like the much older Puck (OE *puca*) whose name in the Middle Ages was a synonym for Satan, Robin was often identified with the biblical devil. He was, as late as Reginald Scott's *Discovery of Witchcraft* (1584) and King James' *Daemonology* (1597), still closely connected with witchcraft and heresy.[58]

But this pagan background did not hinder Robin Goodfellow's popularity in Renaissance literature. Despite his detractors, Robin remained essentially a good sprite. Although in *Grim the Collier* (Dod. VIII, 460) he is called a "country devil" and elsewhere "Robin eclyped Imp of Hell or divell," these were basically playful euphemisms for his non-Christian origin; as Grim, the plebeian hero, goes on to say, "Master Robert, you were ever one of the honestest merry devils that ever I saw . . . Why, we two are sworn brothers . . . ," (Dod. VIII, 462).

In these years, as M. W. Latham has noted, Robin became something of a folk hero, well known in popular Renaissance literature—especially in the Elizabethan pamphlet. *Tell-Trothes New-Yeares Gift* (1593), for example, was subtitled, *Being Robin Good-fellowes newes out of those Countries, where inhabites neither Charity nor honesty.* Like Rubin, the Vice, and

Jack Finney's doctor, Robin was well-traveled and familiar with hell—"a place (sayde hee) that is odious, and yet to none but to them that feare it."[59] "Robins salue" offered a cure for real-life maladies; "Robins councell" was "a soueraigne oyle of experience"; "hee meanes . . . to arme you against many pettie aduersaries."[60]

For these reasons Robin was a logical companion and friend to the soothsayer Tell-Troth. Rooted in both mythology and the practical affairs of everyday life, Robin easily adapted to the combination of fantasy and realism that was so fundamental a part of popular dramaturgy. Like the fool in the *mimus,* and the more modern clown, Robin was often used as a vehicle of satire—the very kinds of satire and parody that made Tarlton and Robert Wilson famous. It is no wonder, then, that an Elizabethan pamphlet drew a direct link between Tarlton and Robin: *Tarlton's Newes out of Purgatorie . . . Published by an old companion of his, Robin Goodfellow.*" This, at any rate, is how the dead Tarlton would be thought of:

for although thou see me heere in likeness of a spirite, yet thinke me to bee one of those *Familiares Lares* that were rather pleasantly disposed then endued with any hurtfull influence, as Hob Thrust, Robin Goodfellow and such like spirites, as they tearme them of the buttry, famozed in every olde wives chronicle for their mad merrye prankes. Therefore sith my appearance to thee is in a resemblance of a spirite, think that I am as pleasant a goblin as the rest, and will make thee as merry before I part, as ever Robin Goodfellow made the cuntry wenches at their Cream-boules . . .[61]

It is difficult to determine whether this association reflects a connection made by Tarlton himself, even though there is reason to believe that he may at one time have played the role of Robin or appeared as the hobgoblin's partner.[62] What is clear, though, is that the stylized goblin type readily took on many clowning features, as the *hob* in hobgoblin indicates: OED "hob," "a familiar form of Rob=Robin" and "formerly a generic name for: A rustic, a clown."

But the Puck or Robin type that was assimilated into Renaissance drama was not simply a semimythical Robin Goodfellow. Shakespeare's Puck, for example, was clearly related to the mad Robin of the popular ballads who, with his "ho, ho, ho" reminiscent of the Vice, promised to "make good sport":

> From Oberon, in fairye land,
> The king of ghosts and shadowes there,
> Mad Robin I, at his command,
> Am sent to viewe the night-sports here;
> What revel rout
> Is kept about,
> In every corner where I go,

I will o'er see,
And merry bee,
And make good sport with ho, ho, ho![63]

Likewise, in *A Midsummer Night's Dream,* Oberon calls his "Robin" (III, 2, 355; IV, 1, 43) a "mad spirit" (III, 2, 4). But even though Shakespeare's Robin retains some measure of cheeky impudence and kobold-like maliciousness, he is predominately a good-natured servant to Oberon ("I jest to Oberon and make him smile," II, 1, 44) and definitely not a traditional Vice figure. The old Vice's audience contact emerges, if anywhere, only in song, epilogue, and relatively infrequent ironic asides.

The similarities between the Robin of folk culture and the character Puck in Renaissance drama should not, therefore, overshadow their differences. Shakespeare's use of popular myth, for example, is applied to the creation of truly unique dramatic poetry in *A Midsummer Night's Dream* and *The Tempest.* For Shakespeare, Robin was no longer strictly the mythical creature who survived in folk customs and Christmas games,[64] but something of a practical joker who, although different from the Vice, helped direct the play. He was, following tradition, still connected with "the maidens of the villagery" and "the country proverb known" (III, 3, 458), but his ritualistic costume in *Grim the Collier* would have been incongruous on Shakespeare's Puck:

Enter Robin Goodfellow, in a suit of leather,
close to his body; his face and hands coloured
russet-colour, with a flail.

(Dod. VIII, 442)

Robin's flail may recall Myscheff in his role of "wyntur corn-thresscher" in *Mankind*; his leather suit and "russet-colour" face, like his "Christmas Calues skin" in *Wily Beguiled,* in some ways parallel the popular fool. But although Shakespeare's Puck still retains the ability to change into horse, hound, hog, or bear (III, 1, 101), these are, like Volpone's protean fantasies ("Whil'st we, in changed shapes, act *Ovids* tales," *Volpone* III, 7, 221), skillfully elevated to new levels of poetic imagery. Indeed, in spite of the fact that modern directors have made much of Puck's cultic background, the calf's fell may have already seemed a curious atavism in Shakespeare's time. (Such direct links between mimetic magic and popular drama exist only in a very few isolated cases—Iniquity in *King Darius,* for example, deals "a blowe with a foxe taye"—but even the Vice in *Mankind,* despite Alois Brandl's claim to the contrary, no longer carried the devil's foxtail.)[65]

In *The Tempest* Shakespeare moved farther still from traditional popular mythology. Ariel still bore some resemblance to the mythical kobold, the servant spirit who did his master's bidding, but by this time had become "a spirit too delicate/To act . . . earthy and abhorred commands"

(I, 2, 272–73). Although his dispatch of mundane chores mirrors Puck's domestic doings and his songs often betray a naive and "natural" perspective, Ariel longs for freedom from servitude and would gladly trade the pragmatic for the ethereal. In Puck the traditional element of satire subsides into a highly generalized ironic commentary on the human condition: "Lord, what fools these mortals be!" (III, 2, 115); but in Ariel the element of satire has virtually disappeared altogether. In this way Shakespeare gradually assimilated figures native to the popular imagination in his search to create dramatic worlds unique in their poetic vitality.[66] Gustav Landauer aptly describes Shakespeare's attitude toward the tradition from which he drew: "Shakespeare faces this world of myth, dogma and ritual as a master who is still just able to let himself be mastered; ... as a wise man who can still be as a child."[67]

In not rejecting, but poetically using that which was naive and down-to-earth in the folk mythology, the Renaissance poet illustrated the fact "that within the field of art itself certain important forms are only possible at a less advanced stage of artistic development."[68] But these forms, once they have combined with other traditions, lose their original significance and become something totally new. Thus Shakespeare's Puck was at once a product of the popular imagination as well as a part of the more literary traditions of Cupid and Ovid's *Metamorphoses*. This variety of sources for Puck's character basically reflects the broad sociological foundation upon which the plays as a whole were built; where, as in *A Midsummer Night's Dream*, plebeian craftsmen, upper-middle-class lovers and the ducal couple mix freely, where the May cult becomes a midsummer night's dream and white magic serves as a new vehicle of a great poet's imagination.[69]

6

Renaissance Poetics and Elizabethan Realism:
Vision and Experience

The assimilation and poetic reshaping of the popular tradition within the more literary Renaissance drama reached its height in the twenty or so years that separate *Doctor Faustus* from *The Tempest*. In this the heyday of Elizabethan and Jacobean drama, the art of poetry was integrated in unique ways with a new sense of the world of empirical reality. The "sweet airs" and "voices" of Prospero's magic island are linked, for example, to the more practical exigencies and the problems of colonization; Titania and Oberon share their remote and fantastic midsummer night wood with pedestrian "hempen homespuns" and craftsmen; the phantasmagorical ether generated by the weird sisters in *Macbeth* foreshadows and illuminates brutal political ambition. But the "realism" that emerges from this unity of the imaginative and the mundane is not, ultimately, a realism of subject, in the sense that the fairies in *A Midsummer Night's Dream* are not "real" but the rustics are, or that the witches' chants are not "real" but Duncan's murder is. Rather, it is a new sense of the interdependence of character and society, and a fully responsive interplay between dramatic speech and dramatic action in the process of reproducing the cause and effect of human behavior that defines "realism" in the Renaissance theater.

Interestingly enough, such realism in the linking of speech and action is not to be found in the neoclassical drama or the other forms used and developed by Renaissance scholars and learned authors, but may be detected in a few scenes (such as the Wakefield shepherd scenes) from the popular medieval theater. And yet, this tradition of popular realism in the theater must have found itself in some unexpected (and problematic) correspondence with Renaissance attitudes toward *mimesis*, especially after Paccius' Latin translation of Aristotle's *Poetics* in 1536. For Aristotle, *mimesis* contained impulses common to all poetic arts, and for him the general origin of poetry was due to imitation as a natural activity for man from childhood. Renaissance poetics reflected this basic respect for imitation as the foundation of poetry, but combined it with the general principle of *inventio*. *Imitatio*, then, was not understood to be a simple mirroring. As George Puttenham put it in 1589, "arte is not only an aide and coadiutor to nature in all her actions but an alterer of them, and in some sort a surmounter of her skill." Poetry, in this respect, is like "nature her selfe working by her owne peculiar vertue and proper instinct."[70] According to the famous definition attributed to Cicero and quoted in many editions of Terence and in Ben Jonson's *Every Man out of his Humour* (III, 6, 207), comedy was *"imitatio vitae, speculum consuetudinis, imago veritatis."*

In practice, however, these principles of truthful imitation were not necessarily those which formed the basis of neoclassical dramaturgy. For example, a rigid line had been drawn between tragedy, which was strictly an aristocratic form, and comedy, in which lesser persons or the "ugly" were imitated. If this division was not originally a social one,[71] it did involve a narrowing of subjects suitable for imitation in each particular form. This alone limited the degree to which drama could truthfully represent the diversity of human life and experience. But even more important, the classical ideal of dramatic "truth," as it was developed by Maggi (1550) and Scaliger (1561), amounted really to a justification of scenic illusion, of merely the appearance of truth. Even before Castelvetro's unities of time, place, and action had been formulated and assimilated into English literary criticism, the Aristotelian unity of action had been virtually abandoned in favor of verisimilitude—the *appearance* of unified action. On this account the classical reliance on illusion in, say, Alberti, Serlio, Palladio, and Scamozzi was radically different from the dramatic interplay of scaffold and place in the popular theater.

Although adhering to many humanist attitudes toward poetics, rhetoric, and logic, the popular Renaissance playwright also adopted perspectives that severely challenged the classical notions of decorum, dramatic illusion, and the implicit inclusion and exclusion of social types in particular genres. Consequently, the Renaissance stage saw both clown and king sharing in the effect and the meaning of a single play.

> Manye tymes (to make mirthe) they make a Clowne companion
> with a Kinge; in theyr graue Counsels they allow the aduise of
> fooles; yea, they vse one order of speach for all persons: a grose
> *Indecorum* . . .[72]

It is this mixed style that pervades Shakespeare's greatest tragedies, where, as in *Lear,* the fool speaks in serious consultation with his king, and so plays "a part in maiesticall matters." Sidney objected to this tradition of "mongrell Tragicomedie," which at its core broke so decisively from the learned notion of verisimilitude and the limitations of highly stylized and mannered poetry.[73] But in spite of such popular conventions that challenged neoclassical decorum, unity, and scenic illusion, the humanist conception of *mimesis* did remain an important influence on the public stage. Like Cicero before him, Shakespeare, in Hamlet's address to the players, used the image of the mirror held up to nature [*quae (parvos et bestias) putat esse specula naturae*] to describe "the purpose of playing." In this often-quoted passage Hamlet certainly echoes the Renaissance principle of *imitatio;* and in his subsequent attack on what Hall called the clown's "selfe-resembled show," that is, the excessive improvisation and self-embodiment that make his imitation of humanity so "abominable," Hamlet may well owe something to the principle of verisimilitude as demanded by Scaliger and other Renaissance critics. But for Shakespeare, this is not the only source of dramatic theory; for Hamlet's speech benefits from a more practical concern with a dramaturgy whose principles are perhaps less evident but far reaching indeed.

Speak the speech, I pray you, as I pronounc'd it to you, trippingly on the tongue; but if you mouth it, as many of our players do, I had as lief the town-crier spoke my lines. . . . Be not too tame neither, but let your own discretion be your tutor. Suit the action to the word, the word to the action; with this special observance, that you o'erstep not the modesty of nature; for anything so o'erdone is from the purpose of playing, whose end, both at the first and now, was and is to hold, as 'twere, the mirror up to nature; to show virtue her own feature, scorn her own image, and the very age and body of the time his form and pressure. Now, this overdone or come tardy off, though it makes the unskilful laugh, cannot but make the judicious grieve; the censure of the which one must, in your allowance, o'erweigh a whole theatre of others. O, there be players that I have seen play— and heard others praise, and that highly—not to speak it profanely, that, neither having th' accent of Christians, nor the gait of Christian, pagan, nor man, have so strutted and bellowed that I have thought some of Nature's journeymen had made men, and not made them well, they imitated humanity so abominably.

(III, 2, 1–4; 16–34)

This miniature "art of acting" (here still abbreviated) amounts to the proposition that word and action should be complementary and that neither should overstep the limits of nature. The specific advice about speaking a speech correctly gives way, however, to a generalization on the purpose of all acting, which "both at the first and now, was and is" to imitate nature. But this generalization, which is the crux of the speech, leads again to the specific, to the matter of the actor's accent and gait as they pertain to a proper imitation of humanity.

What is most striking about this speech is its context; for as the Prince addresses the actors he integrates, both literally and theoretically, the scholarly view of *mimesis* (embodied in Hamlet's sophisticated and educated taste) and the popular traditions of acting and stagecraft of the traveling players, who Rosencrantz has told us, have taken to acting on "the common stages" (II, 2, 338). Whether Hamlet actually speaks for Shakespeare in his address to the players is a vexed question. Alfred Harbage has suggested that Hamlet's learned neoclassical point of view simply supports his characterization as a member of the aristocracy. But while this may be so, it seems likely that, taken in its context, the speech does indeed tell us something about Shakespeare's own theory of drama. Accepting what to him appeared valid in Renaissance mimetic theory, Shakespeare here formulates principles of dramaturgy that follow the humanist tradition but were at least partly derived from, and articulated in terms of (and hence modified by), the practical experience of the common actor.

Suiting the action to the word while at the same time exercising a judicious control over words and actions so that they might not upset the balanced unity of speech, gesture, and movement was an artistic achievement that followed the cooperation a decade or so earlier between common players and humanist-trained playwrights. Marlowe and Kyd benefited from and, at the same time, consummated the development of such new standards of realism. Before them, in plays like *King Cambises*, the realistic integration of word and action was restricted to comic or burlesque scenes or to the actions of Vice-like characters. At that stage serious characters were still given to a more descriptive and, as it were, narrative type of speech, a more highly stylized form of rhetorical declamation. Marlowe and Kyd, however, used the interplay of verbal and physical expression that was formerly restricted to the comic parts in the serious scenes as well. As a result, the speech of serious and aristocratic characters became less declamatory and more theatrically effective; formal rhetoric and stylized poses and situations became less rigid; syntax and vocabulary were given greater flexibility, and sometimes simplified or adjusted to conform with everyday usage.

All of these changes facilitated the development of purely dramatic modes of characterization. Insofar as it illuminated the character of the speaker, the way in which a speech was delivered could now be as dramatically significant as what was said. And although such innovations in no way eliminated stock types, these elements now assumed their typicality not only through conventional (and hence easily recognizable) poses or stock rhetorical formulae, but also by revealing specific patterns of behavior through skillfully juxtaposed word and action. As this affected the serious figures in drama, the changing conventions of speech reflected, and contributed to, the emergence of a new conception of character and a new image of the relationship between the individual and society. No longer functioning merely to represent preconceived attitudes or preordained patterns of static conflict such as the allegorical contest of *humanum genus,* the realistic mode of characterization was particularly well-suited to represent the movement (the relations and the struggle) between the world and the ego, environment and character. This involved the task of representing a variety of moral, psychological, and historical factors, a task that was finally achieved through a new dialectic between generality and detail, vision and experience.

It was in Marlowe's plays that the serious hero, through a new realism in the interplay of speech and action, first moved to the foreground as an essentially individual and dynamic (as opposed to an allegorical and static, or unchanging) figure. Poetically heightened and rhetorically stylized, the hero's speech combined homiletic, classical, and contemporary matter with the popular actor's unique freedom of physical movement and stage-awareness. With this combination of idea, *Gestus,* and physical action the dramatic monologue of modern drama triumphantly emerged.

> Settle thy studies *Faustus,* and beginne
> To sound the deapth of that thou wilt professe:
> Hauing commencde, be a Diuine in shew,
> Yet leuell at the end of euery Art,
> And liue and die in *Aristotles* workes:
> Sweete *Analutikes* tis thou hast rauisht me.
> *Bene disserere est finis logices,*
> Is to dispute well, Logickes chiefest end,
> Affoords this Art no greater myracle?
> Then reade no more, thou hast attaind the end:

A greater subiect fitteth *Faustus* wit,
Bid *on cai me on* farewell, *Galen* come:
Seeing, *vbi desinit philosophus, ibi incipit medicus.*
Be a physition *Faustus,* heape vp golde,
And be eternizde for some wondrous cure.
Summum bonum medicinae sanitas,
The end of physicke is our bodies health:
Why *Faustus,* hast thou not attaind that end?
Is not thy common talke sound Aphorismes?
Are not thy billes hung vp as monuments,
Whereby whole Citties haue escapt the plague,
And thousand desprate maladies beene easde,
Yet art thou still but *Faustus,* and a man.
Wouldst thou make man to liue eternally?
Or being dead, raise them to life againe?
Then this profession were to be esteemd.
Physicke farewell, where is *Iustinian?*

(29-55)

The profound originality of Faustus' monologue lies primarily in the fact that it represents, although necessarily in abbreviated form, an intellectual *process* that involves an empirically significant image of change and movement in thought or attitude. Even though this speech condenses years of restless soul-searching, the course of Faustus' thoughts and ambitions is not described, declaimed, or didactically evaluated, but rather dramatically recreated. Faustus relives the relevant decisions of his life: his attraction to logic, medicine, law, and his final rejection of them. The broadest and most general questions about life and the human condition merge with the concrete experience of the speaker and with his actions and gestures upon the stage (such as reaching for a book and reading from it).[74]

Wolfgang Clemen has aptly described this speech as a "soliloquy which moves forward in accordance with the promptings of the moment." In earlier drama, "the rhetorical preparation, arrangement and embellishment of speech had hitherto concealed and deadened the actual process of thought and experience. But now it is possible to see how Faustus thinks while he speaks, how a simultaneity of the process of thought and structure of speech builds up which is extremely important for the further development of his speech. Thus the pattern of the whole appears different: out of the antitheses of argument and counterargument comes an expression of genuine wavering and doubt, out of talking to himself ... a genuine soliloquy, out of embellishing maxims a personal view of things to which Faustus has fought his way."[75]

Far from being an achievement in technique alone, these new verbal modes of representation were predicated upon a changing apprehension of both the function of art and the nature of human reality. They mark a point in Renaissance drama where process and product merge, where a more intense relationship between art and reality informs both the themes and the modes of drama. Therefore, to say that the structure of Faustus' speech is more empirical than, say, that of Everyman is at best a half-truth if it does not embrace an awareness of the underlying changes in the conception of art and reality—changes that involve both abstract ideas and concrete experience and, especially, new modes of correlating them more intimately and yet less directly.

In order to characterize the new dialectic between style and reality, the departure from morality traditions of allegory seems perhaps most significant. The allegorical mode had provided an altogether different mode of relating the idea (*Wesen*) and the appearance (*Erscheinung*) of reality. As in the medieval philosophy of realism, the true reality was thought to be in the concept of things, not in the things themselves. So the poet of allegory started out with a previously established notion of, say, virtue or vice, youth or sin, and the figuring forth of these abstractions in the form of sensuous experience involved that "gulf" (*Abgrund*) between image and meaning of which Walter Benjamin has written so suggestively.[76] But that gulf between sensuous form and general notion was symptomatic of the fact that both the writer and the reader of allegory had accepted previously established modes of poetic generalization and that it was only on the basis of such adopted modes of generalization that the world of immediate personal experience was allowed to enter into the dialectic of art and reality.

In contrast to that, popular Renaissance drama opened up a new mode of poetic discourse which, as it were, demanded, and proceeded through, the individual perceptions of writer, reader, and character. Bridging the chasm between image and meaning, these two aspects became intimately related. The writer and the reader (or spectator), instead of falling back on predetermined modes of synthesis, were called upon to analyze the areas of congruity and incongruity between vision and experience for themselves. The correlation between Faustus' ideas (or his illusions), and the images of his actual experiences, is notoriously problematic, but even so serves as a new means of defining the meaning of the play as a whole. On the one hand the idea of the play can more closely be seen in its unity with a represented world of experiences, as when gestures, vocabulary, imagery, and even speech rhythm and intonation are used to convey some social, spiritual, or psychological meaning. On the other hand, there are new and growing contradictions between vision and experience. For Marlowe (as for Shakespeare) the world of sensuous and individual appearance had become more variegated at a time when their social significance and their historical frame of reference in society (as in trade, nation, government, and ideology) grew more abstract and complex. The areas of correlation seem more tenuous and precarious, partly because their discovery involved so much more deliberate activity on the part of both writers and readers (or spectators). What is needed is an increased amount of intense imaginative activity, so as to identify, for instance, the image of Faustus' magic or his vision of hell with their new and highly complex meaning as revealed through his hopes, and fears, and desperation as part of the larger meaning which is the play itself. The new mode of creating and receiving these postallegorical images demands some appropriation of both the forms of life and the figures of art, and calls for a sharpened sense of the relationship between imagination and life, role and reality.

Thus, the popular Renaissance mode of apprehending the world inverted the traditional medieval ways of relating the ideal and the real. It brought forth an increased interaction between idea and appearance, between the general and the particular—an interaction that opened up new areas of both congruity and incongruity. Marlowe, Kyd, and Shakespeare no longer started from some preconceived idea of virtue, vice, or youth; they looked at the virtuous, the vicious, or the young, and by looking at them proceeded to elaborate their own poetic conceptions of the image *as the meaning* of the representations of youth or vice or virtue, and vice versa.[77] As in contemporary science and some areas of Renaissance philosophy,[78] it was not the empirical approach that superseded an abstract mode of recognition; rather, it was the interaction between detail and generality, sensuousness and vision, by which literature became more concrete than philosophy and more philosophical than history.

What, in this context, deserves to be noted is the degree to which the actual achievement of popular Renaissance drama went beyond the norms and rules of Renaissance poetics. The precept of Aristotelian poetics, so powerful in the later sixteenth century, is well-known. *"Poesie"* (in the words of Sidney) was designed to deal with "the universal consideration," whereas *"Historie"* was thought to be concerned with "the particular."[79] Although in the Italian Renaissance there were those (like Benedetto Varchi, Alessandro Lionardi, Giovanni Battista Pigna, and others) who tended to elevate poetry to the rank of the most universal and comprehensive type of science or art of discourse,[80] the Aristolelian distinction did represent a significant tendency in neoclassical theory. But the most popular of Renaissance works of literature had already broken down the division between poetry and history, in the sense that the particular was no longer confined to historiography and the general ceased to be the exclusive province of an exalted type of literature. Instead, the two opposing aspects entered into a new relationship by which abstraction and sensuousness, the criteria of thought and the standards of life, theory, and practice were more intimately linked and interrelated than ever before in the history of literature.

Again, these were more than mere technical achievements; behind them were a vision of humanity and a new image of man and society that deserve to be emphasized here because once again it was the popular Renaissance drama that made the most far reaching departures from both medieval and neoclassical conceptions of character. The medieval image of man as expressed in a morality figure like *humanum genus* or a hero of romance like Tristan or even Perceval, is in the fullest sense of the word preconceived in whatever degrees of growth there are from innocence to maturity. The creative principle on which the whole mode of medieval characterization was based was not that of the exploration of the individual's relation to nature and society. Consequently, the quality of experience in the hero and the representation of his environment did not consistently affect each other. As a recent student of medieval romance put it, "there is only a limited degree of interaction between him [the hero] and the world around him. The 'character' of a romance-hero is rather a rehearsed interior monologue than a meaningful and unpredictable dialogue with the outside world. To put it briefly, the hero has to realize his potential, not to come to terms with life."[81]

But in popular Renaissance drama and fiction these two aspects (the hero's relations to images of the outside world and his own potential as a character) no longer form any opposition or alternative. On the contrary, a hero like Faustus, Hamlet, or Prospero (or even Panurge, Lazarillo, or Jack Wilton) does have meaningful and sometimes unpredictable dialogues with the outside world. What is more, the nature of their respective dialogues informs their functions and qualities as characters. There is an interaction between the way the hero comes to terms with life and the manner in which his potential as a character is realized. And through this interaction the image of the hero's success or failure in dealing with the world serves as a major element in the growth of a new mode of characterization.[82]

At this point, the popular-humanist insistence on the unity between "action" and "word" (as in *Hamlet*, III, 2, 17 ff.) can be seen to point beyond the actor's practical piece of advice for speaking a speech correctly. What is involved is the technique of the actor as well as the craft of the playwright. But if the dramatist's vision of man was expressed through his craft, the craftsmanship itself and the poetic realism conveyed through it were to be realized in a language that drew on both the sources of rhetoric and of ordinary speech.

As an example, Thomas Kyd's *The Spanish Tragedy* may serve to illustrate some of the elements and problems involved. Even more than in Marlowe's drama, principles of classical rhetoric and conventions of popular stagecraft are integrated into something new:

> What outcries pluck me from my naked bed,
> And chill my throbbing hart with trembling feare,

Which neuer danger yet could daunt before?
Who cals Hieronimo? speak; heare I am!
I did not slumber; therefore twas no dreame.
No, no; it was some woman cride for helpe,
And heere within this garden did she crie,
And in this garden must I rescue her.
But stay! what murdrous spectacle is this?
A man hangd vp, and all the murderers gone!
And in my bower, to lay the guilt on me!

(Manly, II, 4, 63–73)

Here we have the poet's "word" suited to the play's "action," and the "action" suited "to the word." There is a unity of verbal art and stage-craft not to be found in Seneca or the neoclassical drama; for the mode of communication is not simply speech, but speech coupled with action—action that, because of this coupling, is implied by the words themselves.[83] Again the monologue is no longer a static form of utterance: it does not express previously established facts or opinions. Rather, it represents the *process* of thinking and perceiving by which means the character gains knowledge and, because of his increased awareness, acts and changes in the context of the world of the play.

Clearly absent from the speech is the elevated rhetorical declamation that dominated the serious scenes in plays like *King Cambises*, replaced by a basic Anglo-Saxon vocabulary (bed, heart, fear, dream, help, garden, death are the nouns that carry the action forward). Such a vocabulary is only one of many elements reflected in Hieronimo's speech, but it does indicate some measure of inspiration from the traditional sources of the native language, as opposed to classical or rhetorical influence. Dramatic language in the popular Renaissance play was immeasurably enriched by humanist rhetoric, but was not exclusively a product of that one source. It may be assumed that the dramatic uses of language were most heavily indebted to the popular acting tradition where the forms of speech and the modes of action were conjoined, as in Hieronimo's speech, in the course of an essentially theatrical situation.

In light of this, the Elizabethan dramatic synthesis—"the merging of the eventful, stirring, action drama with the tradition of the . . . rhetorical tragedy"[84]—cannot be thought of simply as a combination of popular play acting and classical rhetoric, since classical rhetoric underwent a fundamental change when it was placed in the context of popular dramatic standards of action *and* language. What is more, if the development of an effective interrelationship between word and action drew upon many sources, then the popular uses of language, as associated with Tarlton or Nashe, must be considered more seriously than in the past. Shakespeare may have been closer to these sources than to the nominal style and somewhat bombastic mode of expression in *Gorboduc*, which Sidney described as "well sounding phrases, clyming to the height of Seneca his stile."[85]

This seems pretty obvious, not only in the case of wordplay (as discussed above) but also in Shakespeare's dramatic use of proverbs and even in some of his imagery. Of the proverb alone in Shakespeare no fewer than 2,923 uses have been counted; and these are not by any means confined to comic or trivial matters, but are used also to create tragic or elevated effects. As M. P. Tilley has pointed out, no other writer even approaches Shakespeare's broad knowledge of every kind of proverb.[86] Such extensive use of proverb is significant, not only because Shakespeare retained in it nonliterary syntax and a preference for simple words in colloquial forms,[87] but because they served to express and to counterpoint a mode of perception that had its roots in practical life and in the common man's concrete world of objects and ideas. Small wonder that these proverbs most often appeared in specifically dramatic contexts, such as in repartee and in the quick-fire exchange urging action,[88] as well as in the "aside" and a context that is characterized by the language of the fools and clowns, Hamlet, Iago, Richard III, and other figures related to the Vice tradition.

Like his use of the proverb and wordplay, Shakespeare's imagery reveals much about how his drama is related to the processes of living. It has long been recognized that images taken from nature, animal life, celestial bodies, crafts, agriculture, medicine, and gardening form the foundation of Shakespeare's metaphorical imagination. But whereas the symbolism behind the pictorial vehicle has been studied at great length, the socioaesthetic dimension of Shakespeare's imagery has been largely neglected.[89] But when, to take an example at random, social corruption is spoken of as a festering sore, when civil war is seen as a fever, when England ruled by the barons is pictured as a neglected garden, a definite attitude toward the subject is clearly at work, an attitude that reveals something "decisive about the perspective from which Shakespeare wants something to be seen."[90] When Shakespeare conjures a mental picture of Ajax and Achilles yoked together "like draught oxen" to "plow up the wars" (Troilus and Cressida II, 1, 103) he is able to refer, as Hilda M. Hulme notes, to a whole segment of already formulated experience, thereby "setting his speaker in the real world of practical matters and generalized language."[91] Unlike aristocratic or court poets, or those who wrote for the private stages, Shakespeare preferred what Alfred Harbage described as "the wisdom of experience and first-hand observation, often expressed proverbially and in the idiom of the folk."[92]

This alone, of course, does not account for the departure from Renaissance poetics, but it reflects one basic element in a complex variety of factors by which the new dialectic between detail and generality, image and meaning was achieved. This achievement, let it be repeated, was unthinkable without the Elizabethan interest in rhetoric and a humanist acquaintance with neoclassical conceptions of *mimesis* and the arts of poetry. But this alone was not enough. A more profound correlation of vision and experience seemed impossible without that different type of "Rhetorique" which humanist trained dramatists like Nashe and Greene were obviously unable to find at the University. That was "Tarlton's surmonting Rhetorique" which, as Gabriel Harvey insinuated, was so useful to Nashe's style—a style: "right-formally conueied, according to the stile and tenour of Tarltons president, his famous play of the seauen Deadly sinnes . . . Surely it must needes bee . . . authentical in forme, that had first such a learned president, and is now pleasantlie interlaced with diuers of new-founde phrases of the Tauerne. . . ."[93] The fact that Tarlton and Nashe both made considerable use of the "new-founde phrases of the Tauerne" and that Shakespeare and his contemporaries followed their example, calls attention to more than a source of language: it refers (through the ironic shield of his defensive polemics) to a tradition where the ordinary word and dramatic action so met that there resulted an art form beyond the conception and definition of neoclassical poetics.

VI

SHAKESPEARE'S THEATER: TRADITION AND EXPERIMENT

1

The Platform Stage

The many links between Elizabethan drama and society must be kept in mind when we consider the physical shape and theatrical conventions of Shakespeare's stage. Like the origin of the Elizabethan public theater, its mode of production must be seen in light of the social and cultural synthesis that characterized the highly transitional balance of class forces in the late Tudor period. No longer based on a corporate social structure (like the German Shrovetide play or the Parisian *confrères*), the Elizabethan theater was a national institution in which native popular traditions were enlarged and enriched in many ways by a variety of elements, most notably, Renaissance ideology. It was precisely because the London theater was *not* exclusively a courtly, academic, or guild theater that there developed a stage and a mode of production the theatrical possibilities of which were as diverse as the models and sources from which it drew. Among these were not only the traditional scaffold and innyard stages used by itinerant players, and the medieval pageant wagons, which could also have been arranged for performance in-the-round, but also contemporary *tableaux vivants*, and thus, indirectly, Renaissance visual arts.

Recent research into Elizabethan stage conditions has revealed the limitations of all reductive approaches to Shakespeare's theater and refuted the late Romantic conception of a simple and unsophisticated wooden stage. The so-called "thatch-and-groundling approach" has gradually lost favor since G. R. Kernodle cast new light on the public theater by pointing out its debt to the tradition of the *tableaux vivants* and the Dutch Rederijk theater.[1] Similarly, more recent research by C. Walter Hodges, Richard Southern, Richard Hosley, Glynne Wickham, and others reveals not one standard public theater, but a variety of theatrical institutions.

The most important of the many revisions of the older reconstruction of the Elizabethan stage (as designed, for example, by J. Q. Adams) concerns the existence of an "inner stage," an acting area recessed into the rear stage wall and separated from the main stage by a curtain. Theater historians like A. H. Thorndike and, of course, Adams placed many of Shakespeare's indoor scenes on this inner stage, assuming that it would have facilitated an uninterrupted performance and would have supported the illusionary effect of important scenes and scene changes. Detailed study of the thirty extant plays that were performed in Shakespeare's Globe theater between 1599 and 1608 does not, however, support this assumption. In twenty plays with indoor scenes there is no indication that an inner stage was, or even could have been, used. In only nine of the plays does the text indicate the discovery of a character (and in only three cases a group of two or three figures) concealed by a curtain. In each of these cases, however, the "discovery" serves a tableau effect and not a fully mimetic illusion of speech and action. The space needed would not have been more than four feet in depth; and so, if the rear wall in the Globe theater was anything like the wall in van Buchel's sketch of the Swan theater, the effects indicated in these nine plays could have been achieved by using a doorway.[2]

George F. Reynolds' pioneering study of stage practices in the popular Red Bull supports this reconsideration of the "inner stage." In the Red Bull, curtained movable scaffolds or a scaffoldlike house may have been used instead of an inner stage: "perhaps the 'rear stage' was not a real and permanent structural part of the stage but itself only a removable structure, more non-committal in its outward appearance than shop or tent, but just as easily brought in and removed."[3] This suggestion, reinforced by practical theatrical experiments by Bernard Miles and others,[4] has made possible entirely new visualizations of important Shakespearean scenes, such as Hodges' convincing reconstruction of the death scene in *Antony and Cleopatra* (IV, 14).[5]

The implications of this revised attitude toward the "inner stage" are quite far reaching and lead almost as a matter of course to a reconsideration of traditional notions about the "upper stage." A little more than a generation ago scholars like E. K. Chambers and W. J. Lawrence had reconstructed the upper stage as part of the upper gallery forming a roof over the inner stage. J. C. Adams placed no fewer than five of the twenty-six scenes in *King Lear*, and an average of about one-fifth of the scenes in Shakespeare's other plays, on this upper stage (in a chamber that could be separated from the gallery).[6] Later and more detailed studies by Reynolds, Hosley, T. J. King, and others indicate, however, a far smaller number of upper stage scenes: of 419 scenes in twenty-two of the plays performed by Shakespeare's troupe, only eleven are undoubtedly upper stage scenes.[7] But, as in the Red Bull, the balcony was not essential in these scenes to insure nonstop acting for the sake of illusion. As Reynolds points out, the balcony "was never used to fill in pauses in action on the front stage."[8] And even in the rare cases in which the upper stage was used—as a city wall, a balcony or a window—the scene enacted there was short, with little movement, and so closely connected with what was happening on the front stage that speakers generally stood at the edge or railing and not in the interior (which certainly made their speeches more audible).

Similarly, King demonstrates that out of 276 plays considered only forty-five required "an acting place above the stage." But even then "above" or "aloft" usually served as "an observation post from which one or two actors comment on, or converse with, actors down on the main stage." Consequently, this "above" acting area "should . . . be considered as an auxiliary to the main stage rather than a distinct and separate 'upper stage.'" As Richard Hosley suggests, then, since the same space was used by spectators and was obviously of minor importance if used only about once in a play, the term "upper stage" seems "rather inappropriate and in some respects misleading."[9]

To this date interest in the workings of the upper or the disputed inner stage has made it easy for critics to underestimate the importance and diversity of the front stage. The rapid movement and short scenes so characteristic of Shakespeare's plays were not so much enhanced by movement between inner, upper, and front acting areas as by a continuation of traditional platform stage conventions. The front stage was much more flexible and changeable than has been suggested in the past, for as an acting area it was basically neutral, free of illusion, recognized, even in performance, to be a stage. Scenes were changed and props were shifted in full view of all; and this front, or rather main, stage was used almost without interruption—for indoor as well as outdoor scenes. Such a flexible use of the main stage, surrounded on three or perhaps even four sides by spectators, reflects the constant efforts of the Elizabethan dramatist and actor to keep the play in close touch with the audience's response.

If the inner and upper stages were neither as developed nor essential to the course of the action as had formerly been assumed, it is reasonable that greater attention should be paid to the platform stage. It is easier to understand now why the main acting area was so very large—even by modern standards. Henslowe's contract for the building of the stage at the Fortune theater gives the following measurements: "in length Fortie and Three foote of lawfull assize and in breadth to extende to the middle of the yarde of the saide howse." The platform stage was so large that it could easily have accommodated most of the various scenes that have at one time or another been attributed to the inner or upper stage. This implies, of course, that the platform stage was not a homogeneous acting area, but may have used front, middle, rear, or other specific locations to produce a variety of theatrical effects—effects that can best be understood when related to the continuing interplay of *locus* and "place," *mimesis* and ritual, in the tradition of the popular theater.

In order fully to judge the scenic function of the main stage we must re-examine its original relation to the rear stage wall. As the sketch of the Swan theater seems to show, the entire tiring-house facade was probably not connected to the galleries or circular building at all. The circular building and the tiring-house seem to have been separate structures, probably separate in origin.[10] The circular building corresponded to the medieval round theater or the arena used for bear-baiting and other popular amusements, but the scaffold set up inside this arena and the tiring-house belonging to it may well have had their origins in the booth stages known to have existed all over Europe.[11] These booth stages were furnished with a scaffoldlike rear structure which, on the continent, developed into the imposing and often richly decorated facade of the Dutch Rederijk theater. Of course such a modern approach to the origins of the Elizabethan stage remains in many ways as hypothetical as the older theories it seeks to revise; but even though reasonable counterarguments can be made, this new reconstruction is supported by facts as well as by practical experiments in the staging of Renaissance drama that have greatly enhanced our understanding of Shakespeare's plays.

Since downstage acting brought the actor so far into the midst of his audience, it is conceivable that the pit, or the yard, which had no chairs or benches, might also have been used as an acting area. If only for its sensational effect, it is reasonable to suppose (as Hodges does) that some amount of acting was done in the yard.[12] But while Hodges only suggests the possibility that messengers and riders on horseback may have entered in this way, precedents in the older theater have already demonstrated the theatrical effect achieved when an actor entered in the midst of the audience. This was the case in the mysteries, where "Erode ragis in the pagond and in the strete also" (above p. 72), and in moralities, where the Vice appeared in the yard or sported with those around him (above p. 152). Appearances of this sort may indeed have been sensational, but they possessed more than what Hodges called a "stunt value." Underlying this mode of acting were traditional architectural configurations and conventions of stagecraft with which Shakespeare was almost certainly familiar. (For such a familiarity it was not absolutely necessary for him to have seen the Herod scenes in Coventry, but as J. Q. Adams pointed out, it is most likely that he did.)[13]

Acting in the pit is known to have taken place in *Henry VIII*, where the porter pushes through the spectators to make room for a procession (V, 4).[14] And while critics such as J. W. Saunders conjecture an appearance in the yard in Act II, scene 1 of *Romeo and Juliet* and Act V, scene 2 of *Antony and Cleopatra*, Allardyce Nicoll made the more general suggestion that the stage direction "pass over the stage," found in numerous texts, does not, as was hitherto assumed, mean to move between the doors in the rear stage wall, but from the pit, across the stage, and back into the pit. The starting and finishing points of this passage over the stage might then be the "ingressi" clearly marked in the Swan drawing, and might well have been connected to the rear stage structure.[15]

Although this last suggestion cannot be conclusively proved, when juxtaposed with the other revisions discussed here it confirms the likelihood that the architecture and stagecraft of the Elizabethan public theater were closer in appearance and structure to the native popular theater than critics have been willing to admit. A corollary to this view would posit that the origin of the English picture-frame stage is not to be found in the doubtful inner stage of Shakespeare's theater, but must be sought in the aristocratic theater of the Italian Renaissance court which made its mark on coterie and court stages in England and the stage settings created by Inigo Jones and later Restoration producers. This, and not the Elizabethan inner stage, explains the advent of the modern proscenium stage, its painted backdrops and visual effects.[16]

In explaining the variability of the platform stage, even as it was modified by humanist and Renaissance influences, it is best to recur to the traditional interplay between *platea* and *locus*, between neutral, undifferentiated "place" and symbolic location. Such an interplay accommodates action that is both nonillusionistic and near the audience (corresponding to the "place") and a more illusionistic, localized action sometimes taking place in a discovery space, scaffold, tent, or other *loci* (corresponding to the medieval *sedes*). Between these extremes lay the broad and very flexible range of dramatic possibilities so skillfully developed by the popular Renaissance dramatist.

While Inigo Jones' lavish Italianate scenery was designed to catch the eye and present what was clearly an idealized imitation of nature, the customs of the traditional popular theater presupposed a collaboration between dramatist and audience in the creation and visualization of dramatic setting. In accordance with this, the relationship between the production and the reception of plays in the popular theater was very close indeed. The proximity of actor and audience was not only a physical condition, it was at once the foundation and the expression of a specific artistic endeavor. Unlike the theater of the subsequent three hundred years, the actor-audience relationship was not subordinate, but a dynamic and essential element of dramaturgy. For the Elizabethan playgoer the drama was more than a play taking place on a stage separated from the audience; it was an event in progress in which good listening and watching were rewarded "by a sense of feeling part of the performance."[17]

In Shakespeare's youth the popular actor, especially the comedian with his extemporal wit, performed not so much *for* an audience as *with* a community of spectators who provided him with inspiration and, as it were, acted as a chorus. Such was the case with Richard Tarlton: "it was his custome for to sing extempore of theames given him."[18] The spectator who challenged the actor had the weight of the audience behind him; collectively, they were collaborators in and judges of an elementary theatrical process. The audience was both the challenger and the challenged; even when pelted with apples Tarlton countered with a suitable couplet, just as he answered criticisms from the audience or from his partner in dialogue with nimble wit and wordplay.[19]

The separation of the audience into groups based on rank was not traditional: it was new in Tarlton's and even in Shakespeare's day. As late as in *Henry VIII* (V, 4) the actual audience was identified with the undifferentiated mass of curious spectators who had come to watch the christening of Elizabeth in front of Henry VIII's palace—an indiscriminate fusion of the audience that Beaumont and Fletcher and other coterie dramatists would have frowned upon. In this way the fictive spectators and the actual audience merged and became a vital link between play and real life:

> ⌈The palace yard.⌉
> *Noise and tumult within. Enter* Porter *and his* Man.

Port.	... You must be seeing christenings? Do you look for ale and cakes here, you rude rascals?
Man.	Pray, sir, be patient; 'tis as much impossible, Unless we sweep 'em from the door with cannons, To scatter 'em as 'tis to make 'em sleep On May-day morning; which will never be. We may as well push against Paul's as stir 'em.
Port.	How got they in, and be hang'd?
Man.	Alas, I know not: how gets the tide in?

(V, 4, 8–16)

Probably speaking from the pit, the Porter draws the audience into the play by pushing them aside to make room for the procession. "An army cannot rule 'em," he says to the audience, who by now must have felt a heightened sense of both their relation to the subject of the play and their power as a mass of people unified in a dramatic role that had powerful correlatives in Tudor and, of course, Stuart history.

The traditional readiness and ability of the audience to be drawn into the play which is indicated here is as noteworthy as the willingness of author and actor to speak directly to the audience and to acknowledge basic agreement with its tastes and ideas. These links between the world of the play and the audience's world of experience are further extended in prologue, chorus, and song. Directly and indirectly reinforcing the play-audience relationship, these links illuminate the similarities and differences between dramatic illusion and Elizabethan reality. The world is seen as a stage, the stage, in turn, as an image of the world; and this link between art and society presupposes and fosters a sense of both unity and tension between actor and audience: the play, the product of theatrical activity, and the process of doing it (as well as the process of being involved through watching and listening) have a profound effect on each other. The gain in terms of consciousness does not involve a loss for the reality of its objects.[20]

It was this precariously balanced sense of community in the theatrical experience that gave the popular Renaissance drama its unique mode of production. We can search in vain for the equivalent of the modern stage manager in Shakespeare's theater. The prompter and keeper of the scripts did not have sufficient authority to fill such a position properly; if he was in charge of rehearsals at all, he was certainly not in complete control. The real decisions—choice of plays, procurement of costumes, distribution of roles, etc.—must have been arrived at by agreement within the troupe of actors and shareholders. The Chamberlain's (later the King's) Men were organized along cooperative lines, and even though important decisions could be made by one acting on behalf of the majority, "the ultimate authority was vested solely in the actor-sharers as a group."[21] The principle of joint ownership and joint responsibility accorded fully with the implications and spirit of the Elizabethan theatrical experience. The success and prolonged harmony of Shakespeare's troupe and its most distinguished members testified to the practicability of a collective theatrical and business venture. Too little attention has been paid to the connection between the organization of Shakespeare's troupe and the dramaturgy and artistic principles that made its plays the greatest and most successful experiment in the history of the modern theater.

Most characteristic of this kind of theatrical work was not the virtuoso display of individual talent, but the individual's renunciation of the need to assert himself, and hence the employment of his talent in cooperation with the needs and possibilities of "everyone working in the theater on the joint venture of production."[22] Naturally, the "ability of dramatist

and actor to devote themselves to their joint work, which corresponded
to the spectators' ability to participate creatively, presupposes common
thought and common feeling";[23] in the words of Alfred Harbage,
"Shakespeare wanted to say what his audience wanted him to say." Such
was the delicate balance between dramatist, actor, and audience.
Shakespeare never disingenuously catered to the audience or relied on
purely sensational effects in production primarily because of "his sense
of identity with and responsibility to those thousands of other men who
honored him with their trust."[24] To this audience Shakespeare spoke
directly, for they were the "gentles all" to whom he referred in the
Prologue to *Henry V* in the inspiring speech of the Chorus:

> And let us, ciphers to this great accompt,
> On your imaginary forces work.

Here the great dramatist and the actor modestly subordinate themselves
to the process of consciousness shared by the audience; and through this
communal form of experience, where hopefully with "humble patience"
the play may be "Gently" heard and "kindly" judged, the world of the
play swells to encompass the most complex realities of political experience. "Suppose that you have seen ... O! do but think ... Follow, Follow!
Grapple your minds ... Work, work your thoughts ... Behold ..."
(Chorus, III). Even the slowest and least literate in the audience should
be able to follow along: "Vouchsafe to those that have not read the
story/That I may prompt them ..." (Chorus, V). Thus Shakespeare deliberately raises the level of awareness of his unread spectators; and in
this sense he is truly "Shakespeare, the plebeian driller," as Tatham
wrote in his 1641 poem to Richard Brome.[25] At any rate, Shakespeare
fulfills the end of what Ben Jonson described as a kind of "spear-
shaking" art (à la Pallas Athena); for Shakespeare here is recalled in his
own unique role of popular educator:

> In each of which, he seems to shake a Lance,
> As brandish't at the eyes of Ignorance.

The social consciousness behind the Shakespearean vision was not de-
structively aimed against plebeian narrowmindedness and inconstancy,
but usually served as a means of conquering or challenging the kind of
"Ignorance" that was the source of both.[26]

2

Role and Actor: The Language of Locality and "Place"

The general absence of scenery on the large acting area of the
Elizabethan platform stage placed rigorous demands on the dramatist's

use of language, the actor's use of gesture, and the audience's attentiveness and imagination. Through language the dramatist created atmosphere and locale, establishing the physical as well as the poetic disposition of scene, character and plot.[27] Coupled with his "word scenery" were rhyme, rhythm, and gesture, the integration of which fostered an extremely effective unity of physical action and poetic expression. As Otto Ludwig pointed out, Shakespeare divided a situation "into gestures of thought, speech, position and intonation . . . the language moves visibly, so to speak, the sound itself may be comical. . . . Everything must be visible, audible, tangible, the thought sensation, the sensation word, the word form and form movement."[28]

While the Elizabethan theater did not strive to create a visual illusion of actuality, it did attempt to imitate nature, albeit in poetically heightened terms. A platform stage capable of sustaining both illusionistic and nonillusionistic effects was indispensible to the interplay between realistic and stylized modes of expression, and between a new consistency of *mimesis* and traditional audience awareness. Once the tensions between these various theatrical modes were subsumed within flexible platform dramaturgy, an astonishing variety and richness of language naturally followed.

Such was the case in what has been called the "extraordinary variety"[29] and variability of the Shakespearean monologue. When, for example, an angry and distracted Lear challenges the forces of nature—"You cataracts and hurricanoes, spout"—he uses a stylized and elevated diction. His apostrophe to lightning and thunder is grandiose and rhetorical:

> You sulph'rous and thought-executing fires,
> Vaunt-couriers of oak-cleaving thunderbolts,
> Singe my white head. And thou, all-shaking thunder,
> Strike flat the thick rotundity o' th' world;
> Crack nature's moulds, all germens spill at once,
> That makes ingrateful man.

> (III, 2, 4-9)

But this is immediately followed by a most ordinary kind of prose:

> O nuncle, court holy water in a dry house is
> better than this rain-water out o'door.

> (III, 2, 10-11)

The contrast between elevated metaphor and simple, everyday speech here sharpens the effect of both. But the difference in meter, assonance, and style produces more than a formal contrast; for it signalizes the distance between two basically different themes and two widely divergent attitudes. No sooner has the raging King adjured the "all-shaking

thunder" to flatten the earth and "Crack nature's moulds" than
"natural" common sense comes to the fore in the person of the pragmatic Fool, who would rather compromise principles than face the torrent.

The range of speech serves here to characterize two fundamentally
different attitudes which correspond to different patterns of theatrical
activity and different conventions of character. But even within Lear's
own speech we find a similar range of expressive modes. Whereas here
he uses elevated rhetoric to command the elements, when he awakes to
find Cordelia in Act IV his tone and speech change:

> Where have I been? Where am I? Fair daylight?
> ... I know not what to say.
> I will not swear these are my hands. Let's see.
> I feel this pin prick.
>
> (IV, 7, 52–56)

These words are especially moving when compared with Lear's previously exalted speech. Similar, if not such striking, examples can be
found in the language of almost all of the tragic heroes. The rhetorical
and stylized language of Macbeth, Othello, Cleopatra, and Hamlet is
mixed with everyday syntax and diction in remarks like Macbeth's "I
have done the deed," or "I am afraid to think what I have done" (II, 2,
14, and 51), Othello's "Soft you; a word or two before you go" (V, 2,
341), Cleopatra's "Will it eat me?" or "What should I stay—" (V, 2, 269
and 311), and Hamlet's frequent use of popular images and proverbs.

This extremely effective alternation between rhetorical and mundane
language, stylization and directness, presupposed and helped to perpetuate specific stage conditions such as those offered by the large and
variable platform. A downstage position, for instance, allowed for a
smoother transition from dialogue to monologue[30] and facilitated the
delivery of wordplay and proverbs directly to the audience—a mode of
delivery with obvious precedents in the popular theater. Such transitions
abound in Shakespeare's plays, as, for example, in Hamlet's conversation
with his mother (III, 4):

Queen.	O Hamlet, thou hast cleft my heart in twain.
Hamlet.	O throw away the worser part of it,
	And live the purer with the other half.
	Good night, but go not to my uncle's bed, ...
	For use almost can change the stamp of nature,
	And either curb the devil, or throw him out,
170	With wondrous potency: once more, good night,
	And when you are desirous to be blessed,
	I'll blessing beg of you. For this same lord,
	[pointing to Polonius]
	I do repent; but heaven hath pleased it so,
	To punish me with this, and this with me,

That I must be their scourge and minister.
I will bestow him and will answer well
The death I gave him; so, again, good night.
I must be cruel only to be kind.
Thus bad begins, and worse remains behind. . . .

[*he makes to go, but returns*]

180   One word more, good lady.
    Queen.   What shall I do?[31]

This passage begins as genuine dialogue that leads to Hamlet's first
"Good night" (167), which being repeated a second and a third time
indicates that the passages in between suspend the convention of dialogue in favor of a more generalized, choruslike kind of monologue
(168–70; 173–75; 178–79). Because of its content—the significance and
the consequences of Hamlet's thoughts and actions—this choruslike
speech must be clearly differentiated from the surrounding dialogue;
and indeed the closing couplets accentuate both its departure from the
illusion of conversation and the fact that its content is basically a summary and an interpretation of past, present, and future action. The
manner of delivery and the prophetic content so broaden the nature of
Hamlet's speech that it supersedes the immediate context of dialogue
and functionally becomes a direct address to the audience, in this case,
something like a chorus. The change from one convention of speech to
another does not come unannounced, however; for the *self-expressive*
statements that transcend the illusion of one-to-one conversation follow
the dramatic representation of leave-taking. In moving beyond the limitations of the illusion of conversation, and so in moving away, physically
and psychologically, from his partner in dialogue, Hamlet also distances
himself from the illusionistic modes of causality and locality and assumes
a theatrically more neutral position from which he, as it were, collabo-
rates with the audience. But, again, the traditional patterns of audience
address are integrated into the dialogue with its *mimesis* of verbal exchange and leave-taking. Thus, an old popular stage convention is im-
pressed into the service of a new kind of realism. The final return to
dialogue—"One word more, good lady"—may indeed be interpreted
psychologically by the modern producer as being motivated by Hamlet's
forgetfulness or altered intention (an interpretation that is not unjustified on one level), but such an interpretation is surely one-sided in light
of the potentialities of downstage acting.[32]

A second example illustrates even more strikingly the interchange of
contrasting forms of speech. Speaking to the blind Gloucester, Lear asks

What, art mad? A man may see how this world goes
with no eyes . . . Thou hast seen a farmer's dog bark
155   at a beggar?
    Gloucester.   Ay, sir.

> *Lear.*   And the creature run from the cur? There thou mightst
> behold the great image of authority: a dog's obey'd
> in office.
>
> 160   Thou rascal beadle, hold thy bloody hand!
> Why dost thou lash that whore? Strip thy own back;
> Thou hotly lusts to use her in that kind
> For which thou whip'st her. The usurer hangs the
> cozener.
> Through tatter'd clothes small vices do appear;
> Robes and furr'd gowns hide all. Plate sin with gold,
> And the strong lance of justice hurtless breaks;
> Arm it in rags, a pigmy's straw does pierce it.
> None does offend, none—I say none; I'll able 'em.
> Take that of me, my friend, who have the power
>
> 170   To seal th'accuser's lips. Get thee glass eyes,
> And, like a scurvy politician, seem
> To see the things thou dost not. Now, now, now, now!
> Pull off my boots. Harder, harder—so.
>
>   (IV, 6)

When read in its entirety, this passage can be seen to fall into three parts: first, a dialogue, couched in everyday language in which question and answer heighten the sense of conversation:

> What, art mad? ... Thou hast seen a
> farmer's dog bark at a beggar?
> *Gloucester.* Ay, sir.

This prose passage leads to a monologuelike statement (160–72) elevated in meter and rhetoric the intensity and vision of which are supported by the convention of Lear's madness:

> Thou rascal beadle, hold thy bloody hand!
> Why dost thou lash that whore? Strip thy own back;
> . . .

This iambic verse, which breaks the illusion of dialogue, leads back ultimately to dialogue via the completely unstylized, unrhetorical, and unmetrical, "Now, now, now, now!" As in Act III, scene 4 of *Hamlet,* theatrical convention and poetic vision coalesce in a dialogue accompanied by physical acting which attains an almost naturalistic precision. The unity of "word" and "action" is complete. On the surface a trivial detail, the gesture precipitated by the remark "Pull off my boots . . ." is actually a remarkably profound piece of stage business. Since the visionary ideas just expressed by Lear exist outside the world of "Robes and furr'd gowns," the rebirth of his dignity demands that he abandon all the accoutrements of royal prestige, which he does: "Harder, harder—so." As in the first example, the poetically heightened, nonillusionistic lines

of the body of the speech are framed by a more illusionistic type of
dialogue, which so carries the action forward that detail and generality,
the concrete and the universal, experience and vision are inextricably
fused. The result is no "confusion," nor is it, as T. S. Eliot also thought,
"fundamentally objectionable." Rather, such fusion of "naturalism" and
"convention" serves to enhance a sense of movement and complexity in
the work as a whole.

The sheer scope of Lear's and Hamlet's language—in content, style
and rhythm—illustrates the symbiotic relationship between Shakespeare's verbal art and a flexible stage that could localize the scene in
dialogue but could just as easily neutralize it once again in monologue or
aside. The dramatic change from locality to neutral "place" and back to
locality again corresponds to a verbal change from the dramatic illusion
of conversation to a nonillusionistic, audience-directed generalizing
monologue, and back to dialogue. Such facility in alternating forms of
speech is inconceivable without an equally flexible stage.

This, however, gives only a very general (and certainly oversimplified)
idea of the dramatic function of the monologuelike speech. A more
detailed look at the passage from *Hamlet* (III, 4, 178-79) shows how it
functions, as similar speeches in Shakespeare often do, to underline "an
important state of affairs, bringing it to the fore with more volume of
sound and emphasis."[33] This "volume of sound" does not necessarily
reflect the content of the speech, nor does it result from the acoustics of
the hall; rather it derives from a stage position similar to that from which
the choruslike statement of the Scrivener and Buckingham's self-
contemplation in III, 6 and V, 1 of *Richard III* are delivered. The sum-
marizing effect of Hamlet's words is unmistakably underlined by the
demonstrative use of "Thus";[34] and the nonillusionistic status of the
comment only intensifies the universality of the idea and hence the
possible wordplay on "kind."

Quite different means are used in Lear's speech, but they serve a
similar purpose. His visionary lines ("Thou rascal beadle . . .") dissolve
the illusion of conversation with Gloucester; since they are abstract—
generalized—they are addressed less to a partner in dialogue than to a
general listener (perhaps even to an individual in the audience singled
out by an icy stare or accusing finger).[35] In momentarily turning away
from his partner in dialogue and the on-stage action, Lear effectively
engages the audience in generalized issues that are central to the play's
meaning, issues the immediacy of which are not only visualized dramatically but experienced realistically as the role dissolves and the man behind the actor speaks directly to his fellow man in the audience. In the
final analysis Shakespeare not only strengthens a realistic approach to
the world, but to the world of art as well.

In an earlier section of this book it was pointed out that in a ritual context *mimesis* is not only consecrative but also productive, since the blurring of differences between religion and knowledge (between belief and activity) makes miming a way of coping with the practical world. But even completely outside of the ritual context, as, for example, in Lear's and Hamlet's speeches, *mimesis* not only serves a remarkably similar function, but does so in terms of a similar process of blurring two different kinds of knowing. Here it is not ritual and cognition that are reconciled, but rather the fictive world of the play and the real experience of the audience that are integrated by the alternating modes of dramatic and extradramatic speech. What primitive mimetic magic and Elizabethan *mimesis* have in common is the fact that both rely (in the former intuitively and in the latter empirically) on the acceptance as fundamentally real actions and words that define a supraindividual, or communal reality.

Because of the variety of sources and influences that pervaded Elizabethan dramaturgy, monologue—like dialogue and the aside—was a changing and changeable form of speech that was capable of many different effects depending on the immediate dramatic context. Obviously monologue served both illusionistic and nonillusionistic, naturalistic and stylized functions.[36] It could be used in aside or in the direct address of the prologue, or it could become a form of soliloquy or the kind of thinking out loud in which a character "in solitude renders an account to himself of his innermost thoughts and feelings."[37] In light of the rich and diverse dramatic functions of Shakespeare's language, it is difficult to separate monologue and dialogue too dogmatically. We can say, however, that as a general rule the localization and neutralization of scene and action in downstage acting reflects, respectively, a dissociation from or identification with the audience, and that the structure and style of speech are largely determined by this relationship.

The two extremes of this relationship could, for example, be viewed as the difference between speech delivered by elevated persons from the throne (localized, illusionistic) and the speech of the clowns (neutral, nonillusionistic). Logically, in light of stage action and social convention, the speaker from the throne was raised physically above those around him and did not function on a level of direct audience contact. Claudius' great speech from the throne (*Hamlet* I, 2) and Timon's speech at the banquet (*Timon of Athens* I, 2) do not in any way directly address the audience. Neither speech contains asides, wordplay, couplets, or many proverbs. In terms of theatrical history this mode of presentation corresponded to the use of the scaffold as *locus* where—as in the *Ludus Coventriae*, for example—the ruling and high-born characters sat: a physical social correlative that had already resulted in a more self-contained kind of staging in the circular theater.

But downstage, somewhere in between the socially and spatially elevated Claudius and Timon and the audience, stood characters less inclined to accept the assumptions—social, ideological, and dramatic—of the localized action. These characters, by means of asides, wordplay, proverbs, and direct audience address offered a special perspective to the audience. In the banquet scene of *Timon* this in between position is occupied by Apemantus. During Claudius' speech the position is held by Hamlet, who, through the use of aside, establishes a close initial bond with the audience. A similar in-between-world, albeit different in terms of stagecraft, is established by the gravediggers in *Hamlet*, and the porters in *Macbeth* and *Henry VIII*, and, of course, such clowns as Launce, whose direct address to the audience is couched in ordinary language filled with proverbs and wordplay, and punctuated with phrases like "Look you," "I'll show you," and "You shall judge."

Between the two extremes—the illusion of conversation from a localized setting and nonillusionistic direct address from a neutral "place"—there existed many forms of transition. These involved an infinitely variable conception of dramaturgy based on what Anne Righter called "that equilibrium of involvement and distance characteristic of the Shakespearean attitude towards the audience."[38] The balance achieved by Shakespeare was especially remarkable in light of the general affinity of Renaissance dramatists for the self-contained play. Shakespeare did, of course, move in this direction, but without abandoning the popular heritage. In *Hamlet* there are still signs of direct address (IV, 4, 47), but these are admittedly quite rare. More characteristic of a play like *Hamlet* is an indirect audience contact that operates through an awareness of the theatrical medium itself. Such is the case when Hamlet compares his own inactivity with the effusions of the player moved to tears by the emotion of his role. Here Hamlet judges himself not as a prince but as an actor:

> ... what would he do
> Had he the motive and the cue for passion
> That I have? he would drown the stage with tears,
> And cleave the general ear with horrid speech,
> Make mad the guilty, and appal the free,
> Confound the ignorant, and amaze indeed
> The very faculties of eyes and ears; yet I,
> A dull and muddy-mettled rascal, peak
> Like John-a-dreams, unpregnant of my cause,
> And can say nothing ...
>
> (II, 2, 563–72, ed. J. D. Wilson)

Without departing from his role or deviating from the action, Hamlet here suggests, through his imagery, a full awareness of the effect he would like his speech to have on the spectators in the theater: of stirring up and sharpening their "very faculties of eyes and ears," the full capacity of their physical as well as their moral sensibilities.

Built into Hamlet's complex audience contact, and fundamental to Launce's direct address, was a principle of popular dramaturgy that was already well-developed in Tarlton's day. When Tarlton had his face slapped while playing the role of the Chief Justice in *The Famous Victories* (above p. 189) as an actor he reacted with a double awareness; for to himself and to his audience he was simultaneously Tarlton and the judge: the slap administered to the judge was clearly understood as a slap to Tarlton as well. It is on the basis of this double action, which utilized both the *platea*-like and the localized dimensions of the platform stage, that Tarlton's subsequent reaction may be said to anticipate somewhat the interplay between role and actor and between actor-role and audience already seen in *Hamlet*. Perhaps it is not fortuitous that Hamlet so often appears in a most uncourtly light. It is as if the plebeian *ohm*, or measure, of the popular tradition in acting re-emerges once more in an expression of the *actor's* true self—the self behind the role of prince— when Hamlet compares himself to "John-a-dreams," a popular figure "usually associated by editors with John a Droynes, a country bumpkin" and probably identical to "some forgotten nursery character like Little Johnny Head-in-air."[39]

Considering the universalizing and humanizing effect of Shakespeare's dramaturgy within a play world and upon a real world beset alike by rigid class barriers, the links between his verbal art and his stagecraft seem more significant than any purely formal synthesis that might have been achieved. The profound interaction of poetic imagination and theatrical technique, renewed and refined at almost every level, serves, in Shakespeare, as a mode and a medium of perceiving and comprehending the world as a temporal, spatial, and social experience. The interplay of poetry and theater itself helps to constitute the universalizing pattern of Shakespeare's drama. It helps to provide a basis for a mode of drama by which image and meaning, the particular and the general, the representation and the vision of objects are complementary aspects of the theatrical product. But this product results from, and consummates, a theatrical process from the actor (and the citizen) to the role and the spectator and back again to the actor and the citizens in the audience, all participating in a common cultural and social activity.

Such a view of the dialectic of the "production" and "reception" of poetic drama involves, as a matter of course, a critical position from which several questions follow—questions that should be asked now, even in the concluding chapter, to suggest some of the more explicit answers. For instance, the "effect which interferes with the illusion"[40] has been observed ever since German critics like Kilian and Schücking took up this question: but it has rarely been viewed in a larger context of history and value. Obviously, this effect can no longer be considered to be the "primitive" result of a "naive technique,"[41] even when we have to concede that occasionally it is only the "author's instructions to the audience"[42] that are involved. Is direct and indirect audience contact, as many English and American scholars would hold, the latent manifestation of a submerged "homiletic comment," an element of "homiletic showmanship?"[43] Is Shakespeare's "multi-consciousness" an expression of that "balance of opposites which constitute the universe of Christianity"?[44] To ask these questions in the present context is simply to express the need for a more complex sense of method and approach. The answer, at its most general and provisional level, will, I suggest, have to be looked for where historical analysis and value judgment can be made to relate so that neither the charge of primitivism nor any metaphysical eulogy, neither the bias of the theater of illusion nor a more modern preoccupation with distance and alienation, can serve as altogether adequate points of departure.

3

Figurenposition: *The Correlation of Position and Expression*

Shakespeare used popular audience contact and related elements of traditional platform stagecraft to such varying degrees and in such variable ways that it is difficult to formulate even general observations about the nature and function of popular conventions in his plays. A number of Shakespeare's characters stand out, however, because they draw so clearly from popular tradition or present new ways in which traditional practices were adapted to new dramatic forms and functions. This group of characters, who share little in common with respect to social class, psychology, and length or importance of role, can be considered as a group provided we shift our attention from the more speculative concerns of character analysis to a more objective understanding of *Figurenposition*—the actor's position on the stage, and the speech, action, and degree of stylization associated with that position.

An admittedly incomplete list of these characters would include Launce and his friend Speed, most of the other Shakespearean clowns, the porters in *Macbeth* and *Henry VIII*, the gravediggers in *Hamlet*, Bottom in *A Midsummer Night's Dream*, the nurse in *Romeo and Juliet*, Richard Gloucester, Iago, the Fool, and, partly, Edmund in *King Lear*, Falstaff, Thersites, Apemantus, and—with some reservations—Aaron in *Titus Andronicus*, the Bastard Falconbridge in *King John*, and Autolycus in *The Winter's Tale*. Also belonging to this group are characters whose status within court groupings is temporarily changed or weakened as a result of real or feigned madness (Edgar, Lear, Hamlet, and, to a lesser extent, Ophelia). Taken together, these characters can be identified with a stage position that functions to greater and lesser degrees (and not exclusively, of course) as a means of achieving a special role and meaning within the play.

As an example, Apemantus' stage position during the banquet scene in *Timon of Athens* (I, 2) illustrates some of the potentialities of downstage acting on the Elizabethan platform stage. According to the stage direction "A great banquet served in,"[45] the banqueting table is set up and decked out probably at about the center of the stage. Timon, Alcibiades, and the Senators enter, and "Then comes, dropping after all, Apemantus. . . ." The men of elevated degree sit down at the main table in the middle of the stage, but, at Timon's instruction, the grumbling Apemantus is given "a table by himself" downstage from the banquet table. The action that follows takes place, as the text indicates, on two levels: Timon and his guests delivering high-sounding speeches from the illusionistic area around the banqueting table (a true *locus*), Apemantus speaking usually in such a way that the audience, whom he faces, can hear, but those behind him cannot. Such a reconstruction of the scene in performance explains the flexibility and variability of conventions of speech immediately apparent from the text.

Timon.	I take no heed of thee; . . . prithee let my meat make thee silent.
Apemantus.	I scorn thy meat; 'twould choke me, for I should ne'er flatter thee. O you gods, what a number of men eats Timon, and he sees 'em not! It grieves me to see so many dip their meat in one man's blood; and all the madness is, he cheers them up too. 40 I wonder men dare trust themselves with men. Methinks they should invite them without knives: Good for their meat, and safer for their lives. There's much example for't; the fellow that sits next him, now parts bread with him, pledges the breath of him in a divided draught, is the readiest man to kill him: 't has been proved. If I were a huge man, I should fear to drink at meals, Lest they should spy my windpipe's dangerous notes. 50 Great men should drink with harness on their throats.
Timon.	My lord, in heart; and let the health go round.
2 Lord.	Let it flow this way, my good lord.
Apemantus.	Flow this way? A brave fellow. He keeps his tides well. Those healths will make thee and thy state look ill, Timon. Here's that which is too weak to be a sinner, Honest water, which ne'er left man i'th'mire. This and my food are equals; there's no odds. Feasts are too proud to give thanks to the gods. . . . 60

1 Lord.	Might we but have that happiness, my lord, that you would once use our hearts, whereby we might express some part of our zeals, we should think ourselves for ever perfect.
Timon.	O, no doubt, my good friends, but the gods themselves have provided that I shall have much help from you: how had you been my friends else? . . . 90 O, what a precious comfort 'tis to have so many like brothers commanding one another's fortunes! O joy, e'en made away ere't can be born! Mine eyes cannot hold out water, methinks. To forget their faults, I drink to you.
Apemantus.	Thou weep'st to make them drink, Timon.
2 Lord.	Joy had the like conception in our eyes, 110 And at that instant like a babe sprung up.
Apemantus.	Ho, ho! I laugh to think that babe a bastard.
3 Lord.	I promise you, my lord, you moved me much.
Apemantus.	Much!

Dissociating himself from the feasters at the banquet table, Apemantus neutralizes his own position and so reviews the *locus*-centered action from a perspective something like, but not identical with, that of the traditional "place," from which he seems to say to the audience, "Look at them, and at what their feasting really means." His frequent use of proverb and wordplay, inverting and ironically heightening the meaning of what is said at the banquet table accords nicely with his superior awareness, his choruslike function, and his position on the stage that recalls, in some way, the old Vice (he retains the Vice's scornful "Ho, ho!"). Yet the dramatic effect of this choruslike link between the world of the play and the world of the audience is by no means unsophisticated. Apemantus' keen-edged remarks comment critically on the pomp, the ceremony, and the high-sounding words of the feasters without destroying the theatrical effect of the banquet itself. Thus, two perspectives are presented in such a way that neither alters or obscures the essential integrity of the other. The dual perspective that results acknowledges the sensuous attraction of a dazzling theatrical occasion, but also penetrates the showy surface; for there is in it "a huge zest-for-life and the moral strength to see through its glitter, its hypocrisies, its shame and its rewards."[46]

The process of drawing the audience into the play has become inseparable from the development of a complementary perspective that helps refine basic issues and restructure basic positions; at the same time, the process of differentiating between truth and appearance has become part of the dramatic mode itself. Dramatic images of central conflicts achieve a greater depth when subjected both to mimetic representation and self-expressive enactment; for through this mode the audience is drawn into the tensions between the feast and reality, between words and their meaning, flattery and criticism, enchantment and disenchantment. Of course Apemantus cannot simply tell the audience what to think; his vicious bitterness can hardly be taken at face value. He can, however, through his well-articulated counterperspective, expand the audience's awareness and establish new, perhaps deeper and more comprehensive dramatic tensions that in their turn expand the meaning of the play as a whole.[47]

Actually, Shakespeare seldom kept up this kind of complementary perspective from a *platea* level of acting for very long. Even in *Timon of Athens* Apemantus' downstage position is only temporary; and his choral function obviously suffers when his physical proximity to the audience dissolves in more illusionistic acting. But another example can perhaps illustrate that Shakespeare developed the interplay of *platea* and *locus* positions with great freedom and flexibility by going beyond the more direct modes of correlating the two. In Act V, scene 2 of *Troilus and Cressida*, Cressida's meeting with Diomedes is watched from a distance by Troilus and Ulysses, who likewise are being watched by Thersites, as indicated by the direction, *"Enter Troilus and Ulysses, at a distance; after them Thersites."*[48] The primary level of *mimesis*—Cressida's dialogue with Diomedes—is seen and commented upon by Troilus, but the second level of acting—Troilus' dialogue with Ulysses, which is closer in perspective to the audience than the first but still a *locus*-oriented dialogue—is seen and commented upon by Thersites. Thersites observes not only Cressida's faithlessness, but Troilus' disillusioned response as well. Although all three levels of acting are in turn watched by the spectators, the last is certainly the closest to the audience in terms of speech, stage position, and the scope of action that is seen. Not only does Thersites view most nearly what the audience views (from a neutral "place"), he communicates his impressions not in dialogue or through the illusion of soliloquy, but in unpretentious direct address.

> *Diomedes.* How, now, my charge!
> *Cressida.* Now, my sweet guardian! Hark, a word with you.
> *Troilus.* Yea, so familiar!   [*whispers*]
> *Ulysses.* She will sing any man at first sight.
> *Thersites.* And any man may sing her, if he can take her
> clef; she's noted.
>
> (V, 2, 7–12)

Thersites acts from a more nearly neutralized place where he can watch and hear the others but cannot be watched or heard by them. His wordplay here further underlines his unique position since it sarcastically sounds a realistic "note" that sharply contrasts Troilus' bewildered idealism. After summing up Cressida's exit with a couplet—"A proof of strength she could not publish more,/Unless she said 'My mind is now turn'd whore,'" (V, 2, 113-14)—Thersites witnesses the following interchange between Troilus and Ulysses:

> Troilus. Let it not believed for womanhood!
> Think we had mothers. Do not give advantage
> To stubborn critics, apt without a theme
> For depravation, to square the general sex
> By Cressid's rule; rather think this not Cressid.
> Ulysses. What hath she done, prince, that can soil our mothers?
> Troilus. Nothing at all, unless that this were she.
> Thersites. Will 'a swagger himself out on's own eyes?
> Troilus. This she? No; this is Diomed's Cressida.
>
> (129-37)

Troilus would gladly close his eyes to what he has just seen, but Thersites' comment keeps the audience from doing the same by quashing any sentimental response to, let alone identification with, Troilus' wishful thinking. Like Apemantus and the Vice figure before him, Thersites is a *provocateur* of truth, not a moral judge. And like the characters whose madness, feigned or real, forces dormant truths to the surface, his debunking and skeptical commentary serves to offer viable alternatives to the main or state view of things. In this sense, characters like Apemantus and Thersites help point out that the ideas and values held by the main characters are relative to their particular position in the play,[49] while by projection the audience realizes that this is equally true of the counter-perspectives offered by the plebeian intermediaries who occupy a *platea*-like position. This basic recognition of the relationship between character and circumstance, like so much else in Shakespeare, is a profoundly original observation that must be seen in connection with the dramatist's awareness of the tensions between society and the individual, the general, and the particular, from which an essential element of Shakespeare's universality derived.

Although *Love's Labour's Lost* offers unique problems as one of Shakespeare's most stylized works (both formally and linguistically), Act IV, scene 3 is remarkable for its clever dramatic treatment of the complexities and potentialities of yet another form of *Figurenposition*. The scene opens not with dialogue but with one of the most boldly punning monologues in Shakespeare's plays. In it, Berowne reveals the true nature of his feelings and brings the audience up to date as to his own activities, but his position is still relatively removed from the audience's perspective. When the King enters, however, Berowne hides; and this is where the sheer comedy of his *Figurenposition* really starts. As the King begins to read, Berowne's new role as eavesdropper necessarily establishes a fundamental link with the audience, a perspective from which he can and does distance himself from the illusion of the represented *locus* (in much the same way as Apemantus and Thersites). When Longaville enters and the King hides, not only does the King, now an eavesdropper also, move closer to the audience in perspective, but Berowne, since he is watching the King watch Longaville, moves closer still to the audience. At this point the scene must have looked something like the scene from *Troilus and Cressida* discussed above. But everyone's perspective is changed once again when Dumaine enters, since Longaville assumes the King's perspective (watching but unaware of being watched), the King Berowne's (watching, aware that a watcher is being watched, but unaware that he himself is being watched), and Berowne another perspective closer still to the audience (so aware of the watcher/watched regression that he speaks freely to those who watch him from the audience). What results is a series of comments spoken in aside whose status relative to the two spatial and verbal extremes—Dumaine's monologue and Berowne's perspective so close to the audience—even the most clearheaded observer could have confused. We might suppose, if this is true, that Shakespeare was not only parodying the inconstancy of the "scholars" (on the level of plot and theme), the ludicrousness of excessive sonneteering (on the level of language), but also, on the level of structure and stagecraft, the traditional interplay between *locus* and *platea*, representation and self-expression.

In light of this effect, it seems possible to reinterpret Berowne's gleeful comment:

> All hid, all hid, an old infant play,
> Like a demie God, here sit I in the skie,
> And wretched fooles secrets heedfully ore-eye.
>
> (F₁ IV, 3, 78–80)

From the scenic circumstance it is clear that the first line refers, as most editors acknowledge, to some children's game like hide-and-go-seek. But since the first line is not separated grammatically from the second and third (although the punctuation in modern editions has been changed to suggest that it is) it is possible that the word "play" in the first line is also a pun on "dramatic performance." "An old infant play," then, could refer to the older, but less artistically developed mystery plays (see *OED* "Infant": "In its earliest stage, newly existing, ungrown, undeveloped, nascent...") in which a demigod (a pun on the fact that the actor who played *Deus* was indeed mortal) sat in the "heavens" looking down upon and judging the actors.⁵⁰

More interesting still is the probability that Berowne, in his successive changes of perspective, moved from a mere "aside" position to a position closer to the audience and above the other actors to accord with his direct address, "here sit I in the skie." Perhaps a good way to visualize his movement would be to picture Berowne climbing one of the downstage columns, such as the ones indicated in the Swan drawing, or some other downstage scaffold structure—although an upstage balcony might have come closer in appearance to the conventional "heavens" associated with the hut-roof area and so heightened the parody of the traditional representation of God in heaven.

But however the scene is reconstructed (and these are only a few of many possibilities) it remains remarkable because it reveals an interest in and a thorough understanding of the potentialities of a stagecraft that hinges on deliberately varied degrees of dissociation from illusionistic action, all within the context of perhaps the most stylized, rhetorical, and intellectually self-conscious play of Shakespeare's career. That Shakespeare used this clever device so early in his career supports and in part explains his more dramatically effective use of similar perspectives in his later works.

The downstage position of Apemantus, Thersites, and in his own uniquely involved way, Berowne, is achieved by the interplay of theatrical and verbal conventions which we have called, for lack of a satisfactory English term, *Figurenposition*. This *Figurenposition* should not be understood only in the sense of the actor's physical position on the stage, but also in the more general sense that an actor may generate a unique stage presence that establishes a special relationship between himself and his fellow actors, the play, or the audience, even when direct address has been abandoned. Hamlet's behavior during the scene in Gertrude's closet already discussed above, for example, is certainly continuous with the action of the play and does not require a second level of acting like that in the banquet scene in *Timon of Athens*. Yet in terms of speech patterns Hamlet and Apemantus have much in common; notably, their emphatic use of couplets and wordplay. As long as Hamlet can set himself apart from the more self-contained dialogue by using couplets, wordplay, and similar illusion-breaking speech patterns, his position relative to his fellow actors remains extremely flexible, and he can fall back on conventions of both *locus* and *platea* stagecraft. His *Figurenposition* is therefore defined verbally as well as spatially, as we see in his first lines, which immediately hint at a unique perspective.

> King.   ... But now, my cousin Hamlet, and my son—
> Hamlet. [*Aside*] A little more than kin, and less than kind.
> King.   How is it that the clouds still hang on you?
> Hamlet. Not so, my lord; I am too much in the sun.
> Queen. Good Hamlet, cast thy nighted colour off,
>   And let thine eye look like a friend on Denmark.
>
>   (I, 2, 64–69)

Hamlet's riddling first line flatly rejects Claudius' assumptions about their relationship, while the second—both a proverb and a pun—is a further clever departure from the King's meaning and point of view. These early breaks with the conventional form and content of continuous dialogue complement Hamlet's unusual relationship with the court already suggested by his entrance after courtiers of lesser degree and by the dark clothes of mourning that only he still wears. Certainly by his speech, but probably also spatially, Hamlet stands apart from his peers as well as his fellow actors through a *Figurenposition* that, while not at all impairing the range of his relations to the play world, establishes a functional link between himself and the audience (almost certainly reinforced by a downstage position).

Still, Hamlet's position on the stage is so complex that the "aside" added by the modern editor hardly does it justice. To begin with, there is really no essential difference between Hamlet's first line, designated "aside," and his second, which can be considered an impertinent reply—"impertinent" in the sense that I have used the word in regard to the Vice's speech. The wordplay in Hamlet's second line reflects and maintains the same dissociation from the *locus* of the court and the same degree of contact with the audience as the first. The functional unity of both lines is much more important than any purely technical differentiation that the modern director or editor might be inclined to make between the literal aside and the impertinent answer. The punning phrase, "I am too much in the sun," links up, of course, with Claudius' question, but after the fashion of the Vice who had a fondness for taking symbolic or metaphoric expressions literally and so inverting them by wordplay. What is misleading about the term "aside" as it refers to the first line, then, is that it suggests that Hamlet and the rest of the court are initially more closely integrated than we might have cause to assume, since "aside" implies that Hamlet is standing with the group and merely turns his head for a moment to make this one remark. This simply skirts the issue by subordinating Hamlet's ambiguous relationship with the court to a single dramatic gesture.

The ritual identification between actor and audience was, to be sure, a thing of the past in Shakespeare's day; and so although Hamlet's rapport with the audience may be linked to the self-introduction characteristic of the figures who traditionally acted on the *platea*, by the time Shakespeare made use of it, it had taken on entirely new forms and served entirely new functions. What has been termed the "extra-dramatic moment" in the Renaissance theater,[51] then, was the product of both tradition and the new Renaissance conception of drama, by which means the connection between action and character became much more effective. Apemantus not only *stands apart* in space, he is, as a character with values, ideas and attitudes, *different* from Timon and his friends. Ther-

sites is not only a sarcastic commentator, he is a character whose fundamental assumptions—like those of Falstaff or Iago—exist outside of the
heroic, courtly, or romantic ethos of the main or state action.

In the same way Hamlet's speech patterns and his related *Figurenposition* reveal not only surface differences with his peers, but a more basic
kind of contradiction between his position, his character, and theirs.
Their difference is first suggested in a highly original form of self-
introduction in which traditional *platea*-conventions are transformed
into something strange and new. Compared with Hamlet's opening lines
(I, 2, 65 and 67), the impertinent mode is almost discontinued after the
opening "Seems"; the principle of inversion, however, is not surrendered but, as it were, turned inward. Almost unprovoked, he snatches
the word "seems" from the lips of the Queen, only to give it an entirely
nonpertinent, that is, egocentric meaning and function within the negative terms of his self-definition:

> *Hamlet.* Seems, madam! Nay, it is; I know not seems.
> 'Tis not alone my inky cloak, good mother,
> Nor customary suits of solemn black,
> Nor windy suspiration of forc'd breath,
> No, nor the fruitful river in the eye,
> Nor the dejected haviour of the visage,
> Together with all forms, moods, shapes of grief,
> That can denote me truly. These, indeed, seem;
> For they are actions that a man might play;
> But I have that within which passes show—
> These but the trappings and the suits of woe.
>
> (I, 2, 76-86)

The attributes of his appearance ("inky cloak," "solemn black") are still
self-expressed, still self-introduced, but with a difference: they are mentioned only to be dismissed as some outward and insufficient definition
of self. They are mere attributes of a potential *role* that cannot "denote
me truly." Hamlet's self-introduction is designed to dissociate himself
from "actions that a man might *play*." Rejecting "seems" and "play" as
modes of his existence, the actor makes his own role problematic. The
function of illusion is questioned from within, though not destroyed
from without. In other words, the traditional dialectic between representation (playing, seeming) and self-embodiment ("that within which
passes show") is used and almost deliberately quoted, but all within the
symbolic frame of reference of Renaissance *mimesis*: Hamlet's special
Figurenposition, his being apart from the *locus* (and the "illusion") of court
society, has a real (theatrical) as well as an imaginative (characterizing)
significance. And so, spatial position assumes a moral function: the actor's rejection of illusion is turned into the character's honesty "which
passes show."

Thus, traditional forms of dramaturgy are turned into modern modes of characterization; the paradox being that Hamlet, who knows no "seems," has to develop his *platea*-like *Figurenposition* within the "seems," that is, the illusionistic frame of the Renaissance play. So he is made to use the most traditional conventions of a *platea*-like embodiment—here, the verbal modes of his antic disposition—as a deliberate "show," a psychological illusion, a strategy for discovery and survival. Hamlet's madness has a function in the play only because he *seems* mad. The resulting contradictions are obvious; but by not suiting the action to the words Hamlet reveals his dilemma to be both one of the theater and one of character. The complexity of the interplay between the two aspects is the measure of the dramatist's achievement in combining innovation and tradition. The continuing contradiction between role and self-expression (which is the virtual *Leitmotiv* of his self-introduction) serves as a basic and most powerful impulse for bringing forth and maintaining the effectiveness of the links between stagecraft and verbal art.

Figurenposition, then, involves a variety of factors and cannot be defined dogmatically in terms of the function of any one set of verbal conventions. No single proverb, pun, instance of wordplay, or use of the aside can be isolated from other elements of plot, character, and language in order to argue the existence of a traditional actor-audience relationship. But if the aside and related verbal conventions go together they usually do more than simply pass on information to the audience. Besides filling the audience in on what has happened, what will happen, or what is being contemplated at the moment, devices like the aside are capable of generating powerful ironies, particularly in the building up of character—where a character's thoughts or how much he knows about his own circumstance (what Bertrand Evans called "artistically graded awareness") can create dramatic tensions in light of what the audience has already seen or heard. When, to some degree or other, verbal conventions such as these break the dramatic illusion and create the so-called "extra-dramatic moment," the effect achieved can be a complex one involving conventions of both acting and characterization, that is, spatial and sometimes moral positions.[52]

And yet, this says very little about the functional relationship between the aside and the kinds of speech considered here: the couplet, the proverb, and wordplay. As our examples suggest, these frequently serve functions similar to earlier forms of exposition and self-introduction. But unlike traditional direct address, Shakespeare's couplets, proverbs, and wordplay are, for the most part, well-integrated into the dialogue, even when they should not necessarily be read as the expression, say, of a poetic spirit or a lively personality. We must recognize, then, that between nonrepresentational speech and psychological realism there is a vast and often misunderstood threshold where the traditional and the modern mix rather freely; and only after the full extent and significance of this mixture is understood can we even approach passages like the Fool's puzzling prophecy in *King Lear* and the more perplexing aspects of Hamlet's "antic disposition."

The transitional role of the couplet or wordplay between realistic dialogue and the convention of audience contact is difficult to establish when what is said relates directly to the action of the play. Hamlet's couplet in III, 4, 178–79, for example, is essentially a veiled prophecy, while just prior to this he aptly sums up his double role as "scourge and minister." A statement likewise related to the course of the action that follows is Hamlet's famous couplet at the end of the first act:

> Let us go in together;
> And still your fingers on your lips, I pray.
> The time is out of joint. O cursed spite,
> That ever I was born to set it right!
> Nay, come, let's go together.
>
> [Exeunt.]
> (I, 5, 187–91)

Although the couplet usually comes at the very end of the scene, giving it additional emphasis and so underlining its meaning, this couplet is followed by one more line. Hamlet, on his way out, abandons the illusion of dialogue after his repeated request for secrecy. (The couplet that follows is too generalized and too far removed from the context of the preceding conversation to have been directed solely at his companions.) But the couplet itself is followed by a return to genuine dialogue. Hamlet's last line clearly refers to the previous "Let us go in together;" and so it is obvious that Horatio and the others have been waiting while Hamlet delivered the couplet and now stand aside to let him exit first. Hamlet rejects this perfectly appropriate court etiquette, however, and repeats, "let's go together."

What is of interest is the way in which Shakespeare integrates the couplet into dialogue. Here he breaks with the convention of the *concluding* couplet only in order to end the scene in a representational mode that allows him to re-emphasize an important aspect of Hamlet's character. Whereas Hamlet in his first and succeeding scenes clearly dissociated himself from the court (and such courtiers as Polonius and Osric), here he just as clearly reassociates himself with his friends and those of lesser degree. Hamlet's rejection of etiquette seems important enough to warrant a return to dialogue in the last line, which return, in its own way, recalls his final resumption of dialogue with his mother—"One word more, good lady"—following several choruslike reflections likewise in couplet form. In both scenes the attempt to integrate the hero in a more self-contained mode of drama and the endeavor to delineate his character as an image of human personality go together, but they do not preclude the continuity, in a new context, of *platea*-derived popular conventions and attitudes.

Usually a couplet occurring at the end of a scene does in fact conclude it; and often enough the speaker of the couplet is the last actor to leave the stage, sometimes even with a clear "Away!" (*Troilus and Cressida* III, 2, 205). It is true that the couplet spoken at this point has the effect of summing up or emphasizing important ideas, that it made last lines easier to hear as the actor retreated toward the rear doors, and that structurally it signalized the break between scenes. But although these functions became more important in Shakespeare's day, quite different functions rooted in traditional platform stagecraft were still at work beneath the surface. In pursuing this point we must remember that in the pre-Shakespearean popular theater illusion was achieved only in the course of a scene and could not be assumed at the very beginning. On a platform stage surrounded by spectators on three or even four sides, with the possibility of spectators seated on the stage itself, the fiction of location had to be built up at the beginning of the scene and more or less abandoned at the end, when the illusion dissolved and the stage returned to the reality of the communal occasion in the playhouse. Since the actors who turned the "word scenery" and related gestures into a locality left that *locus* at the end of the scene, the locality itself—having been created solely by words and the physical presence of the actors—vanished, faded away "into air, into thin air," like "the baseless fabric of this vision" (*The Tempest* IV, 1, 148 and 151). The end of a scene, therefore, was a return to the beginning. And it is in light of such renewed neutrality on the stage that the *platea* position of figures like Richard III, Hamlet, Iago, Thersites, and Prospero allowed a special relationship with the audience throughout most of the play.

The actor delivering a concluding couplet in the presence of others—as Hamlet did—spoke from a *Figurenposition* functionally very much like the aside; for he established audience contact without departing from his role. (This kind of aside spoken upon leaving the stage or ending a scene was so common that special terms have been coined for it, such as "exit aside" or "end-of-scene aside.")[53] The frequency of the concluding couplet corresponds to the no less frequent aside at the beginning of a scene. This is logical if the traditional theatrical process of gradually building illusions on the platform stage is kept in mind. Although less effective dramatically, "since they postpone the establishment of a relationship through dialogue,"[54] the aside spoken by the actor entering for the first time or the aside at the beginning of a scene must have served equally traditional functions of *platea*-derived staging. Since locality did not exist at the beginning of the scene and could not be sustained per se beyond the end of the scene, the introductory and concluding *Figurenpositionen* tended to be physically or dramatically close to the audience. It was already traditional for the Vice figure to open the scene or play with an extended self-introduction that had no representational significance whatsoever.

Kyd, Marlowe, and Shakespeare dispensed to a considerable degree with this unveiled opening and closing audience contact. Marlowe went so far as to begin *in medias res* the introductory monologue in *The Jew of Malta*; Shakespeare often opened scenes in the middle of a dialogue. But traditional stagecraft still exerted a strong influence, and the non-dialogue opening (like Berowne's opening of Act IV, scene 3 in *Love's Labour's Lost* discussed above) remained always an important element of construction.

Since for reasons of characterization or social or dramatic decorum not all characters were allowed the forms of speech that correspond to a *platea* mode of performance, it is not surprising that some types of figures concluded scenes more frequently than others. Although there is no hard and fast rule about this we could note, for example, that Thersites, who is definitely in touch with the audience, concludes scenes with marked frequency. Since he speaks in prose Thersites does not conclude with couplets, but his comments at the end of four scenes (III, 3; V, 1; V, 2; V, 4) fulfill what is obviously a comparable function: sarcastic summary or evaluation of what has happened, spoken after the actors engaged in dialogue have left the stage. In *Timon of Athens*, concluding lines are likewise significant, not only because Timon, Alcibiades, and a Senator share the task of ending scenes with Apemantus (I, 2), the steward Flavius (II, 2; IV, 2), the servant Flaminius (III, 3), and a soldier (V, 3), but because these lesser characters are often only marginally integrated into the action of the play, and as such are well-suited to dismissing the illusion of *locus* and marking the return to the actual platform stage.

Similar observations can be made about the use of other forms of speech, such as the proverb. If M. P. Tilley's dictionary of proverbs is used as a basis for analysis, their distribution can be found to back up the relationship between *Figurenposition* and dramatic speech postulated here. *Hamlet*, for example, contains more proverbs than any other Shakespearean play; and it is noteworthy that Hamlet himself speaks seventy-one of the one hundred and four found in it. Likewise, the Fool in *King Lear* (who we must remember drops out of the play at the end of Act III) delivers twenty-one proverbs, Lear twenty-five, and Kent fourteen. This can be contrasted with Goneril's six, Edmund's two and Regan's three. In *Twelfth Night* Feste speaks twenty-nine proverbs and Sir Toby eighteen, while Malvolio is given a mere five. Thus, the use of proverbs functions as an effective means of characterization. In the case of Goneril, Regan, Malvolio, and other similar characters, the relative absence of proverbial speech suggests "the new age of scientific inquiry and industrial development,"[55] whose representatives, for better or worse, discard the form and content of popular wisdom.

As in the case of Iago and Richard III, the new mode of characterization and the traditional *Figurenposition* can be combined and made to enhance each other. But they can also create awkward tensions, as, for example, those between Edmund as we first see him (the bastard making scornful and inverting comments to the audience) and Duke Edmund as he appears later in the play (no longer in touch with the audience). From the point of view of stagecraft Edmund fulfills a variety of functions, like the very different Duke in *Measure for Measure*, when the downstage position takes on original, and no longer traditional, functions. Thus, insofar as the popular legacy ceases to have an effect in such experimental transformations and is used in a way no longer consonant with its original context, Shakespeare's achievement consists in having combined the new poetic realism with modified and experimental versions of traditional stage practices.

Turned in on themselves and imprisoned by their own egotism, Malvolio, Regan, and Goneril represent a new individualism. They are so far removed, not only in moral outlook but also in physical space, from the plebeian audience and its collective understanding of the world and of art that they occupy a *Figurenposition* that permits knavish speech and self-revealing aside but not that type of proverb and wordplay that is rooted in the common experience and inherited traditions of the people. In fact, they are not given any forms of speech that recall the festive element and ritual origins of audience contact. Unlike Thersites, Apemantus, the servants, and the fools, their outlook, regardless of how brilliantly it is presented, does not permit any sustained downstage position. That is one reason why they do not conclude the play. For Shakespeare it is not these representatives of egotism, but rather lovers and cheerful characters or those who are sad but wise who generally have the last word and sustain the audience rapport into and beyond the play's ending.[56]

4

"Mingling Kinges and Clownes": The Complementary Perspective

As the extradramatic dimension of the *platea* tradition was increasingly integrated into Elizabethan dramaturgy it affected the structure as well as the verbal texture of the plays. At that point the *platea*-like dimension of the platform stage was still reflected in traditional modes of aside or in impertinent and proverbial speech and their related *Figurenposition* but no longer exclusively or even primarily so. Instead, the *platea* heritage began to affect the overall dramatic structure in ways more varied, subtle, and profound than the basic morality conflict with its hybrid extensions of seriousness versus farce had ever allowed. After *Cambises* it was less customary to have "A Lamentable Tragedy Mixed Full of Pleasant Mirth" in which the structure of the "mixture" was so rigid that the Senecan rhetoric of the tragedy and the low comedy of the farce were often separated in neatly juxtaposed scenes.

At the same time, the *platea* mode of acting ceased to be so clearly distinct from the *locus*-centered modes of representation: kings and clowns were more thoroughly "mingled," for the clown himself was designed "to play a part in majesticall matters." Sidney's well-known complaint continued with the assertion that "neither the admiration and Commiseration, nor the right sportfulnesse is by their mongrell Tragicomedie obtained"[57]—a reflection of the fact that the elements of *mimesis* and catharsis (the "Commiseration" resulting from dramatic representation) and the "Mirth" and "sportfulnesse" (that is, the heritage of ritual and self-embodiment) were no longer "served in several dishes." Instead, "our Comedients" suspended the "contrarietie"[58] between the two: the neoclassical chasm that existed between "delight" and "laughter," "Commiseration" and "sportfulnesse," or, as Dryden put it, between "concernment" and "mirth."[59] The *locus*-centered modes of "concernment" and illusion and the *platea*-mode of sport and game began to have a greater structural effect on each other. The Elizabethan platform stage did not divide or dovetail the two modes with anything like the consistency that can be found, say, in the medieval theater of the *Ludus Coventriae* or an early morality like *The Castle of Perseverance*.

In order to understand both the changing context and the impact of the *platea* tradition in terms of Elizabethan dramatic structure, it seems best to think not of a second level in acting or composition but rather of a second dramatic process or dimension that tends to be integrated into the drama as a whole. This second process almost always relates to the main plot of heroic, romantic, or courtly action, but varies widely in function: supplementing, enriching, modifying, inverting, criticizing, or generally distancing the main action. Of the many vehicles of this structural multidimensionality four stand out in the work of Shakespeare: (1) the low comedy subplot, which among other things was used effectively to support, contrast, or parody the main action; (2) the interlude scene, in touch with the audience, usually serving a choric function (as, for example, the porters in *Macbeth* and *Henry VIII*, the gravedigger-clowns in *Hamlet*, the gaoler in *Cymbeline*); (3) the integration of comic figures who are close to the audience within the ranks of the aristocratic or romantic main characters (the best examples are Apemantus, Thersites, the nurse in *Romeo and Juliet*, and the fools in *King Lear*, *Twelfth Night*, and *As You Like It*); and (4) the assimilation of popular elements in the actions and attitudes of the main characters themselves (as in Richard III's and Falconbridge's rapport with the audience, in Edgar's disguise, Lear's madness, and, of course, Hamlet's "antic disposition").

Of all these popular elements, the clown subplot and the comic or choric interlude are, from a structural point of view, the most distinctive, and they certainly have received the widest critical attention. But if, as William Empson suggested, the comic interlude is "the earliest form of double plot,"[60] this helps us to understand that among these structural forms there are no hermetic barriers, only moments of transition and elements of common function. The comic interlude as well as the low comedy subplot must be viewed together insofar as they relate in their overall function to the other forms ([3] and [4]) of integrating traditional modes of "game and sport," and sometimes self-embodiment, into the patterns of romantic, heroic, or courtly action. All of these serve to convey a larger vision that is related to the *platea* tradition in the popular theater and which involves what for want of a better term we may call the "complementary perspective."

Such a term is of course somewhat imprecise, but it does suggest that the function of these popular forms of composition is a complex one in that through them the principle of inversion is transformed into, but also suspended by, a dimension of dramatic structure. The resulting "two-eyedness" has many aspects, and they all affect the levels of plot and characterization. As in *Troilus and Cressida*, "the two parts make a mutual comparison that illuminates both parties."[61] "Mutual comparison" of this sort involves elements of low comedy and romantic pathos (with varying degrees of both tension and congruity, and compromise between them), and must have suggested itself especially in the transitional context of the Elizabethan theater at the turn of the century. It was then that the reassertion of popular traditions in a Renaissance theater was strongest, and the convention of "tragic king"-"comic people" thrived by virtue of its very "contrarietie," and served the combined functions of "Commiseration" and "sportfulnesse," "admiration" and "laughter."

Thus, the fact that up to a certain period the comic persona was usually drawn from the lowest social class was a sociological phenomenon of some consequence. For it is not simply the plebeian status associated with the gravediggers in *Hamlet*, the porter in *Macbeth*, or the gaoler in *Cymbeline* that is significant; rather, out of their own "sportfulnesse" these clowns challenge or complement some of the basic values in the play as a whole. Facing the doubtful privilege of "a gentlewoman" ("she should have been buried out a Christian burial") the first Clown in *Hamlet* punningly and deliberately relates himself to the world of "great folk": "There is no ancient gentlemen but gard'ners, ditchers, and grave-makers; they hold up Adam's profession" (V, 1, 28–31). If, as the

English and German revolutionary peasant movements held, there were no "great folk" while Adam delved and Eve span, and if the "houses" that a gravemaker builds "lasts till doomsday," both the beginning and the end of the human race can be viewed in an egalitarian perspective. The logic of the clown's position seems hard to contradict; but what we must ultimately realize is that the inverting structure of the comic interlude scene affects the theme and vision of the Prince's tragedy. Hamlet himself draws the lesson: "To what base uses we may return, Horatio!" (V, 1, 197); and he also notes that "the age is grown so picked that the toe of the peasant comes so near the heel of the courtier, he galls his kibe" (V, 1, 134–37). In fact the wit of the clown comes so near the experience of the courtier that it affects his language. Hamlet's observation underlines the fact that the social foundations of "mongrell Tragicomedie" were, of a sort, historical: "This three years I have took note of it," says Hamlet, taking up the clown's theme for himself and transporting it from the timelessness of the riddling pun to the personal sense of an empirical perception—a sense of measurable time as associated with a *locus*-like position.

Whereas in most of the late moralities and hybrid plays the *platea* tradition of "sportfulnesse" was hardly integrated into the *locus*-centered modes of "Commiseration" and into the serious matter, in Shakespeare this structural integration was most fruitfully developed. In *Hamlet*, for instance, one of the basic themes ("The time is out of joint") is given a complementary gloss ("the age is grown so picked") by which the play's meaning itself is affected. By matching "Horne Pipes and Funeralls" the clowns continue to do precisely what Sidney feared they would: "they stirre laughter in sinfull things."[62] Their impact on the main action is, from the point of view of ideology, of such a quality that prebourgeois standards of social equality are brought to bear on the privileges and divisions characteristic of class society; in that, the gravediggers in *Hamlet* look back to Jack Cade's political Saturnalia ("And Adam was a gardener"—"But then are we in order when we are most out of order" [2 *Henry VI* IV, 2, 128; 184–85]) which, however, presented a case of the mocker mocked, the inversion of the inverter. But the gravediggers are more deeply integrated into the play's positive meaning, and as such look forward also to the gaoler in *Cymbeline* who, even more than the second clown in *Hamlet*, uses both the theme of death and the gallows as analogous images of finality: "But a man that were to sleep your sleep, and a hangman to help him to bed, I think he would change places with his officer" (V, 4, 172–74). The language of "sleep" and death is reminiscent of Hamlet, and the inverting "change places" comically harkens back to Lear's mad speech: "change places and, handy-dandy, which is the justice, which is the thief?" (IV, 6, 153–54). In *Cymbeline* there is an almost utopian tone in the equalizing position of the gaoler: "I would we were all of one mind, and one mind good" (V, 4, 203–4).

Thus, Shakespeare's integration of popular structural forms achieved a sense of "contrarietie" involving new areas of meaning that resulted from a popular complementary perspective. But at the same time, the low comedy interlude and subplot became part of a multiple plot structure in which the significance of the conventions of speech and action associated with the *platea* was considerably diminished by more self-contained modes of dramatic composition. The low comedy subplot found its place among the emerging varieties of the multiple plot, such as "direct contrast plots," "three-level hierarchies," and "equivalent plots,"[63] and became integrated into a larger framework of Renaissance structural form the origin and background of which was predominantly literary.

However, emphasizing the complex Renaissance context of Shakespeare's dramatic structure and being aware of the total design as the ultimate determinant of drama is quite different from attempting to define the changing function of the comic subplot without viewing it in correlation to the *platea* tradition out of which it undoubtedly developed. Perhaps we should be wary of reading the plays—especially Shakespeare's—in too abstract a way, as if the popular infusion into the Renaissance structure must have served *either* as a foil *or* a parody of the serious matter. In light of the traditional methods of correlation between *platea* and *locus*, the foil relationship by which the "comic people" set off the "tragic king" and the parody analogy do not seem necessary alternatives.

In this, Elizabethan dramatic theory is not very helpful;[64] for contemporary theory was normally and logically an expression of the poetics of literary drama. The popular tradition of theatrical inversion was hardly likely to be articulated in terms of dramatic theory. An occasional statement on the mimetic dimension and thematic weight of the *locus*-oriented action might well be expected; but the counterperspective of popular inversion and theatrical license remained outside the theoretical awareness of the Elizabethan dramatist. For that reason alone (which is to say nothing of the more practical exigencies resulting from Elizabethan censorship and establishment pressure), contemporary evidence seems dangerously biased and can hardly be used indiscriminately or as an adequate reflection of contemporary practice.

The extreme position "that low comedy usually functions as a foil,"[65] or even a "safety-valve to purge anti-social tendencies,"[66] seems to be grounded in the experience of twentieth-century drama and the debased quality of modern "popular" art forms. From a position like this it may indeed be "very difficult to believe" that "any one character is being both elevated and mocked."[67] But that is precisely what happened to central characters like Herod and Pilate, or even a morality figure like Mercy in *Mankind*. If the low comedy subplot and interlude do contain the most archaic elements in the later drama, then one of the most traditional aspects of the popular theater, namely, the connection between enchantment and disenchantment, is transferred to the level of structure.

To reconsider the comic subplot in terms of this traditional dimension of popular acting is not simply to take the background of ritual mocking and the "magical ideas" of the subplot more seriously, a background that, according to modern criticism, cannot be disputed. These traditional elements must be seen as more profoundly integrated into the dramatic structure itself. Perhaps "the old-fashioned term 'comic relief' might be said to describe one of the clown's magical effects,"[68] but the actual function of the subplot must be understood in terms of the whole. Instead of offering "a kind of emotional vacation from the more serious business of the main action,"[69] the dramatic structure of popular comedy made the representation of serious business appear in a more comprehensive perspective, a perspective of comic or grotesque counterpoints, but in the last resort one more true to the realities of living, then and now. Once the comic interlude and subplot are viewed as constituent parts of the play's form and pressure rather than as a "safety-valve" to relieve the audience and the play's social tension, they can be seen as *structurally* very like the uncomic interlude, the conventions of madness and disguise, and the assimilation of popular figures and attitudes within the actions and attitudes of the main characters themselves. To be aware of the common structural function shared by all of these elements, and to relate them to some overall vision as the center of the play's meaning, is to go beyond the notion of "foil" or "safety-valve." The popular conventions could hardly have been designed to "set off" the main action when the "mingling" of "Kinges and Clownes" went so far that the resulting gallimaufry affected not only the relationship between prince and peasant but the language and the attitudes of the prince as well. Hamlet, for instance, is so receptive to the insights of the clowns because "there is in him a very effective gravedigger."[70]

The richness, the complexity of the play's vision of reality, is inseparable from what we have called the complementary perspective. Of this there are examples that can easily be multiplied. This is the case, for instance, in *The Two Gentlemen of Verona*, where the high-sounding declarations of love by the characters of degree are stripped of their illusions by Speed's sarcastic wordplay (II, 1) and Launce's catalogue of womanly virtues (III, 1). In so doing, these clowns do not replace the concept of courtly or romantic love with something better, or even with something more realistic; neither do they gratuitously poke fun at a fashionable pattern of behavior merely for the sake of making fun. Rather, they instill in the audience that views a variety of love relationships a sophisticated yet simply engineered sense of the complexity of experience—as regards love and other things as well.

This dual perspective, which encompasses conflicting views of experience, is no less important in the history plays, the tragedies, and, at least in part, the Roman plays. The structural importance of the Hotspur-Falstaff polarities has already been convincingly argued. A similar complementary perspective can be found in *Henry V*, where the image of the shining hero is confronted with "a heavy reckoning" of "all those legs and arms and heads, chopped off," and where the common soldier, on the eve of battle, expresses the unheroic truth that "there are few die well that die in a battle" (IV, 1, 142). In *Antony and Cleopatra* the heroine's "immortal longings" are contrasted with a "simple countryman's" lively mother wit, as he remarks, shortly before Cleopatra applies the asp, "his biting is immortal; those that do die of it do seldom or never recover" (V, 2, 246). Even moving pathos has two dimensions. In *Romeo and Juliet*, Juliet's grace and the elevated nature of her love are delicately balanced by the robust tenor of the nurse's bawdy wit:

> She could have run and waddled all about;
> For even the day before, she broke her brow;
> And then my husband—God be with his soul!
> 'A was a merry man—took up the child.
> 'Yea,' quoth he 'dost thou fall upon thy face?
> Thou wilt fall backward when thou hast more wit . . .
>
> (I, 3, 38–43)

In a more discreet and subtle sense, Juliet—much like Rosalind in *As You Like It*—is still being "both elevated and mocked." At any rate, elevated love does not preclude common fun. Here, as in the other examples, the complementary perspective, the second "dimension," is predicated on a down-to-earthness that is not regressive or reductive but rather expansive. In *The Winter's Tale* the reawakening of the courtly world through the life and customs of country folk is as necessary a part of the process of understanding as the perception of the ideal through the image of nature is to art in general.

These few examples, chosen for their diversity, reflect fundamental assumptions about the quality, form, and function of dramatic art that are operative to some degree or other in all of Shakespeare's plays, assumptions that give them what has been generally recognized as their all-embracing quality and the humanity of their image of experience. It would have been quite inconceivable for the aristocratic or academic stages to have fostered such a dramatic form; close adherence to neoclassical poetics and humanist norms of rhetoric, together with a strongly held notion of decorum—both social and generic—precluded the "individable" quality of Shakespeare's scene and the "unlimited" range of his poetry.

Shakespeare's was a dramaturgy of kings and clowns, of "mongrell Tragicomedie," a theater in which the localized throne was nonetheless functionally connected with the more downstage *platea* position. Apemantus, Thersites, Falstaff, Launce, the gravediggers, the simple countrymen, the nurse, the clowns, and fools, were figures not altogether of the past but, at least in part, of the present, not entirely of the fiction of the play but also of the reality of the theatrical experience. The result of this was a significant measure of dramatic anachronism, especially as it was reflected in particular speech patterns. The clowns could, at least on one level, understand the rhetorical, stylized speech of central characters, but on another they could intentionally misunderstand it, invert it, garble it, or incorporate it into wordplay that revealed either a more deeply knowing or a naive complementary view. Above all they spoke the language of the audience; for their images they drew on the experience of country folk and craftsmen. When the porter in *Macbeth* opened the gates of the Castle of Inverness he did so in the England of the Gunpowder Plot, in the year of the splendid harvest of 1606. When in *King Lear* Kent calls Oswald a "base football player," the remark, which is certainly perplexing to many modern readers, was just as certainly an understandable anachronism to Shakespeare's audience.

Although Shakespeare was well aware of the dramatic effect of verisimilitude, anachronism remained an essential artistic principle in his drama. The functions of this anachronism, closely linked with the two-dimensionality of the plays, make it unlikely that such low comedy was merely a "safety-valve," or "a kind of emotional vacation," or even a concession to "make his art palatable to his audience."[71] Once anachronism is considered as an aesthetic phenomenon it is possible to discover in its structure an element of contrast and polarity that mirrors the larger structure of Shakespearean drama as a whole. The power of the porter's scene in *Macbeth*, for example, rests in large measure on the contrast and connection between the truly horrifying and the grotesque, between the tragic and the comic paraphrase of the tragic. This is the case in many of the scenes already mentioned, especially where the "second dimension" does not constitute a farcical counterpoint, but rather follows, in form and appearance, elements in the main plot. The comical, the grotesque, the anachronistic are not arbitrarily grafted onto the serious. They appear at well-chosen points in the course of the plays, often at crucial moments: when Cleopatra prepares herself for death, or just after the murder of Duncan, or as Ophelia's grave is dug. As a result of this careful placement, the "second dimension" does not merely comment upon the main action but enters into a highly complex relationship with it that is indispensable to the larger meaning. This is most clearly evident in the porter's scene: in the way that the staggering porter views the gate to Macbeth's castle as hell gate; in the way that his repetitions of the word "equivocator" provide a grotesque prelude to Macbeth's two-faced protestations of innocence that follow. What we have here is not only a contrast, but also a unity of contrasts, not only a polarity, but also polarity as a structural principle. As Otto Ludwig has pointed out, "Shakespeare's entire art is based on contrast."[72] The opposition between inner and outer, the antagonistic arrangement of characters, the antithetic build-up of character (Robert Fricker),[73] the counterpoint between reality and appearance (Wolfgang Clemen), between the real and the unreal (Max Lüthi),[74] all reflect in one way or another this dual structure.

Of course, many explanations for this phenomenon have been offered: the unwritten poetics of popular drama (for example, Dekker's idea that sometimes tears and sometimes smiles should be elicited from the audience); the contrast between virtue and vice, good and evil, in the moralities; the euphuistic tradition of rhetorical speech; the principle of *altercatio*; and the like.[75] But although each of these suggestions certainly has something to recommend it, they all fall short of accounting for the driving force *behind* the effect of contrast and duality which derived at least in part from the *platea*-like dimension and the resultant dialectic in the stagecraft of the platform stage. Shakespeare's "gift for playing up one language level against another but nonetheless maintaining the unity of style of the play as a whole"[76] is obvious enough, but this tells us little when the source and medium of this unified duality is sought in the verbal structure of the dramatic text alone. What is involved is, rather, a dialectical relationship between the theater and verbal art, and their functions in society. In Shakespeare the poetic and the theatrical interact; but their interaction is so effective and comprehensive because it reflects the needs and possibilities of a society that for the first time in history brought forth a hitherto unknown variety of social relationships and, with it, that unique wealth of conflict and contrast that characterizes the social context and the dramatic quality of the popular tradition in the Renaissance theater.[77]

This, however, is only one factor, albeit a basic one, that makes for the duality of structure in the sixteenth-century drama. As long as the Elizabethan clown continued to carry on a secularized, postcultic element of self-embodiment (what Joseph Hall called his "selfe-resembled show"), the age-old contradiction between ritual and *mimesis*, which lived on in the contradiction between the actor and his role, survived—a survival facilitated by the Elizabethan social context. Thus, a more ancient duality was involved: the tension between imitation and expression, between representation and self-realization, rooted in miming culture since the beginning of the division of labor. This traditional form of dramatic two-dimensionality took on added strength and realized new possibilities in the Elizabethan period, especially at a time when the national and cultural "mingle-mangle" was about to reach its climax. The full dramatic scope of Shakespearean multidimensionality would have been impossible without the deeply rooted contradictions of the Elizabethan social order; but the complementary perspective was not exclusively or directly derived from it. It was the potent connection between a highly transitional social structure and the rapidly changing dialectic between the representation of society and the self-expression of its agents in the theater that accounted for the viability and the richness in cultural functions of the multidimensionality in Shakespearean drama.

5

"Naturalism" vs. "Convention"? A Critical Conclusion

Shakespeare's changing relation to the popular tradition in the theater raises a number of critical and theoretical problems—problems that are best understood with respect to the history of the late Elizabethan and early Jacobean theater. At least two innovations of this period must have forced Shakespeare to reassess the use and usefulness of England's popular dramatic heritage: the emergence and temporary vogue of children's companies, and the increasing influence of the more expensive and socially exclusive indoor theater. When the King's Men themselves took over a "private" stage they could not, and did not, abandon the modes of performance that they had practiced and perfected through the years at the public Globe theater. But the popularity of the children—decried in *Hamlet* as "little eyases" (II, 2, 336)—certainly precipitated a significant rivalry. These children's troupes primarily reflected the taste of courtly and upper-class society, with its preference for refinement, especially in dance and song. Physically, the scenery in the private theater was "more carefully designed than the corresponding stage scenes in the public theaters,"[78] a tendency toward fine decoration that led ultimately to the elaborate stage designs (including the more illusionistic painted wings) of Inigo Jones.

But as innovative as the private theater undoubtedly was, as much as it embraced a greater sense of theatrical illusion at the expense of a well-established popular tradition of *platea*-oriented performance, the common features of public and private stagecraft still outweighed the differences. Points of contact must have been especially strong between theaters like the Globe and the Blackfriars, where the same company of adult actors performed the same kinds of plays. And even the children's theater, despite the influence of Italian taste, was based on the traditional principle of scenic simultaneity: fixed "houses" combined with movable scaffolding in a flexible mode of dramaturgy that relied, in many important respects, on public stage conventions.[79] Such basic points of contact made it possible for plays written for the public stage to be performed in private theaters, and even at court. True, it is likely that "when Shakespeare wrote his plays, he had in mind not only the Globe but also the several royal entertainment halls," but it is equally likely, as G. E. Bentley has pointed out, that there were "no significant differences in the staging requirements of the various [professional] companies and that the stage equipment needed was much simpler than has been thought."[80]

If such points of contact embraced common principles of a traditional dramaturgy, this does not mean that there were not considerable (and growing) differences in ideology. It is not surprising, for example, that Alfred Harbage, in his book on *Shakespeare and the Rival Traditions*, contrasts the social and ethical standards of the popular theater with what he calls the "theatre of a coterie." However, in not taking into account the common ground that existed between these two theatrical institutions in questions of dramaturgy, Harbage draws a division that, although useful as a general border between public and private theater, provides a rather rigid and somewhat uncritical approach to the poetic and dramatic achievements of both. Harbage is, of course, justified in preferring the "theatre of a nation" to aristocratic entertainment; but opinions about the ethical and political perspectives represented in the drama do not by themselves provide the sole critical basis for judging the theatrical modes used to achieve such perspectives.[81] We must be careful in assessing the significance of a specific dramatic mode if the difficult task of evaluating Elizabethan theatrical forms is to make sense at all. Any discussion of the popular theater is bound to be misleading if, as in S. L. Bethell's *Shakespeare and the Popular Dramatic Tradition*, it proceeds on the assumption that the popular theater is superior, merely by virtue of its "conventional" stagecraft, to a theater of illusion. The popular theatrical tradition, despite its ritual antecedents and its corresponding emphasis on "convention," was also in many ways a realistic theater (as the characterizations of Mak and the Garcio and Vice types have shown). "Convention" and "naturalism," like ritual and imitation, were contradictory but they were not mutually exclusive. Their coexistence, in fact, fostered that extremely effective balance between dramatic enchantment and disenchantment which we have encountered so often in the varying forms of the popular theater. Any interpretation that assumes such categories as "convention" and "illusion" (or "naturalism") to have constituted two completely separate kinds of drama therefore makes an assumption that is both historically and theoretically unjustified.

When S. L. Bethell sets the "spontaneous complexity of popular drama" in opposition to "the naturalistic position," and associates the latter with both the classical theater and the philosophical naturalism of Darwin and Huxley, he proceeds on the almost metaphysical assumption that the "naturalistic position" reflects a "cultural decline" and an "inadequacy as a method of writing drama." At the expense of the theater of Molière, Schiller, and Chekhov, Bethell elevates "the dramatic subtleties made available by a conventional tradition." But must we really depreciate one dramatic mode in order to understand and value another? Have we made any progress as critics when we allow T. S. Eliot's disregard for realism to take the place of William Archer's naturalistic bias or Tolstoy's and Schücking's estimation of the popular theater as "primitive"?[82]

These two contradictory points of view reflect the two extremes from which the popular tradition has in the past been generally evaluated. Elizabethan stage practices were criticized either for being "conventional" and not sufficiently "naturalistic" (that is, for being "primitive" in not offering—in William Archer's words—"any pictorial exactness of reproduction"),[83] or they were charged with containing elements that were thought to be "naturalistic" and not sufficiently "conventional." However, the lack of consistency is not due primarily to varying principles of Elizabethan dramaturgy but to contradictions in twentieth-century conceptions of progress and modernity. Today, few would care to echo Archer's negative statement that "primitive peoples felt with Goethe . . . that 'art is art because it is not nature.' "[84] But it is only from the point of view of a historical criticism that is fully aware of its own social function and contemporaneity that the embarrassing logic of any such position ("The great Elizabethan tradition is an incubus to be exorcised")[85] can finally be overcome. The dialectic of past significance and present meaning is—as I have argued in the Introduction—an extremely complex and changing one. And we must face the fact that while the Italian and English aristocratic theater drew inspiration from the new science and from new attitudes toward visual perception and geometry, Shakespeare's stage, as Franz Mehring pointed out many years ago, "still had one foot in the Germanic Middle Ages."[86]

In other words, the pre-Shakespearean place-and-scaffold theater, with its principle of multiple and simultaneous presentation, was grounded in basically prescientific assumptions about the perception of reality. In this sense popular dramaturgy supported the underlying assumptions that the plays themselves articulated about the nature of society. As L. E. Pinskij has shown, the "epic" mode of Shakespeare's tragic heroes, that is, the relative unity of their public and private spheres, the various links between the hero and his followers, and what Engels once termed the *Falstaffscher Hintergrund*,[87] are inconceivable without the continuing impact of a state of society that precluded the achievements of the new science and at least some of the divisions of modern class society.[88] We must be careful, however, not to confuse a prescientific perspective with an antiscientific one; for to confuse these is to misunderstand completely the meaning of the ritual background and the social quality and function of some of the late ritual elements in the popular theater. At that stage, there simply was no antinomy between the social functions of art and science, between "ritual" and "realism"; the modes of ritual and the standards of *mimesis* were not mutually exclusive, or at least no more so than the social functions of magic and those of "science" in prefeudal societies.

If this was so, some of the most basic assumptions about the popular dramatic tradition must surely be reconsidered, especially the evolutionary approach to the relationship between "ritual" and "realism." A much more fruitful approach to this matter would emphasize the continuing interplay between embodiment and representation rather than the replacement of one at the expense of the other. What is more, we must not continue to misconstrue the undoubted tensions between the conventional modes of multiple staging and the realism of mimetic verisimilitude as some metaphysical or deplorable contradiction between "convention" (good because atemporal and acausal) and "naturalism" (bad because affected by the new science). To say that the popular tradition was incompatible with "scientific naturalism" is a dangerous half-truth, especially when Shakespeare's achievements in the creation of a dramatic illusion of the reality of human character or action are subsequently dismissed as so many "lapses into naturalism."[89] Such a conclusion is no more accurate or helpful than the diametrically opposed charge of "primitivism." Indeed, nostalgia for some medieval form of "organic community" and blind belief in scientific progress are equally unacceptable points of departure; for both perspectives ignore the fact that, as Marx wrote, "within the field of art itself certain important forms are possible only at an undeveloped stage."[90] If we are to avoid both the absolutism of the unhistorical critic and the relativism of the uncritical historian, the entire conception of the incompatibility between the "epic" theater of multiple convention and the theater of illusion must be rejected once and for all—rejected as both incorrect for the theater of the past and unhelpful as a concept for the possibilities of the theater of the present.

This, of course, is to challenge the already diminished authority of T. S. Eliot and, at the same time, to avoid the unhelpful alternatives that have emerged from the Brecht-Lukács debate. Eliot, to begin with, refused to consider the interplay of "naturalism" and "convention" as a fruitful element in the Elizabethan dramatic mode. Instead, he viewed it as an example of "impure art."[91] Eliot's claim that "in the Elizabethan drama there has been no firm principle of what is to be postulated as a convention and what is not" is in one sense well-taken; but it is also profoundly misleading since it suggests that "this confusion of convention and realism" is a confusion of poetic principles, an arbitrary fluctuation that reflects "their desire for every sort of effect together."[92] In Shakespeare's tragedies, as in the comedies and the histories, there is no confusion, only flexibility; and such flexibility cannot be called arbitrary when its structure is so vitally related to the worldview and the dramatic vision that made Shakespeare the "soule of the age" and so great a source of inspiration in the history of modern drama.

From altogether different points of view, Brecht and Lukács have provided opposing perspectives by which Shakespeare can be viewed as either the playwright in the "epic" theater of multiple convention or the poet in the theater of illusion. Lukács, in his emphasis on empathy and *Einfühlungsästhetik*, follows the tradition of German Shakespeare criticism, for instance that of Goethe who dismissed the Shakespearean stage as a primitive "scaffold where all was meaning but no spectacle" (*ein Gerüste, wo man wenig sah, wo alles nur bedeutete*) and even denied that the "stage was a worthy foundation for his genius" to unfold.[93] Lukács, who likewise ignores the theater as a social institution, follows some of the implications of Goethe's *Natürlichkeitsforderung* by emphasizing the profoundly individual mode of the form and content of Shakespeare's art. The dramatist, he writes, is "mainly concerned with creating such people (*Menschen*) and placing them in such situations where the character's words [Othello's] *naturally* flow from his mouth."[94]

Obviously, such emphasis on "realism" (more precisely, on the nineteenth-century realist tradition) cannot do justice to what Lukács himself calls Shakespeare's *Volksverbundenheit*,[95] since this entirely ignores, as Brecht does not, the Elizabethan theater of multiple convention. But whereas Lukács, in his preoccupation with the mimetic modes of a realistic representation of reality, never reaches the vital sources of Renaissance dramaturgy, Brecht in his turn fails to penetrate to the precariously flexible basis on which is decided "what is to be postulated as a convention and what is not." But although he, like Eliot, remained puzzled, he did have intimations (as early as 1927) that "the best things in Shakespeare, being opposed to our current aesthetics and beyond the grasp of the theater of the present, today cannot be produced on the stage." In referring to "that epic element which ... makes the theatrical reproduction of these plays so difficult," Brecht again singles out one aspect, for him "the only style for today's theater to bring out the actual, that is, the philosophical meaning"[96] in Shakespeare's drama. To emphasize convention and stylization may be one way to counter the Romantic obsession with character, but this still falls short of a sense of the complexity of Shakespearean dramaturgy, even though Brecht concedes "that stylization should not cancel, but rather should enhance, natural expression (*das Natürliche*)."[97] This is from *Kleines Organon* (1948), and it does suggest one basic aspect of the popular Renaissance fusion of vision and experience. But it stops short of that Renaissance form of the artistic transaction, the place "where process and product turn inside out to offer a style of illusion opposed to that which we customarily understand when we speak of the illusion of reality created in mimetic art." Whether the style in question is one of "illusion" or not may be a matter of controversy, but it certainly is a mode in its own right "which demands as much from the process of the seeing eye as from the patterns of the object itself"—a mode "in which both dimensions are preserved without prejudice as complementary phases of a single perception of reality."[98]

This involves history as well as a mode of dramaturgy, and so points to a Renaissance style as valid in contemporary prose[99] as in the structure of dramatic meaning where "a pair of polar opposites"[100] are made to contradict each other in such a way that the *result* (inseparable from the *process* of achieving and perceiving it) is as broad as the newly universal vision of ideas and relationships within postfeudal society. If the poet, as I have suggested, could dramatically juxtapose and evaluate the ideals or attitudes of both service and individualism, honor and property, sophistication and simplicity, cynicism and naivety, these attitudes were useful in dramatic composition precisely because the resulting tensions were not blurred but transformed into tragic conflict or comic incongruity. Shakespeare was in a position to do this because he possessed, as a touchstone to test his material, a standpoint more freely, more critically, more richly apprehended than the particular social attitude or moral concept in question. Shakespeare's universal vision of experience was so secure and remained essentially unshaken because he had access to the fully developed techniques and values of a popular theater turned into a national institution. Amidst the "mingle-mangle" of late Tudor and early Jacobean society these techniques helped to define and achieve a social and artistic position more comprehensive and more vital in the areas of both its independence and its relatedness, its skepticism and its freedom. It is in this larger context of a transitional age that the popular theater, with its ritual heritage and its enchanting and disenchanting modes of *mimesis*, could make so powerful an impact on the nation's drama and enhance the tension as well as the unity between "naturalism" and "convention." The two modes, far from being mutually exclusive, helped to constitute the universalizing pattern in Shakespeare. They provided a basis for the humanizing quality of his achievement whereby experience and vision, the image of reality and the consciousness of the imagination were related without loss to each other. In fact, they were so interrelated that there resulted a heightened sense of both the congruity and the incongruity between the *mimesis* of society and the expression, no longer the embodiment, of self.

APPENDIX

Laughing with the Audience:
A Note on The Two Gentlemen of Verona
and the Popular Tradition in Shakespeare's Comedy

If the popular tradition contributed so much to the peculiar qualities of Shakespeare's stage and dramaturgy and even to some of the modes of his verbal art and dramatic composition, how, it may finally be asked, did it affect the nature of genre? An answer to this question has already been suggested as far as the principle of tragic composition was, for Shakespeare, that of "mongrell Tragicomedie." In regard to Elizabethan tragedy it must suffice here to refer to *Doctor Faustus* and *Richard III* where the popular tradition can be shown to be a constituent factor of genesis. But to proceed to argue for some analogy between the late ritual element of death and rebirth in the folk play and the peculiar mold of the "tragic glass" in Elizabethan tragedy seems to push the argument for the popular tradition onto rather tenuous and speculative ground. It is of course true that the ceremonial death and resurrection pattern or the seasonal cycle, particularly the summer-winter opposition, may point to some more general analogues in myth, but these inform neither any late ritual conventions in the theater nor a tradition of the popular reception of myth on which Shakespeare was in any precise sense of the word able to draw. The reasons for that—as our discussion of the folk play and the medieval drama has shown—are not difficult to determine: the narrative dimension of myth (its potential as story) remained undeveloped in early English drama. Whatever echoes of non-Christian myth we have are incidental, and the much greater impact of late ritual traditions was such that comedy rather than tragedy benefited.

If, even so, Shakespeare, especially in the late plays, seems to develop the theme of death and resurrection, the theatrical context is altogether changed. This is not to deny that in this respect as in several others Shakespeare was perfectly capable of perceiving and developing patterns of tragic action which, even when the context was entirely secular, might have been suggested by some tradition of classical, biblical, or medieval narrative or myth. But if they were so suggested (and this is not the place to inquire how far or to what effect that was the case), these patterns were secondary rather than primary to the dramatic representations and poetic transmutations of the secular and political world. In any case, the context in which Shakespeare developed such tragic mythopoetic analogies was certainly not one of a living popular tradition of myth and ritual in the theater.

In comedy the question is altogether different. But even here (with the possible exception of a traditional body of lower myth, above, chapter V, section 5) the impact on the formation of genre is almost exclusively that of late ritual release and festive custom. The social functions of festival and the traditions of a utopian "green world" of freedom and release have been brilliantly explored in C. L. Barber's *Shakespeare's Festive Comedy*. Most of the conclusions in this book are so definitive that there seems little point in reviewing and elaborating positions that have been developed so cogently. As for a consideration of the nature of genre, however, there is room for further explorations in light of the fact that the functions and structures of Shakespearean comedy were deeply affected by the social context of the actor-audience relationship.

At this point, it is probably more convenient to begin with the theoretical problem, a problem to which John Dover Wilson pointed many years ago when he remarked that Shakespeare "gets his audience to laugh, quite as often *with* his characters as *at* them."[1] The type of comedy that is associated with the principle of laughing with the audience is markedly different from what has traditionally been called "New Comedy." In the largely neoclassical tradition of Menander, Jonson, Molière, Lessing, Ostrowski, and Ibsen, the audience, if indeed it laughs at all, definitely laughs *at* but never *with* the comic figure. The comic figure so laughed at usually is the comic *character* of dramatic illusion, but hardly ever the comic *actor*. The resulting laughter is inspired not by a more or less traditional feeling of social unity between audience and *actor* but by a critical view of the contradictions between the norms of society and the unconventional standards of comic *characters*, be they the dupes or intriguers, the cheats or butts of society. The comic vision that informs this attitude is essentially critical (or satirical, ironical, etc.) because the resolutions it offers are so many ways of exposing the human inadequacy of the antisocial attitude of hypocrisy, vanity, snobbery, bureaucracy, as well as all kinds of mechanical or inorganic forms of isolation from the norms of living.

It is, at any rate, this kind of comedy that writers such as Meredith discussed; and it is the psychology of this kind of comic effect with which Bergson was concerned in *Le Rire*. While some of the more important recent studies on the subject, such as Jurij Borew's *On the Comic*, follow this tradition and consider laughter mainly as a "weapon" directed "against any phenomenon which deserves to be criticised and condemned,"[2] we have to go as far back as Hegel to find a more relevant, though still very general, theory of what for the sake of brevity we may call laughing with the audience. Hegel, in his *Aesthetics*, draws attention to the fundamental distinction in comedy: "whether the acting characters are comic to themselves or whether they appear so only to the audience."[3] While the latter appear merely ridiculous to Hegel, the former are more truly comic in the sense that they enjoy the "blessed ease of a subjectivity which, as it is sure of itself, can bear the dissolution of its own ends and means" (*die Seligkeit und Wohligkeit der Subjektivität, die, ihrer selbst gewiss, die Auflösung ihrer Zwecke und Realisationen ertragen kann*). Hegel gives no examples, but is probably thinking of the security and ease of such comic characters as Aristophanes' Dikaiopolis in *The Acharnians* or Trygaios in *Peace*. Such a comic figure is truly comic when "the seriousness of his will and purpose is not to himself serious," and when his own mode of existence is free from any *Entzweiung*, any disunion or disruption of self and society.[4] This theoretical approach to comedy, very much oversimplified here, suffers in our present context from several weaknesses that result from the highly speculative nature of these theories, but especially from the fact that they completely ignore the practical and historical experience of the theater as a social and technical institution. As the preceding sections of chapter VI have shown, Shakespeare's platform stage was, historically speaking, a highly complex and transitional institution in which there was room for a true gallimaufry of medieval and traditional as well as Renaissance and classical conventions from which no single formula of comedy can be abstracted. The most recent writer on the subject has for very good reasons emphasized the diversity of traditions in Shakespearean comedy—traditions that he has shown to have involved various literary sources from Menander to the Italians.[5] Consequently, laughter in Shakespearean comedy cannot be reduced to any one comic pattern, structure, or mood. To realize this is to realize the limitations of any typological system and the limited extent to which Shakespeare's comedy can be fitted to the categories of such a system.

At this point, an example may be more helpful than theory. In *The Two Gentlemen of Verona* the dramatic functions of laughing with the audience can be fruitfully studied because it serves, for the first time in Shakespeare's work, as an essential means of organizing, controlling, and evaluating experience through a larger comic vision. Here, in this early and experimental but seminal comedy, laughing with the audience assumes something of a structural significance. Being part of a larger whole, it is limited and defined by a complex context of speech, character, and plot. To study the popular mode in comedy, then, is to be aware of the traditional elements in this dramatic context which, in *The Two Gentlemen*, are largely furnished by several conventions of "monologue" and disguise, and various degrees and means of audience awareness, such as are mainly associated with the characters of Speed, Launce, and Julia.

To suggest the significance of this context we can consider first of all the series of comic "asides" by Speed in the opening scene of the second act. Valentine, addressing Silvia in the style of courtly romance, greets her as "Madam and mistress" with "a thousand good morrows"—which Speed, turning aside, echoes as "a million of manners" (II, 1, 88 ff.). While Silvia and Valentine are exchanging their high-flown compliments and Silvia is wooing her Valentine, in Speed's words, "by a figure" (the figure of his self-written love letter), the clown continues to comment in "aside." These comments are not overheard by Silvia and Valentine; they form no part of their dialogue; nor are they in the nature of monologue or self-expression. Rather, they address the audience in the manner of a chorus; and it is through the choric quality of Speed's comments that a dramatic interplay between the wit of the audience and the wittiness of the clown is achieved. The resulting laughter, both in the yard and on the scaffold, shares the same perspective toward its object. The object (Silvia's and Valentine's high-flown addresses) is part of the play world, but the perspective of his comic "asides" links the clown with the real world of everyday experience. This involves some contact not simply between the audience and the character Speed, but between the audience and the actor of Speed's part who, as comic chorus, enjoys a level of awareness that is not strictly limited by the play world. The resulting unity of mirth between the audience and the actor-character cannot be dismissed as a clowning concession to the groundlings or as so much genial atmosphere; for it turns out to be highly functional and quite relevant to a reading of the play as a whole. Its functional achievement can be measured by the degree to which it succeeds in building up a wider comic vision through which the main theme of friendship and courtly love (underlined in this scene by words such as "mistress" and "servant")[6] is dramatically controlled and comically evaluated.

Another and different kind of context in which the audience laughs with, rather than at, a comic person is marked by Launce's famous leave-taking speech (II, 3). Again, this is in the tradition of direct address, and, since it is spoken on Launce's first entrance, still harkens back to the extended self-introduction of the older comic figure in Tudor drama. But the way in which this speech achieves a comic concurrence of actor and audience is quite different from Speed's asides which, while they provoke laughter on the stage, direct this laughter at others. Launce, however, enters by himself, and while he and his family experience are the objects of his own mirth, he is also its free and willing subject—subject in the sense of *Subjekt*, or ego, or self. His, indeed, is what Hegel called the "blessed ease of a subjectivity which, as it is sure of itself, can bear the dissolution of its own ends." For the comic tension between the ridiculousness of the object and the hilarity of the *Subjekt* of this speech is remarkable, and it points to the dramatic quality of its comic achievement. This achievement can be measured by the degree to which the tension between the fictitious object and the actual medium of this speech is resolved in terms of the unity and the contradiction between the character Launce and the actor behind the character. That Launce becomes the clowning object and the laughing subject of his own mirth and that of the audience reveals an astonishing stability in his relations to the social whole. These relations connect the character and the actor, illusion and reality, so that the imaginative flexibility of his relation to the play world has much to do with the security of his relation to real society. And it was one of Shakespeare's supreme achievements in *The Two Gentlemen* to have made these two relations not simply coexist, but so interact that the resulting phenomenon attained a dramatic coherence and artistic integrity that is hardly surpassed in any of the mature comedies.

Launce, much like Falstaff, is not merely witty in himself but the reason that others have and enjoy their own wit. The audience, or at least a certain section of it, is made to share the implicitly burlesque approach to the experience of leave-taking, but the actor, in performing this, shares the audience's bemusement over the scene so enacted. The clowning actor has, as it were, a public capacity for distancing the dramatic illusion and for undermining the social prestige of the main theme of courtly love and friendship; he is, at any rate, still very close to the social attitudes of a popular audience. The members of the audience, however, are not passive spectators but sharers in the postritual community of theatrical mirth. The comic actor, in fact, does not merely play *to* the audience: to a certain degree he still plays *with* the audience, though already much less directly than Richard Tarlton did when he took his cue from a so-called "theamer" among the onlookers, or when he reacted to comment from the audience with a piercing couplet.[7] The tradition of the "self-misformed lout's . . . selfe-resembled show" (about which Hall so scornfully spoke) reaches, of course, much farther back than Tarlton. The background of this tradition is suggested by Shakespeare himself when to Launce's quibbling speech Speed replies: "Well, your old vice still: mistake the word . . ." (III, 1, 279). The allusion, which is itself in the form of a pun, is unmistakable.

Of Shakespeare's three explicit references to the Vice, the one in *The*

Two Gentlemen is the earliest, and it is here that, after the Plautine servants in *The Comedy of Errors* and the dictionary humor of Costard in *Love's Labour's Lost*, Shakespeare first harkens back quite unmistakably to the most popular figure in the morality tradition. Launce has been called by Isaacs "the beginning of the true Shakespearean clown"; and as such he is of course no Vice: with Tarlton before him, not even his direct descendant. But the dramatic function of his laughter and audience awareness are very much indebted to the farcical-allegorical antihero of the morality plays. If contemporaries viewed Will Kempe as "Jestmonger and Viceregentgenerall to the Ghost of Dick Tarlton," then this witty phrase itself was a quibbling reminder of the continued relevance of the Vice tradition which, as early as *Mankind*, revealed the comic concurrence of audience and actor.

Shakespeare, using and experimenting with the Vice and Tarlton traditions, also absorbed the clown's "laughter at his selfe-resembled show," but he did so critically, on a newly limited and functional basis. For the comic acting of William Kempe, even though Kempe was acclaimed as Tarlton's "Viceregentgenerall," was increasingly integrated into a socially much more heterogeneous division of theatrical labor. Accordingly, the clown Launce—if indeed acted by Kempe—no longer carried the comedy before him, but, more modestly and more effectively, assumed a functional role in a larger whole, thereby fulfilling—much as Speed did—the structural task of helping to organize and control the play's larger comic perspective. He became, as did Speed, an important element in the "implicit judgment" of the play.[8]

As has recently been shown by Harold F. Brooks,[9] this involves a series of comic parallels between the clowning and the romantic scenes—a burlesque kind of parallelism that is quite essential to any understanding of the peculiar poise of the play's meaning, including the vexed problem of the play's denouement through Valentine's outrageous generosity (which of course can be and has been variously understood in terms of textual corruption, or source study, or the history of ideas on friendship, etc.).[10] Whatever the explanation, the resulting comic vision of courtly love yields a highly complex image in which the joint actor-audience perspective of laughter helps to define and to control, though not necessarily to belittle, the main theme of love and friendship.

The question, then, is not whether Shakespeare absorbed the clown's "selfe-resembled show," but how this tradition was integrated into the much more self-contained structure and the larger meaning of Shakespearean comedy. To attempt an answer to this question one might first of all suggest that in *The Two Gentlemen of Verona* the real performance of the comic actor's true clowning is achieved through the role of Proteus' comic servant. The real performance of the actor and the imaginative role of the servant interact, and they achieve a new and very subtle kind

of unity. Within this unity the character's relations to the play world
begin to dominate, but the comic ease and flexibility of these relations
are still enriched by some traditional connection between the clowning
actor and the laughing spectator—a connection that has its ultimate
origins in the rituals of a less divided society. The continuity and the
flexibility of this position (which, in the last resort, involves some kind of
freedom from shame and isolation) are remarkable.

To be sure, such freedom is a social and historical phenomenon that
has a lot to do with, say, Elizabethan economic history, the contemporary
division of labor, the extent of the enclosure of the commons, etc., but
this freedom becomes so meaningful to the art of Shakespeare's comedy
precisely because it finds an imaginative equivalent in the structure and
the dramaturgy of the play itself. To illustrate the dramatic nature of
this equivalent one can observe that the joint actor-audience perspective
of the play world involves a mutual extension of awareness. Such awareness reflects and interconnects both the social quality of the *actor's* relation to the real world and the imaginative and spatial dimension of the
character's relation to the play world, his implicit insight into and criticism
of the action of the play.

This extension of mutual awareness, or what I have called the comic
concurrence of actors and audiences, is of course not restricted to
Speed's "asides" or Launce's direct address. A more exhaustive treatment of the subject would have to consider Julia and the problem of
disguise—a vast problem, although like the clowns, the disguised person
is the character who is usually laughed with but rarely laughed at by the
audience. Julia's disguise, just like Speed's "asides" and Launce's direct
address, forms perhaps the most sustained context in which the comic
character is comic for himself, that is to say, in which that character
himself enjoys the comic situation that he is watching (as Speed does) or
creating by himself (as in the case of Launce).

In *The Two Gentlemen of Verona*, as in the mature comedies, this awareness is as characteristic of the disguised person as it is of the clown or
fool. In our examples it is shared by Speed, who alone can interpret the
figure of the self-written love letter by which his master is wooed; but it is
also, if more indirectly, shared by Launce, whose privileged perspective
is implicit in the burlesque quality of his parallel action, so that, in a later
scene, again in direct address, he can say quite explicitly:

> I am but a fool, look you, and yet I have the
> wit to think my master is a kind of knave: but
> that's all one, if he be but one knave . . .
>
> (III, 1, 262 ff.)

Here Launce is utterly secure in the actor's awareness of his own comic
function; but at the same time he remains a character, and as a character

he is equally secure in his awareness of other characters: he is aware—as Valentine is not—of the true significance of Proteus' action.

To express this awareness, he, like the old Vice, uses two very reveal-ing figures: a proverb and a pun. The proverb, as the New Cambridge editor notes, goes, "Two false knaves need no broker"; but Proteus, being but one knave, does need his broker, that is, his go-between. In using the proverb in this quibbling or perhaps riddling fashion, Launce renews and emphasizes his comic concurrence with the audience and he again appeals, from within the world of the romantic comedy, to the Elizabethan world of everyday experience. But by using the incomplete proverb as a riddle he does more than simply express his privileged awareness: he uses this awareness to make the audience participate in the playing of the game (in this case the solution of the riddle). Basically, this invites the same kind of participation that the gravediggers in *Hamlet* provoke with their quibbling, riddling question as to who was the first gentleman, or that the porter in *Macbeth* precipitates with "and drink, sir, is a great provoker of three things" (II, 3, 24 ff.). Through these riddling jests, of which Tarlton was the supreme master, the audience in their turn, being still very keen on sports and mirth, were imaginatively in-vited to join in the development of the comic vision of the play.

This perspective could still arise out of the dramatic treatment of a festive occasion (in which, of course, disguise always figured largely), but it was no longer identical with or confined to the dramatic image and social practice of festivity. With Shakespeare something more universal and at the same time more particular is achieved. The peculiar qualities of Shakespearean comedy, its genial tone as distinct from the bitter humor of, say, Jonson's comedies, the laughter of solidarity rather than that of satire, have much to do with the social context of the Elizabethan theater. In its theatrical functions and some of its dramatic structures Shakespeare's comedy is older than the Elizabethan age; and it points to a state of society, or, more likely, to a vision of Utopia that precludes any *Entzweiung* or alienation between the self and the social. The function and the structure of the genre are most deeply affected by some of the past echoes and future perspectives which, in Shakespeare's time, were possible in the context of the Renaissance reception and transmutation of the popular tradition in the theater.

ABBREVIATIONS

Dod.	Dodsley, *A Select Collection of Old English Plays* . . .
EETS	Early English Text Society
ELH	*English Literary History*
El. St.	*The Elizabethan Stage* (by E. K. Chambers)
JEGPh	*Journal of English and Germanic Philology*
Md. St.	*The Mediaeval Stage* (by E. K. Chambers)
MLN	*Modern Language Notes*
MLR	*Modern Language Review*
MP	*Modern Philology*
OED	*Oxford English Dictionary*
PMLA	*Publication of the Modern Language Association of America*
RES	*Review of English Studies*
SP	*Studies in Philology*
TLS	*The Times Literary Supplement*
ZAA	*Zeitschrift für Anglistik und Amerikanistik*

NOTES

INTRODUCTION

1. Karl Marx and Friedrich Engels, *Werke*, supplemental vol. 1 (Berlin, 1959 ff.), pp. 53–54.

2. For the preceding paragraph I have drawn on my "Shakespeare: Theater and Society. Notes Towards A New Synthesis," *Shakespeare Newsletter* (September–November 1974), p. 41.

3. *Shakespeare in a Changing World*, ed. Arnold Kettle (London, 1964), p. 10.

4. For a more recent discussion of the relationship between past significance and present meaning see my *Structure and Society in Literary History* (Charlottesville, Va., 1976), pp. 18–56.

5. See Leopold Schmidt, *Das deutsche Volksschauspiel* (Berlin, 1962), pp. 12, 32, 53.

6. Leo Salingar, *Shakespeare and the Traditions of Comedy* (Cambridge, 1974), p. 26: "In broad terms, the romantic elements in his plots spring from the Middle Ages, while his sense of comic irony stems from the Roman playwrights and his feeling for comedy as festivity expresses the culture of the renaissance."

7. Cf. Michael Hamburger's paper on *"Gestus* and the Popular Theatre," submitted to the seminar "Marxist Interpretations of Shakespeare and Society" at the International Shakespeare Association Congress in Washington, D. C., 24 April 1976.

8. *The Complete Works of John Lyly*, ed. R. W. Bond (Oxford, 1902), p. 115.

9. J. S. Tunison, *Dramatic Traditions of the Dark Ages* (Chicago, 1907); cf. Janet Spens, *An Essay on Shakespeare's Relation to Tradition* (Oxford, 1916), p. 38. Spens makes the overstated claim that "Shakespeare used a folk-play habitually as the nucleus of his comedies."

10. S. L. Bethell, *Shakespeare and the Popular Dramatic Tradition* (London, 1944), p. 19.

11. Gilbert Murray, "Hamlet and Orestes," *The Classical Tradition in Poetry* (London, 1927), pp. 205–40; Francis Fergusson, *The Idea of a Theater* (Princeton, 1949), pp. 98–142. I have commented on and criticized Northrop Frye's position in my *Literaturgeschichte und Mythologie* (Berlin, 1971), pp. 342–63, and elsewhere. On this whole question, see Robert Hapgood, "Shakespeare and the Ritualists," *Shakespeare Survey* 15 (1962): 111–26.

12. Madeleine Doran, *Endeavors of Art: A Study of Form in Elizabethan Drama* (Madison, Wis., 1954), pp. 25, 346.

13. E. M. W. Tillyard, *Shakespeare's History Plays* (Harmondsworth, 1960), pp. 161, 141, 321.

14. J. S. Smart, *Shakespeare: Truth and Tradition* (London, 1929), pp. 130, 157, 167 ff.

15. Hermann Reich, *Der Mimus: Ein litterar-entwickelungsgeschichtlicher Versuch* (Berlin, 1903), p. 5.

16. Glynne Wickham, *Early English Stages: 1300 to 1600*, vol. 1 (London, 1959), p. xxi.

17. L. L. Schücking, "Shakespeare als Volksdramatiker," *Internationale Monatsschrift für Wissenschaft, Kunst und Technik* 6 (1912): 1516.

18. D. M. Bevington, *From 'Mankind' to Marlowe: Growth of Structure in the Popular Drama of Tudor England* (Cambridge, Mass., 1962), p. 1.

I

THE *MIMUS*

1. In addition to J. G. Frazer's *The Golden Bough* (London, 1923–27) and E. K. Chambers' *The Mediaeval Stage* (London, 1903), see Hans Neumann, *Primitive Gemeinschaftskultur: Beiträge zur Volkskunde und Mythologie* (Jena, 1921); George Thomson, *Aeschylus and Athens: A Study in the Social Origins of Drama* (London, 1941); Christopher Caudwell, *Illusion and Reality: A Study of the Sources of Poetry* (reprint ed., London, 1955); Bronislaw Malinowski, "Culture," *Encyclopaedia of the Social Sciences* 9 (1931): 621–46. For the following paragraphs, cf. Karl Marx, "Einleitung zur Kritik der politischen Ökonomie," Karl Marx and Friedrich Engels, *Werke*, vol. 13 (Berlin, 1961), pp. 640 ff.; Karl Bücher, *Arbeit und Rhythmus*, 6th ed. (Leipzig, 1924), esp. pp. 376–414; Oskar Eberle, *Cenalora: Leben, Glaube, Tanz und Theater der Urvölker* (Olten/Freiburg i. Br., 1955), pp. 13, 44 ff., 322 ff., 384 ff. Although Eberle's general thesis and his conclusions (pp. 485–547) are highly illuminating, his interpretation of the "illusion" (p. 511) created by primitive "actors" and their "complete metamorphosis into the roles" (p. 505) seems unconvincing. See also A. D. Avdeev, *Proizchoždenie teatra* (Leningrad, 1959), esp. pp. 39–83. For a more recent study of the general subject covered in this chapter see Helmut Weimken, *Der griechische Mimus* (Bremen, 1972). For my theoretical position on the relationship between myth and ritual see "Literaturwissenschaft und Mythologie" in my *Literaturgeschichte und Mythologie* (Berlin, 1971), pp. 364–427. The discussion of this relationship has involved a good deal of controversy, at least since Clyde Kluckholm's "Myths and Rituals: A General Theory," *Harvard Theological Review* 35 (January, 1942): 45–79.

2. Cf. Jacob and Wilhelm Grimm, *Deutsches Wörterbuch* sub *Nachahmen* (imitate)—"the physical sense of 'measure, verify' was carried over into the abstract sense 'to produce a similar example according to measurement or from a plan'"; cf. also ibid., sub OHM (O. H. G., âma, ôma; M. H. G., âme, ôme; Netherlandish, aam)—"a fluid mass of a determined size." So also AHMEN or OHMEN—"determine the size of a container." On the etymology and cultural history of *mimos*, cf. Hermann Koller, *Die Mimesis in der Antike: Nachahmung, Darstellung, Ausdruck* (Bern, 1954), pp. 12, 119, 75; G. F. Else, "Imitation in the Fifth Century," *Classical Philology* 53 (1958): 73–90; Göran Sörbom, *Mimesis and Art: Studies in the Origin and Early Development of an Aesthetic Vocabulary* (Upsalla, 1966), esp. pp. 22–40. In an unpublished manuscript (Berlin) Gustav von Wangenheim has investigated the problem of *mimesis* in the light of his long experience as an actor and dramatist. The present discussion is indebted to him for some valuable suggestions.

3. Arnold Hauser, *Sozialgeschichte der Kunst und Literatur*, vol. 1 (Munich, 1953), p. 88. It is in this sense that the concept of a *popular* tradition is understood throughout this present study; or, to use Richard Axton's more recent definition: "The word 'popular' is commonly used in this context in two senses: 'by the people' and 'for the people' ("Popular Modes in the Earliest Plays," *Medieval Drama*, ed. Neville Denny [London, 1973], p. 15.). But even though I agree with Hauser's (and, of course, Axton's) definition, Hauser's sociological approach has its dangers; cf., for instance, the differing views on drama and society in ancient Greece by Marxist scholars such as Thomson (*Aeschylus and Athens*, passim, and Jack Lindsay, *The Clashing Rocks: A Study of Early Greek Religion and Culture and the Origins of Drama* [London, 1965], esp. on Aristophanes' *The Birds*, pp. 353 ff., 383).

4. Erich Bethe, *Die griechische Dichtung* (Potsdam, 1929), p. 365. On the following, cf. Hermann Reich, *Der Mimus* (Berlin, 1903), p. 27, and Arthur Kutscher, *Die Elemente des Theaters* (Düsseldorf, 1932), pp. 81–93.

5. Reich, p. 29; cf. pp. 18, 111–12, 239–41, 321. For the following, see Allardyce Nicoll, *Masks, Mimes and Miracles: Studies in the Popular Theatre* (London, 1931), pp. 81, 122. On the tradition of mythological burlesque, cf. pp. 25 ff., 34, 40, 47, 50–58, 67 ff., 121 ff. On parodic vase painting, cf. H. Heydemann, "Die Phlyakendarstellungen auf bemalten Vasen," *Jahrbuch des kaiserlich-deutschen archäologischen Instituts*, vol. 1 (1886), pp. 260–313:

"The clothing and costume of the figures depicted point to the theater and characterize them as actors, and indeed as comic actors" (p. 262). Heydemann assumes that there is as little basis for connecting them to Old Comedy as to Middle Comedy (p. 270); for a different opinion, see T. B. L. Webster, "South Italian Vases and Attic Drama," *The Classical Quarterly* 42 (1948): 15–27, and A. D. Trendall, *Phlyax Vases*, University of London Institute of Classical Studies, Bull. Supp. 8 (London, 1959). The origin of the Phlyax farce is almost as disputed as that of the pre-fifth century Doric farce; cf. Lennart Breitholtz, *Die dorische Farce* (Upsalla, 1960), pp. 55, 74, 124, 181, et passim, in which no doubt is left that "the parody of myth occupied an important place" in Epicharmos, and that such forms offered "an inexhaustible source of joy for the Phlyaka" (p. 66).

6. Reich, pp. 82, 92.

7. Paul Lehmann, *Die Parodie im Mittelalter* (Munich, 1922), p. 19.

8. For instance, mystery plays in Italy degenerated into "holy farces"; see C. F. Floegel, *Geschichte des Grotesk-Komischen*, ed. F. W. Ebeling, 4th ed. (Leipzig, 1887), pp. 201–05, 240 ff.

9. Glynne Wickham, *Early English Stages: 1300 to 1600*, vol. 1 (London, 1959), p. xl; cf. the typological outline of the world theater in Richard Southern's *The Seven Ages of the Theatre* (London, 1962), which is based on similar assumptions. But see Southern's *The Medieval Theatre in the Round* (New York, 1958), in which profound interrelations between art, theater, and society are brilliantly explored.

10. See Aristophanes, *The Eleven Comedies* (New York, 1934), esp. *The Acharnians*, pp. 88, 93, 104–5, etc.; Socrates in *The Clouds*, pp. 311 ff.; Dionysus in *The Frogs*, p. 207. In Menander and Plautus this audience contact lived on, as a rule, only in entrance and exit lines; for instance, see Menander's *Dyskolos*, trans. and intro. by Rudolf Schottlaender (Berlin, 1961), pp. 11, 59. More rarely the public was called upon as a "witness" (p. 45).

11. See G. W. F. Hegel, *Ästhetik* (Berlin, 1955), p. 1075; cf. pp. 1091 ff. Wolfgang Heise ("Hegel und das Komische" in *Sinn und Form* 16 [1964]: 814) suggests that such nonsatirical laughter reflects some undivided human totality and some primitive freedom from aliena-tion: it "does away with the fear of fate and the pale emotion of passive pity." On the "unity of comic subjects and objects," cf. F. T. Vischer, *Ästhetik*, vol. 1, 2nd ed. (Munich, 1922), p. 483, as well as André Bonnard, *Die Kultur der Griechen*, trans. Gitta Frenzel (Dresden, 1964), esp. Chap. 8, "Das Lachen des Aristophanes," 1: 223–51: both the satirical and the sympathetic laughter of Old Comedy derive from "ancient popular traditions" (p. 231); both possess a "healing force" and a "therapeutic" value (p. 224). For valuable suggestions on the utopian dimension of Aristophanic comedy I am indebted to Wilhelm Girnus, whose radical challenge of Georg Lukács' mimetic theory of literature (cf. *Sinn und Form* 19 [1967]: 175–210) has an important bearing on the present problem. On the transition from Old to New Comedy, cf. Katherine Lever, *The Art of Greek Comedy* (London, 1956), pp. 162–201, and Northrop Frye, "Old and New Comedy," *Shakespeare Survey* 22 (1969): 1–5. On sympathetic laughter as a principle of Shakespearean comedy, cf. J. D. Wilson, *Shake-speare's Happy Comedies* (London, 1962), pp. 23 ff. Cf. the Appendix of this book, "Laugh-ing with the Audience: A Note on *The Two Gentlemen of Verona* and the Popular Tradition in Shakespearean Comedy."

12. Menander, *Epitrepontes* (Arbitration), *Griechische und römische Komödien*, ed. Hans Kleinstück, trans. Alfred Körte (Weimar, 1959), p. 41.

13. See Alfred Klotz, *Geschichte der römischen Literatur* (Bielefeld/ Leipzig, 1930), p. 73. Plautus, *Komödien*, vol. 1, trans. W. Binder, ed. Walter Hofmann (Weimar, 1963), pp. 10, 20, 26.

14. Otto Crusius, *Untersuchungen zu den Mimiamben des Herondas* (Leipzig, 1892), pp. 1–2, 6, 186. Cf. Reich, pp. 79, 478, 875, et passim. Did the "utopian fantasies" (Crusius, p. 72) of the stylized *Mimiamben* find some correspondence in the true *mimus*? The "material debt" of the *mimus* to New Comedy seems to exclude this possibility; but, on the other hand, if the *mimus* itself reinfluenced later comedy (through Sophron) it must not be understood as its offshoot. Cf. Otto Crusius, *Die Mimiamben des Herondas*, ed. R. Herzog (Leipzig, 1926), pp. 42, 51.

15. Eduard Norden, *Einleitung in die Altertumswissenschaft*, vol. 1, ed. Alfred Gercke and Eduard Norden (Leipzig/Berlin, 1910), p. 472; cf. Reich, pp. 77–78, 434. As Kutscher says in *Die Elemente des Theaters*, p. 89: "Popular art is unthinkable without an ethic."

16. Here the otherwise illuminating studies of Shakespeare's fools do not seem to be of much help; cf. R. H. Goldsmith, *Wise Fools in Shakespeare* (Liverpool, 1958); C. S. Felver, *Robert Armin, Shakespeare's Fool* (Kent, Ohio, 1961). More comprehensive inquiries, from C. F. Floegel's *Geschichte der Hofnarren* (Liegnitz/Leipzig, 1789) to Enid Welsford's *The Fool: His Social and Literary History* (New York, 1961) devote little space to the dramatic and theatrical functions of the fool. William Willeford's *The Fool and His Scepter: A Study in Clowns and Jesters and their Audience* (Evanston, Ill., 1969) was published after this note was first printed.

17. Reich, pp. 448, 587 ff., 861.

18. S. Sudhaus, "Der Mimus von Oxyrhynchos," *Hermes* 41 (1906): 247–77; cf. p. 270.

19. Cf. *Herondae Mimiambi* etc., ed. Otto Crusius (Leipzig, 1905), pp. 107–8. This text follows the English translation and stage directions in Nicoll, p. 116.

20. Reich, p. 28.

II

THE FOLK PLAY AND SOCIAL CUSTOM

1. Margaret Dean-Smith, "The Life Cycle or Folk Play," *Folk-Lore* 69 (1958): 235–36.

2. R. J. E. Tiddy, *The Mummers' Play* (Oxford, 1923), pp. 91–92. On the following, cf. E. K. Chambers, *The English Folk-Play* (Oxford, 1933), pp. 185–92. In this connection, Chambers, among others, overlooks the fact that a play like *Grim the Collier* "resounds with echoes of the mumming plays" (K. M. Briggs, *The Anatomy of Puck* [London, 1959], p. 77). For a critique of Chambers, cf. Violet Alford, *Sword Dance and Drama* (London, 1962), pp. 50–53. A comprehensive historical and critical study of English folk drama is lacking, despite Alan Brody's illuminating study of *The English Mummers and Their Plays: Traces of Ancient Mystery* (Philadelphia, 1970), as is a well-grounded work on "Folklore in the Literature of Elizabethan England." J. W. Ashton's essay of this title (*Journal of American Folklore* 70 [1957]: 10–15) promises more than it is equipped to deliver.

3. Brody, p. 51. With E. K. Chambers' cautious dating, contrast Alford, pp. 51 ff., 62, as well as C. R. Baskerville, "Dramatic Aspects of Medieval Folk Festivals in England," *Studies in Philology* 17 (1920): 19–87, esp. pp. 20, 32.

4. Brody, p. 10.

5. The texts are scattered in the well-known studies and anthologies. Cf. J. M. Manly, *Specimens of the Pre-Shaksperean Drama*, vol. 1 (Boston/London, 1900), pp. 279–311; J. Q. Adams, *Chief Pre-Shakespearean Dramas* (Boston, 1924), pp. 345–64; R. J. E. Tiddy, *The Mummers' Play* (Oxford, 1923), pp. 141–257. The plays mentioned above are hereafter cited according to Chambers' text in *The English Folk-Play*, pp. 132–49; 42–48; 105–120; 92–98; but the Oxfordshire St. George play is cited according to Adams, pp. 353–54.

6. R. H. Hilton and H. Fagan, *The English Rising of 1381* (London, 1950), pp. 62–63.

7. George Thomson, *Aeschylus and Athens: A Study in the Social Origins of Drama* (London, 1941), passim; Jack Lindsay, *The Clashing Rocks: A Study of Early Greek Religion and Culture and the Origins of Drama* (London, 1965), esp. pp. 206–7, 349–50, 353–57, 380–87. On the continuity of the prefeudal tradition in Old and Middle High German literature, cf. Henrik Becker, *Bausteine zur deutschen Literaturgeschichte: Ältere deutsche Dichtung* (Halle, 1957), pp. 17–22, 60–66, 109–111, 119–24; but the same author's *Warnlieder*, 2 vols. (Leipzig, 1953) pushes the case too far.

8. Friedrich Nietzsche, *Die Geburt der Tragödie aus dem Geiste der Musik*, Musarionausgabe, vol. 3 (Munich, 1920), pp. 25–26. Recent research on Dionysus has of course modified, but also confirmed this. Nietzsche's "simplification and reduction to a spiritual condition— more precisely the condition of drunkenness" has been rejected as untenable by Karl Kerényi, *Die Herkunft der Dionysosreligion nach dem heutigen Stand der Forschung* (Köln/ Opladen, 1956), p. 10. Dionysus' great age and pre-Apollonian origin have been confirmed, even though Erwin Rohde saw Dionysus as a young divinity and Wilamowitz placed his origin "at the earliest in the 8th century." According to W. F. Otto (*Dionysos: Mythos und Kultus* [Frankfurt am Main, 1933], p. 56), "the god must have been established in Greek culture at least by the end of the second millenium." If this cult, "which binds

humans, animals, plants, and elements in eternal unity" (p. 188), was connected with "ancient, repressed desires of the oppressed populace" of pre-Homeric Greece (M. P. Nilsson, 1955, quoted in Kerényi, p. 11), it may well have been, according to the recently successful deciphering of the tablets of Knossos (ca. 1500 B. C.), of Cretin origin: "Thus, in Greek religious history Dionysus opposes all the Olympians" (Kerényi, p. 8). In contrast to them, the old deity is a god of promise, an "epiphany" god (Otto, p. 75) at whose arrival "the divinely inspired draw milk and honey from the rivers" (p. 90). Here we have the utopian theme, closely associated with the idea of "the fullness of life and the power of death" (p. 131), and the unity of both, which does have a certain distant correspondence in the folk play's memories of Cokaygne and its death and resurrection motifs. But more importantly, this tradition established itself in popular music, dance and prophecy; for Dionysus was a god of prophecy, "and the bacchic ecstasy is full of the prophetic spirit" (p. 91)—witness as late a play as Euripides' *Bacchae*, where Dionysus appears as a strange deity entering Greece and, in the magnificent opening chorus (reminiscent of the *kōmos*), as a "tumultuous" or "noise-spreading god." It is in comparative reference to certain functional equivalents and structural correspondences among the "unofficial" elements of medieval popular culture that I have used, *metaphorically rather than causally*, the concept of "Dionysian" attitudes and standards.

9. I have cited the Cokaygne poem from *Altenglische Sprachproben*, vol. 1, ed. Eduard Mätzner (Berlin, 1867), pp. 148–52. Cf. A. L. Morton's *The English Utopia* (London, 1952), pp. 11–34. Morton, however, overlooks the ambivalence in the vision of Cokaygne as some hoped-for land of the future. Cf. Robert C. Elliott, "Saturnalia, Satire, and Utopia," *Yale Review* 55 (1965–66): 521–36. On the motif of "topsy-turvydom," cf. Tiddy, pp. 84–85, 117.

10. E. K. Chambers, *The Mediaeval Stage*, vol. 1 (Oxford, 1903), p. 236, n. 3. Hereafter cited as *Md. St.*.

11. C. F. Floegel, *Geschichte des Grotesk-Komischen*, ed. F. W. Ebeling, 4th ed. (Leipzig, 1887), pp. 201–2. In England, John Selden was perhaps the first to compare the Saturnalia to the modern Lord of Misrule, mistakenly suggesting the origin of the latter in the former. Cf. W. C. Hazlitt, *Faiths and Folklore: A Dictionary of National Beliefs, Superstitions and Popular Customs etc.*, vol. 2 (London, 1905), p. 370.

12. *Md. St.*, 1:325; cf. Enid Welsford, *The Fool: His Social and Literary History* (New York, 1961), pp. 203–4.

13. *Md. St.*, 1:366. On the Feast of Fools and Boy Bishop, cf. ibid, pp. 274–371; C. M. Gayley, *Plays of Our Forefathers and Some Traditions Upon Which The Plays Were Founded* (London, 1908), pp. 47–69; John Brand, *Observations on the Popular Antiquities of Great Britain*, vol. 1, revised and enlarged by Henry Ellis (London, 1848), pp. 137, 422–31.

14. Enid Welsford, *The Court Masque: A Study in the Relationship Between Poetry and the Revels* (Cambridge, 1927), p. 21.

15. *Md. St.*, 1:181; see Hazlitt, *Faiths and Folklore*, 2:368 ff.

16. *Phillip Stubbes's Anatomy of Abuses in England in Shakspere's Youth*, ed. F. J. Furnivall, Part 1 (London, 1877-79), p. 147.

17. C. L. Barber, *Shakespeare's Festive Comedy: A Study of Dramatic Form and its Relation to Social Custom* (Princeton, 1959), p. 29.

18. See Lily Weiser, *Altgermanische Jünglingsweihen und Männerbünde* (Bühl [Baden], 1927), pp. 49 ff., as well as Otto Höfler, *Kultische Geheimbünde der Germanen*, vol. 1 (Frankfurt am Main, 1934), passim, whose conclusions, however, want a good deal of reconsideration. According to Enid Welsford the Lord of Misrule was a combination of "the court jester and the clown of the traditional festivals" both of which probably go back to "a common ancestor, the sacred or possessed man" (*The Fool*, pp. 199–200).

19. Quoted in E. W. Talbert, *Elizabethan Drama and Shakespeare's Early Plays* (Chapel Hill, 1963), p. 10.

20. C. R. Baskerville, *The Elizabethan Jig and Related Song Drama* (Chicago, 1929), pp. 47, 62; also 28, 81.

21. Ibid., pp. 164, 101.

22. A good many references to suppressions are collected by Baskerville, *The Elizabethan Jig*, pp. 43–56. Cf. Talbert, pp. 9 ff., 330–31; A. P. Rossiter, *English Drama from Early Times to the Elizabethans* (London, 1950), pp. 117–18.

23. Cf., e.g., John Stow, *The Survey of London* (London, 1923), p. 89, which refers to an aristocratic variant of the Lord of Misrule.

24. Glynne Wickham, *Early English Stages: 1300 to 1600*, vol. 1 (London, 1959), p. 202. Cf. Welsford, *The Court Masque*, pp. 20, 25 ff., 85 ff. On Oldcastle and the masquerade for Richard II, cf. *Md. St.*, 1:394-95.

25. Wickham, 1:203. The Tudor Law is quoted in Hazlitt, *Faiths and Folklore*, p. 428. Cf. Welsford, *The Court Masque*, p. 37: "Whatever its origin, in the thirteenth century the mumming was a popular amusement which was looked at askance by the authorities."

26. See *Md. St.*, 1:177, 180-81. Above quote from Nicholas Bownd is cited in Keith Thomas, *Religion and the Decline of Magic* (New York, 1971), p. 164.

27. On the social background of the Robin Hood tradition, see E. J. Hobsbawm, *Primitive Rebels: Studies in Archaic Forms of Social Movements in the 19th and 20th Centuries* (Manchester, 1959), pp. 13-29, esp. 23-24; Maurice Keen, *The Outlaws of Medieval Legend* (London, 1961), p. 3; E. K. Chambers, *English Literature at the Close of the Middle Ages* (Oxford, 1945), p. 136; R. H. Hilton, "The Origins of Robin Hood," *Past and Present* 14 (1958):37. The position shared by historians like Hilton, Keen, and Hobsbawm is disputed by J. C. Holt in "The Origins and Audiences of the Ballads of Robin Hood," *Past and Present* 18 (1960):89-110, where he stresses the connection between the ballads and the lesser gentry. Cf. also the rejoinder by Maurice Keen, "Robin Hood—Peasant or Gentleman?" *Past and Present* 19 (1960):7-15. Margaret Murray emphasizes the mythological origins of Robin Hood in *The God of the Witches* (London, 1933), pp. 35-41. Maurice Keen, however, believes that "the material simply will not bear mythological interpretation" (p. 221). See C. J. Sisson's chapter on "The May Game" in *Lost Plays of Shakespeare's Age* (Cambridge, 1936), pp. 157-85: "First, Robin stood for the assertion of an Englishman's notion of freedom from tyranny, and so could well take the May Lord's place. And secondly, the Robin Hood story was a frequent theme of popular dramatic art, and doubtless such a play was often acted at the May Games. Why not make Robin and Marian preside?" (p. 160).

28. Hobsbawm, p. 24; Keen, *The Outlaws of Medieval Legend*, p. 92.

29. See, for example, the plays at Kempsford and Shipton-under-Wychwood; Tiddy, pp. 209-11, 249-53; the Robin Hood scenes in Manly, 1: 279-95. On their possible romance origins cf. *Md. St.*, 1: 171 ff.

30. Noted only by Adams; cf. *Chief Pre-Shakespearean Dramas*, p. 347.

31. See Southern, *The Seven Ages of the Theatre* (London, 1962), pp. 57-60.

32. Sisson, p. 159.

33. *Md. St.*, 1:192; Brand, 1: 263-64. Francis Douce, in his *Illustrations of Shakespeare and of Ancient Manners: With Dissertations on the Clowns and Fools . . .* (London, 1839), plate 2, figures 1, 3; plate 4, figures 3, 4, assembled graphic materials that depict the bird-heads, cockscombs, and ass' ears related to the fool's cap.

34. H. M. Flasdieck, *Harlekin: Germanischer Mythos in romanischer Wandlung*, reprinted from *Anglia* (Halle, 1937), pp. 97, 105. On its pagan ancestry, ibid. pp. 13, 18-19, 21 ff., 32. Cf. A. K. Dshiwelegow, *Commedia dell'Arte*, trans. R.-E. Riedt (Berlin, 1958), pp. 154 ff.; see also Allardyce Nicoll, *The World of Harlequin* (Cambridge, 1963).

35. Kurt Meschke, *Schwerttanz und Schwerttanzspiel im germanischen Kulturkreis* (Leipzig/Berlin, 1931), p. 158.

36. Cf. A. B. Gomme, "The Character of Beelzebub in the Mummers' Play," *Folk-Lore* 40 (1929):292-93; Stuart Piggott, ibid., pp. 193-95; R. L. Thompson, *The History of the Devil: The Horned God of the West* (London, 1929), pp. 127-37. But note Chambers' skepticism in *The English Folk-Play*, p. 164.

37. Montague Summers, *The History of Witchcraft and Demonology* (reprint ed., New York, 1956), p. 277.

38. See Thompson, *The History of the Devil*, p. 124; Maximilian Rudwin, *The Devil in Legend and Literature* (Chicago/London, 1931), p. 265: "The Devil . . . is said to have interfered in favour of the peasants or serfs against the feudal lords. The Fiend appears in the folklore of all European countries as the defender of accused innocence." But certainly not *only* as protector! Elements of parody in these practices are suggested by Summers (esp. pp. 43, 122, 143 ff., 154 ff.), who quite uncritically comments on the "hateful mockery of God's holy Sacraments" and notes that "the ritual of Holy Mass was elaborately burlesqued in

almost every detail" (p. 151). In this connection he mentions animal skins and other ritual costumes (pp. 29, 134–35, 163). Although in the meantime the *Encyclopedia Britannica* has accepted the ritual background of witchcraft, scholars are by no means agreed on this subject. See, e.g., R. H. Robbins, *The Encyclopedia of Witchcraft and Demonology* (London, 1959), and the same author's "The Imposture of Witchcraft," *Folklore* 74 (1963):545–62. There are, of course, Margaret Murray's speculative studies, such as *The Witch-Cult in Western Europe* (Oxford, new ed. 1963), esp. pp. 124–85, which emphasize the continuity of vegetation magic in the witch-cult as a version of "the old religion." On the other hand, there are serious and indeed definitive reservations against what has been called Margaret Murray's "totally false picture." See, e.g., A. D. J. Macfarlane, *Witchcraft in Tudor and Stuart England* (New York, 1970), whose detailed examination of those accused of witchcraft in Essex does not lend "any support to the argument that there really was an underground pagan cult" (p. 10). See also Keith Thomas, *Religion and the Decline of Magic* (London, 1971), esp. pp. 435–583, who says with great authority that although there were "many pagan survivals—magic wells, calendar customs, fertility rites" and "many types of magical activity," these practices "did not usually involve any formal breach with Christianity" (p. 516). Since "acceptable evidence for the literal reality of ritual devil-worship . . . is extremely scanty," it seems likely that English witchcraft "was neither a religion nor an organization" (ibid.). This does not mean that practices associated with witchcraft were not—from a sociological point of view—meaningful. Beliefs in witches served "a function in early modern England similar to that which they perform in many primitive societies"; they were conservative social forces "upholding the norms of village life" (ibid., p. 566). In the words of E. E. Evans-Pritchard (cited by Macfarlane, p. 249), the witch "epitomized the older social sanctions, the collectivist tradition in which every man was responsible for his neighbors." It is in this sense that it can be said that "there is no doubt that the hundreds of references to witchcraft in the literature of our period derived, directly or indirectly, from a true body of folk belief, deep rooted in the traditions of Europe" (K. M. Briggs, *Pale Hecate's Team* [London, 1962], p. 221).

39. Summers, pp. 14, 13.

40. Arthur Brown, "Folklore Elements in the Medieval Drama," *Folk-Lore* 63 (1952):77.

41. I use Tiddy's text; see pp. 163–68; pp. 176, 230.

42. The Cokaygne poem is cited from Eduard Mätzner's edition of *Altenglische Sprachproben*, vol. 1 (Berlin, 1867), p. 152. Above quote from Chambers, *The English Folk-Play*, p. 48.

43. Chambers' text; see *The English Folk-Play*, pp. 108–9.

44. The Clayworth Play, ed. Tiddy, p. 246. Hereafter cited for this edition.

45. Chambers, *The English Folk-Play*, p. 95; *Md. St.*, 2:277; cf. the words of the Turkish Knight in Adams, p. 355.

46. The "You hash me and smash me," etc., is, of course, quite conventional: cf. Tiddy, pp. 161, 175, 181. But can it be said that behind the club stands the weapon of a more primitive culture? Cf. *Folk-Lore* 40 (1929):292–93.

47. A heathen refrain from Guernsey which survives in our time goes like this: "Har, har, Hou, Hou, danse ici." A witches' chorus noted by Bodin likewise goes: "Har, har, diable, diable, saute ici . . ." (cf. Murray, *The Witch-Cult in Western Europe*, p. 165; Summers, p. 42).

48. The text is that of Adams, pp. 355–56. For the following, cf. T. F. Ordish ("English Folk-Drama," *Folk-Lore* 4 [1893]:152), who concludes from a study of the Nordic tradition of Widhug that the dragon can be viewed as the protector of a spring; he notes that performances of the folk dramas often took place near a stream or water conduit. Although such a locality can point to quite different functions and contexts (cf. *Md. St.*, 1:122–23) the original water- and life-giving powers of the dragon are manifested in varying myths the world over: "The dragon was originally a concrete expression of the divine powers of life-giving" (G. E. Smith, *The Evolution of the Dragon* [Manchester, 1919], p. 234, 81 ff.).

49. Cf. Smith, p. vii, and the preceding note. On the equation of the heathen dragon with the Christian devil, cf. ibid., pp. 137–38. In *Revelation* (20:2) we find: "And he laid hold on the dragon, that old serpent, which is the Devil, and Satan, and bound him a thousand years." In the *Apocrypha*, the dragon is expressly mentioned as a heathen, a

"living god" (23). On the dragon as an "unmasked demon," cf. J. B. Aufhauser, *Das Drachenwunder des Heiligen Georg* (Leipzig, 1911), p. 69. Liberation from the dragon is sometimes equated with liberation from the devil (p. 132), but always with conversion to Christianity.

50. Unless otherwise noted, all Shakespeare citations are hereafter taken from William Shakespeare, *The Complete Works*, ed. Peter Alexander (reprint ed., London/Glasgow, 1962).

51. Years ago (1864) Cowdan Clarke thought this to be "a scrap of ribaldry tacked on by the actor who played the Fool, to please 'the barren spectators.'" Such an attitude was based on a misunderstanding of the theatrical process: "The fact of the Fool's present speech occurring *after* Lear has left the stage alone serves to condemn it as spurious" (A New Variorum Edition, *King Lear*, ed. H. H. Furness [New York, repr. 1963], p. 179). On the "parody" of the "pseudo-Chaucerian verses," cf. The Arden Edition, ed. Kenneth Muir (London, 1963), p. 111.

52. Cf. Meschke, pp. 30–31, 63.

53. See Wolfgang Clemen's suggestive study *Sein und Schein bei Shakespeare* (Munich, 1959). There is an English version in Clemen's *Shakespeare's Dramatic Art* (London, 1972), pp. 163–88.

54. Text in Chambers, *The English Folk-Play*, p. 140. This is a context to which, of course, C. L. Barber has first drawn our attention in his very suggestive *Shakespeare's Festive Comedy*.

55. Chambers, *The English Folk-Play*, pp. 137–38.

56. Cf. Brand, 1:264, 505, 511.

57. F. R. Schröder, *Germanentum und Hellenismus: Untersuchungen zur germanischen Religionsgeschichte* (Heidelberg, 1924), pp. 50 ff; cf. Meschke, p. 147. Cf. Ernesto Grassi, *Kunst und Mythos* (Hamburg, 1957), p. 99.

III

THE MYSTERY CYCLES

1. R. S. Loomis and Gustave Cohen, "Were there Theatres in the Twelfth and Thirteenth Centuries?," *Speculum* 20 (1945):92–98. This question is answered in the negative by many scholars (e.g., Dino Bigongiari, *Romanic Review* 37 [1946]:201–24). Benjamin Hunningher (*The Origin of the Theater* [Amsterdam, 1955], pp. 74–93) postulates cooperation between mimes and clerics, but suggests that the secular theater had an independent existence. Cf. the careful sifting of some of the scanty evidence by Mary H. Marshall, "Theatre in the Middle Ages: Evidence from Dictionaries and Glosses," *Symposium* 4 (1950): 1–39, 366–89. See also J. D. Ogilvy, *"Mimi, Scurrae, Histriones:* Entertainers of the Middle Ages," *Speculum* 38 (1963):603–19: "The balance of both probability and the evidence, even with the most cautious interpretation, seems to me to favor the continuance of some sort of secular dramatic performance" (p. 615). For more recent contributions, see Alan H. Nelson, *The Medieval Stage* (Chicago, 1974), pp. 72–81; Rosemary Woolf, *The English Mystery Plays* (London, 1972), pp. 39 ff.; on this question, see Richard Axton, *European Drama of the Early Middle Ages* (London, 1974), and, especially, his study of "Popular Modes in the Earliest Plays" (*Medieval Drama*, ed. Neville Denny [London, 1973]:13–40), where the popular elements in the precycle traditions are given the best survey that I have seen and where, in this connection, he notes "that the most 'popular' modes of acting (and those closest to the traditions of folk-drama) found in the fifteenth-century plays are the ones that dominate the thirteenth- and fourteenth-century fragments" (p. 39). See also Stanley Kahrl, *Traditions of Medieval English Drama* (London, 1974), esp. pp. 27–52.

2. See Allardyce Nicoll, *Masks, Mimes and Miracles* (London, 1931), pp. 135–75, as well as the same author's *World Drama* (London, 1954), p. 147; Wilhelm Creizenach, *Geschichte des neueren Dramas*, vol. 1 (Halle, 1911), p. 387; E. K. Chambers, *The Mediaeval Stage*, vol. 1 (Oxford, 1903), pp. 23–86 (hereafter cited as *Md. St.*); J. S. Tunison, *Dramatic Traditions of the Dark Ages* (Chicago/London, 1907), p. 114; Hermann Reich, *Der Mimus* (Berlin, 1903), pp. 862 ff., and the same author's *Der Mann mit dem Eselskopf: Ein Mimodrama vom klassischen Altertum verfolgt bis auf Shakespeares Sommernachtstraum* (Weimar, 1904).

3. Cf. R. M. Wilson, *The Lost Literature of Medieval England* (London, 1952), p. 240.
4. Hunningher, esp. p. 83.
5. A ninth-century glossary calls a *theatrum* a wooden structure *ubi ludent homines et spectacula faciunt*; according to Aelfric (eleventh century) it was "wafungstede," a place for sights, where some sort of raised platform may have been used for a similar purpose; cf. Marshall, pp. 14 ff. Bigongiari (p. 222) shows that *theatrum* could have meant simply "scaffolding" or "platform."
6. Cited in Ogilvy, p. 614.
7. Cf. ibid., pp. 612 ff.
8. Cf. *Md. St.*, 1:383, 2:190; further, the same author's *The Elizabethan Stage*, vol. 2 (Oxford, 1923), p. 355, n. 1 (hereafter cited as *El. St.*). Cf. C. G. Coulton, *Social Life in Britain from the Conquest to the Reformation* (Cambridge, 1919), p. 493, on the significance of this *theatrum*, which could not have been a modern, fixed stage.
9. On horns as an attribute of demons, cf. M. D. Anderson, *Drama and Imagery in English Medieval Churches* (Cambridge, 1963), p. 175. On hornblowing by wild hunters on black horses, cf. *Two of the Saxon Chronicles: A Revised Text*, ed. Charles Plummer and John Earle, vol. 1 (Oxford, 1892), p. 258, where twenty or thirty nocturnal "horn blaweres" are mentioned. On the wild hunt in England, cf. E. A. Philippson, *Germanisches Heidentum bei den Angelsachsen* (Leipzig, 1929), pp. 63 ff. Above quotation from Richard Wolfram, *Schwerttanz und Männerbund* (Kassel, 1936), p. 227.
10. *Md. St.*, 1:59-63; cf. 2:262: "Tria sunt histrionum genera. Quidam transformant et transfigurant corpora sua per turpes saltus et per turpes gestus, vel denudando se turpiter, vel induendo horribiles larvas, et omnes tales damnabiles sunt, nisi reliquerint officia sua. Sunt etiam alii qui nihil operantur, sed criminose agunt, non habentes certum domicilium, sed sequuntur curias magnatum et dicunt opprobria et ignominias de absentibus ut placeant aliis . . . Est etiam tertium genus histrionum qui habent instrumenta musica ad delectandum homines, et talium sunt duo genera. Quidam enim frequentant publicas potationes et lascivas congregationes, et cantant ibi diversas cantilenas ut moveant homines ad lasciviam, et tales sunt damnabiles sicut alii. Sunt autem alii, qui dicuntur ioculatores, qui cantant gesta principum et vitam sanctorum . . ."
11. Cited in W. C. Hazlitt, *The English Drama and Stage* (London, 1869), p. 22.
12. Cited in *Md. St.*, 2:260.
13. Ibid., p. 261. Other "miscreants who continued to disgrace the name of minstrel" are mentioned by W. L. Woodfill in *Musicians in English Society from Elizabeth to Charles I* (Princeton, 1953), p. 127. On the decline of "hospitality," ibid., p. 67. H. C. White compiles many contemporary complaints on this subject in *Social Criticism in Popular Religious Literature of the Sixteenth Century* (New York, 1944), pp. 123, 194-95, 268-69.
14. Gabriel Harvey, quoted in *El. St.*, 2:5.
15. *Montaignes Essayes (1603)*, (London, 1634), p. 140. Cited from Furnivall's "Notes" to the edition of *Phillip Stubbes's Anatomy of Abuses in England in Shakspere's Youth*, part 1 (London, 1877-79), p. 303. I have assembled further evidence on this in my *Drama und Wirklichkeit in der Shakespearezeit* (Halle, 1958), pp. 147-56, where I first suggested the connection between the uprooted *rudes Agricolae* and the "freshe starteupp comedanties."
16. *The Selected Works of Robert Crowley*, ed. J. M. Cowper (EETS, E. S. 15) (London, 1872), p. 10. Cf. Maurice Beresford, *The Lost Villages of England* (London, 1954), esp. pp. 337-93; J. B. Black, *The Reign of Elizabeth: 1558-1603* (reprint ed., Oxford, 1949), p. 223; Paul Meissner, *England im Zeitalter von Humanismus, Renaissance und Reformation* (Heidelberg, 1952), p. 408.
17. Woolf, pp. 3-24.
18. Chambers, *Md. St.*, 2:80.
19. See John M. Manly's pioneering study of "The Miracle Play in Mediaeval England," *Transactions of the Royal Society of Literature* (London, 1927), N.S., VII, 113-52. For more recent criticism, see Madeleine Doran, *Endeavors of Art: A Study of Form in Elizabethan Drama* (Madison, Wis., 1954), pp. 102-4, who says that "The chief line of influence from the medieval drama comes . . . from the miracle play" (p. 104); cf. Leo Salingar's chapter "Medieval Stage Romances," in his *Shakespeare and the Traditions of Comedy* (London, 1974), pp. 28-75, who thinks it "very likely that in choosing romantic plots . . . [Shakespeare] was

responding to some of the plays he had seen from his boyhood on, which may have awakened his own desire to work in the theatre" (p. 30).

20. Salingar, p. 31.

21. Nelson, pp. 9, 13-14, passim.

22. Mary H. Marshall, "The Dramatic Tradition Established by the Liturgical Plays," *PMLA* 56 (1941): 991.

23. This basic problem has of course been reopened by O. B. Hardison, Jr., in *Christian Rite and Christian Drama in the Middle Ages* (Baltimore, 1965)—a book that became accessible to me shortly before my original German manuscript went to press. In several respects Hardison's book can be seen as complementary to this present study, but it is also, I think, problematic in some of its basic assumptions. No doubt Hardison has made a number of important points, for instance in his valid objections to the evolutionary methodology in Chambers, Young, and Craig; in his critique of "impersonation" as "a nineteenth-century concept" (p. 32); and, above all, in his view of medieval drama as an "effort to express ritual form in representational terms" (p. 287)—all of which involve a sorely needed awareness of methodology. But the difficulty with Hardison's book is that in his justified attack on *evolutionary* concepts of development he tends to minimize the *historical* element of change in favor of an "intrinsic" (p. x) approach. As a result, he radically underrates the structural distance from liturgy to the mystery cycles and, again, from the cycles to Renaissance drama. Considering the Mass as "sacred drama" (p. 35) and the Church as practically the *only* source of the early dramatic tradition, he suggests (wrongly, I think) "the persistence of ritual form inherited from the Mass and the liturgy" (p. 288) through the morality play down to Shakespeare's histories and tragedies. Apart from the fact that such emphasis on "the continuity of ritual form" (p. 291)—more precisely, on *one* orthodox tradition of ritual form—tends to underrate the elements of change and new growth, several questions remain unanswered. For instance, can these problems be approached from an intrinsic or, at least, a predominantly literary point of view? Says Hardison: "From the point of view of the literary critic, perhaps the most important fact about the early history of medieval drama is that the ritual structure characteristic of the Mass and the Church year carries over unchanged into representational plays" (p. 284). Here, the concept of "ritual structure," as derived from Gilbert Murray's well-known "Excursus," is perhaps a concept too abstract and even reductive. As such it can be made to correspond to the Christian pattern of pathos, peripety, and theophany, so that the vast and clashing Gothic tensions of the medieval cycle, or a play like the Digby *Conversion of St. Paul*, are viewed as an "enlargement of the Resurrection play" (p. 287). What is more, "the pathos-peripety-theophany structure of ritual" (p. 288) is made to account for the "'universal form' of the morality play," which ("for both theoretical and practical reasons") is taken to be the same as that of the "liturgical play" (p. 289)! Hence, "the persistence" of this type of ritual form is claimed in "Shakespeare's religious imagery," in "his use of morality-play techniques" (p. 290), and the more general "archetypal form of Christian drama" (p. 291) which—if we follow Hardison—re-emerges in Shakespeare's comedies, histories, tragedies, and last plays. But such generalizations seem not only too sweeping but also, I think, somewhat inaccurate. Hardison's view of "the transition from ritual to representational drama" (p. 178) is highly suggestive and often extremely stimulating but not, perhaps, historically concrete and theatrically complex enough. The question must be asked, can "ritual form" be "expressed" and, consequently, studied "in representational terms" (p. 287) without the critic paying his utmost attention to *the total modes of correlation* (and other changing social functions) between the elements of ritual and those of representation? The modern critic with his predominantly literary and symbolic perspective may feel fascinated by such thematic, symbolic, or mythological patterns as pathos or peripety, but the historical equivalent and correlative of ritual is dramaturgy and stagecraft, and without a consideration of the actual verbal, spatial, and social *processes* in the theater one arrives, once more, at the "fearful symmetry" of symbolic patterns that are no longer good enough for an understanding of the early history of modern drama. See my critique of Northrop Frye and some counterproposals for a theoretical approach to myth and ritual in *Literaturgeschichte und Mythologie* (Berlin/Weimar, 1971), pp. 342-427. For a theoretical critique of O. B. Hardison's position (which critique, at least in part, runs counter to my own) see Rainer Warning,

"Ritus, Mythos und geistliches Spiel," *Poetica* 3 (1970):83–114. Warning stresses "die Verwurzelung des Dramas im kultischen Ritual"; for his suggestive but also highly speculative approach to "'Spiel' als funktionale *Äquivalenzklasse*," see his *Funktion und Struktur: Die Ambivalenzen des geistlichen Spiels* (Munich, 1974), pp. 12, 244. George E. Wellwarth ("From Ritual to Drama: The Social Background of the Early English Theatre," *Journal of General Education* 19 [1968]:297–328), although on quite different assumptions, also follows that narrow criterion of *mimesis* that has so long been established by the lingering nineteenth-century perspective on drama in English and American criticism: "Drama is, therefore, the act of conscious, deliberate, and controlled impersonation. . . . Karl Young is correct when he names impersonation as the sole criterion of drama" (pp. 300–301). But does not a serious interest in the "Social Background" of the early theater, such as "popular dramatic entertainment" (p. 298), lead us to revise the illusionistic perspective, especially if the "transition from ritual to drama" (p. 299) is conceived not as an *evolutionary* progress, but rather viewed as a *recurring* process, that is, a permanent contradiction, involving both history and structure?

24. Cf. H. C. Gardiner, *Mysteries' End: An Investigation of the Last Days of the Medieval Religious Stage* (New Haven, 1946), pp. 54 ff.; F. M. Salter, *Medieval Drama in Chester* (Toronto, 1955), pp. 35 ff., et passim; Hardin Craig, *English Religious Drama of the Middle Ages* (Oxford, 1955), p. 185; cf. also the older studies by F. W. Cady, "The Liturgical Basis of the Towneley Mysteries," *PMLA* 24 (1909):419–69, and P. E. Kretzmann, *The Liturgical Element in the Earliest Forms of the Medieval Drama* (Minneapolis, 1916), among others. The pre-eminence of biblical matter and Christian sentiment is of the highest importance, but even so one should not jump to conclusions about the dramatic method, poetic form, and ideological content of individual mystery plays. In this respect the otherwise welcome and, indeed, overdue re-evaluation of the medieval drama (especially in Prosser, Hardison, and others) goes astray. Cf. below notes 38 and 63. For some recent perspectives on this problem, see V. A. Kolve, *The Play Called Corpus Christi* (Stanford, 1966). In his study of *Shakespeare's Dramatic Heritage* (London, 1969), Glynne Wickham again considers "the possibility that a secular dramatic tradition could have come into existence independently of the religious tradition and grown up alongside it" (p. 24). For Wickham this is the tradition of the Tournament, the Revels, and the great Hall, whereas "the groundswell of a ritualistic pattern" is seen to be associated solely with "the drama of the Real Presence within the liturgy," which "remains ritualistic," and the "imitative drama of Christ's Humanity in the world" (pp. 6, 23; see his *Early English Stages: 1300 to 1600*, vol. 1 [London, 1959], p. 314).

25. Hans-Jürgen Diller, "The Craftsmanship of the 'Wakefield Master,'" *Anglia* 83 (1965):287 ff. The same author has taken these questions further in what is the most detailed and, I think, perceptive study of the subject that we have: *Redeformen des englischen Misterienspiels* (Munich, 1973). For a historical approach to the meanings of the terms used above, see Erwin Wolff, "Die Terminologie des mittelalterlichen Dramas in bedeutungsgeschichtlicher Sicht," *Anglia* 78 (1960):1–27.

26. *Everyman and Medieval Miracle Plays*, ed. A. C. Cawley (London, 1956), p. xvi.

27. Alexander Hohlfeld, "Die Altenglischen Kollektivmisterien," *Anglia* 11 (1889):240. Cf. E. Lipson, *The Growth of English Society*, 3rd ed. (London, 1954), pp. 22, 29, 31.

28. Chambers' early date (*Md. St.*, 2: 108–9) is convincingly disputed by Salter (pp. 12, 42, 118–19) on the basis of renewed source studies in Chester.

29. Cf. *El. St.*, 4:291.

30. See A. J. Doyle, "The Social Context of Medieval English Literature," *The Age of Chaucer*, ed. Boris Ford (reprint ed., Harmondsworth, 1963), p. 95; Arnold Williams, *The Drama of Medieval England* (Michigan, 1961), pp. 94–95; Salter, pp. 76–77.

31. Williams, *The Drama of Medieval England*, p. 130.

32. Arnold Williams, *The Characterization of Pilate in the Towneley Plays* (Michigan, 1950), p. 40. Williams makes the point that "the social import of the whole passion group is that it presents a picture of the common man, Jesus, in the grip of the law" (ibid.).

33. Unless otherwise noted, I quote from the following well-known editions of the cycles: York (L. T. Smith), Chester (Hermann Deimling and G. W. Matthews), Towneley (George England and A. W. Pollard), *Ludus Coventriae* (K. S. Block), the Coventry Scenes (Hardin Craig, 1902), and the Digby Plays (F. J. Furnivall). See Bibliography. Cf., however,

note 39 below. The references in the text are as follows: York, XXXV, 62 should be read as the edition of L. T. Smith, scene 35, line 62.

34. R. J. E. Tiddy, *The Mummers' Play* (Oxford, 1923), pp. 96–97; Chambers, *The English Folk-Play* (Oxford, 1933), pp. 169–70.

35. A. C. Cawley, ed. *The Wakefield Pageants in the Towneley Cycle* (Manchester, 1958), pp. xxiii ff. Even Roy Pascal goes too far when he writes that "the most that can be said is that the theme of the Resurrection itself embodied the emotional functions of tribal initiation" ("On the Origins of the Liturgical Drama of the Middle Ages," *MLR* 36 [1941]:383). There is as yet no definitive study of the relationship between the mysteries and the culture of the folk, and it may still be said, as F. M. Tisdel noted years ago, that "the subject has not been sufficiently developed" ("The Influence of Popular Customs on the Mystery Plays," *JEGPh* 5 [1903–5]:323). See, e.g., Arthur Brown, "Folklore Elements in the Medieval Drama," *Folk-Lore* 63 (1952):65–78; Tiddy, pp. 94–107; Nicoll, *Masks, Mimes and Miracles*, pp. 178 ff.; Chambers, *The English Folk-Play*, pp. 161 ff.; John Speirs, "The Mystery Cycle: Certain Towneley Plays," *Medieval English Poetry: The Non-Chaucerian Tradition* (London, 1957), pp. 307–75 (cf. *Scrutiny* 18 [1951–52]: 86–117, 246–65), as well as his essay in *The Age of Chaucer*, ed. Boris Ford, pp. 49–50, 167 ff.; further, Millicent Carey, *The Wakefield Group in the Towneley Cycle* (Baltimore, 1930), pp. 165–84; Kenneth Richmond, *Poetry and the People* (London, 1947), pp. 59–71; Irena Janicka, *The Comic Elements in the English Mystery Plays Against the Cultural Background (particularly Art)* (Posnan, 1962), pp. 48, 65, 93 ff., 108 ff.; Violet Alford, *Sword Dance and Drama* (London, 1962), pp. 48–49; among others. More recently, Richard Axton ("Popular Modes in the Earliest Plays," p. 39), although he assumes that the early "clerical drama of the church co-operated with a popular tradition" (p. 28), suggests that the Corpus Christi plays "were in some ways a *reaction* on the part of orthodoxy to a long and flourishing tradition" of secularizing popular miracle plays.

36. A. P. Rossiter, *English Drama From Early Times to the Elizabethans* (London, 1950), pp. 73–74 (above quotation pp. 69, 71). Cf. Janicka, pp. 50 ff., 109.

37. Therefore, the emphasis on the dramatic "effort to express ritual form in representational terms" (Hardison, *Christian Rite and Christian Drama*, p. 287) remains one-sided, since there is still a complementary effort to express representational form in ritual terms, i. e., an effort to comprehend and "represent" reality in grotesque and burlesque form, beyond the terms of verisimilitude. To speak of "a fusion of the techniques of representation derived from vernacular tradition with the ritual form characteristic of Latin religious drama" (ibid., p. 285) is to overlook somewhat the complexity and the interrelatedness of these dramatic structures. See above, n. 23.

38. See Rudolf Stamm, *Geschichte des englischen Theaters* (Bern, 1951), pp. 25–26; W. F. McNeir, "The Corpus Christi Passion Plays as Dramatic Art," *SP* 48 (1951): 614, 623. Starting from these premises, modern scholars tend to view—and to dismiss—the interest in the comic and the realistic as merely a modern preoccupation, as, for instance, the "modern enjoyment of the broad fun in the Mak episode" (p. 614). Unfortunately, the facile interpretation of the comic and realistic as "broad fun" permeates the whole reevaluation of the mystery plays; see, e. g., Martin Stevens, "The Dramatic Setting of the Wakefield *Annunciation*," *PMLA* 81 (1966):193–98, who simply takes for granted that the elements of comedy and realism have no structural function as part of a larger whole which, in fact, they help to constitute.

39. Hereafter I quote from A. C. Cawley's edition of *The Wakefield Pageants in the Towneley Cycle* (Manchester, 1958), but I retain the scene and line numbering of the EETS edition. See above, n. 33.

40. See W. E. Tomlinson, *Der Herodes-Charakter im englischen Drama*, "Palaestra 195" (Leipzig, 1934); J. Q. Adams, *Chief Pre-Shakespearean Dramas* (Boston, 1924), pp. 32–40, esp. p. 33. For the liturgical context of the tradition of *Herodes iratus*, see Karl Young, *The Drama of the Medieval Church*, vol. 2 (Oxford, 1933), p. 68; cf. pp. 74, 81, 84, 91–92, 99, 114, among others. See below, n. 45.

41. Katharine Garvin ("A Note on Noah's Wife," *MLN* 49 [1934]:88–90) points out the pre-Norman sources of the tradition; A. J. Mill ("Noah's Wife Again," *PMLA* 56 [1941]:613–26) finds parallels in folklore and heretical versions "as early as the fourth century" (p. 615; cf. p. 624).

42. *Md. St.*, 1:313; 2:56-57. On the Herod at Padua, cf. Young, 2:99-100. John Speirs goes too far when he sees, as does Tiddy, an "unmistakable resemblance" between Herod-Pilate and the "Turkish Knight" ("A Survey of Medieval Verse," *The Age of Chaucer*, p. 50). Arnold Williams' interpretation seems equally speculative: "The old God reappears in the tyrants, especially Herod" (*The Drama of Medieval England*, p. 134). Thus, it is claimed that Herod's "boasting and ranting . . . has its antecedents in the berserks and Flyting contests so common in early Scandinavian story" (ibid.).

43. G. R. Owst, *Literature and Pulpit in Medieval England* (Cambridge, 1933), p. 493; cf. R. E. Parker, "The Reputation of Herod in Early English Literature," *Speculum* 8 (1933):59-67. Bruce Erlich, to whose highly perceptive comments the English version of this book owes so much, draws my attention to Erich Auerbach's essay on "Figura" in *Scenes from the Drama of European Literature*, trans. Ralph Manheim (New York, 1959), pp. 11-56.

44. As against Hardison's position; see above, n. 37.

45. D. C. Boughner, *The Braggart in Renaissance Comedy: A Study in Comparative Drama from Aristophanes to Shakespeare* (Minneapolis, 1954), p. 132. Against Boughner (pp. 137-38) and other critics like Creizenach (1:56) is the conception of the Herod scenes as comic farce: cf. Hermann Graf, *Der "Miles Gloriosus" im englischen Drama bis zur Zeit des Bürgerkrieges* (Rostock, 1892), p. 13; F. T. Wood, "The Comic Elements in English Mystery Plays," *Neophilologus* 25 (1940): 42, 196-97, 205. Craig (*English Religious Drama*, p. 297) views Herod in terms of his "bad pre-eminence in low comedy."

46. For some empirical and referential dimensions of the role, see Sir John Paston's letter with the description of Suffolk's wrath in court: "there was never no man that playd Herod in Corpus Crysty play better" (*The Paston Letters*, ed. James Gairdner, 5:321; cited by Cawley in *The Wakefield Pageants*, p. 115). According to Cawley, the poet's image of Herod "has no doubt gained zest from his own observation of contemporary magnates" (ibid.).

47. Anne Righter, *Shakespeare and the Idea of the Play* (London, 1962), p. 23.

48. T. McAlindon, "Comedy and Terror in Middle English Literature: The Diabolical Game," *MLR* 60 (1965): 324, 329. The "parody-motif of game and sport" as "the most outstanding common trait" (p. 332) can be viewed through its "connection with popular entertainments such as the Beast Disguisings and the Feast of Fools" (ibid.). Cf. H. L. Savage, "The Feast of Fools in *Gawain*," *JEGPh* 60 (1962):537-44. The impact and astonishing persistence of "comedy and terror" and the tradition of "eldritch diabolism" (M. C. Bradbrook) through Tarlton and Marlowe seem noteworthy. They finally reach the Viennese *Volkstheater* where a similar mixture of "Komik und Grauen" survives (Otto Rommel, *Die Alt-Wiener Volkskomödie* [Vienna, 1952], p. 302). Cf. M. C. Bradbrook, "Marlowe's *Doctor Faustus* and the Eldritch Tradition," *Essays on Shakespeare and Elizabethan Drama: In honour of Hardin Craig*, ed. Richard Hosley (London, 1963), pp. 83-90.

49. Wickham, *Early English Stages*, 1:150. See Nelson, *Medieval English Drama*, pp. 59, 72-81, esp. 77. See also Alan H. Nelson, "Some Configurations of Staging in Medieval Drama," in *Medieval English Drama*, ed. Jerome Taylor and Alan H. Nelson (Chicago, 1972), pp. 116-48. For some interesting new evidence on the strength of the round earth-work tradition see Kenneth M. Dodd, "Another Elizabethan Theater in the Round," *Shakespeare Quarterly* 21 (1970): 125-56. For a more skeptical but unconvincing view involving a reconsideration of Southern's reconstruction of the medieval theater in the round see Natalie Crohn Schmitt's "Was There A Medieval Theatre in the Round? A Re-examination of the Evidence," *Theatre Notebook* 23 (1968-69):130-42, and 24 (1969-70):18-25. See n. 52.

50. Southern, *The Seven Ages of the Theatre* (London, 1962), p. 109.

51. Williams, *The Drama of Medieval England*, p. 98.

52. Stevens, p. 193. Cf. the introduction to *The Wakefield Mystery Plays*, ed. and trans. Martial Rose (London, 1961). The theory of the platform carts as the "equivalent of the spacious *platea* of the fixed Miracle stage" is in Wickham, *Early English Stages*, 1:171 ff. It seems characteristic of the conflicting and still largely inconclusive results of recent research that a scholar like Alan H. Nelson (following J. W. Walker, *Wakefield, its History and People*, vol. 1 [Wakefield, 1939], pp. 150-51) considers the possibility, as previously suggested by him for York, of indoor production, but concludes by saying that "perhaps the wisest course is to confess how little is actually known or even knowable concerning the

production of the Wakefield dramatic cycle" ("The Wakefield Corpus Christi Play: Pageant Procession and Dramatic Cycle," *Research Opportunities in Renaissance Drama* 13-14 [1970-71]:230). Similarly, A. C. Cawley in his paper "Pageant Wagon Versus Juggernaut Car" (ibid., pp. 204-8) warns against "the present preoccupation with multiple staging in the round" if only because it tends to minimize "the great variety of production methods—indoors, out of doors, in the round, in a rectangular acting area, on pageant wagons and booth stages, with the 'house' (or symbols of locality) distributed around the acting area or in a semi-circle or straight line before the audience" (p. 204). This is a bewildering generalization which, however, seems not quite as futile in connection with the results of recent scholarship as that of Nelson, Cynthia Tyson, Richard Axton, Kenneth Cameron, Martin Stevens, Martial Rose, and others.

53. Richard Hosley, "Three Kinds of Outdoor Theatre Before Shakespeare," *Theatre Survey* 12 (1971):26.

54. See Richard Southern, "The Contribution of the Interludes to Elizabethan Staging," *Essays on Shakespeare and Elizabethan Drama: In honour of Hardin Craig*, ed. Richard Hosley (London, 1963), pp. 3-14. Cf. T. W. Craik, *The Tudor Interlude: Stage, Costume, Acting* (Leicester, 1958), esp. pp. 7-26.

55. T. S. Eliot, *Selected Essays: 1917-1932* (London, 1932), pp. 114, 116.

56. Cf. the analysis in Enid Welsford's *The Fool: His Social and Literary History* (New York, 1961), pp. 231 ff. Cf. also Barbara Swain, *Fools and Folly During the Middle Ages and the Renaissance* (New York, 1932), p. 63, where the fool in French mystery plays is shown to have "made the realistic comment upon the solemn or idealistic efforts of the heroes." On the Adam play, cf. *Md. St.*, 2:80, 85, as well as Gustave Cohen, *Historie de la mise en scène dans le théâtre religieux Français du moyen age*, expanded ed. (Paris, 1951), p. 62.

57. Craik, p. 23.

58. Cf. Erich Auerbach, *Mimesis: Dargestellte Wirklichkeit in der abendländischen Literatur*, 3rd ed. (Berlin/Munich, 1964), p. 313. There Christ is shown to have appeared not as a hero and king but as a man of the lowest social class: his "disciples were fishermen and artisans . . ." (p. 73). Auerbach links the rise of the serious element in the *sermo humilis* with the rise in early Christianity of "a spiritual movement in the depths of the common people" (p. 46).

59. Richard Southern, *The Medieval Theatre in the Round* (New York, 1958), pp. 11, 119 ff.

60. Cf. *Md. St.*, 2:79, 83-84. Cf. the French *mansions* (Cohen, pp. 89-90).

61. See "On the Use of the 'Place' and the 'Platea' . . . ," Appendix in Southern, *The Medieval Theatre in the Round*, pp. 219-36. See the slight modification of the earlier definition in the same author's *The Staging of Plays Before Shakespeare* (London, 1973), pp. 186-87, according to which "place" in Tudor Interludes was used to refer to "that part of the floor [of a Great Hall] which could be claimed as the acting-area," but "of course there was no demarcation of any such area" (p. 187).

62. As does W. F. McNeir in "The Corpus Christi Passion Plays as Dramatic Art," *SP* 48 (1951):601-28.

63. McNeir and Eleanor Prosser (*Drama and Religion in the English Mystery Plays: A Re-evaluation* [Stanford, 1961]) are among those who attempted a re-evaluation of the cycles not as "literary curiosities" or as "primitive works of art but as the final outcome of a slowly developed growth" (McNeir, pp. 601-2). The "new estimate of it as literature" (p. 602) and indeed as "dramatic artistry" (p. 628) is welcome, but this "artistry" is profoundly one of the theater, not of the pulpit. Thus, the unity of the *Secunda Pastorum* is aesthetic, not, as W. M. Manly would have it, "religious" ("Shepherds and Prophets: Religious Unity in the Towneley *Secunda Pastorum*," *PMLA* [1963]:151-55). This orthodox approach affects, despite his totally different frame of reference, some of the conclusions of M. M. Morgan, "'High Fraud': Paradox and Double-plot in the English Shepherds' Plays," *Speculum* 39 (1964):676-89.

64. A. P. Rossiter, *Angel With Horns and Other Shakespeare Lectures* (London, 1961), p. 286. Arnold Williams maintains that the "social satire" and the "rough humor" of the *Secunda Pastorum* are not "completely functional" (*The Characterization of Pilate*, p. x).

65. Leopold Kretzenbacher, "Schlangenteufel und Satan im Paradeisspiel," *Masken in Mitteleuropa*, ed. L. Schmidt (Vienna, 1955), p. 74.

66. Thomas Beard, *The Theatre of God's Judgements* (London, 1631), pp. 206-7, quoted in Righter, p. 17.

67. All references are to Cawley's edition, *The Wakefield Pageants in the Towneley Cycle*, pp. 43-63.

68. Carey, p. 109; cf. Manly, 1:vii; et al.

69. Cawley (p. 106) reads the "ye" not as an address to the audience but as pure dialogue.

70. See below Chapter VI, parts 2 and 3. It has been said of the York master (and the same is true, in a different way, of Shakespeare) that "his realism is exceptional, but did not constitute a break with tradition." All of them, in their different contexts, "took to its logical conclusion a tendency inherent in medieval drama" (J. W. Robinson, "The Art of the York Realist," *MP* 60 [1962-63]:241-50).

71. Cf. J. H. Smith, "Another Allusion to Costume in the Work of the 'Wakefield Master,'" *PMLA* 52 (1937):901-2. Smith views this scene as "a sustained and raucous jeer at the system of maintenance."

72. R. C. Cosbey, "The Mak Story and its Folklore Analogues," *Speculum* 20 (1945): 310-17, esp. 315-16. According to Speirs (*Medieval English Poetry*, pp. 335-48), the sheep in the cradle is connected with the "horned god" of the witches; Mak is believed to be associated with "Loki and the wolf," and, with reference to line 197 ("... a man that walkys on the moore"), it is said that "He [Mak] is the wild man of the moor...." But this reference is more likely to the motif of the shepherd's life as described in line 10 ("Bot we sely husbandys that walkys on the moore"). To overemphasize the ritual and symbolic aspects at the expense of the mimetic ("the Mystery Cycle . . . is still as a whole in the ritual phase," p. 316) seems in line with a somewhat idealistic and purely literary reading of the cycles which considers the play as a "dramatic poem" (pp. 324, 326, et passim).

73. Carey (pp. 109-10), having traced only one verbal parallel with the Bible in the *Second Shepherd's Play*, comes to the conclusion that "the plays are composed largely from nonbiblical sources" (p. 112).

74. Auerbach, p. 309. This points to one of the major presuppositions of the rise of realism in the literature of the Renaissance to which the popular tradition helps to contribute. Cf. Roman Samarin, "Zum Problem des Realismus in der westeuropäischen Literaturen der Renaissance," *Probleme des Realismus in der Weltliteratur*, Institut für Slawistik der DAdW (Berlin, 1962), p. 351. See Miklós Szenczi, "The Nature of Shakespeare's Realism," *Shakespeare Jahrbuch* 102 (1966):37-59, who surveys related positions in Soviet criticism.

75. M. E. Aston ("Lollardy and Sedition, 1381-1431," *Past and Present* [April, 1960]:1-44) demonstrates the relationship between social sedition and religious dissent (p. 36). See J. A. F. Thomson, *The Later Lollards, 1414-1520* (Oxford, 1965), esp. pp. 35, 245, 247; Montague Summers, *The History of Witchcraft and Demonology* (New York, 1956), pp. 13, 36 ff., 43, et passim; A. L. Morton, *A People's History of England* (London, 1951), pp. 132 ff.; G. M. Trevelyan, *English Social History* (London, 1945), p. 79. A reviewer of *The Later Lollards* in *TLS* (3.2.1966, p. 79) spoke of the "intangible widespread subversion" which, though not well organized, was deep-rooted. Naturally the heresy was not confined to England, and its continental origins and traditions were old and widespread; see, in particular, the work of Marxist historians such as Gottfried Koch, *Frauenfrage und Ketzertum im Mittelalter* (Berlin, 1962), Theodora Büttner and Ernst Werner, *Circumcellionen und Adamiten* (Berlin, 1959); or that on the heresy of the "free spirit" which has been described as "the ideology of the plebeian classes" (Martin Erbstösser and Ernst Werner, *Ideologische Probleme des mittelalterliched Plebejertums* [Berlin, 1960], p. 47). Karl Kautsky is quite off the mark when he defines the Lollards as a "communist sect" (*Vorläufer des neueren Sozialismus*, vol. 1, *Kommunistische Bewegungen im Mittelalter* [Berlin, 1947], pp. 249-68), but there *were* powerful leveling tendencies which emerged in 1381. The famous "When Adam delved and Eve span, who was then the gentleman?" finds as late an echo as the gravedigger scene in *Hamlet* (V, 1, 23-29). On the tradition of prophetic and heretical "primitive communism" in *King Lear*, cf. J. F. Danby, *Shakespeare's Doctrine of Nature: A Study of King Lear* (London, 1961), pp. 185-89.

76. Carey, p. 146. Thomson has shown "how the name Lollard could be used as a term of abuse, even by those accused of it" (*The Later Lollards*, p. 29).

77. Hilton, pp. 60 ff., 125.

78. A. G. Dickens, *Lollards and Protestants in the Diocese of York: 1509–1588* (Oxford, 1959), pp. 245, 251; see the same author's *The English Reformation* (London, 1964), pp. 9, 36, 16–52, 222–35, et passim. Dickens sums up his study of York ecclesiastical proceedings against popular heretics in these words: "The most interesting and novel part of our inquiry has concerned heresy and Protestantism amongst the common people and middle classes. . . . In this corner of society, time seems almost to have stood still. The world of popular heresy had survived, much of it oddly oblivious to royal and episcopal propaganda, Protestant, Catholic, and Erastian. A major revelation of our story is this failure of both Church and State to establish anything approaching spiritual uniformity or to bind the laity, as they had bound the clergy, to their chariots. At no stage, not even under Elizabeth, did English authority accomplish this feat, though it was left to our egregious second Stuart king to make the national Church so uncomprehensive as to lose a respectable minimum of control over a turbulent scene" (*Lollards and Protestants*, pp. 240, 250 ff.). At this point, as Christopher Hill has shown so convincingly, the Civil War was to unleash an absolute host of long-repressed utopian and heretical ideas and attitudes; see, e.g., *The World Turned Upside Down: Radical Ideas During the English Revolution* (London, 1972).

79. Thomson, *The Later Lollards*, pp. 30, 67, 71, 241, 244.

80. Quoted in Dickens, *Lollards and Protestants*, p. 17.

81. John Speirs, "The Towneley *Shepherd's Plays,*" *The Age of Chaucer*, ed. Boris Ford, p. 168; ibid.: "This make-believe abundance—their own make-believe, it seems—is not there as a mockery of them in the season of deprivation. The tone is rather one of jollity as if what is seen is a promise of the spring abundance that is indeed certain. The buffoonery of the Shepherds is, apparently, a significant Christmas game in this Christmas play—a game intended perhaps magically to help to induce the abundance it prefigures." Cf. Speirs, *Medieval English Poetry*, p. 329. A folklore tradition serves as source; cf. *Shakespeare Jest-Books*, vol. 3 (London, 1864), pp. 4–5. See H. A. Eaton, "A Source for the Towneley *Prima Pastorum,*" *MLN* 14 (1899):265–68.

82. The utopian theme in no way contradicts the Christian content of the scene; rather it is subtly intertwined with the biblical prophecy (332–405) culminating in the words of the third shepherd: "And I hold it trew, for ther shuld be, When that kyng commys new, peasse by land and se" (403–4). But does this mean that "they [the shepherds] have assumed *la voix de l'Église*?" (E. C. Dunn, "The Proleptic Principle in the Towneley *Prima Pastorum,*" *Linguistic and Literary Studies in Honor of Helmut A. Hatzfeld*, ed. A. S. Crisafulli [Washington, 1964], p. 123).

83. A. C. Cawley, "The 'Grotesque' Feast in the *Prima Pastorum,*" *Speculum* 30 (1955): 213, 215. Cawley maintains, as does M. M. Morgan, that the meal is make-believe food, but ignores the context of theme and dramaturgy.

84. Salter, p. 77.

85. The burlesque effect of song must not obscure the much greater significance of the actual church hymn as "an integral, dramatic factor in the plays." In Chester there are at least twenty-three songs in fourteen scenes, in Wakefield nineteen in ten, in York twenty-seven in twelve (Fletcher Collins, "Music in the Craft Cycles," *PMLA* 47 [1932]: 613–21).

86. B. J. Whiting, *Proverbs in the Earlier English Drama* (Cambridge, Mass., 1938), p. 18.

87. Cf. ibid., p. 21.

IV

MORALITIES AND INTERLUDES

1. See Paul Meissner, *England im Zeitalter von Humanismus, Renaissance und Reformation* (Heidelberg, 1952), p. 411; G. W. Wallace, *The Evolution of the English Drama up to Shakespeare* (Berlin, 1912), pp. 13, 21–86; E. K. Chambers, *The Mediaeval Stage*, vol. 2 (Oxford, 1903), p. 187 (hereafter cited as *Md. St.*).

2. These broad historical generalizations are based on my *Drama und Wirklichkeit in der Shakespearezeit* (Halle, 1958), pp. 13–139; cf. below, Chapter V, part 1.

3. See Richard Southern, *The Staging of Plays Before Shakespeare* (London, 1973), pp. 25, 48, 142, 186–87, et passim; E. K. Chambers, *The Elizabethan Stage*, vol. 3 (Oxford, 1923), p.

23 (hereafter cited as *El. St.*); further, T. W. Craik, *The Tudor Interlude: Stage, Costume, Acting* (Leicester, 1958), pp. 9-10.

4. *El. St.*, 3: 23; cf. Glynne Wickham, *Early English Stages: 1300 to 1600*, vol. 1 (London, 1959), pp. 243, 247. The distinction between an aristocratic upper middle class indoor theater and a popular or "universal" outdoor theater made by Wickham does not seem helpful when the secular "theatre of social recreation" is opposed to the cultic "theatre of worship" on the basis of those categories (pp. xliii, 179-80, et passim). The mystery plays, and certainly a morality such as *Mankind*, encompass both of these functions. For more recent studies, see Glynne Wickham's *Shakespeare's Dramatic Heritage: Collected Studies in Mediaeval, Tudor and Shakespearean Drama* (London, 1969), pp. 24-41, and especially David M. Bevington's "Popular and Courtly Traditions on the Early Tudor Stage," *Medieval Drama*, ed. Neville Denny, Stratford-upon-Avon Studies 16 (London, 1973):91-108, who admirably balances a sense of the "separateness of these traditions" by an awareness of "the continuity between popular and courtly [staging] tradition" (p. 93). But such continuity was due to "the happy fact that the English ruling class never isolated itself from the kinds of drama that also appealed to popular audiences" (p. 92).

5. *El. St.*, 3:23-34; Craik, pp. 20, 23; cf. further, Elisabeth Lauf, *Die Bühnenanweisungen in den englischen Moralitäten und Interludien bis 1570*, Dissertation (Münster, 1932), which in part anticipates (e.g., p. 14) some of D. M. Bevington's important conclusions in *From 'Mankind' to Marlowe: Growth of Structure in the Popular Drama of Tudor England* (Cambridge, Mass., 1962).

6. Bevington, *From 'Mankind' to Marlowe*, pp. 52-53; on the traditional quality of the *place* in *Magnificence*, cf. the edition of R. L. Ramsay (EETS, E.S. XCVIII) (London, 1906), ll. 824, 828, 1327, 1796. Ramsay comments on the political content as a pivot for formal innovations (pp. cvi-cvii). Since the German edition of this book was published, Richard Southern (*The Staging of Plays Before Shakespeare*, pp. 180-201) has amply confirmed the continuity of popular modes of staging in this indoor play.

7. *A Select Collection of Old English Plays*, originally published by Robert Dodsley, 4th ed., 15 vols., ed. W. C. Hazlitt, vol. 1 (London, 1874-76), p. 10.

8. Ibid., p. 2.

9. On the social background of the dramatists, cf. A. W. Reed, *Early Tudor Drama* (London, 1926), pp. 22, 29, 46, 52, 102 ff.

10. See Bevington, *From 'Mankind' to Marlowe*, pp. 128, 133, 148, 151.

11. M. C. Bradbrook, *The Growth and Structure of Elizabethan Comedy* (London, 1961), pp. 6-7, my italics. Cf. P. W. Biesterfeldt, *Die dramatische Technik Thomas Kyds: Studien zur inneren Struktur und szenischen Form des elisabethanischen Dramas* (Halle, 1936), p. 17. See below Chapter V, passim.

12. These and following quotations from Henry Medwall, *Fulgens and Lucres*, ed. F. S. Boas and A. W. Reed (Oxford, 1926).

13. C. R. Baskerville, "Conventional Features of Medwall's *Fulgens and Lucres*," *MP* 24 (1926-27):435; cf. the same author's "Some Evidence for Early Romantic Plays in England," ibid., 14 (1916-17): 229-51, 467-512.

14. Baskerville ("Conventional Features . . . ," p. 442) naturally sees the piece "independently of classical models," and Reed and Boas state emphatically that the "form of this play is uninfluenced by classical models . . . *Fulgens and Lucres* owes nothing like *Johan Johan* to French farce or like *Ralph Roister Doister* to Roman comedy" (p. xxvii). On the other hand, Medwall was acquainted with classical literature, and his earlier Morality, *Nature*, contains references to Ovid and Aristotle.

15. Cf. E. Th. Sehrt, *Der dramatische Auftakt in der elisabethanischen Tragödie: Interpretationen zum englischen Drama der Shakespearezeit* (Göttingen, 1960), pp. 61-62.

16. Boas and Reed ed., p. xxiv. See Eduard Eckhardt, *Das englische Drama im Zeitalter der Reformation und Hochrenaissance* (Berlin/Leipzig, 1928), p. 58: "The subplot operates as a burlesque parallel to the main plot."

17. For reasons that cannot be developed in a note, I am reluctant to follow Richard Southern (*The Staging of Plays Before Shakespeare*, pp. 143-44) in his claim that *Mankind* "was performed in a hall before screens." Even if the unknown author had envisioned an indoor performance, the dramatic substance and meaning of the play (which Southern hardly considers) point to a different social context.

18. My interpretation challenges the assumption of the "decadence" of the piece which has been advocated by scholars like Hardin Craig (e.g., in "Morality Plays and Elizabethan Drama," *Shakespeare Quarterly* 1 [1950]:69), who considered *Mankind* as "a very badly degenerated version of what was once a typical morality." I have argued against this conception at some length in the German version of this book agreeing with D. C. Boughner when he writes: "Obviously the accepted judgment that *Mankind* is an example of the morality in decadence is mere critical perversity" ("Vice, Braggart and Falstaff," *Anglia* 72 [1954]:39). There is less need now to vindicate the play since its remarkably successful revival in Toronto (1966) and since recent criticism has come to emphasize its historical importance (most cogently in the work of David Bevington) as well as the structural qualities and functions of its dramatic images (as by Paula Neuss). See *Medieval Drama*, ed. Denny, pp. 96–99 and 41–67.

19. *Mankind* is easily accessible in most anthologies: J. M. Manly, *Specimens of the Pre-Shaksperean Drama*, vol. 1 (Boston/London, 1897), pp. 315 ff.; J. Q. Adams, *Chief Pre-Shakespearean Dramas* (Boston, 1924), pp. 304 ff.; Alois Brandl, *Quellen des weltlichen Dramas vor Shakespeare* (Strassburg, 1898), pp. 37 ff.; David Bevington, *Medieval Drama* (Boston, 1975), pp. 901–38. I quote from Adams, but supplement from *The Macro Plays*, ed. Mark Eccles (EETS, O.S. 262) (London, 1969), pp. 153–84. I have occasionally glanced at J. S. Farmer's edition in *Early English Dramatists: 'Lost' Tudor Plays* (London, 1907).

20. W. K. Smart, "Some Notes on *Mankind*," *MP* 14 (1916–17):48–55, 306–7.

21. J. Ray, *A Collection of English Proverbs* (1742), p. 55, quoted in Smart, p. 300.

22. Cf. Brandl, p. xxxii; Lauf, p. 12; Adams, p. 304; Smart, "Some Notes on *Mankind*," p. 306. Eccles notes that "Although Pollard thought it was played in the inn yard, it may have been played inside the inn" (p. xlii). For "the real possibility that *Mankind* was taken indoors," see D. M. Bevington's summary in *Medieval Drama*, ed. Denny, pp. 98–99.

23. W. K. Smart, "*Mankind* and the Mumming Plays," *MLN* 32 (1917):21–25.

24. The apparent parallel between *Piers Plowman* and the spade scene in *Mankind* is not convincing proof of any influence, despite M. H. Keiller's suggestion in "The Influence of *Piers Plowman* on the Macro Play of *Mankind*," *PMLA* 26 (1911):339–55.

25. L. W. Cushman, *The Devil and the Vice in the English Dramatic Literature Before Shakespeare* (Halle, 1900), p. 111.

26. These and corresponding references in the text follow Dodsley's *Select Collection of Old English Plays*: Dod., I, 49 should be read as Dodsley's edition, volume 1, page 49.

27. Walter Benjamin, *Ursprung des deutschen Trauerspiels* (Berlin, 1928), p. 175.

28. K. M. Briggs, *The Anatomy of Puck: An Examination of Fairy Beliefs Among Shakespeare's Contemporaries and Successors* (London, 1959); cf. her chapter on "The Fashion for the Miniature," pp. 56–70.

29. *Hamlet*, ed. J. Dover Wilson, "The New Shakespeare" (reprint ed., Cambridge, 1961), p. 276. Lollard heresy, with its attacks on priests, saints, and relics, amply documented by A. G. Dickens, J. A. F. Thomson, and other historians, here finds an echo unmatched in its "foolish" intensity; it is Protestant propaganda via popular Saturnalian release. Hypocrisy's catalogue is worth quoting if only because of its length:

> *Hypocrisy.* ... Under the name of holiness and religion
> That deceived almost all.
> As holy cardinals, holy popes,
> Holy vestments, holy copes,
> Holy hermits and friars,
> Holy priests, holy bishops,
> Holy monks, holy abbots,
> Yea, and all obstinate liars:
> Holy pardons, holy beads,
> Holy saints, holy images,
> With holy, holy blood,
> Holy stocks, holy stones,
> Holy clouts, holy bones;
> Yea, and holy holy wood.

Holy skins, holy bulls,
Holy rochets and cowls,
Holy crouches and staves,
Holy hoods, holy caps,
Holy mitres, holy hats;
Ah good holy holy knaves.
Holy days, holy fastings,
Holy twitching, holy tastings,
Holy visions and sights,
Holy wax, holy lead,
Holy water, holy bread,
To drive away spirits.
Holy fire, holy palm,
Holy oil, holy cream,
And holy ashes also;
Holy brooches, holy rings,
Holy kneeling, holy censings,
And a hundred trim-trams mo.
Holy crosses, holy bells,
Holy relics, holy jewels,
Of mine own invention;
Holy candles, holy tapers,
Holy parchments, holy papers:
Had not you a holy son?   (Dod., II, 65–66)

31. Henry Chettle, *Kind-Hartes Dreame*/William Kemp, *Nine Daies Wonder,* ed. G. B. Harrison (London, 1923), p. 7.

32. The influence of the classical source must in no way be denied, but the oft-repeated assertion that "the theme of madness . . . goes back all the way to Seneca's *Hercules furens*" (Wilhelm Berghäuser, *Die Darstellung des Wahnsinns im englischen Drama bis zum Ende des 18. Jahrhunderts,* Dissertation [Giessen, 1914], p. 5) appears, in the exclusiveness of its claim, to be as one-sided as E. R. Curtius' treatment of related *topoi,* such as "poetic furor" as unchanging emanations of the "Greek Spirit" (*Europäische Literatur und Lateinisches Mittelalter* [Bern, 1948], pp. 469–70). The exaggeration of Seneca's influence has been brilliantly refuted by G. K. Hunter ("Seneca and the Elizabethans: A Case-Study in Influence," *Shakespeare Survey* 20 [1969]:17–26), who has shown that the "tradition of the vernacular drama, unlike that of the neo-classical drama, was already a theatrical tradition." Hence, Seneca "could contribute nothing more than occasional sententiae to this stage-tradition." What is more, the preoccupation with classical sources overlooks the social context as well as the related fact, first demonstrated to my knowledge by John Corbin (*The Elizabethan Hamlet* [London/New York, 1895], esp. p. 29), that "the mad [and potentially tragic] scenes had a comic aspect now ignored." This comic component was part of a native "eldritch tradition" that was continued in the Vice's unity of horror and laughter. To disregard this tradition as one of the constituent factors in Hamlet's madness can be seriously misleading, as when Hamlet—as was so common in late Victorian criticism—is considered strictly in terms of neuropathology. L. B. Wright points in a better direction when he considers madness as a source of Elizabethan entertainment ("Madmen as Vaudeville Performers on the Elizabethan Stage," *JEGPh* 30 [1931]:48–54)—a point of view that need not preclude, but can in fact complement, a view of madness in its dramatic role as "an isolating device" (J. T. McMullen, "Madness and the Isolation of Characters in Elizabethan and Early Stuart Drama," *SP* 48 [1951]:206). The same author's dissertation, not available to me, examines *The Functions or Uses of Madness in Elizabethan Drama Between 1590 and 1630* [North Carolina, 1948]. Madness, according to the abstract, is viewed as a "protection for satire.") See Petra Böse's *"Wahnsinn" in Shakespeares Dramen: Ein Unterschung zu Bedeutungsgeschichte und Wortgebrauch.* Vol. 10 ("Studien zur engl. Philologie," N. F.), as well as Sidney Thomas, *The Antic Hamlet and Richard III* (New York, 1943), pp. 3–7.

33. Gilbert Murray, "Hamlet and Orestes," *The Classical Tradition in Poetry* (London, 1927), esp. pp. 227–35.

34. Francis Fergusson, *The Idea of a Theater* (Princeton, 1949), p. 114.

35. L. L. Schücking, *Die Charakterprobleme bei Shakespeare* (Leipzig, 1932), p. 170. With the modification of the sources "the motive for the Prince's pretensions to madness was omitted" (*Hamlet*, English and German, ed. L. L. Schücking, "Sammlung Dieterich" [Leipzig, 1941], p. xxx). On the other hand, Hamlet is not wholly identifiable with the melancholic type. For instance, his sarcastic attitude toward women cannot be seen exclusively as having derived from the "woman-hating rationalizing melancholic" (p. 188) since the Vice's enmity toward women and marriage, as Cushman shows (p. 87), furnished a powerful dramatic precedent that had a continuity up to Iago and Richard III, and, so, up to Hamlet.

36. M. P. Tilley, *A Dictionary of the Proverbs in England in the Sixteenth and Seventeenth Centuries* (Ann Arbor, 1950). It is noteworthy that Hamlet alone is given more proverbs than appear in the whole of *The Comedy of Errors* (which contains fifty-three) or *Titus Andronicus* (which contains sixty-three). Cf. Horst Weinstock, *Die Funktion elisabethanischer Sprichwörter bei Shakespeare* (Heidelberg, 1966). On Hamlet's images, see M. M. Morozov, "The Individualization of Shakespeare's Characters Through Imagery," *Shakespeare Survey* 2 (1949):93–101.

37. M. M. Mahood, *Shakespeare's Wordplay* (London, 1957), p. 166. On the following cf. William Farnham (*The Medieval Heritage of Elizabethan Tragedy* [reprint ed., Oxford, 1956], p. 436), who notes Hamlet's "capacity for vulgar, sometimes bawdy clowning." See also the same author's more recent *The Shakespearean Grotesque: Its Genesis and Transformations* (Oxford, 1971), where, in his chapter on "Hamlet among Fools" (pp. 97–127), he says that "there is in [Hamlet] a very effective gravedigger" (p. 109).

38. L. C. Knights, *Drama and Society in the Age of Jonson* (Harmondsworth, 1962), pp. 261–74.

39. As does, e. g., Sister Miriam Joseph, *Shakespeare's Use of the Arts of Language* (New York, 1947), p. 171.

40. Here my argument must be tentative in the face of an obvious lacuna in Shakespeare criticism. The pioneer work by Leopold Wurth (*Das Wortspiel bei Shakespeare* [Vienna/Leipzig, 1895]) offers little in regard to the structure, function and origin of the pre-Shakespearean pun. Miriam Joseph (*Shakespeare's Use of the Arts of Language*, pp. 164–73) views wordplay only in relation to Renaissance rhetoric. Helge Kökeritz (*Shakespeare's Pronunciation* [New Haven, 1953]) makes accessible an extraordinary amount of new material, but primarily considers "The Homonymic Pun as Evidence of Pronunciation" (pp. 53 ff.). Only Lyly is mentioned in connection with the pre-Shakespearean pun. M. M. Mahood, in her study of *Shakespeare's Wordplay*, is concerned with the poetic and dramatic functions of wordplay; she finds in it "a valuable means of access to the heart of the drama" (p. 55), but views the ultimate sources of wordplay in depth psychology ("punning releases a desire to talk nonsense which was suppressed in the nursery," p. 30), as does Michel Grivelet ("Shakespeare as 'Corrupter of Words,'" *Shakespeare Survey* 16 [1963]: 70–76). To be sure, such an approach appears less schematic than the modern typologies which posit "the thirty-two kinds of triple context puns which must exist" (James Brown, "Eight Types of Pun," *PMLA* 71 [1956]:23). If these classifications appear excessive, the basic division into "semantic" and "homonymic" puns seems to be more helpful (Kökeritz, p. 57; cf. also Wurth, p. 8), partly because it parallels the basic distinction between the semantic and phonetic levels of wordplay. The latter can be separated, according to Wurth (p. 108), into play with rhyme, alliteration, assonance, and play with word distortions, which already, at least in part, must be considered along with semantic puns, and which I term here—insofar as it sets the literal against the metaphorical—"image-play." I will add only one other to these traditional concepts: that of the "jingle," which describes a "foolish" or nonsensical play with sound and alliteration. This relates to Kökeritz' definition ("the *jingle*, a wordplay in which neither meaning nor identity of sound but rather the effective balancing of like-sounding words are of primary concern," p. 58) but is limited—in contrast to Kökeritz' list (pp. 68–85)—to nonsensical sound-play with alliteration, rhyme, and vowel gradation. There is a printed West German dissertation that defines this element under the larger term ("Oberbegriff") of *Sprachspiel*; see Norbert Kohl, *Das Wortspiel in der Shakespeareschen Komödie: Studien zur Interdependenz von verbalem und aktionalem Spiel in den frühen Komödien und den späten Stücken*, Dissertation (Frankfurt a. M, 1966), p. 62.

41. T. W. Baldwin, *Shakspere's Small Latine and Lesse Greeke*, vol. 2 (Urbana, Ill., 1944), pp. 680, 670.
42. Joseph, p. 165.
43. For instance, F. P. Wilson, "Shakespeare and the Diction of Common Life," *Proceedings of the British Academy* 27 (London, 1941).
44. I have taken this further in some suggestions "Towards a Historical Approach to Shakespeare's Imagery," in my *Structure and Society in Literary History* (Charlottesville, Va., 1976).
45. See Mahood, pp. 31, 52: "Words such as great, high, blood, state and grace have restricted meanings of social approbation, but Shakespeare undermines their social prestige by recalling for us their generalized meanings or other restricted senses which supply a critical overtone."
46. See preceding note.
47. A. W. von Schlegel, "Uber dramatische Kunst und Literatur," 27th lecture, *Sämtliche Werke*, ed. Eduard Böcking, vol. 7 (Leipzig, 1846-47), pp. 193-94.
48. Robert Petsch, *Das deutsche Volksrätsel* (Strassburg, 1917), pp. 16 ff.
49. Ibid., pp. 16, 45.
50. Cf. *Tarlton's Jests and News out of Purgatory* (London, 1844), pp. 6, 10, 11, 15, 18, among others. To set and resolve riddles was the most popular festival game in the Roman Saturnalia; see M. P. Nilsson, "Saturnalia," *Paulys Real-Enzyklopädie der classischen Altertumswissenschaft*, new ed., 2nd series, vol. 3 (Stuttgart, 1921), col. 204.
51. See C. S. Felver, *Robert Armin, Shakespeare's Fool: A Biographical Essay* (Kent State University, 1961), pp. 37, 28; cf. Wurth, pp. 190-91.
52. See Alois Brandl, "Shakespeares *Book of merry Riddles* und die anderen Rätselbücher seiner Zeit," *Shakespeare Jahrbuch* 42 (1906):64; cf. pp. 1, 6. For suggestions on the sociology of wordplay see Wurth, pp. 187-88, 192, 194; Kökeritz, p. 55; Kenneth Muir, "The Uncomic Pun," *The Cambridge Journal* 3 (1949-50):483. On the national reception of the clowning tradition, see Kempe's *Nine Daies Wonder*, pp. 10, 12, 14-15, 17, 22-23.
53. See Wurth, p. 153.
54. A. C. Cawley, ed., *The Wakefield Pageants in the Towneley Cycle* (Manchester, 1958), p. 91. Garcio belongs to "the same oppressed class of inferior servants as . . . Slawpase in the *Prima Pastorum*, and Froward in the *Coliphizachio*" (p. 106). All quotations from *Mactacio Abel* are from this edition.
55. There is as yet no comprehensive study of the "cheeky boy" or Garcio type. His relationship to Jack Finney is noted by E. K. Chambers, *The English Folk-Play* (Oxford, 1933), p. 170; Arthur Brown, "Folklore Elements in the Medieval Drama," *Folk-Lore* 63 (1952):68; R. J. E. Tiddy, *The Mummers' Play* (Oxford, 1923), pp. 96-97, 111; Irena Janicka, *The Comic Elements in the English Mystery Plays Against the Cultural Background (particularly Art)* (Poznan, 1962), pp. 93 ff. Cf. O. M. Busby, *Studies in the Development of the Fool in the Elizabethan Drama* (London, 1923), pp. 19-20; Robert Withington, "The Ancestry of the 'Vice,'" *Speculum* 7 (1932):525-29; and the same author's "The Development of the Vice," *Essays in Memory of Barrett Wendell* (Cambridge, Mass., 1926), esp. pp. 161-62, among others. On the relationship between Garcio in Wakefield and Brewbarret in York, cf. Margaret Trusler, "The York *Sacrificium Cayme and Abell*," *PMLA* 49 (1934):956-59; M. G. Frampton, "The Brewbarret Interpolation," *PMLA* 52 (1937):895-900, which views Brewbarret as "a late product of the York school of comedy" (p. 900) and argues, with Margaret Trusler, against the older interpretation of Millicent Carey (*The Wakefield Group in the Towneley Cycle* [Göttingen/Baltimore, 1930], pp. 215 ff.) whereby the York scenes were believed to be based on an original version at Wakefield. This would indirectly confirm the folklore origins and the corresponding wide dissemination of the Garcio-Brewbarret type.
56. Quoted in Ludwig Wirth, *Die Oster- und Passionsspiele bis zum XVI. Jahrhundert* (Halle, 1889), p. 206. The German oil merchant's play helps to illuminate some comparable elements in the genealogy of the Garcio-Rubin type: the same rapport with the audience, the song and direct address (p. 184), as well as a similar gesture of defiance against gentlemen and the oil merchant (p. 181), who, for his part, like Jack Finney's doctor, has traveled far and "makes the blind speak." Cf. C. Reuling, *Die komische Figur in den wichtigsten deutschen Dramen bis zum Ende des 17. Jahrhunderts*, Dissertation, Zürich (Stuttgart, 1890), pp. 13, 27-28.

57. Wirth, p. 180.

58. Quotations in the text are taken from *The Digby Plays* (EETS, E. S. LXX), ed. F. J. Furnivall (London, 1896).

59. Wirth, p. 175.

60. Quotations in the text are from *Chief Pre-Shakespearean Dramas*, ed. J. Q. Adams (Boston, 1924).

61. Thomas Lupton, *All for Money*, ed. Ernst Vogel, *Shakespeare Jahrbuch* 40 (1904), ll. 1008–9.

62. Cf. Adams' comment on line 461 of his text.

63. Colle's enumeration of the sicknesses healed by his master "savours very much of the list in the Mummers' Play" (Chambers, *The English Folk-Play*, p. 170). Rubin's mockery of his master's skill corresponds to this; cf. Wirth, pp. 175 ff.; Reuling, p. 12.

64. G. W. F. Hegel, *Ästhetik* (Berlin, 1955), pp. 1079, 1039–40.

65. Citations in the text are from *Specimens of the Pre-Shaksperean Drama*, ed. J. M. Manly (London/Boston, 1897).

66. Citations follow Vogel's edition, see above n. 61.

67. Citations follow Brandl's edition, see above n. 19.

68. Cf. Kökeritz, pp. 56–57. Freud's interpretation of wordplay is, no doubt, illuminating, and sometimes profoundly so; but how relevant is the psychological approach to a collective tradition antedating the rise of individualism?

69. J. A. F. Thomson, *The Later Lollards, 1440–1520* (Oxford, 1965), p. 33.

70. Cited in ibid., p. 251.

71. Cited by Douglas Hewett, "The very Pompes of the Divell: Popular and Folk Elements in Elizabethan and Jacobean Drama," *RES* 25 (1949):13.

72. This touches on the links between the Vice and the jig, in which "the fool was conventionally the cleverest dancer." This allowed for "the triumph of the fool over those of social standing"—at least in wooing (C. R. Baskerville, *The Elizabethan Jig and Related Song Drama* [Chicago, 1929], pp. 355, 253, 256; on the nonsense element in the jig, cf. ibid., pp. 60 ff.). The origin and background of these links have hardly been explored; but for evidence of "three plain examples of the use of the term 'the Vice' in connection with folk games," see F. H. Mares, "The Origin of the Figure called 'the Vice' in Tudor Drama," *Huntington Library Quarterly* 22 (1958): esp. pp. 21–25, as well as his important, though unpublished B Litt thesis, "The Origin and Development of the Figure Called the 'Vice' in Tudor Drama" (Lincoln College, Oxford, 1954), pp. 49, 53–54, which goes beyond the suggestions of scholars like R. J. E. Tiddy or Robert Withington, but tends to underrate the allegorical heritage of the Vice and the way it actually seems to thrive on the grotesque contradictions of Christian orthodoxy and pagan heresy.

73. Except of course in song, where the beautiful "hey, and a ho, and a hey nonino" (*As You Like It* V, 3, 15) or Ophelia's "Hey non nonny, nonny, hey nonny" (*Hamlet* IV, 5, 162) continue the popular tradition, but to a vastly different poetic effect.

74. Wolfgang Clemen, *Kommentar zu Shakespeares Richard III* (Göttingen, 1957), p. 175. This "diminishing of the unrealistic aspects of the aside" is here considered as Shakespeare's original achievement. In this connection, Clemen and his school have (for all their valuable contributions) somewhat overemphasized the impact of rhetoric and the Senecan tradition. See especially the work of Schmid, Gruner, Förg, and others, on which I have commented in *Shakespeare und die Tradition des Volkstheaters* (Berlin, 1967), pp. 485 ff.

75. The wide-branching family tree of the Elizabethan clown and fool is outlined by O. M. Busby (pp. 8–24), who greatly overestimated, however, the direct influences of the "Sottie" and the Feast of Fools. On the complex genealogy of the fool, cf. Enid Welsford, *The Fool: His Social and Literary History* (New York, 1961), and the more recent study by William Willeford of *The Fool and His Scepter: A Study in Clowns and Jesters and their Audience* (Evanston, Ill., 1969).

76. F. J. Furnivall and A. W. Pollard, eds., *The Macro Plays*, (EETS, E. S. XCI) (London, 1904), p. xvii.

77. *Phillip Stubbes's Anatomy of Abuses*, ed. F. J. Furnivall, part 1 (London, 1877–82), pp. 141, 143.

78. Cushman, p. 76.

79. L. B. Wright, "Social Aspects of Some Belated Moralities," *Anglia* 42 (1930):111. On

the continuation of the morality in Ben Jonson, primarily in his "humours," cf. C. R. Baskerville, *English Elements in Jonson's Early Comedy*, University of Texas Bull., 178 (Austin, 1911), esp. pp. 17–42. Cf. L. C. Knights, *Drama and Society in the Age of Jonson* (Harmondsworth, 1962), pp. 179–99.

80. For the unity of "merriment" and "satire" in Shakespeare, cf. O. J. Campbell, *Shakespeare's Satire* (New York, 1943), p. 23.

81. Bevington, *From 'Mankind' to Marlowe*, pp. 80 ff.

82. All preceding citations from Bernard Spivack, *Shakespeare and the Allegory of Evil* (New York, 1958), pp. 109, 192, 186, 110, 189, 199, 168, 339, 405, 178, 286, 303. Behind such inflation of the word "homiletic" there is, of course, the authority of G. R. Owst, but perhaps Spivack overlooks the fact that Owst—who is not concerned with the dramaturgy of the Vice—nonetheless remarks about this allegorical figure that "No doubt, it was not the Bible in the first instance, but some deeper and more ancient racial attachment to folk-lore and pagan demonology that gave rise to these spiritual abstractions, and endowed them with a history of their own" (*Literature and Pulpit in Medieval England* [Cambridge, 1933], p. 86; cf. pp. 526–47). But then the homiletic approach to the Vice dominated well before G. R. Owst and Bernard Spivack (See e. g., T. E. Allison, "The Paternoster Play and the Origin of the Vices," *PMLA* 39 [1924]: 789–804).

83. Spivack, pp. 122, 199.

84. Otto Rommel, *Die Alt-Wiener Volkskömodie* (Vienna, 1952), p. 157.

85. From the Anti-Martin pamphlet *A Whip for an Ape* (1589); cf. John Lyly, *The Complete Works*, ed. R. W. Bond, vol. 3 (Oxford, 1902), p. 419.

86. Günter Reichert, *Die Entwicklung und die Funktion der Nebenhandlung in der Tragödie vor Shakespeare* (Tübingen, 1966), p. 9. This whole context might provide a historical perspective on the problem of Shakespeare's "complementarity" on which Norman Rabkin has written so perceptively in *Shakespeare and the Common Understanding* (London/New York, 1967).

87. Clemen, *Kommentar zu Shakespeares Richard III*, p. 24.

V

THE ELIZABETHAN DRAMA

1. The following sections draw on my essay "The Soul of the Age: Towards a Historical Approach to Shakespeare," *Shakespeare in a Changing World*, ed. Arnold Kettle (New York, 1964):17–42.

2. Cf. the evidence I have assembled in *Drama und Wirklichkeit in der Shakespearezeit* (Halle, 1958). For some helpful synthesis see Leonard Goldstein's unprinted *Habilitation* dissertation "George Chapman: Aspects of Decadence in Early Seventeenth Century Drama," Humboldt University (Berlin, 1965).

3. A. L. Rowse, *The England of Elizabeth*, vol. 1, "The Structure of Society" (London, 1950), p. 243; J. B. Black, *The Reign of Elizabeth: 1558–1603* (Oxford, 1949), p. 226.

4. *Harrison's Description of England in Shakespeare's Youth*, ed. F. J. Furnivall, part 1 (London, 1877–1908), pp. 259–60. Harrison, in the first edition of his *Description* (1577), had characteristically qualified the absolute statement of 1587: "the ground of the parish is *often* gotten vp..." (cf. on this ibid., p. 260, ed. n. 1).

5. *Phillip Stubbes's Anatomy of Abuses*, ed. F. J. Furnivall, part 1 (London, 1877–82), p. 149. Cf. C. L. Barber, *Shakespeare's Festive Comedy: A Study of Dramatic Form and its Relation to Social Custom* (Princeton, 1959), pp. 22–23.

6. The statute resulted from a compromise between the strictly conservative draft of the Privy Council and the progressive amendments of the lower house; see S. T. Bindoff, "The Making of The Statute of Artificers," *Elizabethan Government and Society*, ed. S. T. Bindoff, et. al. (London, 1961), pp. 56–94. Above quotation from Lujo Brentano, *Geschichte der wirtschaftlichen Entwicklung Englands*, vol. 1 (Jena, 1927–29), p. 282; W. J. Ashley, *An Introduction to English Economic History and Theory*, vol. 1, part 2 (London, 1892), pp. 101–2.

7. W. H. B. Court, *The Rise of the Midland Industries: 1600–1838* (Oxford, 1938), p. 51; J.

U. Nef, *The Rise of the British Coal Industry*, vol. 1 (London, 1932), pp. 19 ff., 123 ff., 165 ff.; Paul Sweezy, *Monopoly and Competition in the English Coal Trade, 1550-1850* (Cambridge, 1938). H. R. Schubert, *History of the British Iron and Steel Industry (450 B. C. -1775)* (London, 1957), p. 157; Jürgen Kuczynski, *Die Geschichte der Lage der Arbeiter unter dem Kapitalismus*, vol. 22, ("England: 1640-1760") (Berlin, 1964), pp. 54-67.

8. Kuczynski, p. 79; W. G. Hoskins ("The Rebuilding of Rural England, 1570-1640," *Past and Present* 4 [1953]:44-59) speaks of "the Great Rebuilding" and "the Housing Revolution," especially after 1570; cf. the same author's *The Midland Peasant: The Economic and Social History of a Leicestershire Village* (London, 1957), esp. pp. 149, 285-99.

9. S. Kramer, *The English Craft Guilds: Studies in their Progress and Decline* (New York, 1927), pp. 74, 69, 72-73; cf. E. K. Chambers, *The Mediaeval Stage*, vol. 2 (Oxford, 1903), p. 110 (hereafter cited as *Md. St.*).

10. Salter, p. 50.

11. See J. Buxton, *Sir Philip Sidney and the English Renaissance* (London, 1954); E. Rosenberg, *Leicester: Patron of Letters* (New York, 1955); E. H. Miller, *The Professional Writer in Elizabethan England* (Cambridge, Mass., 1959), chap. 4. The position of the new aristocracy is well presented by Paul Siegel, *Shakespearean Tragedy and the Elizabethan Compromise* (New York, 1957), pp. 12 ff.

12. W. G. Zeeveld, *Foundations of Tudor Policy* (Cambridge, Mass., 1948), p. 6. See also F. Caspari, *Humanism and the Social Order in Tudor England* (Chicago, 1954), pp. 132 ff.

13. Karl Marx and Friedrich Engels, *Revolution in Spain* (New York, 1939), p. 25.

14. *James Harrington's Oceana*, ed. S. B. Liljegren (Heidelberg, 1924), p. 49. A. T. Rubenstein, *The Great Tradition in English Literature: From Shakespeare to Shaw* (New York, 1953), p. 7; Andrew Browning, *The Age of Elizabeth* (London, 1928), p. 197; J. R. Seeley, *Growth of English Policy*, vol. 1 (Cambridge, 1895), p. 183. For a more detailed discussion of the Tudor compromise in legislation and religion, see my *Drama und Wirklichkeit in der Shakespearezeit* (Halle, 1958), pp. 34-139.

15. Cf. Wilfrid Mellers, "Words and Music in Elizabethan England," *The Age of Shakespeare*, ed. Boris Ford (Harmondsworth, 1956), p. 387: "These various media and conventions involved different types of musical experience directed towards different types of audience. Yet the strength of Elizabethan musical culture consists in the fact that these different audiences were not mutually exclusive . . . folk-songs could be used by learned composers in their motets and masses without any feeling of self-consciousness. The learned composer accepted folk-song as *his* music, not as the property of a special class called 'the people.'" Cf. E. H. Meyer, *English Chamber Music* (London, 1946). On related trends in architecture and the arts, cf. Eric Mercer, *English Art: 1553-1625* (Oxford, 1962).

16. See G. W. Wallace, *The First London Theatre: Materials for a History* (Lincoln, Neb., 1913) passim; J. Q. Adams, *Shakespearean Playhouses* (Boston, 1917), pp. 27-74; E. K. Chambers, *The Elizabethan Stage*, vol. 2 (Oxford, 1923), pp. 383-400, esp. 387 ff. (hereafter cited as *El. St.*). Against "the covetousness of Alleyn" (Adams, p. 63) stood "such hopes of great gain" (p. 40) that an embittered commercial war was unavoidable.

17. Cf. T. F. Ordish, *Early London Theatres* (London, 1894), pp. 35-40.

18. Alfred Harbage, *Shakespeare's Audience* (New York/London, 1964), p. 41.

19. Stubbes, part 1, pp. 141, 144. The singularly forceful lingering of the blasphemous effect of theatrical performances ("scoffingly, flowtingly, and iybingly") is significant. On the Puritan polemic see E. N. S. Thompson, *The Controversy between the Puritans and the Stage* (New York, 1903); on its relative justification see Douglas Hewitt, "The very Pompes of the Divell: Popular and Folk Elements in Elizabethan and Jacobean Drama," *RES* 25 (1949): 13 ff.

20. *El. St.*, 4:278, 283-84, 287-88, 295 ff.

21. *El. St.*, 4:300.

22. *Documents Relating to the Office of the Revels in the Time of Queen Elizabeth*, ed. A. Feuillerat (Louvain, 1908), p. 409. Cf. C. J. Sisson, *Le goût public et le théâtre élisabéthain jusqu' à la mort de Shakespeare* (Dijon, n.d.), p. 49; Alfred Harbage, *Shakespeare and the Rival Traditions* (New York, 1952), pp. 19, 116.

23. Armin-G Kuckhoff, *Das Drama William Shakespeares* ("Schriften zur Theaterwissenschaft," vol. 3) (Berlin, 1964), p. 822.

24. *The Selected Works of Robert Crowley*, ed. J. M. Cowper (EETS, 1872), p. 132.

25. From Laneham's letter: see its discussion by M. C. Bradbrook, *The Rise of the Common Player* (London, 1962), pp. 141–61.

26. *The Complete Works of John Lyly*, ed. R. W. Bond, vol. 3 (Oxford, 1902), p. 115.

27. Scoloker's remark (1604), cited by E. K. Chambers, *William Shakespeare: A Study of Facts and Problems*, vol. 2 (Oxford, 1930), p. 215.

28. Harbage, *Shakespeare's Audience*, p. 144; similarly C. J. Sisson, H. S. Bennett, and more recent writers on Shakespeare's audience. But Marxist critics have done well to point to the contradictions involved in this unity: cf. Anselm Schlösser (on the populace in Shakespeare) in *ZAA* (1956), 4:148–71; Leonard Goldstein (on Elizabethan acting) in *Bull. New York Publ. Libr.* 62 (1958): 330–49; Alexander Anikst (on Shakespeare as playwright of the people) in *Shakespearovski Sbornik* (Moscow, 1958), pp. 7–44.

29. Crowley, p. 11.

30. *Harrison's Description of England*, ed. F. J. Furnivall, part 1 (London, 1877), p. 132.

31. Cf. *El. St.*, 4:291.

32. *The Works of Christopher Marlowe*, ed. C. F. Tucker Brooke (Oxford, 1910): *Faustus*, ll. 104–5; *Tamburlaine*, part 1, ll. 872–76. Future references are cited from this edition.

33. F. L. Lucas, *Seneca and Elizabethan Tragedy* (Cambridge, 1922), p. 103.

34. This is based on my more detailed discussion of "Thomas Nashe and Elizabethan Humanism," in *Filológiai Közlöny* (Budapest, 1962), 7:285–99, with English summary in *Supplément*, pp. 40–44. The above Nashe quotations are taken from *Works*, ed. R. B. McKerrow (London, 1904–10), 2:64; 1:37, 22.

35. Cited according to *Tarlton's Jests and News out of Purgatory* (London, 1844), p. xix; on "Greenesse," cf. *Elizabethan Critical Essays*, ed. G. G. Smith, vol. 2 (Oxford, 1904), p. 431.

36. Still, it should be borne in mind that Marlowe's treatment of Faustus was already part of a larger context—that of the popular culture of the English Renaissance. Consequently, the distance between Johann Faust, the impious sorcerer of the Frankfurt *Historia* (1587), and the Marlovian Renaissance figure was already narrowed considerably in the *English Historie of the Damnable Life and Deserved Death of Doctor Iohn Faustus*. In the German *Historia*, the hero's mind is characterized as follows: "Daneben hat er auch einen thummen, unsinnigen unnd hoffertigen Kopf gehabt . . ." (ed. W. Braune [Halle, 1878], p. 12). In the English prose version the passage reads: "Faustus fell into such frenzies and deepe cogitations that . . ." etc. Where the German narrator reproves his arrogance, the English adaptation says, "his speculation was so wonderful!" (cf. *The Historie of the Damnable Life . . .* , ed. H. Logeman [Amsterdam, 1900], pp. 2–3).

37. Edmund Creeth (*Mankynde in Shakespeare* [Athens, Ga., 1976], p. 115) tends to minimize "the obvious fossils of archaic technique preserved in *Faustus*" but heavily emphasizes the "recrudescence of moral play structure in Shakespeare" as an "impulse to justify the popular dramatic tradition" against "coterie playwrights like Marston and Webster" (pp. 169–70). But is not Webster's Flamineo alone a most complex and devastatingly original response to the popular Vice? See my comments on Harbage (*Shakespeare and the Rival Traditions*) who Creeth here follows rather uncritically.

38. For Meres, cf. *Elizabethan Critical Essays*, 2:318; for Dryden, *Of Dramatic Poesy and Other Critical Essays*, 1:258; for Rymer, *Critical Essays of the Seventeenth Century*, 2:234; for Pope, *Eighteenth Century Essays on Shakespeare*, ed. D. N. Smith (Oxford, 1963), p. 46.

39. This differentiation is adopted from Tawney's analysis of the muster in Gloucester (1608). Cf. Harbage (*Shakespeare's Audience*, p. 54). See Christopher Hill, *The Century of Revolution, 1603–1714* (Edinburgh, 1961), pp. 17f., where Gregory King's data is helpfully discussed. Lawrence Stone, in *The Crisis of the Aristocracy: 1558–1641* (Oxford, 1965), distinguishes two large "lower groups below the level of the gentry" (p. 51) among which a good deal of mobility should be assumed.

40. *A Second and Third Blast*, quoted in W. C. Hazlitt, *The English Drama and Stage Under the Tudor and Stuart Princes: 1543–1664* (London, 1869), p. 139.

41. H. C. White, *Social Criticism in Popular Religious Literature of the Sixteenth Century* (New York, 1944). Above quotation from Engels, *Der Deutsche Bauernkrieg*; Marx and Engels, *Werke*, vol. 7 (Berlin, 1959 ff.), pp. 338, 344. Of these "unlettered masses" (which, according to Lawrence Stone [p. 51], "probably comprised well over half the population") it is possible to say that they "had not lost touch with the treasures of popular culture handed

down by oral tradition, folklore, legends. . . . Nothing came amiss to them that had gone into the ballads, the songs, the pageants, the old wives' tales, the school horn-books, the almanacks, the sermons, the chapbooks, proverbs, anecdotes, and jests." (Henri Fluchère, *Shakespeare and the Elizabethans*, trans. Guy Hamilton [New York, 1956], p. 23.)

42. Cf. *Tarlton's Jests and News out of Purgatory*, pp. viii–x; A. H. Thorndike, *Shakespeare's Theater* (New York, 1916), p. 375.

43. Cf. E. W. Talbert, *Elizabethan Drama and Shakespeare's Early Plays* (Chapel Hill, 1963), pp. 342–43. The attitudes and ideas involved in the origin and development of the Elizabethan fool are, as Barbara Könneker (*Wesen und Wandlung der Narrensidee im Zeitalter des Humanismus* [Wiesbaden, 1966]) demonstrates, not derived from humanism, but from beneath: from jest books and folk customs (pp. 361–74), not from Erasmus.

44. C. R. Baskerville, *The Elizabethan Jig and Related Song Drama* (Chicago, 1929), p. 28.

45. Cf. W. J. Lawrence, "On the Underrated Genius of Dick Tarleton," *Speeding Up Shakespeare* (London, 1937), p. 38.

46. Baskerville, *The Elizabethan Jig*, p. 101. To the above excerpt, cf. pp. 28, 47, 61–62, 68, 164–65.

47. *Tarlton's Jests and News out of Purgatory*, pp. 24–25.

48. On S. L. Bethell's interpretation (*Shakespeare and the Popular Dramatic Tradition* [London, 1944]), see my critique above.

49. Annemarie Schöne, "Die weisen Narren Shakespeares und ihre Vorfahren," *Jahrbuch für Ästhetik und allgemeine Kunstwissenschaft* 5 (1960):207; cf. also O. M. Busby, *Studies in the Development of the Fool in the Elizabethan Drama* (London, 1923), p. 29.

50. A. P. Rossiter, *Angel with Horns and other Shakespeare Lectures* (London, 1961), pp. 52, 63. Rossiter complements recent Marxist interpretations of *Henry V*; cf. Anselm Schlösser, "Der Widerstreit von Patriotismus und Humanismus in *Heinrich V*," *ZAA* 12 (1964):244–256; Zdeněk Stříbrný, "*Henry V* and History," *Shakespeare in a Changing World*, pp. 84–101.

51. Rossiter, *Angel with Horns*, p. 286.

52. J. Dover Wilson, *The Fortunes of Falstaff* (Cambridge, 1964), p. 39.

53. Lawrence, "On the Underrated Genius of Dick Tarleton," pp. 18, 29. Above quotation from J. A. Bryant, "Shakespeare's Falstaff and the Mantle of Dick Tarlton," *SP* 51 (1954):151. Bryant, to be sure, overlooks the incommensurable girth of Falstaff, which was derived from the native Lord of Misrule, the blasphemous Vice, as well as the classical *miles gloriosus*. Cf. on this, Dover Wilson's study of Falstaff (p. 20), D. C. Boughner's "Vice, Braggart and Falstaff," *Anglia* 72 (1954): 61, as well as James Monaghan, "Falstaff and his Forbears," *SP* 18 (1921):353–61.

54. Joseph Hall, *Virgidemiarum* (1597), cited according to Lawrence, p. 31.

55. The popularity of charms and spells and related superstitious beliefs is only one example of the importance of lower myth in everyday life. Cf. Felix Grendon, "The Anglo-Saxon Charms," *American Folklore* 22 (1909) 84 (April–June):105–237; Oswald Cockayne, *Leechdoms, Wortcunning, and Starcraft of Early England* (London, 1864).

56. Marx, introduction to *Kritik der politischen Ökonomie*, p. 269. The comparison between ancient myth and that in the work of Shakespeare is implied but not developed by Marx. It is noteworthy that one of the most popular humanists of Shakespeare's time was well aware of the parallel. Thomas Nashe (1592) saw the figures of popular myth—"the Robbin-goodfellowes, Elfes, Fairies, Hobgoblins of our latter age"—as the equivalent of that "which . . . the fantastical world of Greece ycleped Fawnes, Satyres, Dryades and Hama-dryades." Cf. Thomas Nashe, *Works*, ed. R. B. McKerrow, vol. 1 (London, 1904–10), p. 347.

57. K. M. Briggs, *The Anatomy of Puck: An Examination of Fairy Beliefs among Shakespeare's Contemporaries and Successors* (London, 1959), p. 6: "Various things contributed to make the late Elizabethan times our great period of fairy literature, but the rise of the yeoman writer was perhaps chief among them." Cf. pp. 17 ff. Further, M. W. Latham, *The Elizabethan Fairies: The Fairies of Folklore and the Fairies of Shakespeare* (New York, 1950), p. 14: "the time of the greatest flourishing of the fairies in literature extended approximately from the years 1570 to 1625." Similarly, Alfred Nutt, *The Fairy Mythology of Shakespeare* (London, 1900), p. 2, places the high point in "the wonderful half-century: 1580–1630." On the evolution of the role of the middle class author from about 1580, cf. E. H. Miller, *The Professional Writer in Elizabethan England* (Cambridge, Mass., 1959), pp. 8 ff.

58. Cf. Latham, pp. 227-28, 258. On the fairies as "peasant deities," cf. Nutt, pp. 8 ff. In contrast to Briggs and others Latham does not consider Robin Goodfellow as a fairy. Philippson (pp. 74-78) characterizes Puck, and also Hob and Robin, as goblins, but notes that the Celtic belief in small, underground sprites, both good and evil, is closely related to the Germanic belief in elves and indeed is hardly to be differentiated therefrom. In the absence of a definitive and truly satisfying study of English folklore, imprecision in terminology is difficult to avoid.

59. Quoted from Tell-Trothes New-Yeares Gift, ed. F. J. Furnivall (London, 1876), p. 3. The extent to which the appearance of Robin Goodfellow could arouse the expectations of an audience is evident in the opening sentence of this work: "I Marry, sir, now you looke as if you expected newes: me thinks I see your eares open to heare what Robin good fellow will tel you; . . . ." The ballad character Tom Telltruth was also associated with nonsense and satire; cf. Baskerville, The Elizabethan Jig, p. 62, n. 3.

60. Tell-Trothes New-Yeares Gift, pp. 38, 45.

61. Tarlton's Jests and News out of Purgatory, p. 55.

62. Baskerville, The Elizabethan Jig, pp. 92-93, 99; cf. Talbert, p. 337.

63. John Brand, Observations on the Popular Antiquities of Great Britain, rev. and greatly enlarged by Henry Ellis, vol. 2 (London, 1848), p. 509. Cf. also J. O. Halliwell, Illustrations of the Fairy Mythology of A Midsummer Night's Dream (London, 1845), p. 165. On Puck, cf. T. F. Thiselton Dyer, Folk-Lore of Shakespeare (London, 1883), pp. 5-8; more recently, Dorelies Kersten, "Shakespeares Puck," Shakespeare Jahrbuch 98 (1962):189-200.

64. According to Ben Jonson's Love Restored; cf. G. L. Kittredge, "The Friar's Lantern and Friar Rush," PMLA 15 (1900):415-41, especially p. 426, n. 1; further, Baskerville, The Elizabethan Jig, p. 22, n. 2. Robin's "Christmas Calues skin" in Wily Beguiled should be treated as an indication of his participation in Christmas customs: See Wily Beguiled, Malone Society Reprints (Oxford, 1912), p. 313; cf. 1255 ff. where Robin says, "Ile go put on my diuelish roabes,/I meane my Christmas Calues skin sute."

65. Cf. F. H. Mares, "The Origin of the Figure Called 'the Vice' in Tudor Drama," Huntington Library Quarterly 22 (1958):17. In reference to line 455 ("Kepe yowur tayll, in goodnes, I prey you, goode brother!") Alois Brandl writes "Die Teufel hatten Schwänze" (Quellen des weltlichen Dramas in England vor Shakespeare [Strassburg, 1898], p. xxxiii). This misinterpretation (mistaking tail for tale) has been adopted by later scholars. Eduard Eckhardt (Die lustige Person im älteren englischen Drama [Berlin, 1902], p. 102), for example, uses the attribution of a tail to the Vice as the cornerstone of his argument, finding it well-suited to his hypothesis as to the Vice's ancestry. But the Vice is not as nearly related to either the devil or to the folk fool as Eckhardt assumes.

66. Cf. The Tempest, ed. Frank Kermode, Arden Edition (London, 1954), appendix B: Ariel "often behaves like a native English fairy." But "Many elements are mixed in Ariel, and his strange richness derives from the mixture" (p. 143). R. L. Green holds a similar opinion in "Shakespeare and the Fairies," Folklore 73 (1962):93: "we have a new fairy-world made out of the floating traditions both literary and popular." The line between tradition and originality is, however, hard to draw, for Ariel as well as for the fairy characters, which Green says are "Apparently Shakespeare's most original addition to fairy literature . . . though there it is probable that Shakespeare was using the actual country traditions" (ibid.). The contradiction is not one of the formulation: it reflects a creative concurrence of originality and tradition. As Wilhelm Girnus put it, "Il n'y a point de véritable tradition sans modernité et inversement . . . Echte Traditionen sind demnach . . . Ausgangspunkte" ("Deutsche Klassik und literarische Tradition," Natur und Idee, dedicated to Andreas Bruno Wachsmuth, ed. Helmut Holtzhauer [Weimar, 1966], p. 84).

67. Gustav Landauer, Shakespeare, vol. 2 (Potsdam, 1948), p. 276.

68. See Karl Marx, introduction to Kritik der politischen Ökonomie.

69. Cf. Barber's interpretation of A Midsummer Night's Dream (p. 139): "dramatic art can provide a civilized equivalent for exorcism. The exorcism represented as magically accomplished at the conclusion of the comedy is accomplished, in another sense, by the whole dramatic action, as it keeps moving through release to clarification."

70. For above ref. to Aristotle, The Basic Works of Aristotle, ed. Richard McKeron (New York, 1941), De Poetica, trans. Ingram Bywater, p. 1457. On the Elizabethan reception of

mimetic theory, cf. *Elizabethan Critical Essays*, vol. 1, pp. 5–45 (Ascham), p. 158 (Sidney), vol. 2, p. 3 (Puttenham); quotation ibid., pp. 188 and 191. Before and beside the undeveloped comic theory of Aristotle, Donatus, and the commentaries on Terence (based on Horace, Cicero, and Quintilian) had the greatest influence in England. Cf. M. T. Herrick, *Comic Theory in the Sixteenth Century* (reprint ed., Urbana, Ill., 1964), which places the onset of Aristotelean influence "by 1579" (p. 224). Unfortunately, the most significant among modern theories of *mimesis*, that of Georg Lukács (*Die Eigenart des Ästhetischen* [Neuwied, 1963], 1 (half) vol., pp. 352–851), sets up impenetrable barriers between *mimesis* and the elements of an ancient Dionysian culture, such as the ecstatic dance (p. 390).

71. J. E. Spingarn, *A History of Literary Criticism in the Renaissance*, 2nd ed. (New York, 1924), p. 87; cf. p. 128. But see Vernon Hall, Jr., *Renaissance Literary Criticism: A Study of its Social Content* (Gloucester, Mass., reprint ed., 1959), p. 181: "Essentially, decorum is a class concept."

72. George Whetstone, dedication to *Promos and Cassandra* (1578); quoted from Smith, vol. 1, pp. 59–60.

73. *An Apology for Poetry*; quotation ibid., p. 199.

74. Cf. on this, E. Th. Sehrt, *Der dramatische Auftakt in der elisabethanischen Tragödie* (Göttingen, 1960), pp. 85 ff.

75. Wolfgang Clemen, *Die Tragödie vor Shakespeare: Ihre Entwicklung im Spiegel der dramatischen Rede* (Heidelberg, 1955), p. 129.

76. Walter Benjamin, *Ursprung des deutschen Trauerspiels* (Berlin, 1928), p. 164.

77. See M. C. Bradbrook, *Shakespeare and Elizabethan Poetry* (Harmondsworth, 1964), p. 48.

78. Earnan McMullin, "Empiricism and the Scientific Revolution," *Art, Science and History in the Renaissance*, ed. Charles I. Singleton (Baltimore, 1970), p. 334; cf. Earnan McMullin, "Medieval and Modern Science: Continuity or Discontinuity?" *International Philosophical Quarterly* 5 (1965): 103–29.

79. *The Prose Works of Sir Philip Sidney*, ed. Albert Feuillerat (Cambridge, 1912), 3: 16.

80. See Bernard Weinberg, *A History of Literary Criticism in the Italian Renaissance* (Chicago, 1961), 1: 1–37, et passim.

81. John Stevens, *Medieval Romance: Themes and Approaches* (London, 1973), p. 170.

82. I have taken this point further in "Strukturen epischer Weltaneignung in der Renaissance," *Synthesis* 3 (Bucarest, 1976):47–64.

83. Here, I follow Clemen, *Die Tragödie vor Shakespeare*, who has cogently demonstrated how Kyd has the "Deklamationsmonolog mit der Handlung, der Bühne verklammert," p. 99.

84. Ibid., p. 21.

85. *The Prose Works of Sir Philip Sidney*, 3: 38. On this whole question, see George Hunter's important article, "Seneca and the Elizabethans: A Case-study in 'Influence,'" *Shakespeare Survey* 20 (1967), esp. p. 24. See also Hunter's more recent study of "Seneca and English Tragedy" (*Seneca*, ed. C. D. N. Costa [London, 1974]:166–204) where he accounts for "the real hostility of received English dramatic patterns to the nature of his [Seneca's] plays" (p. 181) in historical as well as in structural terms: "The perspectives of the ordinary world are essential to Shakespearean tragedy; they are quite absent from Seneca" (p. 170). Obviously, the difference has to do with a more profoundly dramatic sense of reality and individuality: "It is not any Senecan machinery but this power to show emotion turning into action by the mysterious alchemy of free personal choice that gives *The Spanish Tragedy* and *Hamlet* and *Titus Andronicus* their grip on the audience" (p. 185).

86. M. P. Tilley, *A Dictionary of the Proverbs in England in the Sixteenth and Seventeenth Centuries* (Ann Arbor, 1950), p. viii. Cf. Martin Lehnert's detailed discussion and enumeration in *Zeitschrift für Anglistik* 5 (1957): 200–208. Horst Weinstock (p. 209) notes that Shakespeare avoids "abstract sentenzhafte Sprichwörter zugunsten psychologisch vertiefter, bildhaft anschaulicher Erfahrungssprichwörter aus dem Alltagsleben."

87. D. S. Bland, "Shakespeare and the 'Ordinary' Word," *Shakespeare Survey* 4 (1951):50; Cf. F. P. Wilson, *Shakespeare and the Diction of Common Life*, Proceedings of the British Academy, vol. 27 (London, 1941); Hilda M. Hulme, *Explorations in Shakespeare's Language* (London, 1962), esp. pp. 39–150. Martin Lehnert, *Shakespeares Sprache und Wir* (Berlin,

1963), pp. 7, 51 ff. Wilhelm Franz, *Shakespeare-Grammatik*, 4th ed. (Halle, 1939), p. 9, emphatically says that "Shakespeare schöpfte aus dem lebendigen Born der Volkssprache, und daher hat sein Englisch die Kraft, die Frische, die Poesie in Ausdruck und Bild. . . ."

88. M. M. Mahood, *Shakespeare's Wordplay* (London, 1957), p. 51.

89. I have taken this point further in a recent study of "Metaphor and Historical Criticism: Shakespeare's Imagery Revisited," in my *Structure and Society in Literary History* (Charlottesville, Va., 1976):188-233.

90. Wolfgang Clemen, *Shakespeares Bilder: Ihre Entwicklung und ihre Funktion im dramatischen Werk* (Bonn, 1936), p. 246.

91. Hulme, *Explorations in Shakespeare's Language*, p. 70; the author, it should be noted, relates this to the function of the emblematic proverb.

92. Harbage, *Shakespeare and the Rival Traditions*, p. 148. Cf. Bradbrook, *Shakespeare and Elizabethan Poetry*, pp. 82 ff., 223-24, and 76: "He submitted to learn from experience."

93. *Elizabethan Critical Essays*, 2:431, 232. In his reply Nashe took the reproach seriously and asked (ibid., p. 243), "Is my stile like Greenes, or my ieasts like Tarltons?"

VI

SHAKESPEARE'S THEATER: TRADITION AND EXPERIMENT

1. C. W. Hodges, "The Lantern of Taste," *Shakespeare Survey* 12 (1959), p. 8. Cf. G. R. Kernodle, *From Art to Theatre: Form and Convention in the Renaissance* (Chicago, 1944), pp. 130-53. Cf. L. B. Wright, *Shakespeare's Theatre and the Dramatic Tradition* (Washington, 1958), p. 14: "one cannot escape the conclusion that usage varied and that stage construction in the theatres may have differed in some important details." For a discussion of the flexibility of Shakespeare's theater, see J. L. Styan, *Shakespeare's Stagecraft* (Cambridge, 1967), pp. 7 ff.

2. Richard Hosley, "The Discovery-Space in Shakespeare's Globe," *Shakespeare Survey* 12 (1959):35-46.

3. G. F. Reynolds, *The Staging of Elizabethan Plays at the Red Bull Theater: 1605-1625* (London, 1940), p. 188; cf. pp. 131-63. E. K. Chambers had already postulated the existence of a "curtained structure" in the Swan theater, but had not enlarged upon his theory (*The Elizabethan Stage*, vol. 3 [Oxford, 1923], p. 86, hereafter cited as *El. St.*). C. W. Hodges (n. 5 below) and Leslie Hotson (for example, in *Shakespeare's Wooden O* [London, 1960], pp. 56-57) have gone far beyond this. Doubt about the existence of the rear stage has led to various reinterpretations of individual scenes (for example, Richard Hosley, "The Staging of Desdemona's Bed," *Shakespeare Quarterly* 14 [1963]:57-65) and to the reconstruction of plays with the aid of concealed stages or tents (for example, L. J. Ross, "The Use of a 'Fit-Up' Booth in *Othello*," *Shakespeare Quarterly* 12 [1961]:359-70). The existence of similar structures in plays by Jonson and Chapman has also been postulated; cf. W. A. Armstrong, "The Enigmatic Elizabethan Stage," *English* 13 (1961): 216-20.

4. Bernard Miles and Josephine Wilson, "Three Festivals at the Mermaid Theatre," *Shakespeare Quarterly* 5 (1954):310: "We have learnt that it is impossible to play scenes on the so-called 'inner stage,' or even far upstage at all."

5. C. W. Hodges, *The Globe Restored: A Study of the Elizabethan Theatre* (London, 1953), pp. 58-59. A. M. Nagler (*Shakespeare's Stage* [reprint ed., New Haven, 1964]) characterizes the tentlike structure as "an auxiliary stage, a potential scene of action" (p. 26) and refers to the medieval example of the fixed-roof *pinaculum* in Vigil Raber's sketch of the play at Bozen, 1514 (p. 49).

6. J. C. Adams, *The Globe Playhouse: Its Design and Equipment* (Cambridge, Mass., 1943), p. 294; also the same author's "The Original Staging of King Lear," in *J. Q. Adams Memorial Studies*, ed. James McManaway, et. al. (Washington, 1948), pp. 315-35.

7. G. F. Reynolds, "Was there a 'Tarras' in Shakespeare's Globe?" *Shakespeare Survey* 4 (1951):100, n. 9.

8. Reynolds, *The Staging of Elizabethan Plays . . .* , p. 190.

9. T. J. King, *Shakespearean Staging: 1599-1642* (Cambridge, Mass., 1971), p. 31. Cf.

Richard Hosley, "The Gallery over the Stage in the Public Playhouses of Shakespeare's Time," *Shakespeare Quarterly* 8 (1957): p. 21, and the same author's "Shakespeare's Use of a Gallery over the Stage," *Shakespeare Survey* 10 (1957):77.

10. Cf. the graphic demonstration in Glynne Wickham, *Early English Stages: 1300–1600*, vol. 2 (London, 1959), pp. 161-63. Henslowe's specifications require "a Stadge and Tyreinge howse to be made, erected & settupp *within the saide fframe*" (italics mine; cf. Chambers, *El. St.*, 2:137).

11. See Richard Southern, *The Open Stage* (London, 1953), pp. 15-21, and the drawing by Hodges in appendix A of *The Globe Restored*, pp. 170-77, which was preceded by the publication of "Unworthy Scaffolds: A Theory for the Reconstruction of Elizabethan Playhouses," *Shakespeare Survey* 3 (1951):83-94.

12. *The Globe Restored*, p. 49.

13. J. Q. Adams, ed., *Chief Pre-Shakespearean Dramas* (Boston, 1924), p. 158, n. 1.

14. Cf. J. W. Saunders, "Vaulting the Rails," *Shakespeare Survey* 7 (1954):69-81.

15. Allardyce Nicoll, "Passing Over the Stage," *Shakespeare Survey* 12 (1959):47-55. This has been confirmed by Richard Southern in *The Staging of Plays Before Shakespeare* (London, 1973), pp. 569-70, where he suggests that there were small steps at the corner of the stage to facilitate entrance from and exit to the yard. Still, the evidence is not conclusive; "passing over the stage" may indeed refer to no more than the movement of an actor around the platform from door to door. Since this book was written, work on the Elizabethan stage has continued to grow at an unprecedented rate. For some of the most stimulating contributions, see the collection of essays in *Renaissance Drama* 4 (1972), or the series *The Elizabethan Theatre* (ed. David Galloway [Toronto, 1969 ff.]). For what is perhaps the most rewarding discussion of some of the basic issues, see P. C. Kolin's Report on the 1971 MLA Conference on Renaissance Drama, paneled by Bernard Beckerman, Richard Hosley, and T. J. King (*Research Opportunities in Renaissance Drama* 15-16 [1972-73]:3-14). There are some new emphases and trends toward a consciousness of, for instance, the dramatic and "emblematic" significance of the theatrical "discovery," or, again, a new awareness, as formulated by Bernard Beckerman or Norman Rabkin, of the critical and social implications of historical research into the physical stage. (See, among many others, *Reinterpretations of Elizabethan Drama*, Selected papers from the English Institute, ed. Norman Rabkin [New York, 1969].) But many questions remain unanswered and some previous answers are increasingly questioned, as in Richard Hosley's mounting objections to the "liberal position" of C. W. Hodges and George Reynolds on the use of curtained booths. See Hosley's well-founded emphasis on plays like *Hamlet* as "an 'arras' or 'hanging' play, a purely open stage play" (Kolin's Report, p. 6). Here as elsewhere it may be said that "extensive investigations of the severely limited evidence have won us few widely and easily accepted solutions." See P. C. Kolin and R. O. Watt in the introduction to what is the most useful recent "Bibliography of Scholarship on the Elizabethan Stage Since Chambers," *Research Opportunities in Renaissance Drama* 15-16 (1972-73):33-59. There is a shorter but selective bibliography, together with a summary, by Michael Jamieson, "Shakespeare in the Theatre," *Shakespeare: Select Bibliographical Guides*, ed. Stanley Wells (London, 1973). For a somewhat fuller synthesis, see Andrew Gurr, *The Shakespearean Stage: 1574-1642* (Cambridge, 1970).

16. For a classic statement of the older theory, see A. H. Thorndike, *Shakespeare's Theater* (New York, 1916), p. 77. On the following, cf. Rudolf Stamm, *Geschichte des englischen Theaters* (Bern, 1951), pp. 51, 101, 110, for an extremely balanced statement of the problems involved.

17. J. W. Saunders, "Vaulting the Rails," *Shakespeare Survey* 7 (1954), p. 79.

18. *Tarlton's Jests and News out of Purgatory* (London, 1844), p. 27.

19. Ibid., pp. 14, 22-23, 44. Cf. the jest, "How Tarlton and one in the gallery fell out."

20. Cf. Anne Righter, *Shakespeare and the Idea of the Play* (London, 1962), passim.

21. Alfred Harbage, "The Role of the Shakespearean Producer," *Shakespeare Jahrbuch* 91 (1955), p. 163. Cf. John Russel Brown, *Free Shakespeare* (London, 1974), esp. pp. 48-57, where the significance of such performances without directors and designers is explored. See Bernard Beckerman (*Shakespeare at the Globe: 1599-1609* [New York, 1962], p. 24): "From a common creative act arose the plays that Shakespeare penned and the pro-

ductions that his friends presented. The record of this partnership is contained in the extant scripts, not merely in stage directions or in dialogue, but in the very substance of the dramatist's craft, the structure of the incidents."

22. See Stamm, *Geschichte des englischen Theaters*, p. 55.

23. Ibid. Cf. Jackson I. Cope, *The Theater and the Dream: From Metaphor to Form in Renaissance Drama* (Baltimore/London, 1973), esp. the prologue, "The Rediscovery of Anti-Form in Renaissance Drama," pp. 1-13. (I have reviewed and commented on this suggestive book in *Zeitschrift für Anglistik* 24 [1976]:78-80.)

24. Alfred Harbage, *Shakespeare and the Rival Traditions* (New York, 1952), pp. 296, 307, 298.

25. Quoted from Harbage, ibid., p. 305.

26. Indeed, as Alexander Anikst stresses, Shakespeare was no partisan of popular rule ("Shakespeare—volkstümlicher Schriftsteller," *Shakespearowski Sbornik* [Moscow, 1958], p. 43). Cf. Anselm Schlösser's "Zur Frage 'Volk und Mob' bei Shakespeare," *ZAA* 4 (1956): 148-71, and Brents Stirling's important study of *The Populace in Shakespeare* (New York, 1949). Lorentz Eckhoff, *Shakespeare, Spokesman of the Third Estate* (Oxford, 1954), is an exceedingly problematic book. Above quotation from Ben Jonson in E. K. Chambers, *William Shakespeare: A Study of Facts and Problems*, vol. 2 (Oxford, 1930), p. 209.

27. Cf. Anton Müller-Bellinghausen, "Die Workulisse bei Shakespeare," *Shakespeare Jahrbuch* 91 (1955):182-96; among others.

28. Rudolf Stamm, "Dichtung und Theater in Shakespeares Werk," *Shakespeare Jahrbuch* 98 (1962):12; cf. the same author's *Zwischen Vision und Wirklichkeit* (Bern/Munich, 1964), pp. 9-27.

29. Wolfgang Clemen, *Shakespeare's Soliloquies*, Pres. Address of the Mod. Hum. Research Assoc., (1964), pp. 1, 8, 24; *Shakespeares Monologe* (Göttingen, 1964), p. 5. Cf. also Kenneth Muir, "Shakespeare's Soliloquies," *Ocidente* 67 (1964):45-48; as well as the older studies by M. L. Arnold (1911) and Hermann Poepperling (Dissertation, 1912); cf. Nevill Coghill, *Shakespeare's Professional Skills* (Cambridge, 1964), pp. 128-63.

30. Cf. B. L. Joseph, *Elizabethan Acting* (London, 1952), pp. 122, 132; J. L. Styan, "The Actor at the Foot of Shakespeare's Platform," *Shakespeare Survey* 12 (1959):56-63.

31. J. D. Wilson's text, "The New Shakespeare," (reprint ed., Cambridge, 1961) is quoted, with the exception of the emendation (which follows other editors) "curb" (l. 169) and the folio reading "thus" (instead of Wilson's "this" from Q_2, l. 179).

32. Behind John Dover Wilson's highly detailed stage directions, as M. C. Bradbrook noted, stand "traces of nineteenth century realist staging" (*Elizabethan Stage Conditions: A Study of their Place in the Interpretation of Shakespeare's Plays* [1931] [Hamden, Conn., 1962], p. 136).

33. Wolfgang Clemen, *Kommentar zu Shakespeares Richard III* (Göttingen, 1957), p. 35.

34. Even before Shakespeare such a "thus" is frequently associated with some form of audience address; cf. Bernard Spivack, *Shakespeare and the Allegory of Evil* (New York, 1958), p. 190. This corresponds to the Scrivener's "such" or "Here's" and similar verbal gestures which are used to present and to comment on the play in performance.

35. That the actor of Lear actually spoke to a particular spectator cannot, of course, be proved; but that Shakespeare's audience was familiar with such a tradition is evident from the unmistakable precedents in late Moralities and interludes. In the popular *King Cambises*, Ambidexter says: "I care not if I be maried before to-morrow at noone, / If mariage be a thing that so may be had. / How say you, maid?..." (950 ff.). J. Q. Adams' stage direction, "To one in the audience," is undoubtedly correct. An original instance occurs in Heywood's *The Play of the Weather:* "*Mery-reporte.* My Lord, there standeth a sewter even here behynde,/... He wolde hunte a sow or twayne out of thys sorte./ *Here he poynteth to the women.*" (Adams, ed., 245 ff.).

36. *Elizabethan Acting*, pp. 123 ff., 149. The far reaching generalization ("we have not to do with true dialogue, but with a sequence of alternate declamation," p. 131) contradicts what is, to my mind, a correct interpretation, "that the style must have varied ... according to the needs of individual scenes." But even the fact that "Elizabethan acting varied in accordance with the style of the words to be spoken" (p. 151) does not derive, finally, from conventions of rhetoric, but rather from the scenic and dramatic "mingle-mangle" of the popular theater, which also, of course, admits of rhetoric. Beckerman (pp. 113-21) offers a

convincing total picture and a just critique of the exaggerated claims for rhetoric. See Leonard Goldstein, "On the Transition From Formal to Naturalistic Acting in the Elizabethan and Post-Elizabethan Theatre," *Bull. New York Public Library* 62 (1958):330-49. A similar tendency "from formalism to illusion" is asserted by W. G. McCollom ("Formalism and Illusion in Shakespearean Drama, 1595-1598," *Quarterly Journal of Speech* 31 [1945]:446 ff.), Clifford Leech (*Shakespeare's Tragedies* [London, 1950], p. 56), and others.

37. Eugen Kilian, "Der Shakespearesche Monolog und seine Spielweise," *Shakespeare Jahrbuch* 39 (1903): xviii.

38. Righter, p. 205.

39. Cf. *Hamlet*, ed. Dover Wilson, p. 276.

40. L. L. Schücking, *Die Charakterprobleme bei Shakespeare* (Leipzig, 1932), p. 19.

41. Kilian, p. xxxix.

42. Schücking, pp. 25-26.

43. *Shakespeare and the Allegory of Evil*, pp. 286, 302, 303, 339, 341; Spivack also speaks, with reference to the Vice's relationship to the audience, of "homiletic logic" (p. 168) and even of "homiletic bravura" and "homiletic jest" (p. 405). Cf. above chap. IV, n. 82.

44. S. L. Bethell, *Shakespeare and the Popular Dramatic Tradition* (London, 1944), p. 81.

45. *The Life of Timon of Athens*, ed. J. C. Maxwell, "The New Shakespeare" (Cambridge, 1957).

46. A. P. Rossiter, *English Drama from Early Times to the Elizabethans* (London, 1950), p. 75.

47. Clemen, *Kommentar zu Shakespeares Richard III*, p. 151.

48. Quoted from *Troilus and Cressida*, ed. Alice Walker, "The New Shakespeare" (Cambridge, 1957).

49. Cf. L. C. Knights, "Shakespeare's Politics: With Some Reflections on the Nature of Tradition," *Proceedings of the British Academy* (1957):117.

50. The etymology of "infant" further enhances the possible depth of the pun since the Latin substantive use of *infãns*—"unable to speak"—might be a perfect description of the silent *tableau vivant* effect achieved in some medieval pageantry and dramaturgy. This, at any rate, would support the already playful oxymoron, "old infant": old in the history of the theater, infant, as the etymology suggests, in terms of the mode of performance. (Here I wish to thank my editor, to whom I owe this note as well as the interpretation of Berowne's *Figurenposition*.)

51. See Doris Fenton, *The Extra-Dramatic Moment in Elizabethan Plays before 1616* (Philadelphia, 1930), pp. 113 ff.

52. On the myriad dramatic functions of the aside (interest, characterization, irony, transmission of information, etc.), cf. Wolfgang Riehle, *Das Beiseitesprechen bei Shakespeare: Ein Beitrag zur Dramaturgie des elisabethanischen Dramas*, Dissertation (Munich, 1964), especially pp. 111 ff.

53. Riehle, p. 26.

54. Ibid., p. 27.

55. J. F. Danby, *Shakespeare's Doctrine of Nature: A Study of King Lear* (London, 1961), p. 46.

56. The audience rapport of Gloucester, Iago, and, in part, Edmund derives from other premises. They are, like their predecessor the knavish Vice, the theatrical managers of their own intrigues and dramatic inversions. They continue to challenge the status quo, not so much from any personal motivation (although Shakespeare, somewhat perfunctorily, supplies that, too) but rather for the sake of challenge and negation. They are the great perverters of state, marriage, and filial love, re-enacting the *Geist, der stets verneint*—the Mephistophelean spirit which persistently destroys. In this sense, their audience contact is profoundly in the popular tradition. Their natural ambivalence as well as their insuperable vitality stem to a degree from the exuberance with which they freely exploit the vantage points of both platform and *locus*, ritual and representation.

57. *The Prose Works of Sir Philip Sidney*, ed. Albert Feuillerat (Cambridge, 1912), 3:39.

58. Ibid., p. 40.

59. Here Sidney indirectly anticipates Thomas Rymer: "But the poet must do every thing by contraries . . ." (*A Short View of Tragedy*; cf. *Critical Essays of the Seventeenth Century*, ed. J. E. Spingarn [London, 1908], 2:246) and even the charge that John Dryden was to

make against the histories and plays like *The Winter's Tale*: "which were ... so meanly written that the comedy neither caused your mirth, nor the serious part your concernment" (John Dryden, *Of Dramatic Poesy and Other Critical Essays*, ed. George Watson [London, 1962], 1:172).

60. William Empson, "Double Plots," *Some Versions of Pastoral: A Study of the Pastoral Form in Literature* (Harmondsworth, 1966), p. 29. See Ola Winslow, *Low Comedy as a Structural Element in English Drama from the Beginnings to 1642* (Chicago, 1926), esp. pp. 66-132.

61. Ibid., p. 34.

62. *The Prose Works of Sir Philip Sidney*, 3:41.

63. Richard Levin, *The Multiple Plot in English Renaissance Drama* (Chicago/London, 1971), pp. 21-191.

64. Richard Levin, (ibid., pp. 119, 143) has used this as evidence. See Norman Rabkin, "The Double Plot: Notes on the History of a Convention," *Renaissance Drama* 7 (1964): 55-69.

65. Ibid., p. 114.

66. Ibid., p. 144.

67. Ibid., p. 115.

68. Ibid., p. 139.

69. Ibid., p. 142.

70. Willard Farnham, *The Shakespearean Grotesque: Its Genesis and Transformations* (Oxford, 1971), p. 109.

71. Schücking, *Die Charakterprobleme bei Shakespeare*, p. 17.

72. Otto Ludwig, *Werke*, ed. A. Eloesser (1908), part 4, p. 62, quoted in Horst Oppel, "Kontrast und Kontrapunkt im Shakespeare-Drama," *Shakespeare Jahrbuch* 97 (1961):156.

73. Robert Fricker, *Kontrast und Polarität in den Charakterbildern Shakespeares* (Bern, 1951), especially pp. 115-233.

74. Max Lüthi, "Die Macht des Nichtwirklichen in Shakespeares Spielen," *Shakespeare Jahrbuch* 97 (1961):13-33.

75. L. L. Schücking, *Shakespeare und der Tragödienstil seiner Zeit* (Bern, 1947), p. 153.

76. Oppel, p. 164.

77. Is the polarity of structure in this broad "Kraftfeld" (field of force) determined by the *unmediated* influence of folk drama? It is interesting to speculate on this, as W. B. Thorne does: "The pattern which emerges ... is that of a polarity, the result of the playwright's increasing dependence upon and blend of folk themes with classical or literary tales. The polar plot construction lends itself easily to the formation of an artificial world in which to present the main action, and provides additional perspective from which to evaluate the eventual return to reality in the form of a new equilibrium, or a reassessment of the existing situation" (*The Influence of Folk-Drama upon Shakespearian Comedy*, cf. *Dissertation Abstracts* 25 [1965] pp. 6603 ff.).

78. Stamm, *Geschichte des englischen Theaters*, p. 111, cf. p. 128.

79. Philipp Aronstein, *Das englische Renaissancedrama* (Leipzig/Berlin, 1929), p. 143. The concept of illusion is not used here in the narrow sense of the nineteenth-century theater of illusion. Theatrical illusion arises when the theater inspires an impression of reality that abstracts itself from the audience's sense of attending a theatrical performance—a tendency that begins early and peaks in the unquestioned acceptance of the "fourth wall." But the genealogy of the illusionistic stage is a complex one evolving through continuing conflict with nonillusionistic modes. Of the few preliminary studies in this direction, cf. Margareta Braun, *Symbolismus und Illusionismus im englischen Drama vor 1620: Eine Untersuchung illusionsfördernder und illusionszerstörender Tendenzen, vor allen in den frühen Historien* ... , Dissertation (Munich, 1962), in which the "Perspektive des Realismus" is, however, expounded in terms of a somewhat narrow and one-sided stylistic emphasis. Cf. *El. St.*, 3:144; W. A. Armstrong, *The Elizabethan Private Theatres: Facts and Problems* (London, 1958), p. 13. On the social background of the transformation of the early Jacobean theater, see my paper "Le déclin de la scène 'indivisible' Élisabéthaine," *Dramaturgie et Société*, ed. Jean Jacquot (Paris, 1968), pp. 815-27.

80. On Shakespeare's indoor stage, cf. Irwin Smith, *Shakespeare's Blackfriars Playhouse: Its History and Its Design* (New York, 1964), who notes that "Shakespeare as an individual dramatist responded to the Blackfriars innovations less readily than the King's Men and

their dramatists as a group seem to have done" (p. 239). See G. E. Bentley, *Shakespeare and his Theatre* (Lincoln, Nebr., 1964), p. 85. Some of the cultural and ideological implications of this cleavage were, I think, first noticed by W. J. Courthope (1911), L. B. Wright (1935), and, of course, Alfred Harbage (1952).

81. Harbage himself (*Shakespeare and the Rival Traditions*, p. 295) corrects this somewhat schematic position when he writes of Shakespeare that "There is no mood or idea in the select drama that is unexpressed in his.... He assimilates and transforms the thought of his antagonists at the same time that he excels their art." On the other side, W. A. Armstrong, I think, goes much too far when he claims for Blackfriars "the central place in the overall development of the Elizabethan stage and stagecraft" (*The Elizabethan Private Theatres*, p. 17).

82. Bethell, pp. 25, 22, 15, 25. To Schücking's pioneering work, *Die Charakterprobleme bei Shakespeare*, cf. my reference in *Shakespeare Jubiläum 1964*, ed. Anselm Schlösser (Weimar, 1964), pp. 93 ff.

83. William Archer, *Play-making: A Manual of Craftsmanship* (Boston, 1912), p. 398.

84. Ibid., p. 393.

85. Ibid., p. 395.

86. Franz Mehring, *Beiträge zur Literaturgeschichte*, ed. W. Heist (Berlin, 1948), p. 78.

87. Marx and Engels, *Werke*, vol. 28, p. 603 (letter to Ferdinand Lasalle, 18 May 1859).

88. Cf. L. E. Pinskij, *Realizm epochi vozroždenia* (Moscow, 1961), pp. 258–73. For an entirely different point of view, see Willard Farnham, *The Medieval Heritage of Elizabethan Tragedy* (reprint ed., Oxford, 1956).

89. Bethell, p. 19. Bethell goes so far as to say that "the popular school was guilty of lapses into naturalism."

90. Marx and Engels, *Werke*, vol. 13, p. 640 (Marx, *Einleitung zur Kritik der politischen Ökonomie*).

91. "Four Elizabethan Dramatists," cf. T. S. Eliot, *Selected Essays: 1917–1932* (London, 1932), p. 114.

92. Ibid., p. 116.

93. *Goethes Sämtliche Werke* (Jubiläums-Ausgabe), 37: 48 f. But see his later reservations, 38: 90.

94. Georg Lukács, *Der historische Roman* (Berlin, 1955), p. 119 (italics mine).

95. Ibid., p. 169.

96. Bertolt Brecht, *Schriften zum Theater* (Berlin/Weimar, 1964), 1: 112.

97. Ibid., 7: 61.

98. Jackson I. Cope, *The Theater and the Dream: From Metaphor to Form in Renaissance Drama*, p. 2. Cf. the section on *A Midsummer Night's Dream*, where "the radically double nature of the dramatic experience—at once illusionistic and anti-illusionistic" (p. 223) is perceptively discussed.

99. See Walter R. Davis, *Idea and Act in Elizabethan Fiction* (Princeton, 1969), as well as *Realismus in der Renaissance* (Berlin, 1977) which I have edited and to which I have contributed two chapters on the history and theory of Renaissance prose.

100. Norman Rabkin, *Shakespeare and the Common Understanding* (New York, 1967), p. 12.

APPENDIX

1. John Dover Wilson, *Shakespeare's Happy Comedies* (London, 1962), pp. 23 ff.

2. Jurij Borew, *Über das Komische* (Berlin, 1960), pp. 19, 22, 166.

3. G. W. F. Hegel, *Ästhetik*, ed. Friedrich Bassenge (Berlin, 1955), p. 1091.

4. Ibid., cf. p. 1075.

5. See Leo Salingar, *Shakespeare and the Traditions of Comedy* (Cambridge, 1974). But Salingar's approach remains predominantly literary and as such overestimates the classical heritage; see my forthcoming review in *Modern Language Studies* (1977).

6. Cf. II, 1, 87; 90; 97; 123. This seems unique in Shakespeare. The play's debt to the romance tradition is fully brought out by John Vyvyan, *Shakespeare and the Rose of Love* (1960). See also H. B. Charlton, *Shakespearean Comedy* (1952), pp. 27 ff.

7. Cf. *Tarlton's Jests and News out of Purgatory*, pp. 14, 22–23, 27, 44.

8. See J. R. Brown, *Shakespeare and his Comedies* (London, 1957), pp. 11 ff.

9. H. F. Brooks, "Two Clowns in a Comedy (to say nothing of the Dog): Speed, Launce (and Crab) in *The Two Gentlemen of Verona*," *Essays and Studies* 16 (1963): 91–100.

10. See, for example, R. M. Sargent, "Sir Thomas Elyot and the Integrity of *The Two Gentlemen of Verona*," *PMLA* 65 (1950):1166–82; also the introduction to "The New Cambridge Shakespeare," pp. xiii ff.; Vyvyan, pp. 130 ff.; E. Th. Sehrt, *Wandlungen der Shakespeareschen Kömodie* (Göttingen, 1961), p. 14.

BIBLIOGRAPHY

EDITOR'S NOTE

The bibliography contains most of the literature cited in the original German edition, and so covers relevant publications up to 1966 with some consistency and completeness. Also contained are works cited in the notes to sections that Professor Weimann has revised or enlarged for this new edition as well as some relevant titles that I have added.

Primary

A Select Collection of Old English Plays. Originally published by Robert Dodsley in the year 1744. Edited by W. C. Hazlitt. 15 vols. London, 1874–76.

Specimens of the Pre-Shaksperean Drama. Edited by J. M. Manly. 2 vols. Boston/ London, 1897.

Quellen des weltlichen Dramas in England vor Shakespeare. Edited by Alois Brandl. Strassburg, 1898.

Early English Dramatists. Edited by J. S. Farmer. London, 1905–8.

Malone Society Reprints. W. W. Greg, general editor. London, 1907 ff.

Chief Pre-Shakespearean Dramas. Edited by J. Q. Adams. Boston, 1924.

York Plays. The Plays Performed by the Crafts or Mysteries of York on the Day of Corpus Christi in the 14th, 15th and 16th Centuries. Edited by L. T. Smith. Oxford, 1885.

The Chester Plays. Part 1. Edited by Hermann Deimling, EETS, E. S. LXXI. London, 1897.

Two Coventry Corpus Christi Plays. Edited by Hardin Craig, EETS, E. S. LXXXVII. London, 1902.

The Macro Plays. Edited by F. J. Furnivall and A. W. Pollard, EETS, E. S. XCI. London, 1904.

The Non-Cycle Mystery Plays. Edited by Osborn Waterhouse, EETS, E. S. CIV. London, 1909.

The Chester Plays. Part 2. Edited by Dr. Matthews, EETS, E. S. CXV. London, 1916.

Ludus Coventriae or The Plaie called Corpus Christi. Edited by K. S. Block, EETS, E. S. CXX. London, 1922.

Everyman and Medieval Mystery Plays. Edited by A. C. Cawley. London, 1956.

The Wakefield Pageants in the Towneley Cycle. Edited by A. C. Cawley. Manchester, 1958.

The Macro Plays. Edited by Mark Eccles, EETS, O. S. 262. London, 1969.

Wilson, Robert. *The Cobbler's Prophecy*. Edited by Wilhelm Dibelius, *Shakespeare Jahrbuch* 33 (1897): 9–48.

Wager, W. *The Longer Thou Livest, The More Fool Thou Art*. Edited by Alois Brandl, *Shakespeare Jahrbuch* 36 (1900):14–64.

Lupton, Thomas. *All For Money*. Edited by Ernst Vogel, *Shakespeare Jahrbuch* 40 (1904): 145–86.

Skelton, John. *Magnificence*. Edited by R. L. Ramsay, EETS, E. S. XCVIII. London, 1906.

Wapull, George. *The Tide Tarrieth No Man*. Edited by Ernst Rühl. *Shakespeare Jahrbuch* 43 (1907):1–52.

Medwall, Henry. *Fulgens and Lucres*. Edited by F. S. Boas and A. W. Reed. Oxford, 1926.

The Selected Works of Robert Crowley. Edited by J. M. Cowper, EETS, E. S. XV. London, 1872.

The Works of Thomas Kyd. Edited by F. S. Boas. Oxford, 1901.

The Works of Thomas Nashe. Edited by R. B. McKerrow. 5 vols. London, 1904–10.

The Works of Christopher Marlowe. Edited by C. F. Tucker Brooke. Oxford, 1925.

William Shakespeare: The Complete Works. Edited by Peter Alexander. Glasgow/London, 1951.

Ben Jonson. Edited by C. H. Herford and Percy Simpson. 11 vols. Oxford, 1925–1952.

Secondary

Adams, J. C. *The Globe Playhouse: Its Design and Equipment*. Cambridge, Mass., 1943.

Adams, J. Q. *Shakespearean Playhouses*. Boston, 1917.

Adams, J. Q., ed. *The Dramatic Records of Sir Henry Herbert*. New Haven/London, 1917.

Alexander, Peter. *Shakespeare's "Henry VI" and "Richard III."* Cambridge, 1920.

Alford, Violet. *Sword Dance and Drama*. London, 1962.

Allison, T. E. "The Paternoster Play and the Origin of the Vices." *PMLA* 39 (1924):789–804.

Anders, H. R. D. *Shakespeare's Books: A Dissertation on Shakespeare's Reading and the Immediate Sources of his Works*. Berlin, 1904.

Anderson, M. D. *Drama and Imagery in English Medieval Churches*. Cambridge, 1963.

Anikst, Alexander. *Teatr epochi Shakespeara*. Moscow, 1965.

Anikst, Alexander. "Shakespeare—a Writer of the People." *Shakespeare in the*

Soviet Union. Translated by Avril Pyman. Edited by Roman Samarin and Alexander Nikolyukin. Moscow, 1966:113–39.

Anikst, Alexander. *Shakespeare: Remieslo dramaturga*. Moscow, 1974.

Armstrong, W. A. "The Enigmatic Elizabethan Stage." *English* 13 (1961):216–20.

Aronstein, Philip. *Das englische Renaissancedrama*. Leipzig/Berlin, 1929.

Ashley, W. J. *An Introduction to English Economic History and Theory*. London, 1892.

Ashton, J. W. "Folklore in the Literature of Elizabethan England." *Journal of American Folklore* 70 (1957):10–15.

Aston, M. E. "Lollardy and Sedition, 1381–1431." *Past and Present* (April 1960): 1–44.

Auerbach, Erich. *Mimesis: Dargestellte Wirklichkeit in der abendländischen Literatur*. 3rd ed. Bern/Munich, 1964.

Aufhauser, J. B. *Das Drachenwunder des Heiligen Georg*. Leipzig, 1911.

Avdeev, A. D. *Proizchoždenie teatra: Elementy teatra v pervobytnoobščestvennom stroe*. Leningrad, 1959.

Axton, Richard. *European Drama of the Early Middle Ages*. London, 1974.

Axton, Richard. "Popular Modes in the Earliest Plays." *Medieval Drama*. Edited by Neville Denny. London, 1973:13–40.

Barber, C. L. *Shakespeare's Festive Comedy: A Study of Dramatic Form and its Relation to Social Custom*. Princeton, 1959.

Baskerville, C. R. *English Elements in Jonson's Early Comedy*. Univ. of Texas Bull. No. 178. Austin, 1911.

Baskerville, C. R. "Some Evidence for Early Romantic Plays in England." *MP* 14 (1916–17):229–51; 467–512.

Baskerville, C. R. "Dramatic Aspects of Medieval Folk Festivals in England." *SP* 17 (1920):19–87.

Baskerville, C. R. "Conventional Features of Medwall's 'Fulgens and Lucres.'" *MP* 24 (1926–27):419–42.

Baskerville, C. R. *The Elizabethan Jig and Related Song Drama*. Chicago, 1929.

Baum, P. F. "Chaucer's Puns." *PMLA* 71 (1956):225–46.

Bausinger, Hermann. "Volksideologie und Volksforschung." *Zeitschrift für Volkskunde* 61 (1965):177–204.

Becker, Henrik. *Warnlieder*. 2 vols. Leipzig, 1953.

Becker, Henrik. *Bausteine zur deutschen Literaturgeschichte. Ältere deutsche Dichtung*. Halle, 1957.

Benjamin, Walter. *Ursprung des deutschen Trauerspiels*. Berlin, 1928.

Bentley, G. E. *Shakespeare and his Theatre*. Lincoln, Nebr., 1964.

Beresford, Maurice. *The Lost Villages of England*. London, 1954.

Berghäuser, Wilhelm. *Die Darstellung des Wahnsinns im englischen Drama bis zum Ende des 18. Jahrhunderts*. Dissertation, Giessen, 1914.

Bethell, S. L. *Shakespeare and the Popular Dramatic Tradition*. London, 1944.

Bevington, D. M. *From 'Mankind' to Marlowe: Growth of Structure in the Popular Drama of Tudor England*. Cambridge, Mass., 1962.

Bevington, D. M. *Tudor Drama and Politics: A Critical Approach to Topical Meaning*. Cambridge, Mass., 1968.

Bevington, D. M. "Popular and Courtly Traditions on the Early Tudor Stage." *Medieval Drama*. Edited by Neville Denny. London, 1973:91–108.

Biesterfeldt, P. W. *Die dramatische Technik Thomas Kyds. Studien zur inneren Struktur und szenischen Form des Elisabethanischen Dramas.* Halle, 1936.

Bigongiari, Dino. "Were there Theatres in the Twelfth and Thirteenth Centuries?" *Romanic Review* 37 (1946):201-24.

Bindoff, S. T. "The Making of the Statute of Artificers." *Elizabethan Government and Society.* Edited by S. T. Bindoff, et al. London, 1961:56-94.

Black, J. B. *The Reign of Elizabeth: 1558-1603.* Oxford, 1949.

Bland, D. S. "Shakespeare and the 'Ordinary' Word." *Shakespeare Survey* 4 (1951): 49-55.

Boughner, D. C. *The Braggart in Renaissance Comedy: A Study in Comparative Drama from Aristophanes to Shakespeare.* Minneapolis, 1954.

Boughner, D. C. "Vice, Braggart and Falstaff." *Anglia* 72 (1954):35-61.

Bradbrook, M. C. *Themes and Conventions of Elizabethan Tragedy.* Reprint. Cambridge, 1960.

Bradbrook, M. C. *The Growth and Structure of Elizabethan Comedy.* London, 1961.

Bradbrook, M. C. *Elizabethan Stage Conditions: A Study of their Place in the Interpretation of Shakespeare's Plays.* Reprint. Hamden, Conn., 1962.

Bradbrook, M. C. *The Rise of the Common Player: A Study of Actor and Society in Shakespeare's England.* London, 1962.

Bradbrook, M. C. "Marlowe's 'Doctor Faustus' and the Eldritch Tradition." *Essays on Shakespeare and Elizabethan Drama.* Edited by Richard Hosley. London, 1963:83-90.

Bradbrook, M. C. *Shakespeare and Elizabethan Poetry.* Penguin Books. Harmondsworth, 1964.

Bradner, Leicester. "Stages and Stage Scenery in Court Drama before 1558." *RES* 1 (1925):447-48.

Brand, John. *Observations on the Popular Antiquities of Great Britain.* Revised and greatly enlarged by Henry Ellis. 3 vols. London, 1848.

Brandl, Alois. "Shakespeare's Book of merry Riddles und die anderen Rätselbücher seiner Zeit," *Shakespeare Jahrbuch* 42 (1906):1-64.

Braun, Margareta. *Symbolismus und Illusionismus im englischen Drama vor 1620.* Dissertation. Munich, 1962.

Braune, W., ed. *Historia von D. Johann Fausten.* Halle, 1878.

Brecht, Bertolt. *Schriften zum Theater.* Edited by Werner Hecht. 7 vols. Berlin/ Weimar, 1964.

Breitholtz, Lennart. *Die dorische Farce.* Upsalla, 1960.

Brentano, Lujo. *Geschichte der wirtschaftlichen Entwicklung Englands.* 3 vols. Jena, 1927-29.

Briggs, K. M. *The Anatomy of Puck: An Examination of Fairy Beliefs among Shakespeare's Contemporaries and Successors.* London, 1959.

Briggs, K. M. *Pale Hecate's Team.* London, 1962.

Brody, Alan. *The English Mummers and their Plays: Traces of Ancient Mystery.* Philadelphia, 1970.

Brown, Arthur. "Folklore Elements in the Medieval Drama." *Folk-Lore* 63 (1952): 65-78.

Brown, James. "Eight Types of Pun," *PMLA* 71 (1956):14-26.

Brown, J. R. "Theater Research and the Criticism of Shakespeare and his Contemporaries." *Shakespeare Quarterly* 13 (1962):451-61.

Brown, J. R. *Free Shakespeare*. London, 1974.

Browning, Andrew. *The Age of Elizabeth*. London, 1928.

Bryant, J. A. "Shakespeare's Falstaff and the Mantle of Dick Tarlton," *SP* 51 (1954):149–62.

Bücher, Karl. *Arbeit und Rhythmus*. 6th ed. Leipzig, 1924.

Busby, O. M. *Studies in the Development of the Fool in Elizabethan Drama*. London, 1923.

Bush, Douglas. "Tudor Humanism and Henry VIII." *Univ. of Toronto Quarterly* 7 (1938):162–77.

Bush, Douglas. *The Renaissance and English Humanism*. Reprint. Toronto, 1962.

Büttner, Theodora, and Werner, Ernst. *Circumcellionen und Adamiten*. Berlin, 1959.

Campbell, O. J. *Shakespeare's Satire*. New York, 1943.

Carey, Millicent. *The Wakefield Group in the Towneley Cycle*. Göttingen/Baltimore, 1930.

Caspari, Fritz. *Humanism and the Social Order in Tudor England*. Chicago, 1954.

Caudwell, Christopher. *Illusion and Reality: A Study of the Sources of Poetry*. Reprint. London, 1955.

Cawley, A. C. "The 'Grotesque' Feast in the Prima Pastorum," *Speculum* 30 (1955):213–17.

Cawte, E. C., Helm, Alex, and Peacock, N. *English Ritual Drama: A Geographical Index*. London, 1967.

Chambers, E. K. *The Mediaeval Stage*. 2 vols. Oxford, 1903.

Chambers, E. K. *The Elizabethan Stage*. 4 vols. Oxford, 1923.

Chambers, E. K. *William Shakespeare: A Study of Facts and Problems*. 2 vols. Oxford, 1930.

Chambers, E. K. *The English Folk-Play*. Oxford, 1933.

Chambers, E. K. *English Literature at the Close of the Middle Ages*. Oxford, 1945.

Clemen, Wolfgang. *Shakespeares Bilder. Ihre Entwicklung und ihre Funktion im dramatischen Werk*. Bonn, 1936.

Clemen, Wolfgang. *Die Tragödie vor Shakespeare. Ihre Entwicklung im Spiegel der dramatischen Rede*. Heidelberg, 1955.

Clemen, Wolfgang. *A Commentary on Shakespeare's Richard III*. London, 1968.

Clemen, Wolfgang. *Sein und Schein bei Shakespeare*. Munich, 1959.

Clemen, Wolfgang. *Shakespeares Monologe*. Göttingen, 1964.

Clemen, Wolfgang. *Shakespeare's Soliloquies*. Pres. Address of the Modern Humanities Research Assoc. 1964.

Clemen, Wolfgang. *Shakespeare's Dramatic Art*. London, 1972.

Coghill, Nevill. *Shakespeare's Professional Skills*. Cambridge, 1964.

Cohen, Gustave. *Histoire de la mise en scène dans le théâtre religieux français du moyen age*. Paris, 1951.

Collins, Fletcher. "Music in the Craft Cycles." *PMLA* 47 (1932):613–21.

Collins, Fletcher. *The Production of Medieval Church Music Drama*. Charlottesville, Va., 1972.

Cope, Jackson I. *The Theater and the Dream: From Metaphor to Form in Renaissance Drama*. Baltimore, 1973.

Corbin, John. *The Elizabethan Hamlet: A Study of the Sources and of Shakespeare's*

Environment to Show that the Mad Scenes had a Comic Aspect now Ignored. London, 1895.

Cosbey, R. C. "The Mak Story and its Folklore Analogues," *Speculum* 20 (1945): 310–17.

Coulton, G. C. *Social Life in Britain from the Conquest to the Reformation*. Cambridge, 1919.

Court, W. H. B. *The Rise of the Midland Industries: 1600–1838*. Oxford, 1938.

Craig, Hardin. "Morality Plays and Elizabethan Drama." *Shakespeare Quarterly* 1 (1950): 64–72.

Craig, Hardin. *English Religious Drama of the Middle Ages*. Oxford, 1955.

Craik, T. W. *The Tudor Interlude: Stage, Costume, Acting*. Leicester, 1958.

Creeth, Edmund. *Mankynde in Shakespeare*. Athens, Ga., 1976.

Creizenach, Wilhelm. *Geschichte des neueren Dramas*. vol. 1. Halle, 1911.

Crow, John. "Folk-Lore in Elizabethan Drama." *Folk-Lore* 58 (1947):297–311.

Crusius, Otto. *Unterschungen zu den Mimiamben des Herondas*. Leipzig, 1892.

Crusius, Otto. *Die Mimiamben des Herondas*. Edited by R. Herzog. Leipzig, 1926.

Crusius, Otto, ed. *Herondae Mimiambi, etc*. Leipzig, 1905.

Curtius, E. R. *Europäische Literatur und Lateinisches Mittelalter*. Bern, 1948.

Cushman, L. W. *The Devil and the Vice in the English Dramatic Literature before Shakespeare*. Halle, 1900.

Danby, J. F. *Shakespeare's Doctrine of Nature: A Study of King Lear*. London, 1961.

Denny, Neville, assoc. ed. *Medieval Drama*. Stratford-upon-Avon Studies 16. London, 1973.

Dickens, A. G. *Lollards and Protestants in the Diocese of York: 1509–1558*. Oxford, 1959.

Dickens, A. G. *The English Reformation*. London, 1964.

Diller, Hans-Jürgen. "The Craftsmanship of the Wakefield Master." *Anglia* 83 (1965):271–88.

Diller, Hans-Jürgen. *Redeformen des englischen Misterienspiels*. Munich, 1973.

Dodd, Kenneth M. "Another Elizabethan Theater in the Round." *Shakespeare Quarterly* 21 (1970):125–50.

Donaldson, Ian. *The World Upside-Down: Comedy from Jonson to Fielding*. Oxford, 1970.

Doran, Madeleine. "On Elizabethan 'Credulity.' With Some Questions Concerning the Use of the Marvellous in Literature." *Journal of the History of Ideas* 1 (1940):151–76.

Doran, Madeleine. *Endeavors of Art: A Study of Form in Elizabethan Drama*. Madison, Wis., 1954.

Douce, Francis. *Illustrations of Shakespeare and of Ancient Manners: With Dissertations on the Clowns and Fools. . . .* London, 1839.

Doyle, A. J. "The Social Context of Medieval English Literature." In *The Age of Chaucer*. Edited by Boris Ford. Reprint. Harmondsworth, 1963: 85–105.

Dryden, John. *Of Dramatic Poesy and Other Critical Essays*. Edited by George Watson. 2 vols. London, 1962.

Dshiwelegow, A. K. *Commedia dell'arte*. Translated by R. -E. Riedt. Berlin, 1958.

Duchartre, Pierre-Louis, and Saulnier, René. *L'Imagerie populaire*. Paris, 1925.

Dunn, E. C. "The Prophetic Principle in the Towneley 'Prima Pastorum.'" *Lin-*

guistic and Literary Studies in Honor of Helmut A. Hatzfeld. Edited by A. S. Crisafulli. Washington, 1964:117-27.

Dyer, T. T. F. Folk-Lore of Shakespeare. London, 1883.

Eaton, H. A. "A Source for the Towneley 'Prima Pastorum.'" MLN 14 (1899): 265-68.

Eberle, Oskar. Cenalora: Leben, Glaube, Tanz und Theater der Urvölker. Olten/ Freiburg i. Br., 1954.

Eckhardt, Eduard. Die lustige Person im älteren englischen Drama. Berlin, 1902.

Eckhoff, Lorentz. Shakespeare, Spokesman of the Third Estate. Oxford, 1954.

Eliot, T. S. Selected Essays: 1917-1932. London, 1932.

Elliott, John R. "Medieval Rounds and Wooden O's: The Medieval Heritage of Elizabethan Theatre." Medieval Drama. Edited by Neville Denny. London, 1973:223-46.

Elliott, Robert C. "Saturnalia, Satire, and Utopia." Yale Review 55 (1965-66): 521-36.

Else, G. F. "'Imitation' in the Fifth Century." Classical Philology 53 (1958): 73-90.

Elson, J. J., ed. The Wits or, Sport upon Sport. New York, 1932.

Empson, William. Some Versions of Pastoral. London, 1935.

Erbstösser, Martin, and Werner, Ernst. Ideologische Probleme des mittelalterlichen Plebejertums. Berlin, 1960.

Evans, Bertrand. Shakespeare's Comedies. Oxford, 1960.

Farnham, Willard. The Medieval Heritage of Elizabethan Tragedy. Reprint. Oxford, 1956.

Farnham, Willard. The Shakespearean Grotesque: Its Genesis and Transformations. Oxford, 1971.

Feldman, S. D. The Morality-Patterned Comedy of the Renaissance. The Hague/Paris, 1970.

Felver, C. S. Robert Armin, Shakespeare's Fool. Kent, Ohio, 1961.

Fenton, Doris. The Extra-Dramatic Moment in Elizabethan Plays before 1616. Philadelphia, 1930.

Fergusson, Francis. The Idea of a Theater. Princeton, 1949.

Feuillerat, Albert, ed. Documents Relating to the Office of the Revels in the Time of Queen Elizabeth. Louvain, 1908.

Flasdieck, H. M. Harlekin. Germanischer Mythos in romanischer Wandlung. Separatum from Anglia. Halle, 1937.

Floegel, C. F. Geschichte der Hofnarren. Liegnitz/Leipzig, 1789.

Floegel, C. F. Geschichte des Grotesk-Komischen. Continued by F. W. Ebeling, 4th ed. Leipzig, 1887.

Fluchère, Henri. Shakespeare and the Elizabethans. Translated by Guy Hamilton. New York, 1956.

Förg, Joseph. "Typiche Redeformeln und -motive im vorshakespeareschen Drama." Dissertation. Munich, 1955.

Frampton, M. G. "The Brewbarret Interpolation in the York Play the Sacrificium Cayme and Abell." PMLA 52 (1937):895-900.

Franz, Wilhelm. Shakespeare-Grammatik. 4th ed. Halle, 1939.

Frazer, J. G. The Golden Bough. 12 vols. London, 1923-27.

Fricker, Robert. Kontrast und Polarität in den Charakterbildern Shakespeares. Bern, 1951.

Frye, Northrop. *Anatomy of Criticism: Four Essays*. Princeton, 1957.

Frye, Northrop. *A Natural Perspective: The Development of Shakespearean Comedy and Romance*. New York, 1965.

Frye, Northrop. "Old and New Comedy." *Shakespeare Survey* 22 (1969):1–5.

Furnivall, F. J., ed. *Tell-Trothes New-Yeares Gift*, etc. London, 1876.

Furnivall, F. J., ed. *Harrison's Description of England in Shakespeare's Youth*. 4 parts. London, 1877–1908.

Galloway, David, ed. vols. 1–3, and Hibbard, G. R., ed. vols. 4–5. *The Elizabethan Theatre*. Papers Given at the International Conference on Elizabethan Theatre Held at the University of Waterloo, Ontario. vol. 1, Toronto, 1970; vols. 2–5, Hamden, Conn., 1970–75.

Gardiner, H. C. *Mysteries' End: An Investigation of the Last Days of the Medieval Religious Stage*. New Haven, 1946.

Garvin, Katherine. "A Note on Noah's Wife," *MLN* 49 (1934):88–90.

Gates, William B. "Did Shakespeare Anticipate Comments from His Audience?" *Quarterly Journal of Speech* 33 (1947):348–54.

Gayley, C. M. *Plays of Our Forefathers and Some of the Traditions upon which the Plays were Founded*. London/New York, 1908.

Girnus, Wilhelm. *Deutsche Klassik und literarische Tradition, Natur und Idee*. Festschrift for A. B. Wachsmuth. Edited by Helmut Holtzhauer. Weimar, 1966:79–91.

Goldsmith, R. H. *Wise Fools in Shakespeare*. Liverpool, 1958.

Goldstein, Leonard. "On the Transition From Formal to Naturalistic Acting in the Elizabethan and Post-Elizabethan Theater." *Bull. New York Public Library* 62 (1958):330–49.

Goldstein, Leonard. "George Chapman: Aspects of Decadence in Early Seventeenth Century Drama." Habil.-Schrift. Berlin, 1965.

Gomme, A. B. "The Character of Beelzebub in the Mummers' Play." *Folk-Lore* 40 (1929):292–93.

Graf, Hermann. *Der "Miles Gloriosus" im englischen Drama bis zur Zeit des Bürgerkrieges*. Dissertation. Rostock, 1892.

Granville-Barker, Harley. *Prefaces to Shakespeare*. Paperback ed. 4 vols. London, 1963.

Grassi, Ernesto. *Kunst und Mythos*. Hamburg, 1957.

Green, R. L. "Shakespeare and the Fairies," *Folklore* 73 (1962):89–103.

Greg, W. W. *A Bibliography of the English Printed Drama to the Restoration*. 3 vols. London, 1957.

Grivelet, Michel. "Shakespeare as 'Corrupter of Words.'" *Shakespeare Survey* 16 (1963):70–76.

Gruner, Helene. "Studien zum Dialog im vorshakespeareschen Drama." Dissertation. Munich, 1955.

Gurr, Andrew. *The Shakespearean Stage: 1574–1642*. Cambridge, 1970.

Hall, Vernon, Jr. *Renaissance Literary Criticism: A Study of its Social Content*. Reprint. Gloucester, Mass., 1959.

Halliwell, J. O. *Illustrations of the Fairy Mythology of A Midsummer Night's Dream*. London, 1845.

Halliwell, J. O., ed. *Tarlton's Jests and News out of Purgatory*. London, 1844.

Hapgood, Robert. "Shakespeare and the Ritualists." *Shakespeare Survey* 15 (1962):11-24.

Happé, P. "The Vice and the Folk-Drama." *Folklore* 75 (1964):161-93.

Harbage, Alfred. *Shakespeare and the Rival Traditions.* New York, 1952.

Harbage, Alfred. "The Role of the Shakespearean Producer." *Shakespeare Jahrbuch* 91 (1955):161-73.

Harbage, Alfred. *As They Liked It: A Study of Shakespeare's Moral Artistry.* New York, 1961.

Harbage, Alfred. *Shakespeare's Audience.* New York/London, 1964.

Hardison, O. B., Jr. *Christian Rite and Christian Drama in the Middle Ages: Essays in the Origin and Early History of Modern Drama.* Baltimore, 1965.

Hauser, Arnold. *Sozialgeschichte der Kunst und Literatur.* 2 vols. Munich, 1953.

Hazlitt, W. C. *Faiths and Folklore: A Dictionary of National Beliefs, Superstitions and Popular Customs....* 2 vols. London, 1905.

Hazlitt, W. C., ed. *Shakespeare Jest-Books.* 3 vols. London, 1864.

Hazlitt, W. C., ed. *The English Drama and Stage under the Tudor and Stuart Princes: 1543-1664.* London, 1869.

Hecht, Hans. "Henry Medwalls Fulgens and Lucrece. Eine Studie zu den Anfängen des weltlichen Dramas in England." *Anglia.* Festschrift for Alois Brandl, 2, "Palaestra," 148. Leipzig, 1925:83-117.

Heise, Wolfgang. "Hegel und das Komische." *Sinn und Form* 16 (1964):811-30.

Herrick, M. T. *Comic Theory in the Sixteenth Century.* Urbana, Ill., 1964.

Herrmann, Max. *Forschungen zur Deutschen Theatergeschichte des Mittelalters und der Renaissance.* Part 1. Dresden, 1955.

Herrmann, Max. *Die Entstehung der berufsmässigen Schauspielkunst im Altertum und in der Neuzeit.* Edited by Ruth Mövius. Berlin, 1962.

Hewitt, Douglas. "The very Pompes of the Divell: Popular and Folk Elements in Elizabethan and Jacobean Drama." *RES* 25 (1949): 10-23.

Heydemann, H. "Die Phlyakendarstellungen auf bemalten Vasen." *Jahrbuch des kaiserlich-deutschen archäologischen Instituts* 1 (1886):260-313.

Hill, Christopher, and Dell, Edmund, eds. *The good old cause; the English Revolution of 1640-60; its causes, course and consequences.* London, 1949.

Hill, Christopher. *The Century of Revolution, 1603-1714.* Edinburgh, 1961.

Hill, Christopher. *The World Turned Upside Down: Radical Ideas during the English Revolution.* London, 1972.

Hilton, R. H., and Fagan, H. *The English Rising of 1381.* London, 1950.

Hilton, R. H. "The Origins of Robin Hood." *Past and Present* 14 (1958):30-43.

Hitchcock, E. V., ed. *Harpsfield's Life of More, with an introduction On the Continuity of English Prose...* by R. W. Chambers (EETS, 186), London, 1932: xlv-clxxiv.

Hobsbawm, E. J. *Primitive Rebels: Studies in Archaic Forms of Social Movements in the 19th and 20th Centuries.* Manchester, 1959.

Hodges, C. W. *The Globe Restored: A Study of the Elizabethan Theatre.* London, 1953.

Hodges, C. W. "The Lantern of Taste." *Shakespeare Survey* 12 (1959):8-14.

Höfler, Otto. *Kultische Geheimbünde der Germanen.* vol. 1. Frankfurt a. M., 1934.

Hohlfeld, Alexander. "Die altenglischen Kollektivmisterien." *Anglia* 11 (1889):219-310.

Holt, J. C. "The Origins and Audiences of the Ballads of Robin Hood." *Past and Present* 18 (1960):89-110.

Hoskins, W. G. "The Rebuilding of Rural England, 1570–1640." *Past and Present* 4 (1953):44–59.

Hoskins, W. G. *The Midland Peasant: The Economic and Social History of a Leicestershire Village*. London, 1957.

Hosley, Richard. "The Gallery Over the Stage in the Public Playhouses of Shakespeare's Time." *Shakespeare Quarterly* 8 (1957):15–31.

Hosley, Richard. "Shakespeare's Use of a Gallery Over the Stage." *Shakespeare Survey* 10 (1957):77–89.

Hosley, Richard. "Was There a Music-Room in Shakespeare's Globe?" *Shakespeare Survey* 13 (1960):113–23.

Hosley, Richard. "The Staging of Desdemona's Bed." *Shakespeare Quarterly* 14 (1963):57–65.

Hosley, Richard. "The Origins of the Shakespearean Playhouse." *Shakespeare Quarterly* 15 (1964):2:29–39.

Hosley, Richard. "Three Kinds of Outdoor Theatre Before Shakespeare." *Theatre Survey* 12 (1971):1–33.

Hosley, Richard, ed. *Essays on Shakespeare and Elizabethan Drama: In Honour of Hardin Craig*. London, 1963.

Hotson, Leslie. *The Commonwealth and Restoration Stage*. Cambridge, Mass., 1928.

Hotson, Leslie. *Shakespeare's Wooden O*. London, 1960.

Hotson, Leslie. *The First Night of "Twelfth Night."* London, 1961.

Hulme, Hilda M. *Explorations in Shakespeare's Language*. London, 1962.

Hunningher, B. *The Origin of the Theater*. Amsterdam, 1955.

Hunter, G. K. "Seneca and the Elizabethans: A Case-Study in 'Influence.'" *Shakespeare Survey* 20 (1967):17–26.

Hunter, G. K. "Seneca and English Tragedy." *Seneca*. Edited by C. D. N. Costa. London, 1974: 166–204.

Huppé, B. F. "Petrus, id est Christus: Word Play in Piers Plowman, the B-Text." *ELH* 17 (1950):163–90.

Jameison, Michael. "Shakespeare in the Theatre." *Shakespeare: Select Bibliographical Guides*. Edited by Stanley Wells. London, 1973: 25–43.

Janicka, Irena. *The Comic Elements in the English Mystery Plays Against the Cultural Background (particularly Art)*. Poznan, 1962.

Janicka, Irena. *The Popular Theatrical Tradition and Ben Jonson*. Łódz, 1972.

Jones, E. D., ed. *English Critical Essays*. Nineteenth century. Reprint. Oxford, 1950.

Joseph, B. L. *Elizabethan Acting*. London, 1952.

Joseph, Sister Miriam. *Shakespeare's Use of the Arts of Language*. New York, 1947.

Joseph, Sister Miriam. *Rhetoric in Shakespeare's Time: Literary Theory of Renaissance Europe*. New York, 1962.

Kahrl, S. J., and Cameson, Kenneth. "The Staging of the N-town Cycle." *Theatre Notebook* 21 (1967):122–38, 152–65.

Kahrl, Stanley. *Traditions of Medieval English Drama*. London, 1974.

Kamlah, Wilhelm. "Der Ludus de Antichristo." *Historische Vierteljahrsschrift* 28 (1933):53–87.

Keen, Maurice. "Robin Hood—Peasant or Gentleman?" *Past and Present* 19 (1960):7–15.

Keen, Maurice. *The Outlaws of Medieval Legend*. London, 1961.

Keiller, M. H. "The Influence of Piers Plowman on the Macro Play of Mankind," *PMLA* 26 (1911):339–55.

Kerényi, Karl. *Die Herkunft der Dionysosreligion nach dem heutigen Stand der Forschung*. Köln/Opladen, 1956.

Kernodle, G. R. *From Art to Theatre: Form and Convention in the Renaissance*. Chicago, 1944.

Kersten, Dorelies. "Shakespeares Puck." *Shakespeare Jahrbuch* 98 (1962):189–200.

Kettle, Arnold, ed. *Shakespeare in a Changing World*. London, 1964.

Kilian, Eugen. "Der Shakespearesche Monolog und seine Spielweise." *Shakespeare Jahrbuch* 39 (1903):XIV–XLII.

King, T. J. *Shakespearean Staging: 1599–1642*. Cambridge, Mass., 1971.

Kittredge, G. L. "The Friar's Lantern and Friar Rush." *PMLA* 15 (1900):415–41.

Kluckholm, Clyde. "Myths and Rituals: A General Theory." *Harvard Theological Review* 35 (January 1942):45–79.

Knights, L. C. *Shakespeare's Politics: With Some Reflections on the Nature of Tradition*. Proceedings of the British Academy. 1957.

Knights, L. C. *Drama and Society in the Age of Jonson*. Penguin ed. Harmondsworth, 1962.

Koch, Gottfried. *Frauenfrage und Ketzertum im Mittelalter*. Berlin, 1962.

Kökeritz, Helge. *Shakespeare's Pronunciation*. New Haven, 1953.

Koller, Hermann. *Die Mimesis in der Antike. Nachahmung, Darstellung, Ausdruck*. Bern, 1954.

Kolve, V. A. *The Play Called Corpus Christi*. Stanford, 1966.

Könneker, Barbara. *Wesen und Wandlung der Narrenidee im Zeitalter des Humanismus*. Wiesbaden, 1966.

Kramer, S. *The English Craft Guilds: Studies in their Progress and Decline*. New York, 1927.

Kretzenbacher, Leopold. "Schlangenteufel und Satan im Paradeisspiel." *Masken in Mitteleuropa*. Edited by L. Schmidt. Vienna, 1955: 72–92.

Kuckhoff, Armin-G. *Das Drama William Shakespeares. Schriften zur Theaterwissenschaft*. vol. 3, 1. Berlin, 1964.

Landauer, Gustav. *Shakespeare*. 2 vols. Potsdam, 1948.

Latham, M. W. *The Elizabethan Fairies: The Fairies of Folklore and the Fairies of Shakespeare*. New York, 1930.

Lauf, Elisabeth. *Die Bühnenanweisungen in den englischen Moralitäten und Interludien bis 1570*. Dissertation. Münster, 1932.

Lawrence, W. J. "On the Underrated Genius of Dick Tarleton." *Speeding up Shakespeare*. London, 1937: 17–38.

Leech, Clifford. *Shakespeare's Tragedies*. London, 1950.

Leech, Clifford, and Margeson, J. M. R., eds. *Shakespeare 1971*. Toronto, 1972.

Lehmann, Paul. *Die Parodie im Mittelalter*. Munich, 1922.

Lehnert, Martin. *Shakespeares Sprache und Wir*. Berlin, 1963.

Lennep, William Van. "The Death of the Red Bull." *Theatre Notebook* 16 (1962):126–34.

Lennep, William Van, ed. *The London Stage, Part I: 1660–1700*. Carbondale, Ill., 1965.

Lever, Katherine. *The Art of Greek Comedy*. London, 1956.
Levin, Richard. "Elizabethan Clown Sub-Plots." *Essays in Criticism* 16 (1966): no. i:84-91.
Levin, Richard. *The Multiple Plot in English Renaissance Drama*. Chicago/London, 1971.
Lindsay, Jack. *The Clashing Rocks: A Study of Early Greek Religion and Culture and the Origins of Drama*. London, 1965.
Lipson, E. *The Growth of English Society*. 3rd ed. London, 1954.
Logeman, H., ed. *The English Faust-Book of 1592*. Gand/Amsterdam, 1900.
Loomis, R. S., and Cohen, Gustave. "Were there Theatres in the Twelfth and Thirteenth Centuries?" *Speculum* 20 (1945):92-98.
Lukács, Georg. "Die Eigenart des Ästhetischen." Georg Lukács, *Werke*. vols. 11 and 12 (Ästhetik, part 1). Neuwied, 1963.
Lüthi, Max. "Die Macht des Nichtwirklichen in Shakespeares Spielen." *Shakespeare Jahrbuch* 97 (1961):13-33.
Macfarlane, A. D. J. *Witchcraft in Tudor and Stuart England*. New York, 1970.
Mahood, M. M. *Shakespeare's Wordplay*. London, 1957.
Malinowski, Bronislaw. "Culture." *Encyclopaedia of the Social Sciences*. vol. 4. (1931):621-46.
Manly, W. M. "Shepherds and Prophets: Religious Unity in the Towneley 'Secunda Pastorum.'" *PMLA* 78 (1963): 151-55.
Mares, F. H. "The Origin and Development of the Figure Called the "Vice" in Tudor Drama." B. Litt. Dissertation. Oxford, Lincoln, 1954.
Mares, F. H. "The Origin of the Figure Called "the Vice" in Tudor Drama," *Huntington Library Quarterly* 22 (1958):11-29.
Marshall, M. H. "'Theatre' in the Middle Ages: Evidence from Dictionaries and Glosses." *Symposium* 4 (1950):1-39; 366-89.
Marshall, M. H. "The Dramatic Tradition Established by the Liturgical Plays." *PMLA* 56 (1941):962-91.
Martin, Alfred von. *Soziologie der Renaissance. Zur Physiognomik und Rhythmik bürgerlicher Kultur*. Stuttgart, 1932.
Marx, Karl and Friedrich Engels. *Werke*. 39 vols. Berlin, 1959-1968.
Mätzner, Eduard, ed. *Altenglische Sprachproben*. vol. 1. Berlin, 1867.
McAlindon, T. "Comedy and Terror in Middle English Literature: The Diabolical Game." *MLR* 60 (1965):323-32.
McCollom, W. G. "Formalism and Illusion in Shakespearian Drama: 1595-1598." *Quarterly Journal of Speech* 31 (1945):446-53.
McCullen, J. T. "Madness and the Isolation of Characters in Elizabethan and Early Stuart Drama." *SP* 48 (1951):206-18.
McMullen, Glenys. "The Fool as Entertainer and Satirist on Stage and in the World." *Dalhousie Review* 50 (1970):10-22.
McMullin, Earnan. "Medieval and Modern Science: Continuity or Discontinuity?" *International Philosophical Quarterly* 5 (1965):103-29.
McMullin, Earnan. "Empiricism and the Scientific Revolution." *Art, Science and History in the Renaissance*. Edited by Charles I. Singleton. Baltimore, 1970.
McNeir, W. F. "The Corpus Christi Passion Plays As Dramatic Art." *SP* 48 (1951):601-28.

Mehring, Franz. *Beiträge zur Literaturgeschichte*. Edited by W. Heist. Berlin, 1948.

Meissner, Paul. *England im Zeitalter von Humanismus, Renaissance und Reformation*. Heidelberg, 1952.

Mellers, Wilfrid. "Words and Music in Elizabethan England." *The Age of Shakespeare*. Edited by Boris Ford. Harmondsworth, 1956:386–415.

Meschke, Kurt. *Schwerttanz und Schwerttanzspiel im germanischen Kulturkreis*. Leipzig/Berlin, 1931.

Meyer, E. H. *English Chamber Music*. London, 1946.

Miles, Bernard, and Wilson, Josephine. "Three Festivals at the Mermaid Theatre." *Shakespeare Quarterly* 5 (1954):307–10.

Mill, A. J. "Noah's Wife Again." *PMLA* 56 (1941):613–26.

Miller, E. H. *The Professional Writer in Elizabethan England*. Cambridge, Mass., 1959.

Mokul'skij, S. S. *Chrestomatija po istorii zapadnoevropejskogo teatra*. vol. 1. 2nd. ed. Moscow, 1953.

Monaghan, James. "Falstaff and his Forbears." *SP* 18 (1921):353–61.

Moore, John Brooks. *The Comic and the Realistic in English Drama*. Chicago, 1926.

Morgan, M. M. "'High Fraud': Paradox and Double-plot in the English Shepherds' Plays." *Speculum* 39 (1964):676–89.

Morozov, M. M. "The Individualization of Shakespeare's Characters through Imagery." *Shakespeare Survey* 2 (1949):93–101.

Morton, A. L. *The English Utopia*. London, 1952.

Muir, Kenneth. "The Uncomic Pun." *The Cambridge Journal* 3 (1949–50):472–85.

Muir, Kenneth. "The Dramatic Function of Anachronism." *Proc. of the Leeds Phil. and Lit. Society* 6 (1951):529–33.

Muir, Kenneth. *Shakespeare's Sources*. 2 vols. London, 1951.

Muir, Kenneth. "Shakespeare's Soliloquies." *Ocidente* 67 (1964):45–58.

Muir, Kenneth. "Shakespeare and Politics." *Shakespeare in a Changing World*. Edited by Arnold Kettle. London, 1964:65–83.

Müller-Bellinghausen, Anton. "Die Wortkulisse bei Shakespeare." *Shakespeare Jahrbuch* 91 (1955):182–95.

Murray, Gilbert. "Hamlet and Orestes." *The Classical Tradition in Poetry*. London, 1927:205–40.

Murray, Margaret. *The God of the Witches*. London, 1933.

Murray, Margaret. *The Witch-Cult in Western Europe*. Oxford, 1963.

Nagler, A. M. *Shakespeare's Stage*. New Haven, 1958.

Nef, J. U. *The Rise of the British Coal Industry*. 2 vols. London, 1932.

Nelson, Alan H. "Some Configurations of Staging in Medieval Drama." *Medieval English Drama: Essays Critical and Contextual*. Edited by Jerome Taylor and Alan H. Nelson. Chicago, 1972:116–48.

Nelson, Alan H. *The Medieval English Stage: Corpus Christi Pageants and Plays*. Chicago, 1974.

Neumann, Hans. *Primitive Gemeinschaftskultur. Beiträge zur Volkskunde und Mythologie*. Jena, 1921.

Nicoll, Allardyce. *The Development of the Theatre*. London, 1927.

Nicoll, Allardyce. *Masks, Mimes and Miracles: Studies in the Popular Theatre*. London, 1931.

Nicoll, Allardyce. *The World of Harlequin*. Cambridge, 1953.

Nicoll, Allardyce. "Shakespeare and the Court Masque." *Shakespeare Jahrbuch* 94 (1958):51–62.

Nicoll, Allardyce. "'Passing over the Stage.'" *Shakespeare Survey* 12 (1959): 47–55.

Niessen, Carl. *Handbuch der Theaterwissenschaft*. 3 vols. Emsdetten, 1949–58.

Nietzsche, Friedrich. *Die Geburt der Tragödie aus dem Geiste der Musik*. Berlin, n.d.

Nilsson, M. P. "Saturnalia." *Paulys Real-Enzyklopädie der classischen Altertumswissenschaft*. rev. ed. 2nd series. vol. 3. Stuttgart, 1921.

Nutt, Alfred. *The Fairy Mythology of Shakespeare*. London, 1900.

Ogilvy, J. D. "Mimi, Scurrae, Histriones: Entertainers of the Early Middle Ages." *Speculum* 38 (1963):603–19.

Oppel, Horst. "Kontrast und Kontrapunkt im Shakespeare-Drama." *Shakespeare Jahrbuch* 97 (1961):153–82.

Ordish, T. F. "English Folk Drama." *Folk-Lore* 4 (1893):149–75.

Ordish, T. F. *Early London Theatres*. London, 1894.

Otto, W. F. *Dionysos: Mythos und Kultus*. Frankfurt a. M., 1933.

Owst, G. R. *Literature and Pulpit in Medieval England*. Cambridge, 1933.

Parker, R. E. "The Reputation of Herod in Early English Literature." *Speculum* 8 (1933):59–67.

Pascal, Roy. "On the Origins of the Liturgical Drama of the Middle Ages." *MLR* 36 (1941):369–87.

Peers, E. A. *Elizabethan Drama and Its Mad Folk*. Cambridge, 1914.

Petsch, Robert. *Das deutsche Volksrätsel*. Strassburg, 1917.

Peukert, W. E. *Geheimkulte*. Heidelberg, 1951.

Philippson, E. A. *Germanisches Heidentum bei den Angelsachsen*. Leipzig, 1929.

Pinskij, L. E. *Realism epochi vozroždenia*. Moscow, 1961.

Prosser, Eleanor. *Drama and Religion in the English Mystery Plays: A Re-evaluation*. Stanford, Cal., 1961.

Rabkin, Norman. "The Double Plot: Notes on the History of a Convention." *Renaissance Drama* 7 (1964):55–69.

Rabkin, Norman. *Shakespeare and the Common Understanding*. New York, 1967.

Rabkin, Norman, ed. *Reinterpretations of Elizabethan Drama*. Selected Papers From the English Institute. New York, 1969.

Reed, A. W. *Early Tudor Drama*. London, 1926.

Reich, Hermann. *Der Mimus. Ein litterar-entwickelungsgeschichtlicher Versuch*. Berlin, 1903.

Reich, Hermann. *Der Mann mit dem Eselskopf. Ein Mimodrama vom klassischen Altertum verfolgt bis auf Shakespeares Sommernachtstraum*. Weimar, 1904.

Reichert, Günter. *Die Entwicklung und die Funktion der Nebenhandlung in der Tragödie vor Shakespeare*. Tübingen, 1966.

Reuling, C. *Die komische Figur in den wichtigsten deutschen Dramen bis zum Ende des XVII. Jahrhunderts*. Dissertation. Zürich, Stuttgart, 1890.

Reynolds, G. F. *The Staging of Elizabethan Plays at the Red Bull Theater: 1606–1625*. London, 1940.

Reynolds, G. F. "Was there a 'Tarras' in Shakespeare's Globe?" *Shakespeare Survey* 4 (1951):97–100.

Richmond, Kenneth. *Poetry and the People*. London, 1947.

Riehle, Wolfgang. *Das Beiseitesprechen bei Shakespeare. Ein Beitrag zur Dramaturgie des elisabethanischen Dramas*. Dissertation. Munich, 1964.

Righter, Anne. *Shakespeare and the Idea of the Play*. London, 1962.

Ritson, Joseph. *Fairy Tales, Legends and Romances Illustrating Shakespeare and other Early English Writers*. Edited by W. C. Hazlitt. London, 1875.

Robbins, R. H. *The Encyclopedia of Witchcraft and Demonology*. New York, 1959.

Robbins, R. H. "The Imposture of Witchcraft." *Folklore* 74 (1963):545–62.

Robinson, J. W. "The Art of the York Realist." *MP* 60 (1962–63): 241–51.

Rodgers, Edith Cooperrider. *Discussion of Holidays in the Later Middle Ages*. New York, 1940.

Rommel, Otto. *Die Alt-Wiener Volkskomödie*. Wien, 1952.

Rosenfeld, Sybil. *Strolling Players and Drama in the Provinces: 1660–1765*. Cambridge, 1939.

Ross, L. J. "The Use of a 'Fit-Up' Booth in *Othello*." *Shakespeare Quarterly* 12 (1961):359–70.

Rossiter, A. P. *English Drama From Early Times to the Elizabethans*. London, 1950.

Rossiter, A. P. *Angel with Horns and other Shakespeare Lectures*. London, 1961.

Rowse, A. L. *The England of Elizabeth*. vol. 1: *The Structure of Society*. London, 1950.

Rubinstein, A. T. *The Great Tradition in English Literature: From Shakespeare to Shaw*. New York, 1953.

Rudwin, Maximilian. *The Devil in Legend and Literature*. Chicago, 1931.

Salingar, Leo. *Shakespeare and the Traditions of Comedy*. Cambridge, 1974.

Salter, F. M. *Medieval Drama in Chester*. Toronto, 1955.

Samarin, Roman. *Zum Problem des Realismus in den westeuropäischen Literaturen der Renaissance. Probleme des Realismus in der Weltliteratur*. Edited by Institut für Slawistik der DAdW. Berlin, 1962.

Samarin, Roman. *Realism Shakespeara*. Moscow, 1964.

Saunders, J. W. "Vaulting the Rails," *Shakespeare Survey* 7 (1954):69–81.

Savage, H. L. "The Feast of Fools in 'Gawain.'" *JEGPh* 51 (1952):537–44.

Schlösser, A. "Zur Frage 'Volk und Mob' bei Shakespeare," *ZAA* 4 (1956): 148–71.

Schlösser, Anselm. "Der Widerstreit von Patriotismus und Humanismus in 'Heinrich V.'" *ZAA* 12 (1964):244–56.

Schlösser, Anselm, ed. *Shakespeare Jubiläum 1964*. Weimar, 1964.

Schmidt, Leopold. *Das deutsche Volksschauspiel. Ein Handbuch*. Berlin, 1962.

Schmidt, Leopold, ed. *Masken in Mitteleuropa. Volkskundliche Beiträge zur europäischen Maskenforschung*. Wien, 1955.

Schmitt, Natalie Crohn. "Was there a Medieval Theatre in the Round? A Reexamination of the Evidence." *Theatre Notebook* 23 (1968–69):130–42 and (1969–70):18–25.

Schöne, Annemarie. "Shakespeares weise Narren und ihre Vorfahren." *Jb. für Ästhetik und allg. Kunstwissenschaft* 5 (1960):202–45.

Schröder, F. R. *Germanentum und Hellenismus. Untersuchungen zur germanischen Religionsgeschichte*. Heidelberg, 1924.

Schubel, Friedrich. "Die englischen Bühnen zu Shakespeares Zeit." *Shakespeare: Seine Welt—unsere Welt*. Edited by Gerhard Müller-Schwefe. Tübingen, 1964:24–40.

Schubert, H. R. *History of the British Iron and Steel Industry (450 B.C.-1775)*. London, 1957.

Schücking, L. L. "Shakespeare als Volksdramatiker." *Internationale Monatsschrift für Wissenschaft, Kunst und Technik* 6 (1912):1513-34.

Schücking, L. L. *Die Charakterprobleme bei Shakespeare*. 3rd ed. Leipzig, 1932.

Schücking, L. L. *Shakespeare und der Tragödienstil seiner Zeit*. Bern, 1947.

Schumann, Hildegard. "King Lear." *Shakespeare Jahrbuch* (Weimar) 100-101 (1964-65):192-207.

Schurtz, Heinrich. *Altersklassen und Männerbünde*. Berlin, 1902.

Sehrt, E. Th. *Der dramatische Auftakt in der elisabethanischen Tragödie. Interpretationen zum englischen Drama der Shakespearezeit*. Göttingen, 1960.

Sewell, Arthur. *Character and Society in Shakespeare*. Oxford, 1951.

Sharp, C. J. *The Sword Dances of Northern England*. 3 parts. London, 1911-14.

Siegel, P. N. *Shakespearean Tragedy and the Elizabethan Compromise*. New York, 1957.

Siegel, P. N. *Shakespeare in His Time and Ours*. London, 1968.

Simon, Joan. *Education and Society in Tudor England*. Cambridge, 1966.

Sisson, C. J. *Le goût public et le théâtre Élisabéthain jusqu'à la mort de Shakespeare*. Dijon, n.d.

Sisson, C. J. *Lost Plays of Shakespeare's Age*. Cambridge, 1936.

Smart, J. S. *Shakespeare: Truth and Tradition*. London, 1929.

Smart, W. K. "Some Notes on *Mankind*." *MP* 14 (1916-17):43-58, 101-21.

Smart, W. K. "*Mankind* and the Mumming Plays." *MLN* 32 (1917):21-25.

Smith, D. N., ed. *Eighteenth Century Essays on Shakespeare*. 2nd ed. Oxford, 1963.

Smith, G. E. *The Evolution of the Dragon*. Manchester, 1919.

Smith, G. G., ed. *Elizabethan Critical Essays*. 2 vols. Oxford, 1904.

Smith, Irwin. *Shakespeare's Blackfriars Playhouse: Its History and Its Design*. New York, 1964.

Sörbom, Göran. *Mimesis and Art: Studies in the Origin and Early Development of an Aesthetic Vocabulary*. Upsalla, 1966.

Southern, Richard. *The Open Stage*. London, 1953.

Southern, Richard. *The Medieval Theatre in the Round*. New York, 1958.

Southern, Richard. *The Seven Ages of the Theatre*. London, 1962.

Southern, Richard. "The Contribution of the Interludes to Elizabethan Staging." *Essays on Shakespeare and Elizabethan Drama*. Edited by Richard Hosley: 3-14.

Southern, Richard. *The Staging of Plays before Shakespeare*. London, 1973.

Speirs, John. *Medieval English Poetry: The Non-Chaucerian Tradition*. London, 1957.

Speirs, John. "A Survey of Medieval Verse," *The Age of Chaucer*. Edited by Boris Ford. Reprint. Harmondsworth, 1963:17-67.

Speirs, John. "The Towneley 'Shepherds' Plays.'" *The Age of Chaucer*. Edited by Boris Ford. Reprint. Harmondsworth, 1963:167-74.

Spens, Janet. *An Essay on Shakespeare's Relation to Tradition*. Oxford, 1916.

Spevack, Marvin. "The Dramatic Function of Shakespeare's Puns." Ph. D. Dissertation, Harvard, 1953.

Spingarn, J. E. *A History of Literary Criticism in the Renaissance*. 2nd ed. New York, 1924.

Spingarn, J. E., ed. *Critical Essays of the Seventeenth Century*. 3 vols. Oxford, 1908.

Spivack, Bernard. *Shakespeare and the Allegory of Evil.* New York, 1958.

Stamm, Rudolf. *Geschichte des englischen Theaters.* Bern, 1951.

Stamm, Rudolf. "Dichtung und Theater in Shakespeares Werk." *Shakespeare Jahrbuch* 98 (1962):7–23.

Stamm, Rudolf. *Zwischen Vision und Wirklichkeit.* Bern, 1964.

Steinitz, Wolfgang. "Volkskunde und Völkerkunde." *Forschungen und Fortschritte* 27 (1953):142–45.

Stevens, Martin. "The Dramatic Setting of the Wakefield 'Annunciation.'" *PMLA* 81 (1966):193–98.

Stirling, Brents. *The Populace in Shakespeare.* New York, 1949.

Stone, Lawrence. *The Crisis of the Aristocracy: 1558–1641.* Oxford, 1965.

Stříbrný, Zdeněk. "Shakespeare a lidové tradice." *Časopis por moderni filologii* 40 (1958):65–79.

Stříbrný, Zdeněk. "'Henry V' and History." *Shakespeare in a Changing World.* Edited by Arnold Kettle. London, 1964:84–101.

Stubbes, Phillip. *The Anatomy of Abuses.* Edited by F. J. Furnivall. 2 parts. London, 1877–82.

Stumpfl, Robert. *Kultspiele der Germanen als Ursprung des mittelalterlichen Dramas.* Berlin, 1936.

Styan, J. L. "The Actor at the Foot of Shakespeare's Platform." *Shakespeare Survey* 12 (1959):56–63.

Styan, J. L. *Shakespeare's Stagecraft.* Cambridge, 1967.

Sudhaus, S. "Der Mimus von Oxyrhynchos." *Hermes* 41 (1906):247–77.

Summers, Montague. *The History of Witchcraft and Demonology.* Reprint. New York, 1956.

Swain, Barbara. *Fools and Folly during the Middle Ages and the Renaissance.* New York, 1932.

Sweezy, Paul M. *Monopoly and Competition in the English Coal Trade, 1550–1850.* Cambridge, Mass., 1938.

Szenczi, Miklós. "The Nature of Shakespeare's Realism." *Shakespeare Jahrbuch* (Weimar) 102 (1966):37–59.

Talbert, E. W. *Elizabethan Drama and Shakespeare's Early Plays.* Chapel Hill, 1963.

Thomas, Keith. *Religion and the Decline of Magic.* New York, 1971.

Thomas, Sidney. *The Antic Hamlet and Richard III.* New York, 1943.

Thompson, E. N. S. *The Controversy between the Puritans and the Stage.* New York, 1903.

Thompson, R. L. *The History of the Devil. The Horned God of the West.* London, 1929.

Thomson, George. *Aeschylus and Athens: A Study in the Social Origins of Drama.* London, 1941.

Thomson, J. A. F. *The Later Lollards, 1414–1520.* Oxford, 1965.

Thomson, Katharine. "Elizabethan Popular Songs and the English Musical Tradition." *Marxism Today* 9 (1965):337–45.

Thorndike, A. H. *The Influence of Beaumont and Fletcher on Shakespeare.* Worcester, Mass., 1901.

Thorndike, A. H. *Shakespeare's Theater.* New York, 1916.

Thorne, W. B. "The Influence of Folk-Drama upon Shakespearean Comedy." Ph. D. Dissertation. Univ. of Wisconsin, 1965.

Tiddy, R. J. E. *The Mummers' Play.* Oxford, 1923.

Tilley, M. P. *A Dictionary of the Proverbs in England in the Sixteenth and Seventeenth Centuries.* Ann Arbor, 1950.

Tillyard, E. M. W. *Shakespeare's History Plays.* Harmondsworth, 1960.

Tisdel, F. M. "The Influence of Popular Customs on the Mystery Plays." *JEGPh* 5 (1903-5):323-40.

Tomlinson, W. E. *Der Herodes-Charakter im englischen Drama, "Palestra 195."* Leipzig, 1934.

Trendall, A. D. *Phlyax Vases.* Univ. of London Institute of Class. Studies. Bull. Suppl. 8. London, 1959.

Trevelyan, G. M. *English Social History.* London, 1945.

Trusler, Margaret. "The York 'Sacrificium Cayme and Abell.'" *PMLA* 49 (1934): 956-59.

Tunison, J. S. *Dramatic Traditions of the Dark Ages.* Chicago, 1907.

Velz, J. W. "Some Modern Views of Shakespeare's Classicism." *Anglia* 81 (1963): 412-28.

Wallace, G. W. *The Evolution of the English Drama up to Shakespeare.* Berlin, 1912.

Wallace, G. W. *The First London Theatre: Materials for a History.* Lincoln, Nebr., 1913.

Webster, T. B. L. "South Italian Vases and Attic Drama." *The Classical Quarterly* 42 (1948):15-27.

Weimann, Robert. *Drama und Wirklichkeit in der Shakespearezeit.* Halle, 1958.

Weimann, Robert. "The Soul of the Age: Towards a Historical Approach to Shakespeare." *Shakespeare in a Changing World.* Edited by Arnold Kettle. London, 1964:17-42.

Weimann, Robert. "Laughing With the Audience: *The Two Gentlemen of Verona* and the Popular Tradition of Comedy." *Shakespeare Survey* 22 (1969):35-42.

Weimann, Robert. *Literaturgeschichte und Mythologie.* Berlin, 1971.

Weimann, Robert. "Metaphor and Historical Criticism: Shakespeare's Imagery Revisited." *Structure and Society in Literary History.* Charlottesville, Va., 1976:188-233.

Weinberg, Bernard. *A History of Literary Criticism in the Italian Renaissance.* 2 vols. Chicago, 1961.

Weiser, Lily. *Altermanische Jünglingsweihen und Männerbünde.* Bühl (Baden), 1927.

Wellwarth, George E. "From Ritual to Drama: The Social Background of the Early English Theatre." *Journal of General Education* 19 (1968):297-328.

Welsford, Enid. *The Court Masque: A Study in the Relationship between Poetry and the Revels.* Cambridge, 1927.

Welsford, Enid. *The Fool: His Social and Literary History.* Anchor ed. New York, 1961.

White, H. C. *Social Criticism in Popular Religious Literature of the Sixteenth Century.* New York, 1944.

Whiting, B. J. *Proverbs in the Earlier English Drama.* Cambridge, Mass., 1938.

Wicht, Wolfgang. "Shakespeares 'Julius Caesar' und 'Coriolanus.' Zur Problematik der realistischen Methode in den beiden Römerdramen." Dissertation. Rostock, 1965.

Wickham, Glynne. *Early English Stages: 1300 to 1600.* vol. 1. London, 1959. vol. 2. part 1. London, 1963.

Wickham, Glynne. *Shakespeare's Dramatic Heritage: Collected Studies in Mediaeval, Tudor and Shakespearean Drama*. London, 1969.

Wiemken, Helmut. *Der griechische Mimus*. Bremen, 1972.

Wiley, W. L. *The Early Public Theatre in France*. Cambridge, Mass., 1960.

Willeford, William. *The Fool and His Scepter: A Study in Clowns and Jesters and their Audience*. Evanston, Ill., 1969.

Williams, Arnold. *The Characterization of Pilate in the Towneley Plays*. Michigan, 1950.

Williams, Arnold. *The Drama of Medieval England*. Michigan, 1961.

Wilson, F. P. *Shakespeare and the Diction of Common Life*. Proceedings of the British Academy, 27. London, 1941.

Wilson, F. P. *Marlowe and the Early Shakespeare*. Oxford, 1954.

Wilson, J. D. *Shakespeare's Happy Comedies*. London, 1962.

Wilson, J. D. *The Fortunes of Falstaff*. Cambridge, 1964.

Wilson, R. M. *The Lost Literature of Medieval England*. London, 1952.

Winslow, Ola. *Low Comedy as a Structural Element in English Drama from the Beginnings to 1642*. Chicago, 1926.

Wirth, Ludwig. *Die Oster- und Passionsspiele bis zum 16. Jahrhundert*. Halle, 1889.

Withington, Robert. "The Development of the 'Vice.'" *Essays in Memory of Barrett Wendell*. Cambridge, Mass., 1926:155–67.

Withington, Robert. "The Ancestry of the 'Vice.'" *Speculum* 7 (1932):525–29.

Withington, Robert. "Braggart, Devil, and 'Vice,'" *Speculum* 11 (1936):124–29.

Wolfram, Richard. *Schwerttanz und Männerbund*. Kassel, 1936 ff.

Wood, F. T. "Comic Elements in English Mystery Plays." *Neophilologus* 25 (1940):39–48; 194–206.

Woodfill, W. L. *Musicians in English Society from Elizabeth to Charles I*. Princeton, 1953.

Woolf, Rosemary. *The English Mystery Plays*. London, 1972.

Wright, L. B. "Social Aspects of Some Belated Moralities." *Anglia* 42 (1930): 107–48.

Wright, L. B. "Madmen as Vaudeville Performers on the Elizabethan Stage." *JEGPh* 30 (1931):48–54.

Wright, L. B. *Middle-Class Culture in Elizabethan England*. Chapel Hill, 1935.

Wright, L. B. *Shakespeare's Theatre and the Dramatic Tradition*. Washington, 1958.

Wurth, Leopold. *Das Wortspiel bei Shakespeare*. Vienna/Leipzig, 1895.

Yates, F. A. *The Art of Memory*. London, 1966.

Young, Karl. *The Drama of the Medieval Church*. 2 vols. Oxford, 1933.

Zeeveld, W. G. *Foundations of Tudor Policy*. Cambridge, Mass., 1948.

Zimansky, C. A., ed. *The Critical Works of Thomas Rymer*. New Haven, 1956.

INDEX

Library of Congress Cataloging in Publication Data

Weimann, Robert.
  Shakespeare and the popular tradition in the theater.

  Revised English translation of Shakespeare und die Tradition des Volkstheaters.
  Bibliography: p.
  Includes index.
    1. Shakespeare, William, 1564–1616—Criticism and
interpretation. 2. Folk-drama, English—History and
criticism. I. Title.
PR2978.W413   1978   822.3'3   77–13673
ISBN 0-8018-1985-7